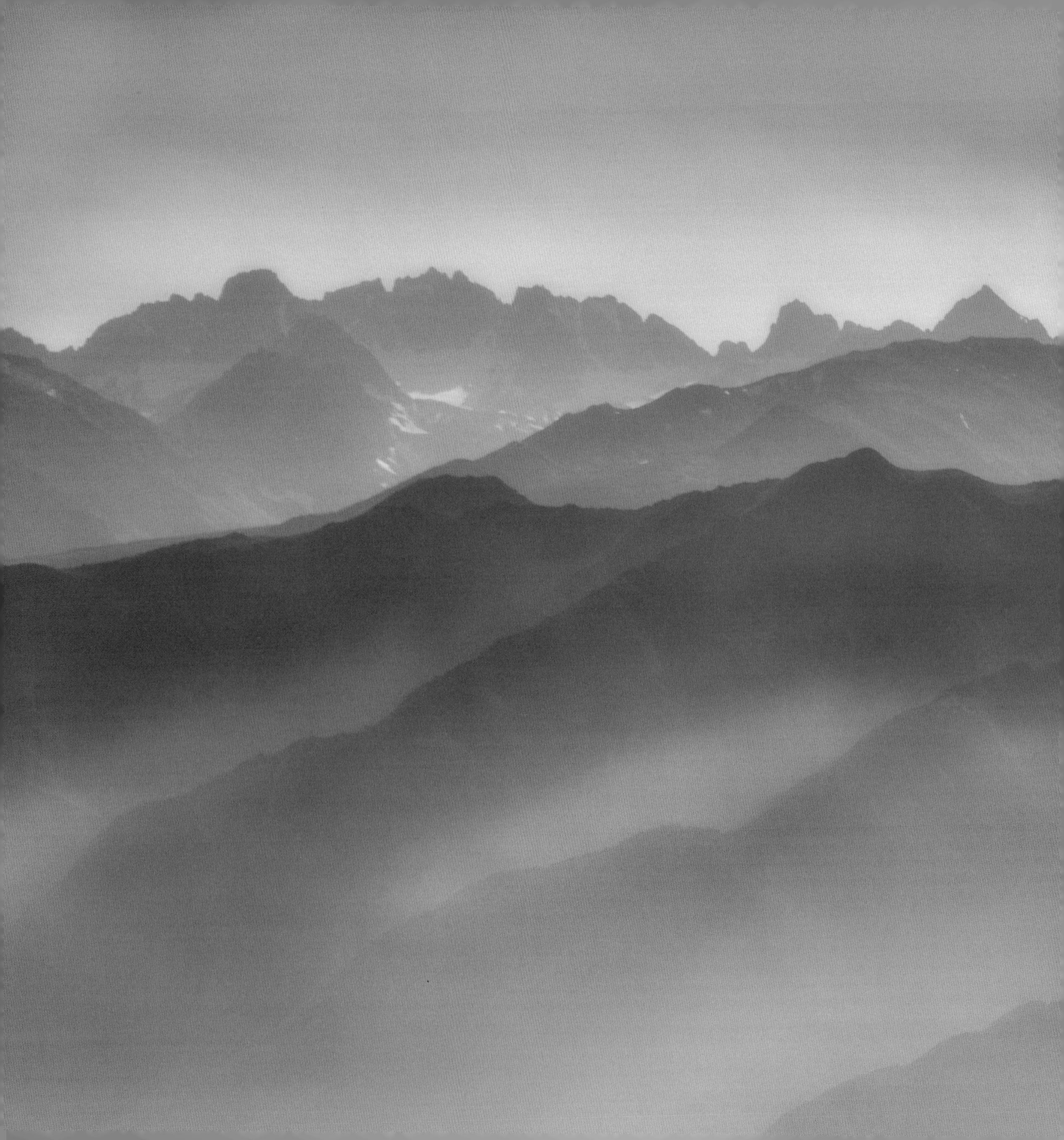

COMPOSITION & PHOTOGRAPHY

WORKING WITH PHOTOGRAPHY USING DESIGN CONCEPTS

HAROLD DAVIS

rockynook

Composition & Photography:
Working with Photography Using Design Concepts

Harold Davis

www.digitalfieldguide.com

ISBN: 978-1-68198-743-9

Rocky Nook Inc.
1010 B Street, Suite 350
San Rafael, CA 94901 USA

www.rockynook.com

Distributed in the UK and Europe by Publishers Group UK
Distributed in the US and all other territories by Ingram Publisher Services

Library of Congress Control Number: 2021944845

Many of the designations in this book used by manufacturers and sellers to distinguish their products are claimed as trademarks of their respective companies. Where those designations appear in this book, and Rocky Nook was aware of a trademark claim, the designations have been printed in caps or initial caps. All product names and services identified throughout this book are used in editorial fashion only and for the benefit of such companies with no intention of infringement of the trademark. They are not intended to convey endorsement or other affiliation with this book.

While reasonable care has been exercised in the preparation of this book, the publisher and author assume no responsibility for errors or omissions, or for damages resulting from the use of the information contained herein or from the use of the discs or programs that may accompany it.

Printed in Korea

CONTENTS

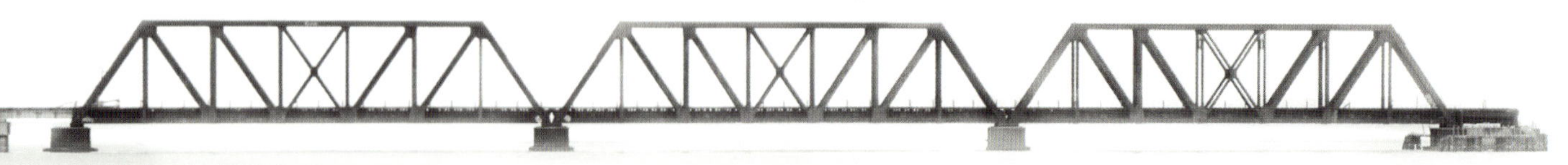

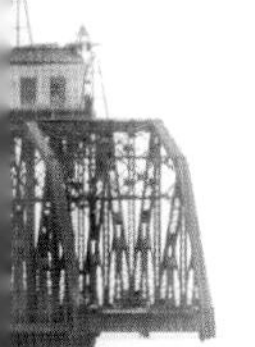

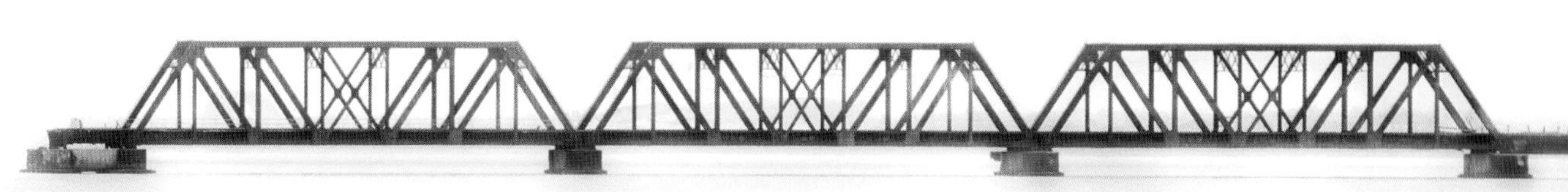

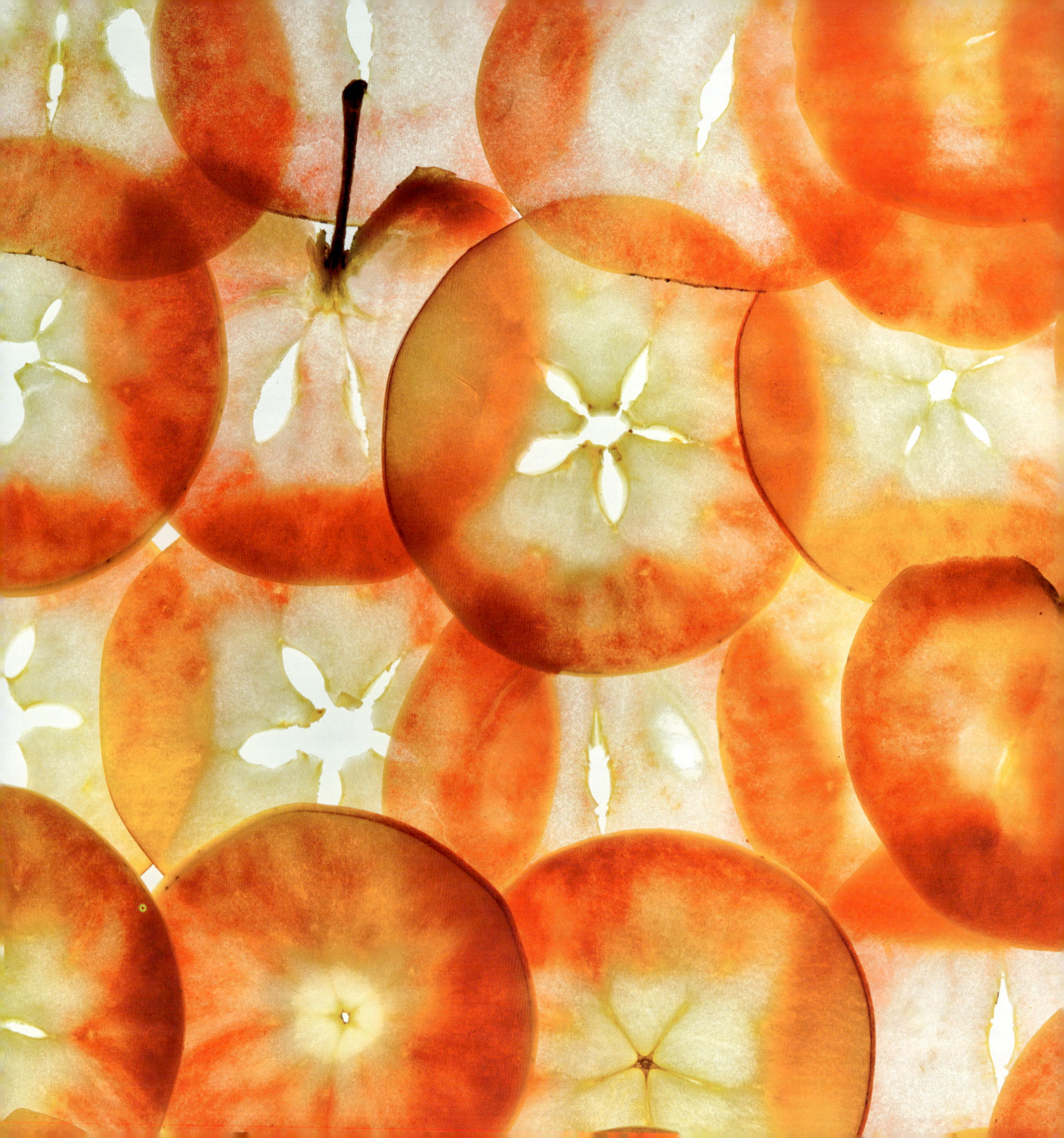

EXPECT THE UNEXPECTED

Of all the magical elixirs that make up a successful photograph—or indeed any visual image—composition is perhaps the most fundamental, and at the same time one of the most elusive. What makes a composition "good"?

We may not know what makes a composition good, but some compositions resonate, and we

There's always one in every barrel!—Thinly slicing fruits and vegetables and putting them on a light box was a grand experiment. With these compositions an important consideration is how to arrange an apparently arbitrary grouping while maintaining an underlying structure. With these Pink Lady apple slices, I intentionally left one apple stem intact so that there was something unique and differentiated for the viewer's eye to begin processing the image.

Nikon D850, 100mm Zeiss Makro-Planar, seven exposures with shutter speeds ranging from 1/40 of a second to 1.6 seconds, each exposure at f/14 and ISO 64, tripod mounted.

instinctively recognize good composition when we see it.

We also know that composition is the fundamental scaffolding of image-making. If you get it wrong in the camera, composition is the hardest element of an image to fix in post-production. Indeed, sloppy compositions often cannot be (and should not be) repaired in Photoshop.

Without an interesting and exciting composition, a photo will appear rudderless, empty, and lack compelling interest. The scene that was captured may be pretty, but the resulting image won't catch the eye and fire the imagination.

Delving a little deeper, after acknowledging the importance of composition, we come to the realization that *the only rule is that there are no rules*. It's indeed hard to create any unified theory of compositional construction that bears up across a wide universe of image-making. But as I already observed, we instinctively recognize good composition when we see it. There is an undeniable strong emotional response when a composition resonates with the subject matter of an image.

As the photographer Henri Cartier-Bresson put it in the context of his own work, in addition to capturing the decisive moment in a composition, there needs to be an instinctive sense of geometry of the situation.

Thus, composition is crucial, and recognizable to both photographers and the viewers of their images. However, attempts to define "good composition" and, more importantly, to convey rules for good compositional construction don't work.

The best compositions contain an element of the unexpected: *Expect the unexpected!*

Embracing the unexpected means becoming comfortable with spontaneity, serendipity, and change as a part your artistic practice.

Expecting the unexpected is probably the only viable "rule" of composition. Codification of composition risks eliminating experimentation and spontaneity, vitiates unexpected serendipity, and violates this "rule."

Hey, there are no rules! So what's the point of this book?

Forgetting about rules, there are ways of looking at subject matter—compositions—that can be very helpful.

Composition is a process, it's not a hard-and-fast set of rules, and it is not just the end result.

Books about composition do tend to teach composition as a subject that can be clearly divided into a system of rules, such as the so-called "rule of thirds." These "rules" are not necessarily wrong, but they are not generally applicable, and they should not be followed slavishly. *Excessively following rules inhibits creativity.*

Composition is not actually a system of rules: it is a process. My goal is to help photographers with the process of composition in the absence of hard-and-fast rules.

While there are many possible ways to interact with photographic composition, the approach I take in *Composition & Photography* is to show how patterns and abstractions can be perceived and encouraged as an underlying and fundamental part of composition.

To abstract something is to reduce the thing to fundamentals, or to show a familiar thing

Window and Shadow—In this deceptively simple and contemplative composition, the photograph delivers a sense of enclosure while looking out the window at a brilliantly lit afternoon. The power of the composition comes from the near symmetry of the lit window and its shadow on a nearby wall in an otherwise unadorned room. This simplicity of composition adds a sense of isolation to the conversation between photographer and viewer.

Apple iPhone 6s.

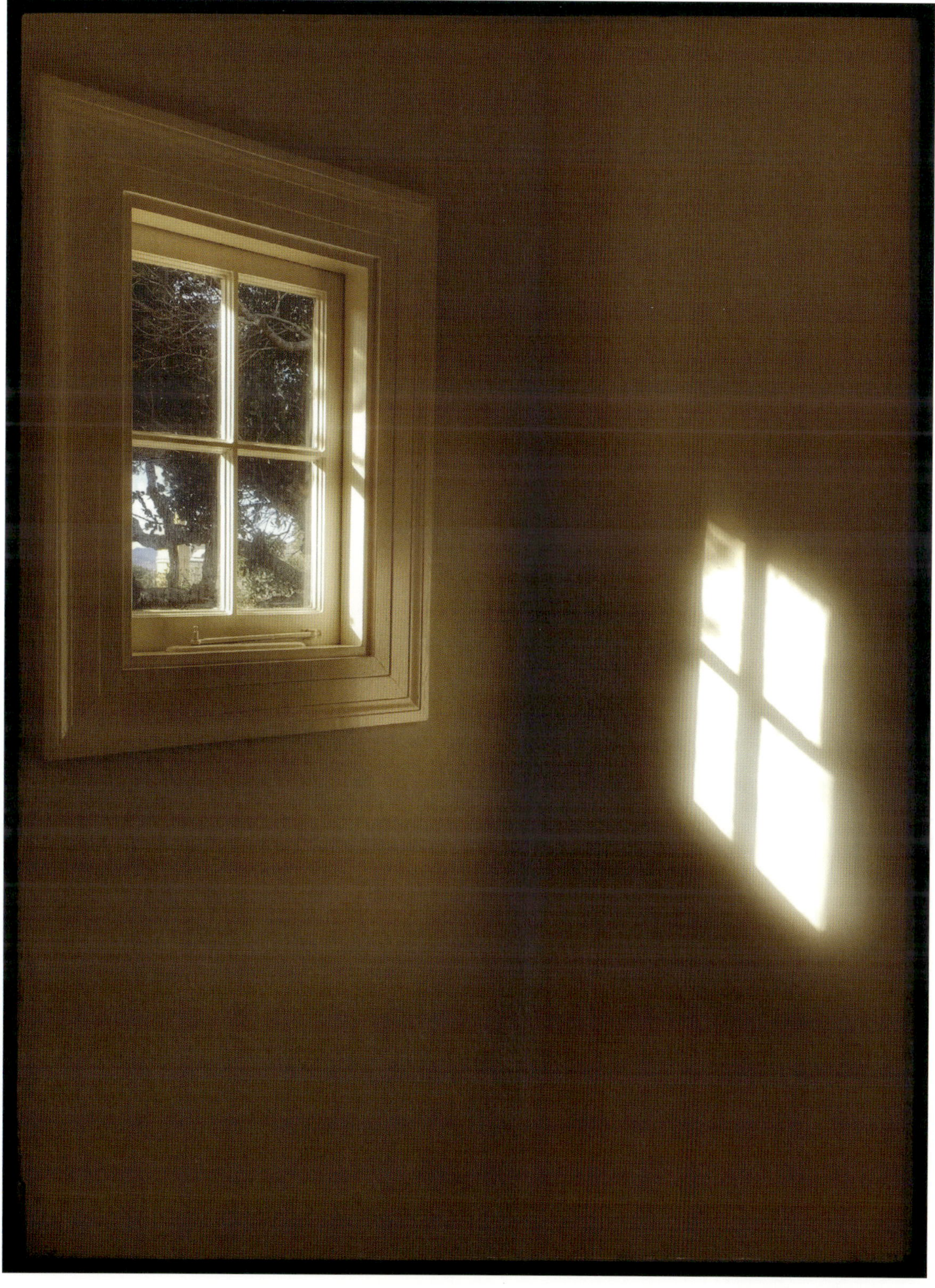

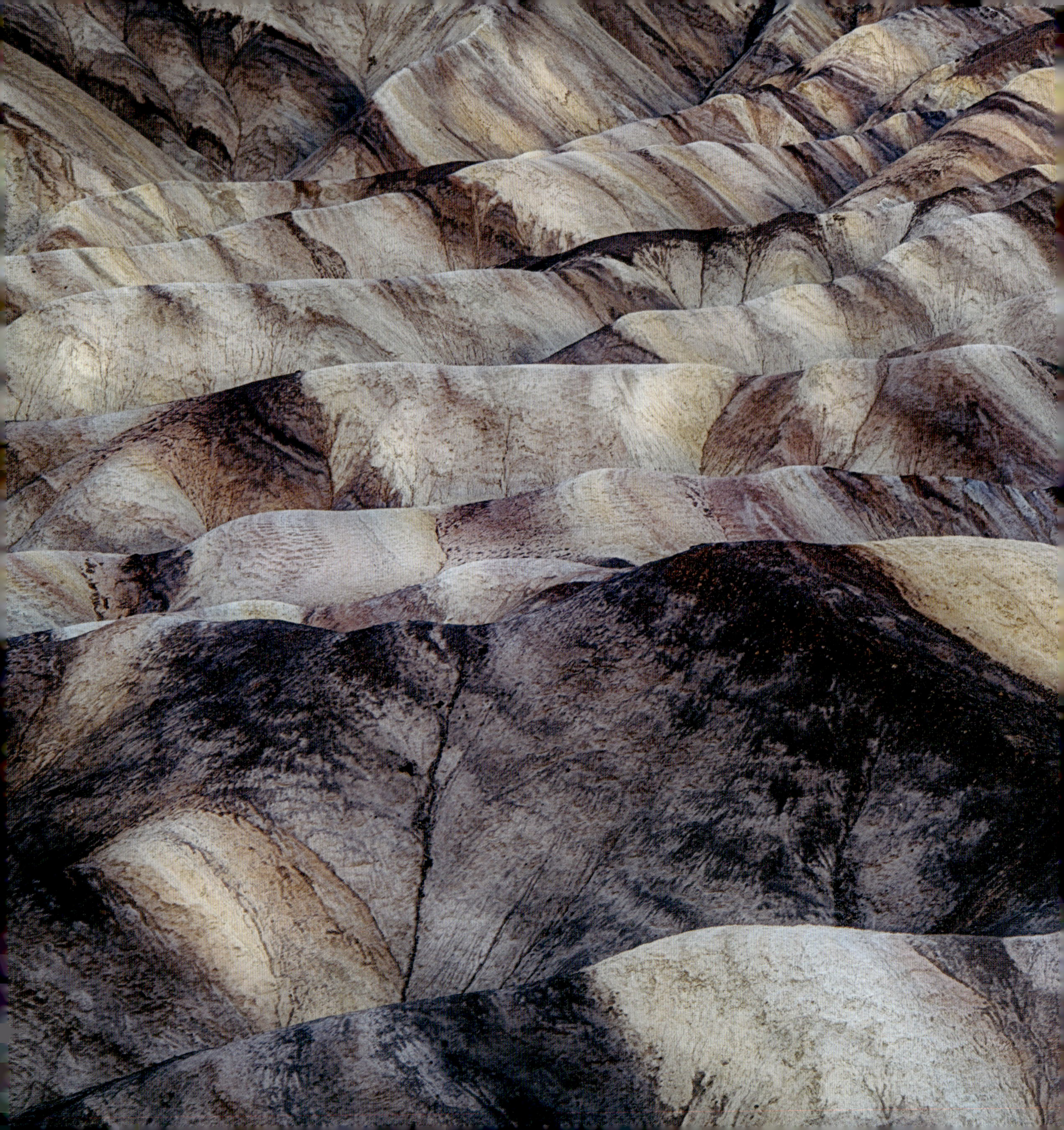

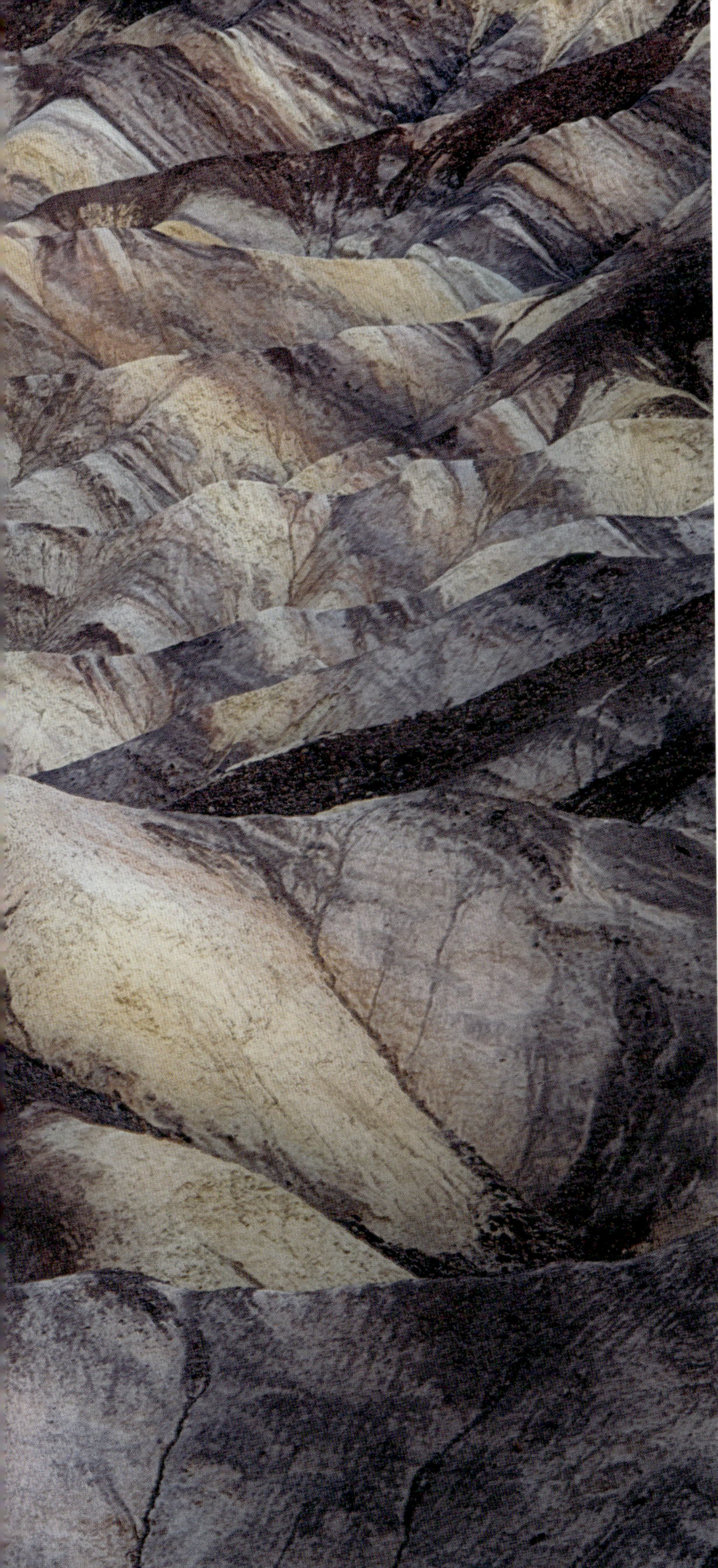

in an unfamiliar light using an interesting and applicable metaphor.

A fundamental goal of composition is to show us things that are new, that we haven't seen before, and to show us a subject in a new way (or in a new light). So in this sense, abstraction is a key tool—and sometimes the overall goal—of composition.

Composition & Photography is a guide to visual conceptualization, and a coach for enhancing your inherent sense of composition.

Folds in the Earth—The challenge in photographing a landscape like this view from Zabriskie Point in Death Valley, California, is creating a cohesive sense of organization from an apparently disorganized system of rocks, canyons, dry river drainages, and the folds of the earth.

In addition, there is the challenge of showing a much-photographed scene in a new and original way.

Standing at Zabriskie Point just before sunset on a late-winter afternoon, I used a moderate telephoto lens (150mm) to isolate a portion of the landscape where the striations and differences between light and dark created an almost checkerboard pattern, particularly when viewed on the diagonal.

This diagonal alternation of lights and darks creates an underlying structure and pattern that provides a compositional armature so that viewers of the image will have an underlying sense that there is an order, albeit perhaps an alien sense of order, beneath the chaos of the anarchic landscape.

Nikon D850, 150mm, five exposures with shutter speeds ranging from 1/8 of a second to 1.3 seconds, each exposure at f/20 and ISO 64, tripod mounted.

When compositional serendipity comes knocking at your photographic door, do you stand ready?

My goal in writing *Composition & Photography* is to empower you to become the best creator of structure and form in your photographs that you can be.

To accomplish this intention, I begin with the very simplest compositional elements, such as lines and circles. As we go along, these elements are combined to make patterns. Finally, I'll show you how to combine techniques and begin visual conversations to create powerful compositions, regardless of the genre and kind of photography you practice.

Along the way, I will show you examples of my work that are illustrations of the compositional design principles explained in the text. Each image is accompanied by caption information and the compositional idea behind the photo.

I've also included exercises and thought pieces with the text and images. Often these may seem open-ended and without a definitive solution. This is in the tradition of the Zen *koan*: with these I intend to provoke thought and test your convictions, rather than supply my solution.

In other words, *Composition & Photography* is intended to spur your creativity and help you begin your internal creative discussion. The examples and exercises are about flexibility, process, and ideas. Please use these ideas to enhance your own inherent creativity!

What is most important to you? You are the artist and this practice is about *your* art. There are no rules, and the job of your compositions is solely to support you, your creativity, and your art.

Own the power of composition, and use composition to make your own unique photographs!

My hope is that this book will help you on your journey to finding the tools and visual vocabulary that will enable you to creatively design the structure behind your imagery. It's worth repeating again that this is *not* a book about rules: this *is* a book about making great photos!

Harold Davis

Berkeley, California

KEY IDEAS

- The only rule is that there are no rules.

- Composition is a process, not a hard-and-fast set of rules.

- Understanding underlying shapes and patterns supports the practice of composition.

- Compositional practice is about *your* art.

- Expect the unexpected! Leave room for serendipity in your compositional practice.

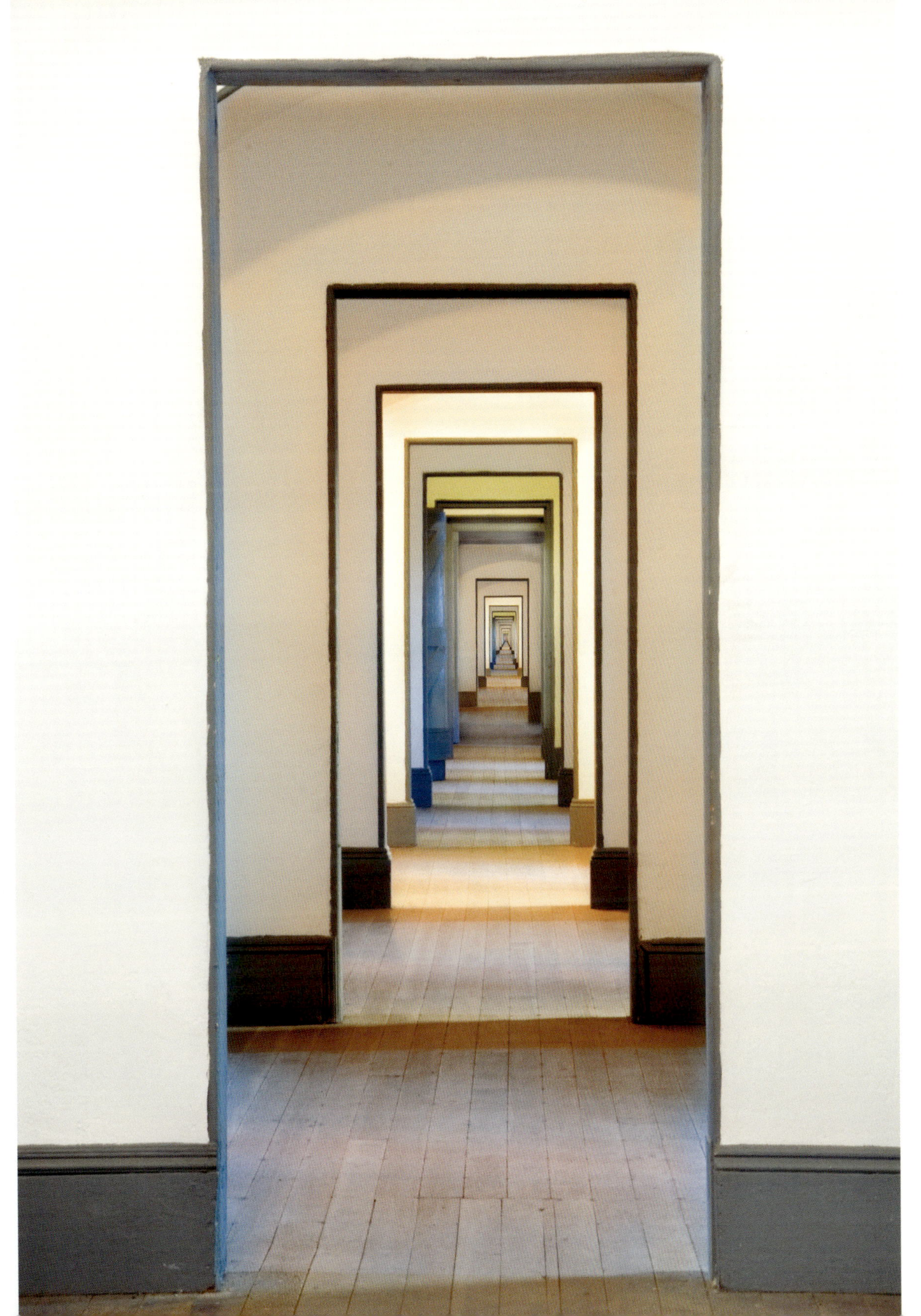

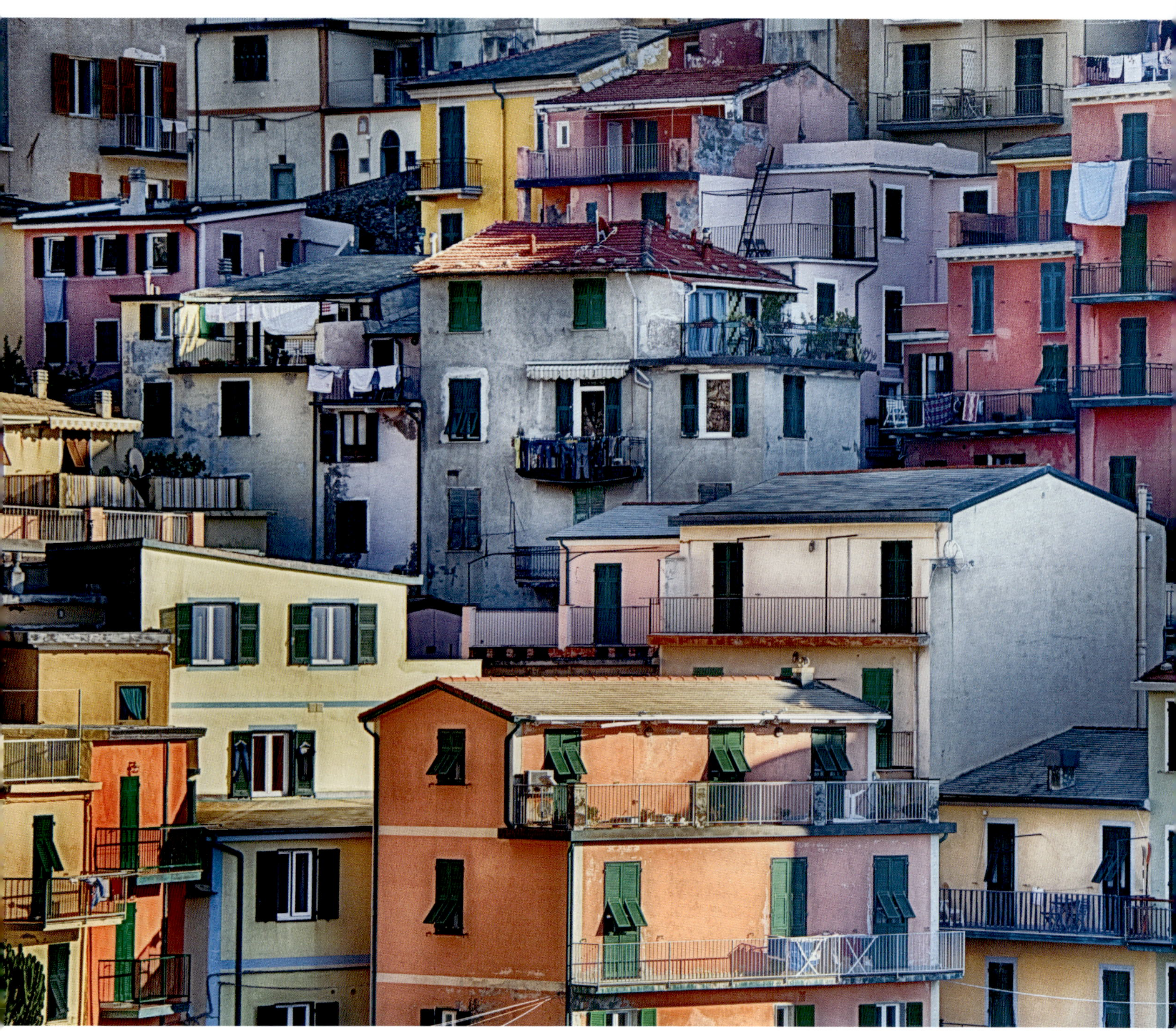

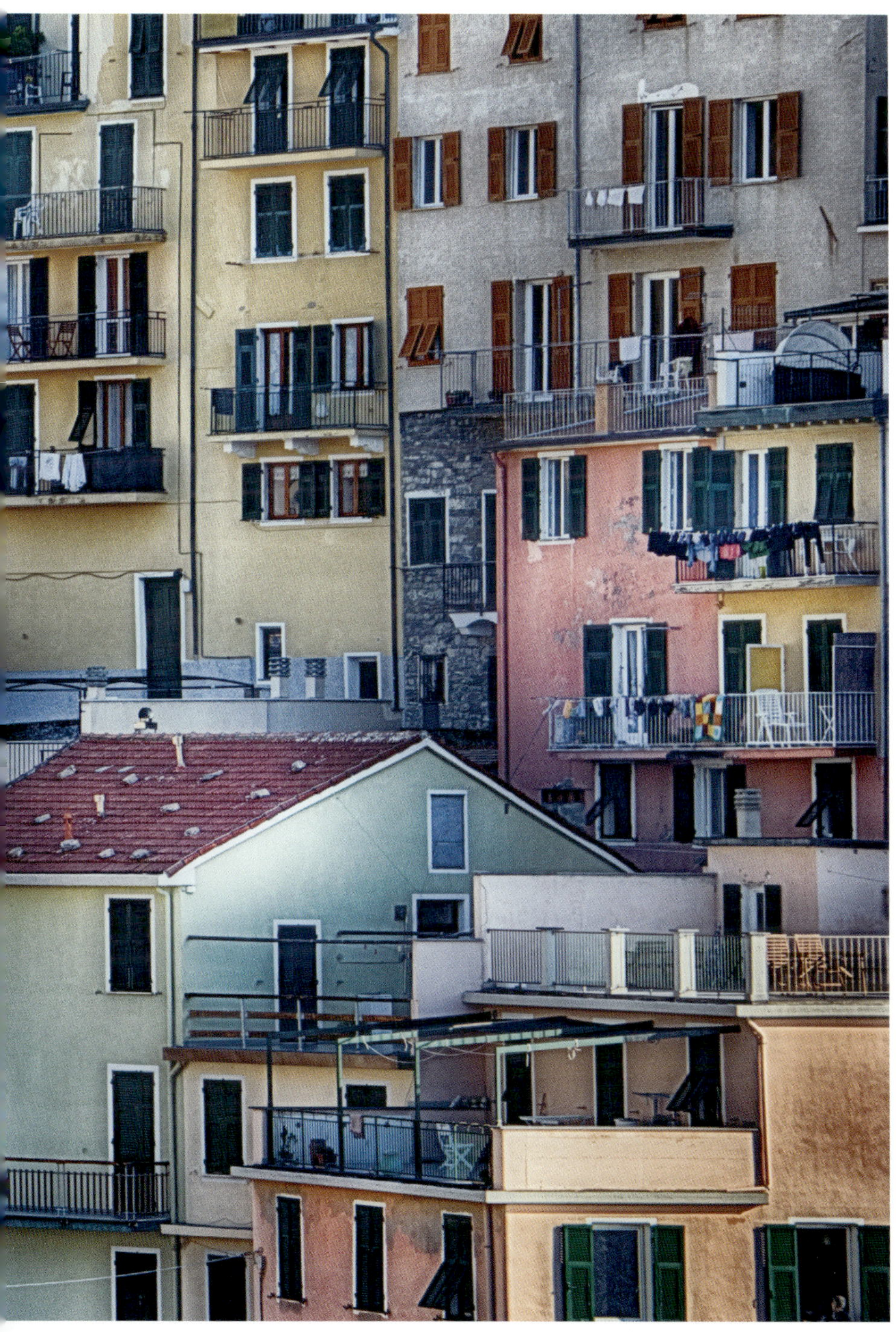

Page 15: *Endless Doors*—The basis for this image uses a moderate telephoto lens (95mm) to capture a series of receding doors in the Officers' Quarters at Fort Point, under the Golden Gate Bridge in San Francisco, California.

When I looked at the resulting photo on my computer, I saw six doorways, and at the end of the progression, a somewhat unattractive display case. To take this composition from mediocre to exciting, in Photoshop I removed the display case and composited the image with itself to extend the sequence of doors.

While this image belies my general tendency to get it right in camera, it was important to keep a set of fresh eyes on the composition so that I could figure out how to make something special of it.

Nikon D200, 95mm, 10 seconds at f/22 and ISO 100, tripod mounted.

Left: *Manarola*—Along the rugged Ligurian coast of the Italian Riviera, the Cinque Terre region stands out for its spectacular mountainous scenery with cliffs running down to the water's edge and colorful seafaring villages.

There are few things more exiting to me in composition than to be able to create some form of geometric order out of apparent disorganization and chaos. It was with this in mind that I framed my image of the interior of historic Manarola village.

Nikon D810, 122mm, five exposures with shutter speeds ranging from 1/250 to 1/4 of a second, each exposure at f/8 and ISO 200, tripod mounted.

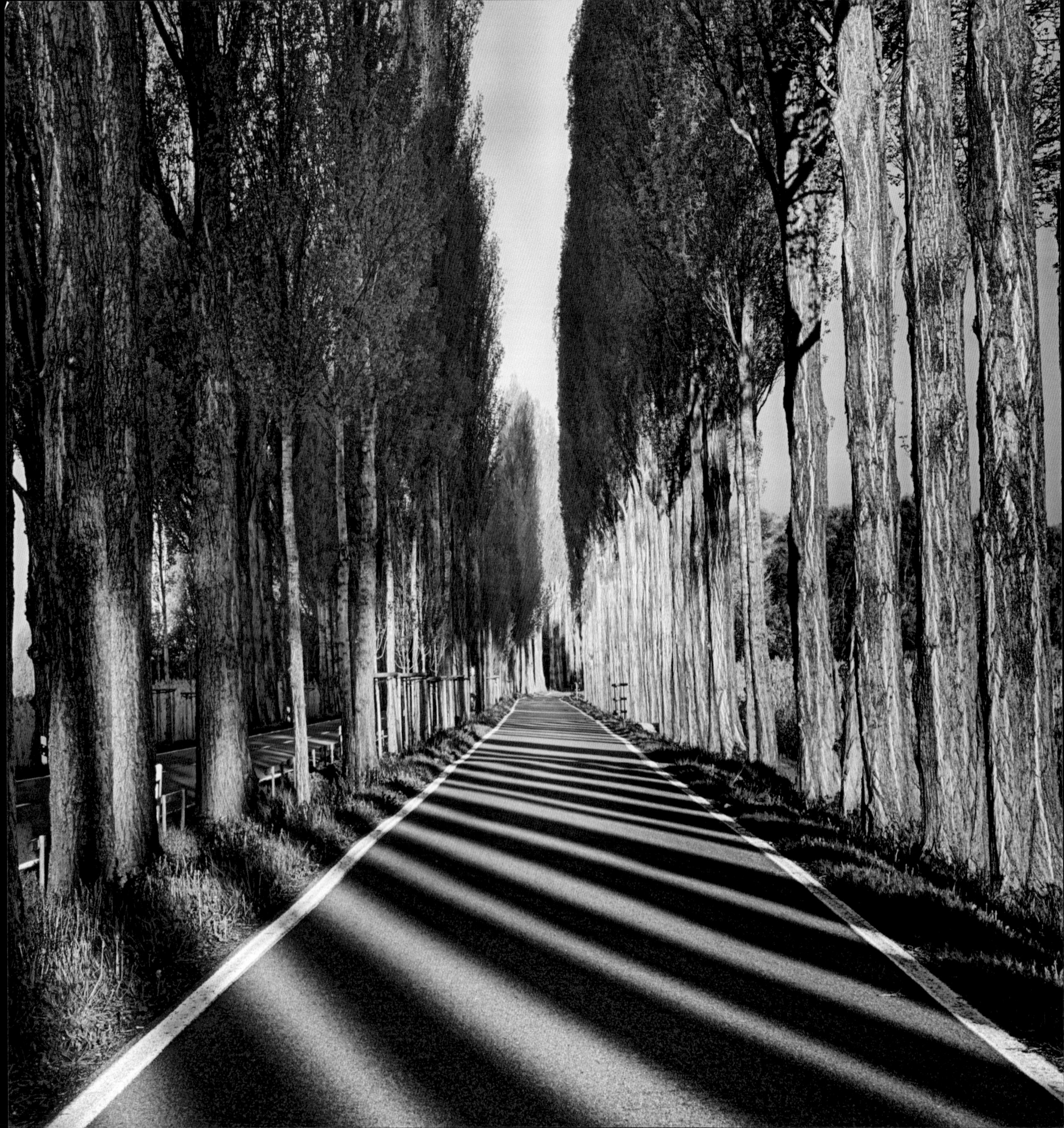

LINE

Consider the line. The line may be the simplest form in geometry. And in our perception.

Or not. Not quite.

The point is simplest. Maybe.

But lines are made up of an aggregation of points.

Points themselves are aggregations of points, until you go down in scale to the molecular, atomic, or subatomic level. To put this another way, zoomed way out, a circular photograph—such as made by an 8mm round, wide-angle fisheye—can appear to be a single point or dot.

Reichenau Causeway—This bike-path causeway leads to Reichenau Island, a World Heritage Site that lies in Lake Constance, which forms the border between Germany, Austria, and Switzerland. The causeway was completed in 1838 and stretches from the ruins of Schopflen Castle and the eastern end of Reichenau Island.

Waking before sunrise, I pulled on some warm clothing and headed out with my gear to the causeway to photograph the lines created by shadows, the rows of trees, and the demarcation of the bike path.

Nikon D850, 28-300mm Nikkor at 92mm, five exposures with shutter speeds ranging from 1/50 to 0.4 of a second, each exposure at f/22 and ISO 64, tripod mounted.

Zooming in, if there is enough resolution, the closer you get, the more you can see the points within that make up the point. Resolution willing—perhaps you are in Photoshop on a large, high-resolution monitor at 1,000 percent magnification—each of these points that you have previously enlarged can themselves be enlarged. And so on. The world at large is composed of worlds in the macro-aggregate. (This concept is illustrated on pages 20–21).

But let's get back to the line. In terms of how we see the world and view photographs, lines are perhaps the most basic of all forms, and are a better starting place in the quest to understand and work with composition than the point.

Starting with a line, you can go almost anywhere.

Aggregations of lines make up shapes. As they make the shapes, lines help provide the illusion of depth, perspective, and contrast. Lines are the hard-working soldiers—you might say, "line workers"—that build the scaffolding that is composition, and form the underlying basis for composition in art.

So, let's consider the line. Particularly the expressive line.

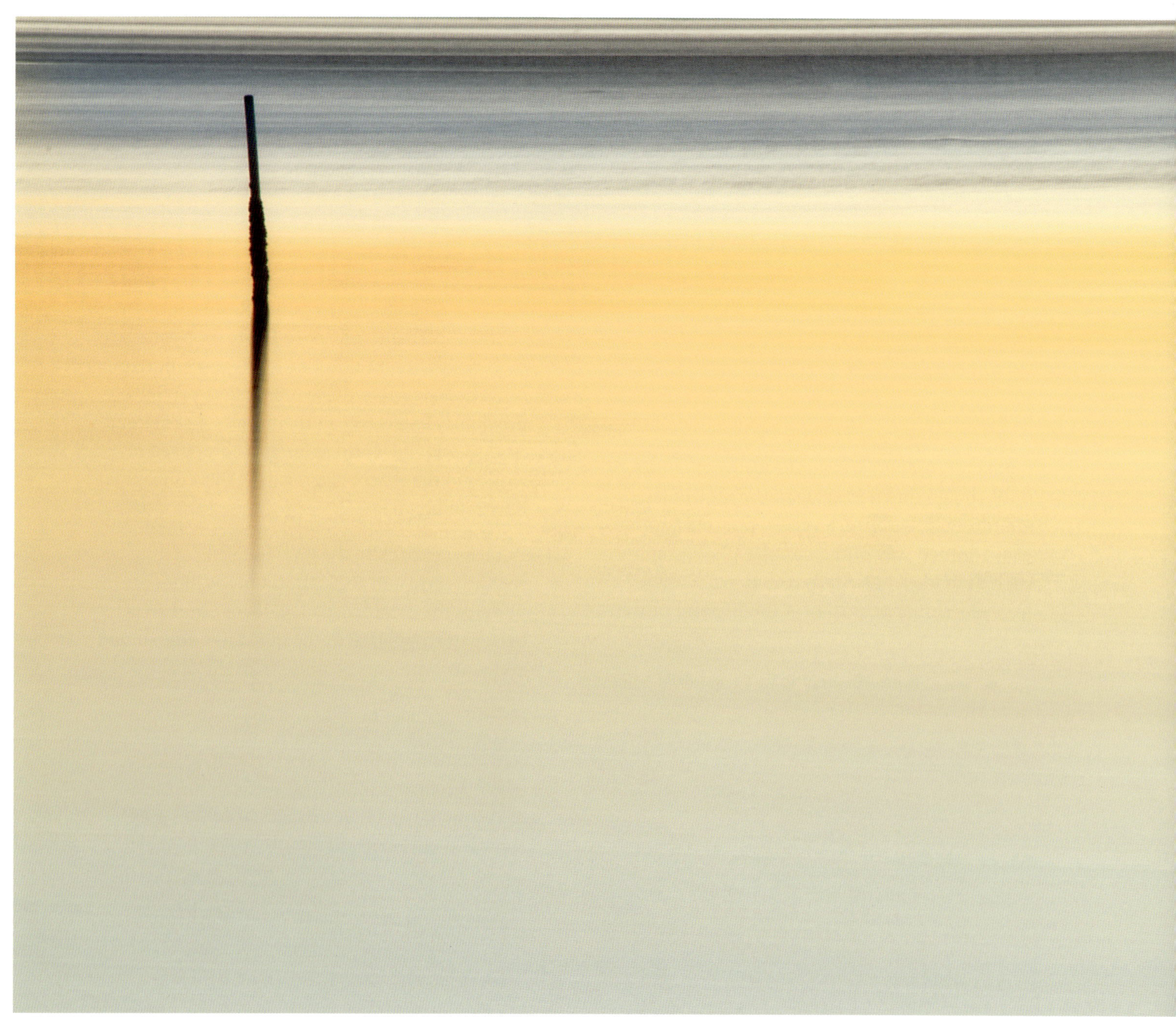

Some lines just sit there. They don't do anything. Think of the light blue horizontal lines on a sheet of notebook paper as an example. These lines are the utilitarian bureaucrats in the world of composition. Basically, one should pay no attention to them unless an image embraces regularity as an underlying scaffolding.

Other, more dynamic and interesting lines convey questions, thoughts, and emotions. These lines are expressive

Line Dance—This image is a seemingly simple composition that presents an irregular upright line and its reflection in the upper-left quadrant. This line was formed by an old piling in San Francisco Bay, with the motion of the bay water calmed and abstracted with a long shutter speed (10 seconds).

The apparent simplicity of the image belies the contrast between the spacial simplicity of the smooth water and the abrupt verticality of the line. In this case, the result works as an image, and appears simple— but this contrast between a straight vertical line and an abstract horizontal background can be tricky to pull off.

The things that bring us the most joy are not overly complicated. Perfection in an image usually involves creating a sense for the viewer of unforced simplicity.

Nikon D300, 18-200 Nikkor at 200mm, 10 seconds at f/32 and ISO 100, tripod mounted.

and have meaning that is conveyed by what they are.

How can a mere line do this? How can a simple line convey so much? To analyze these questions, we can begin by thinking about some characteristics of a line:

- *Weight*—this refers to the thickness of a line and is a holdover from the time when lines were created by pressing a stylus, so the "weight," or thickness, of the line depended on how hard the stylus was pressed.

- *Color*—lines are easier to see in monochromatic composition, but play a vital role in color composition as well.

- *Direction*—even lines that are not explicitly directional often have an implied visual movement and direction.

- *Curvature*—how much or how little the line curves.

The *weight* of a line really means how dark the line is, and thus also involves color. A very dark line splits space, and may convey determination, or possibly anger. When a line is very faint, or light, it might indicate indecision, or even tension over whether the line itself should exist.

A faint line cannot be used to anchor a composition that is primarily linear, as are *Line Dance,* on pages 20–21, and *Reichenau Causeway,* on page 18. If you are going to use lines as the crucial aspect that dominates other shapes of a composition, you must be fearless and bold. The very rarity and unlikeliness of this kind of composition gives it power and grace, but the fewer the elements in the composition, the trickier it is to pull off.

Color may seem to be an obvious characteristic of a line (at least in a color composition). What perhaps is less obvious is that the choice of color conveys an underlying emotion to the viewer. Bright colored lines in oranges and red often are happy, while dark colored lines in black, brown, and somber hues can be unhappy.

Photographically speaking, it is often easiest to see how lines form a composition when working in the absence of color, in black and white. Another way to put this is that our eyes love color, but they are often misled by color, and the underlying composition is best seen and constructed without color; thus, one way to check your composition can be to view your image in monochrome.

A composition that presents an inherently sad subject (perhaps involving loss or memory), but uses bright colors, will strike viewers as dissonant, though they may have no idea why. Conversely, a happy subject in dark colors may often make viewers think that conflict is around the next bend—for example, a storm may be coming.

Almost all lines in a composition have an implicit *direction*. Absent an arrowhead at the end of the line, it may not be fair to say that a line is directional in a cartoonish sense, but the truth is that lines by their very nature guide our vision. We look along lines, and usually we do the looking in one direction only, even if we then retrace the visual path.

Our eye follows the line and we are guided in how to approach the composition, where to enter it, and where to leave it (see pages 136–157). Certainly, as a photographic artist, once one understands the "look along" nature of lines, one realizes that one way, or direction, of looking is usually preferred.

Penobscot Crossing—On a rainy day, I rode the elevator up the tower of the Penobscot Narrows Bridge to the glass-enclosed observatory at the top, which is said to be the highest bridge observatory in the world. In the rain the lines and shapes of this interesting bridge in coastal Maine became an abstraction from above, particularly when crossed with the wake of a motor boat.

Since I was photographing through both glass and moisture, I decided to maximize selective focus and minimize depth of field by choosing f/4 as my aperture. This also enabled me to use a fast enough shutter speed (1/2000 of a second) to freeze the motion of the boat and its wake.

Looking at this composition, its lines are very apparent: the bridge makes a big white vertical line, crossed by the horizontal line of the boat wake.

Nikon D810, 28-300mm Nikkor at 28mm, 1/2000 of a second at f/4 and ISO 800, hand held.

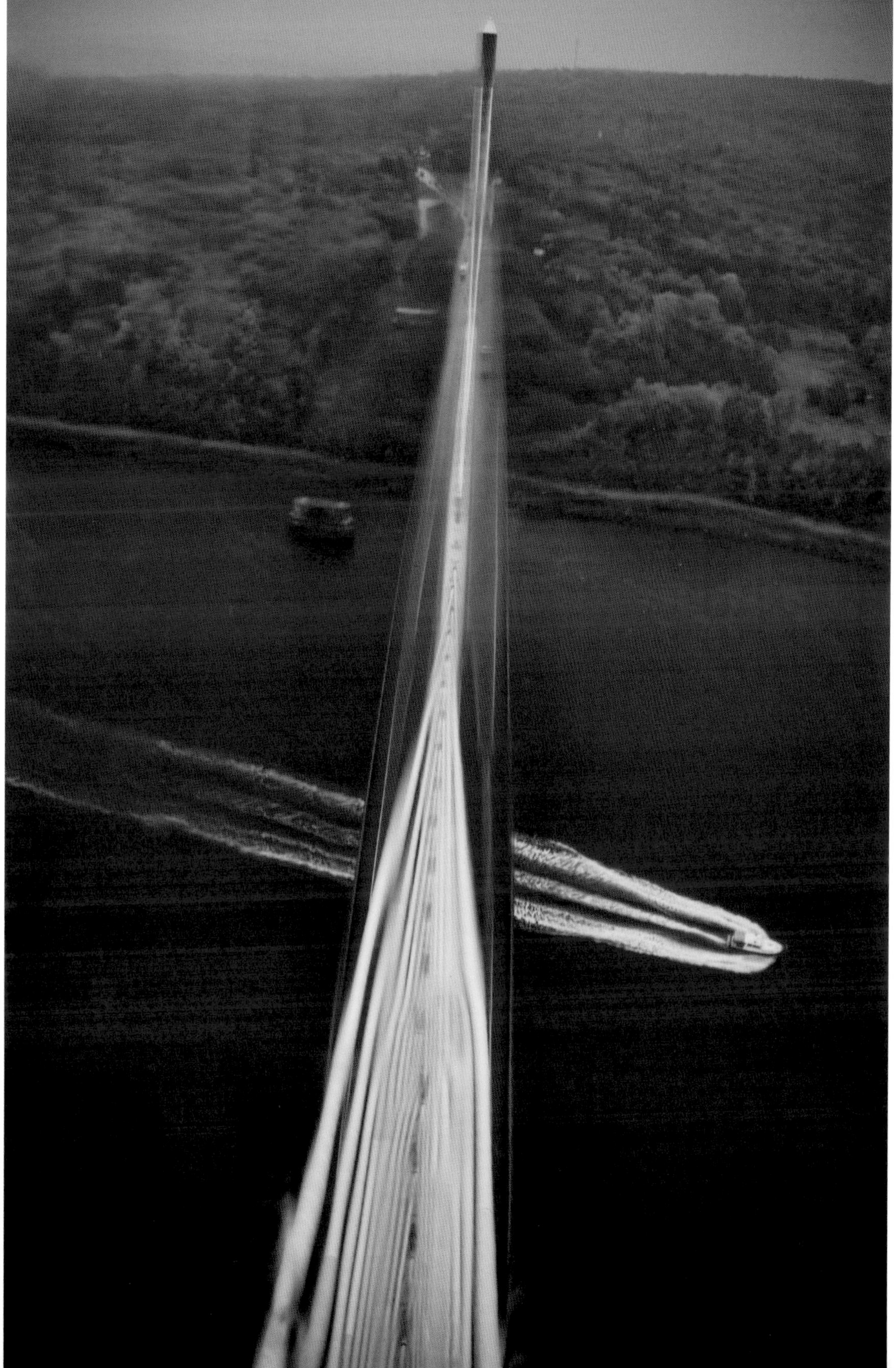

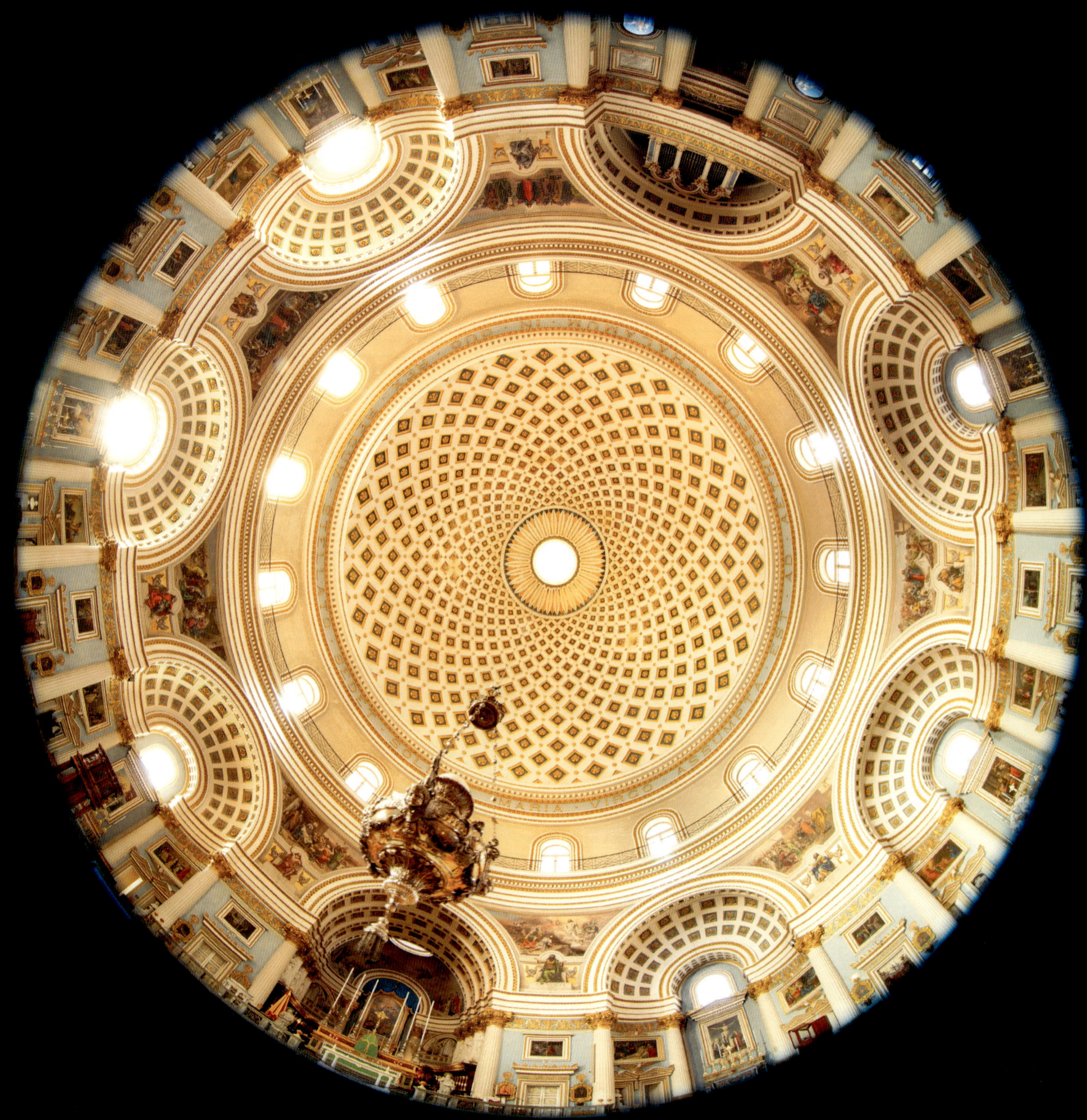

LOOKING AT A DOME AS A DOT

Mosta Dome—During the Second World War, "Fortress" Malta was the redoubt that held out against increasingly intense aerial bombardment by the axis powers. The heroism of the Maltese people earned the entire island nation the British Cross of St. George in gratitude.

Mosta Dome, known as the Rotunda of Mosta, or more formally the Basilica of the Assumption of Our Lady, is a Catholic parish church on the island of Malta. Built in the mid-1800s and patterned after the Pantheon in Rome, it is one of the largest domes in the world.

During the war, the Luftwaffe dropped three large bombs onto Mosta Dome. Two of the bombs slid off the dome harmlessly. The third bomb penetrated the Rotunda where hundreds of congregants were waiting for an early evening mass. Miraculously, the bomb landed next to the altar and did not explode. Detonation experts from the RAF were able to remove the bomb and sink it into the Mediterranean without exploding it.

Today, a replica of the bomb is memorialized in the Basilica's sacristy and the place where the bomb passed through the dome has never been fully repaired because the "Miracle of Mosta Dome" is a point of pride (you can see where the bomb came through the dome in the top image at right).

Reproduced and viewed from a long way out, this fisheye image looks mostly like an undifferentiated yellowish point or dot. The more you magnify, and the closer you get, the more you can see, including the break in the pattern of the dome ceiling where the bomb came through.

The full image on the facing page shows Mosta Dome in all its glory. Magnifying the image to reveal the small area of the dome (top right), shows that the full image itself is comprised of dots. As the image gets smaller and smaller (middle and bottom right), the entire dome becomes like a dot visually (see the text on page 19 for more about points and dots).

Nikon D850, 8-15mm Nikkor at 8mm (circular fisheye), 5 seconds at f/11 and ISO 64, tripod mounted.

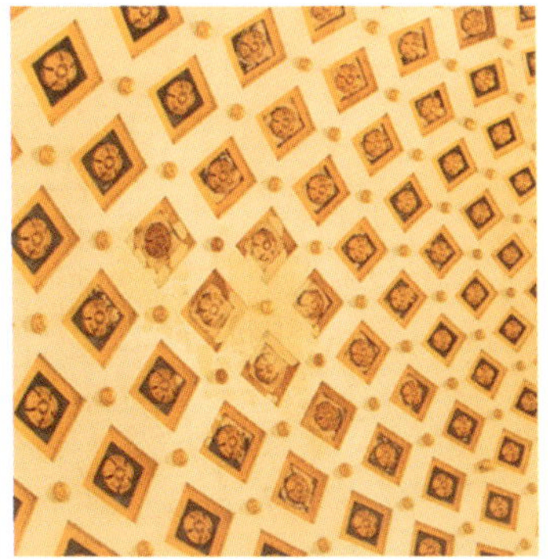

Enlarged, the image itself is made up of dots. The illustration is at 300% and the irregularity in the dome pattern shows where the bomb fell through.

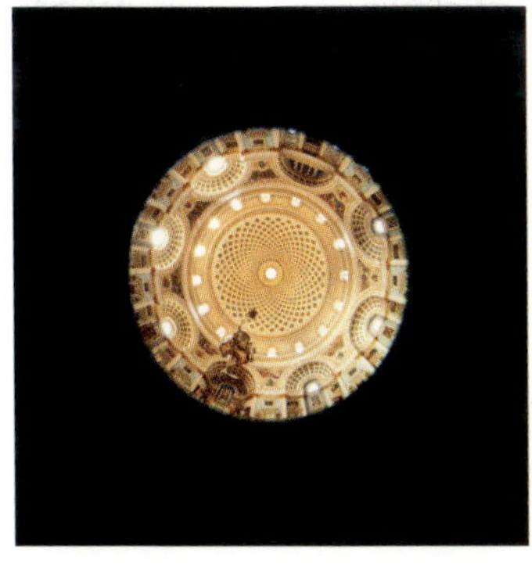

As the round shape gets smaller, the dome appears to be made up of many dots.

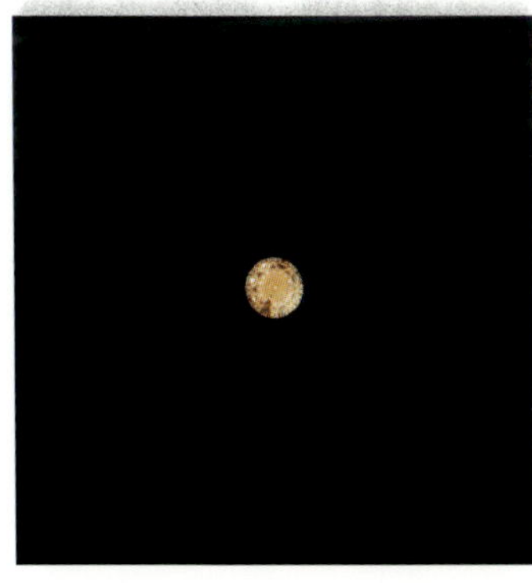

As the image becomes smaller still, it begins to look like a dot or point.

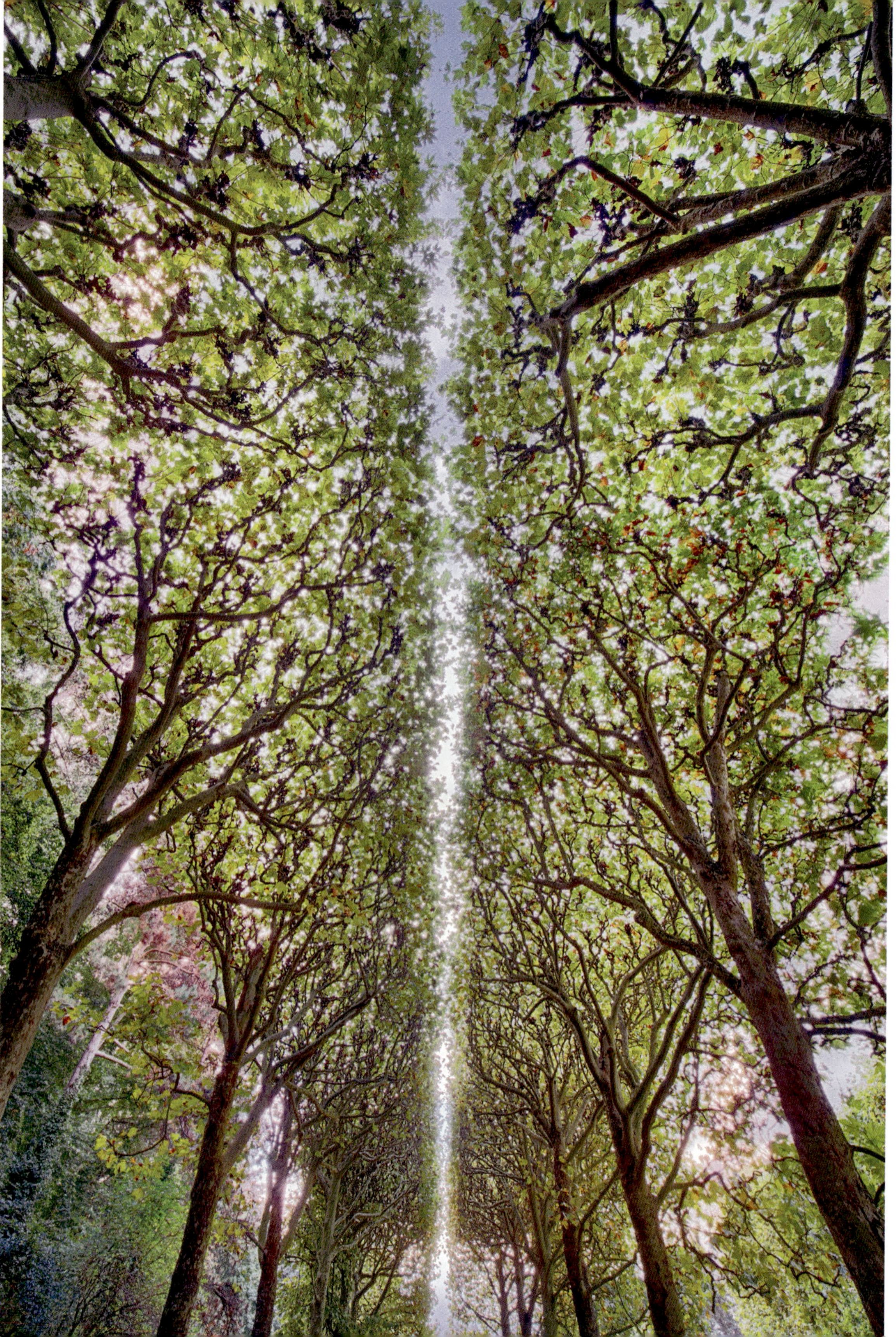

With a preferred direction, one can then work to enhance the directional bias, and to make sure that the entire composition is in sympathy with the implied direction, or at least that the direction is used to enhance the composition.

Using direction in this fashion creates the possibility for entry and exit points in a composition: an entry point is where most viewers start looking at an image, and an exit point is where the gaze leaves the photo, even if this does not occur consciously to the viewer. For more about entries and exits, see pages 136–157.

A straight line is often not considered curved. (Actually, and more technically, a straight line is a kind of curve.) But in order for a line to convey emotion, it is the wiggles and waggles, or simple swoops that count most. Lines without curvature are rare in life and photography, and are almost always man-made. But when they do occur, they can create bold compositions because of the iconoclastic nature of an uncurving line.

A line conveys emotion. A line conveys power. So how can you use the emotive power of lines in your work? Here are some ideas for thought.

Take a simple stylus—such as a pen, pencil, marker, crayon, etc.—and a piece of paper. Draw lines. Which lines matter the most? Which lines convey emotion all by themselves?

With a color landscape photograph, explore the nature of the lines in the landscape. Can you diagram where the lines are, and which lines are important? Next, convert the color landscape to monochromatic. It should be easier to see the role of lines in the composition now. Verify this. Finally, with the role lines play in the black-and-white version of your image made clear, work in post-production to emphasize the impact of lines in this composition.

Create a photograph. Your photo can use any kind of subject matter that makes simple use of what is essentially a single line. In other words, one line or a few lines should be the entire basis of the image.

Want to take this a step further? Make sure the line is essentially straight—and either horizontal or vertical, but not both. In this exercise, the entire composition comes from this "straight" line.

Other than points, lines are probably the most basic shape. We'll be building on lines to understand compositions of far greater complexity. But in the meantime, lines will take you a good distance, and get you started on the important work of understanding the basics of photography as two-dimensional design.

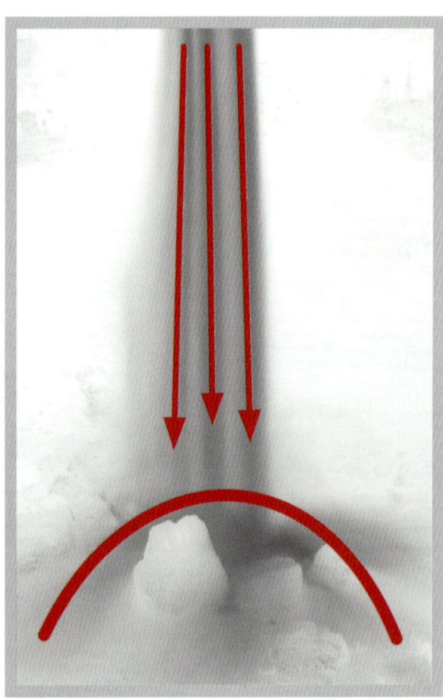

The image of the long-exposure and exposure-duration-bracketed image shown in *Haifoss Variation 4*, opposite, has been photographically stylized into a very simple graphic that can be represented by three downward lines plunging into a semi-circle.

Haifoss Variation 4—On a bright but overcast day in the Icelandic Highlands, my workshop group photographed the magnificent series of waterfalls around the Haifoss Gorge.

As I was exploring the scenery with my camera, it occurred to me that a great way to make an abstract composition from the flowing water would be to isolate the water from the background scenery. Furthermore, I could extend the dynamic range of the final image and add to the effects that long shutter speed durations could make by varying the apparent solidity of the water. Accomplishing this goal in broad daylight would require stopping down the lens, using a low ISO, and adding a neutral density filter. In addition, multiple different exposures would be needed.

I call this effect *exposure-duration bracketing*—this is not exactly HDR because it doesn't blend exposures *per se*, but it is a close cousin to HDR techniques with a bit of added flexibility. Exposure-duration bracketing is one of those photographic techniques that is usually hit-or-miss, meaning that you have to try a number of times before you get good results (as you can see from the title, this one was my fourth variation).

The point of this particular variation of the Haifoss Falls image was to create a highly stylized photo where three lines of water appear to plunge into a pool at the bottom of the image frame. In "real life" at motion-stopping shutter speeds, the water is fast flowing and wild, and does not create the cleanly delineated lines you see in this composition.

Nikon D850, 28-300mm Nikkor at 116mm, +4 neutral density filter, circular polarizer, three exposures, one each at 2.5, 5, and 10 seconds, each exposure at f/36 and ISO 200, tripod mounted and combined in Photoshop.

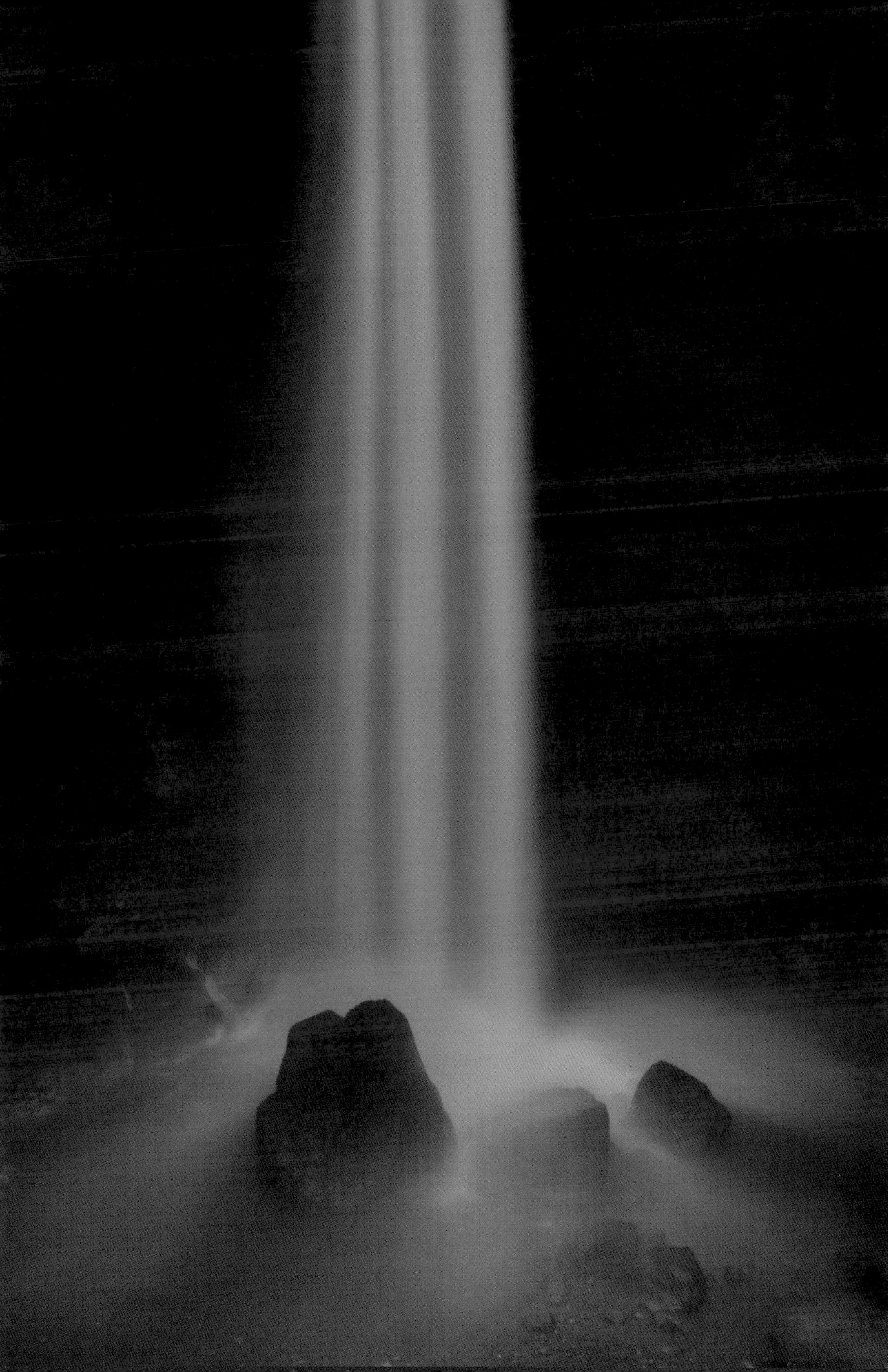

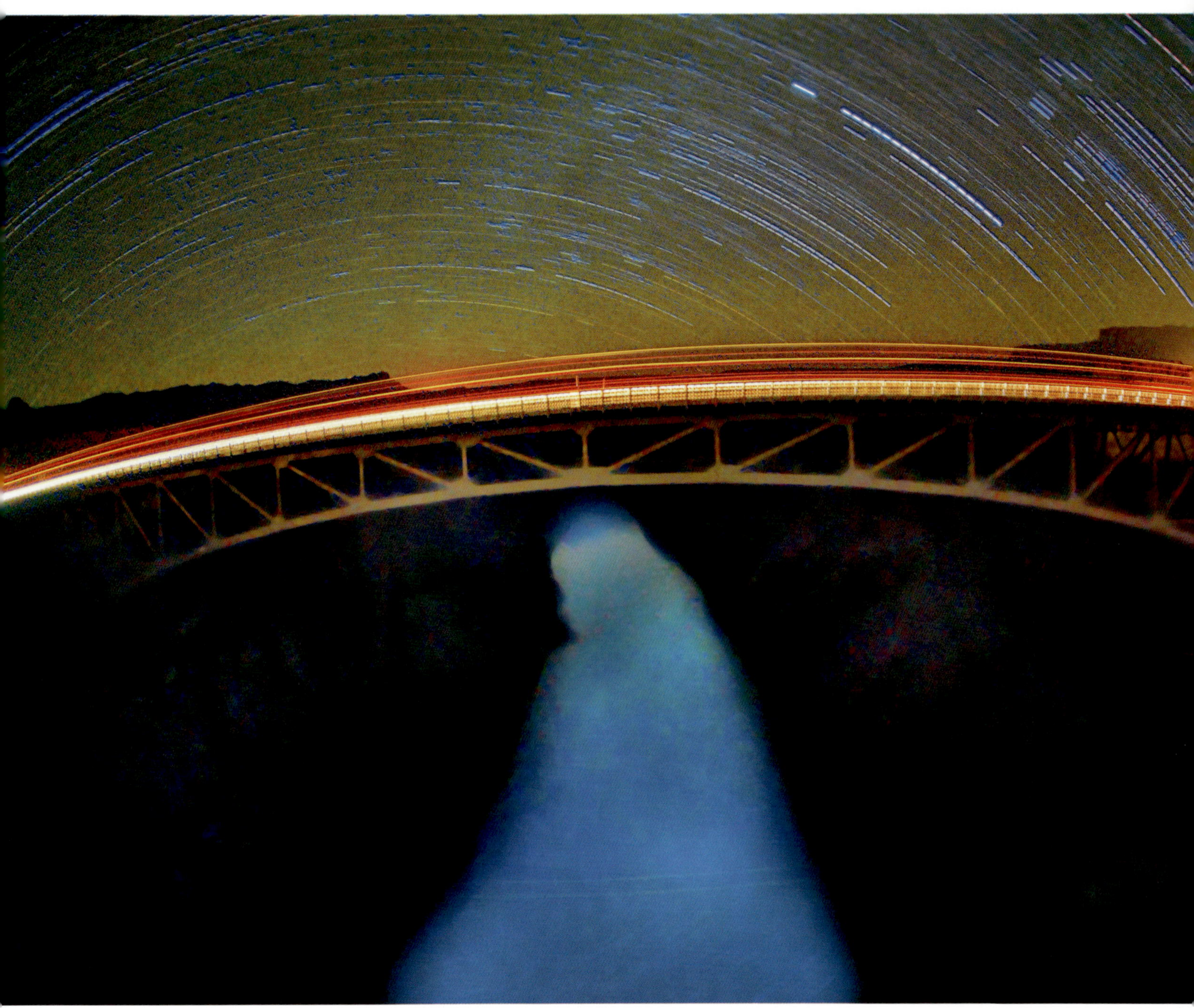

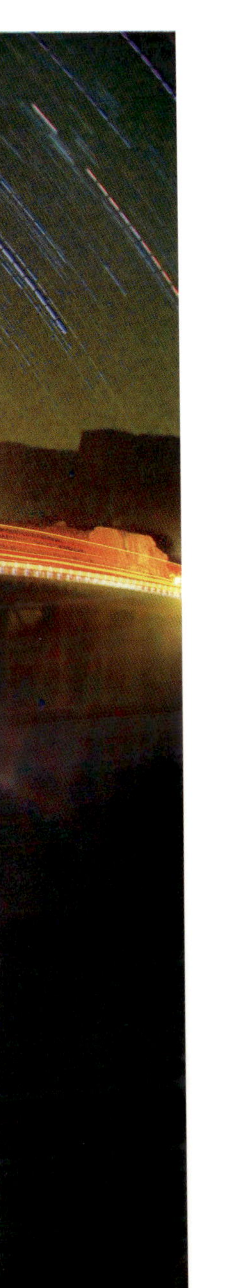

Navajo Bridge at Night—Near Lees Ferry, Arizona, US Highway 89A crosses the Colorado River. Two spans of the Navajo Bridge cross Marble Canyon. Prior to the completion of the Navajo Bridge, the only way to get across the Colorado was by ferry. To this day, there are very few alternative crossings during the long journey of this great river from the Colorado Mountain highlands to the Gulf of Mexico.

The original span of the Navajo Bridge opened in 1929 and today is used as a footbridge. A wider, second span of the bridge was completed in 1995 and is the highway crossing used by cars and other vehicles.

Standing on the footbridge during a dark-of-the-moon night, I turned my camera south to face the newer span and photographed down Marble Canyon as the cars whizzed past. Using a long shutter speed (9 minutes) rendered the car lights as bright horizontal strokes.

Nikon D300, 10.5mm Nikkor rectilinear fisheye, fourteen exposures, each exposure at f/2.8 and ISO 400, tripod mounted; Navajo Bridge and River: single exposure at 9 minutes; Star Trails: created via a stacked composite of thirteen exposures, each exposure at 4 minutes.

FINDING THE LINES

In many images it is easy to see the predominant shapes and lines once you train your eye to do it. *Navajo Bridge at Night*, shown to the left, is a good example because the lines are so clear. The arched star trails in the sky make up one set of lines. The car lights and bridge gently arc across the frame, and are the predominant and brightest element in the image. The Colorado River enters the bottom of the frame at roughly its midpoint and moves perpendicular to the bridge.

This relationship of the important lines in the image can be shown in a schematic diagram like the one below.

To learn more about the design aspects of composition, it's a great idea to take a look at your own images from the point of view of how you would diagram the lines. You can even take this one step further, and "photograph" without a camera by diagramming the lines in a scene in front of you using a pencil and sketchbook.

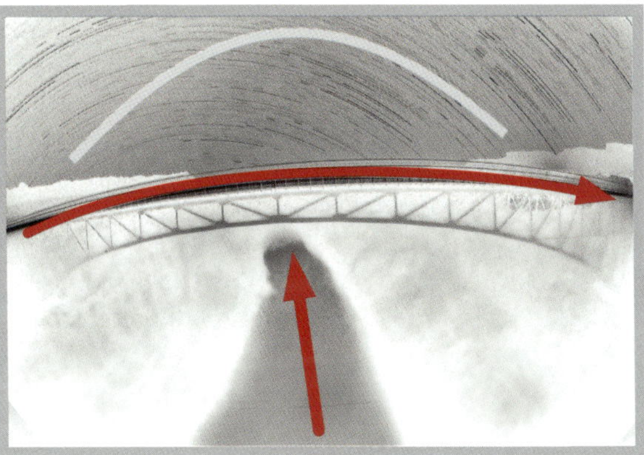

The lines in *Navajo Bridge at Night* show car lights on the bridge, the dome of stars in the sky, and the perpendicular path of the Colorado River. The arrows show the direction of the viewer's eye movement across these elements.

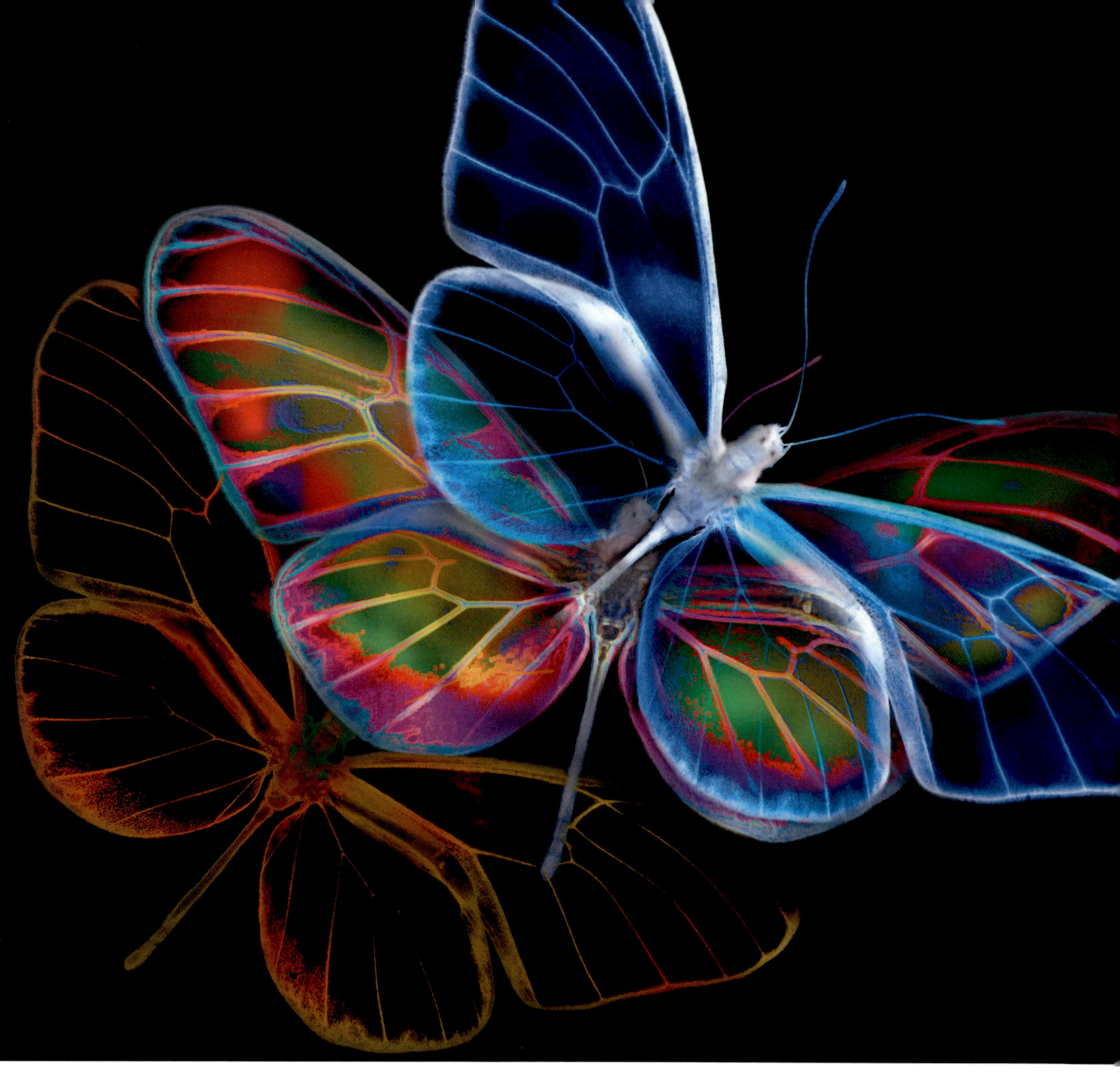

FOUND LINES VERSUS BESPOKE LINES

Let's face it, some lines are pretty obvious. For example, if you are photographing a bench in a park, the slats in the bench will clearly form horizontal lines across your composition. For another example of obvious lines in a photograph, take a look at *Reichenau Causeway* on page 19.

On the other hand, some lines need to be tended and revealed. There are some situations where a subtle line can be "coaxed" into becoming apparent with some gentle photographic nurturing.

I like compositions that rely on the subtle line almost more than those where the line is bold, straightforward, and obvious. There are many tools I can use to bring out the lines in a composition. Some of these include positioning my camera as I did with *Tree Line* on page 26 to make the area between the reaching tree branches into a line of sky between the trees, and using shutter speed to create the long the horizontal lines in *Line Dance* on pages 20–21. By manipulating and using shallow depth of field, I created bold perpendicular lines in *Penobscot Crossing* on page 23.

In addition, post-production often presents a possibility for enhancing the lines in a composition. In *Wings of Man*, opposite, I created three versions of an image, inverted the versions in the LAB color space, and manipulated the colors. Then, I composited the three versions, creating a sense of motion for the eye from bottom left up toward the right.

The goal is to make the lines in the composition your own, so that the composition works for you. In the real world it is often the case that a "bespoke" line— a hidden line that you find and bring to the viewer's attention using your own photographic and post-production creativity—can do this more effectively than the lines that are obviously in "your face."

Incidentally, another way to look at a "found line" going into an image is that it is a visual entry point. For more about entry and exit points, turn to page 136.

Wings of Man—I photographed a specimen butterfly on a light box, and then, using Photoshop, I made three duplicate images and inverted them using the LAB color space. After manipulating the colors using LAB, I composited the three versions to create the sense that the butterfly was coming to life and flying up, off the background.

The diagram to the right shows the line that is the organizing path for this image. In other words, the viewer's eye follows the butterfly's path from the lower left up and toward the right, into flight.

Nikon D300, 100mm Zeiss Makro-Planar, 2 seconds at f/8 and ISO 100, tripod mounted.

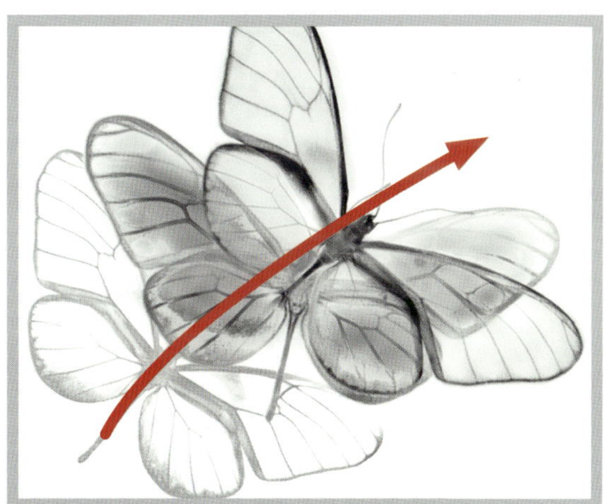

👉 USING LINES IN **YOUR** COMPOSITIONS

Maybe you are saying, "Okay, Harold, I can see how you make lines out of your compositions, but what does this have to do with *my* photographic compositions?" Fair question!

Here's the thing: I think Edward Weston's advice that you don't want to be thinking about formal composition as you make photos is good. As Weston put it, "Now to consult the rules of composition before making a picture is a little like consulting the law of gravitation before going for a walk."

On the other hand, composition is clearly important to photography. For better or for worse, it is impossible to ignore composition.

So what to do?

A good starting place is to learn to see composition in terms of shapes and lines. You can do this by viewing other folks' work, taking a look at the sample images provided in this book (I've described some of my compositional issues in the photo captions), in your own work before you make a photo, and in your own work as you review your photos.

Practice always makes things easier. The better your compositions get, the more you'll see to improve from a compositional viewpoint. Slight movement in terms of the camera position can make a huge positive difference in terms of a final composition. If you take to heart what you learn about composition, your compositional skills can steadily improve.

I like to think that learning to practice composition can be thought of as a bi-directional feedback loop. The more you look at and understand good compositions, the more you will learn to create good compositions without thinking about them in the moment of creation. The more your compositions improve, the better your ability to analyze compositions will become. I like to represent this as a virtuous circular relationship like the one flowing around this circle.

SEEING LINES AND SHAPES

REVIEWING COMPOSITIONS

SPENDING TIME PHOTOGRAPHING

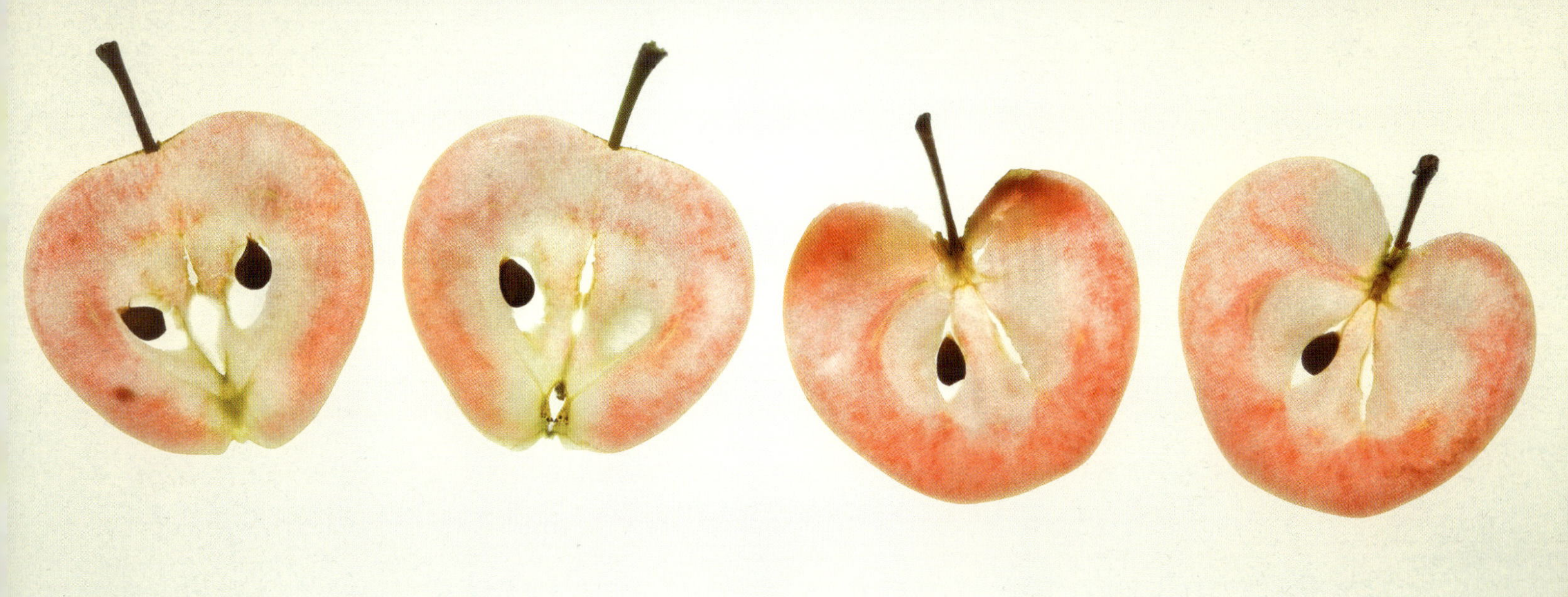

Apple Slice Play Date—It's great fun to photograph fruits and vegetables on a light box. The real hard part is slicing fruits and veggies thin enough without pulling out a box of band-aids!

I was working on an elaborate composition of apples that formed a mandala shape on the light box (for more about mandalas turn to page 49). Four of the apples were particularly interesting looking and I placed them in a compositional line.

The line seemed a little too regular to me so I nudged every other apple slightly on the diagonal. As I looked at the composition that was emerging, it seemed to me that the first apple on the left looked like a mischievous face.

An interesting thing about this composition is that the apples do form a line moving from the left to the right. However, somewhat unusually, there is a "bounce back": after my eye reaches the apple on the right, my gaze returns in the opposite direction along the line back to the apple on the left.

Nikon D850, 50mm Zeiss Makro-Planar, six exposures with shutter speeds ranging from 1/40 to 0.8 of a second, each exposure at f/22 and ISO 64, tripod mounted.

KEY IDEAS

- Lines seem simple, but with a well-designed line you can go anywhere!

- Lines are the basic element of many compositions.

- Most lines have an implied direction.

- Learning to see the lines in compositions is important, and is a skill that can be learned with practice.

- Your work can become richer if you internalize how lines interact, work together, and form visual direction.

- Try to find lines that aren't immediately apparent and use photographic and post-production techniques to make them an important part of your composition.

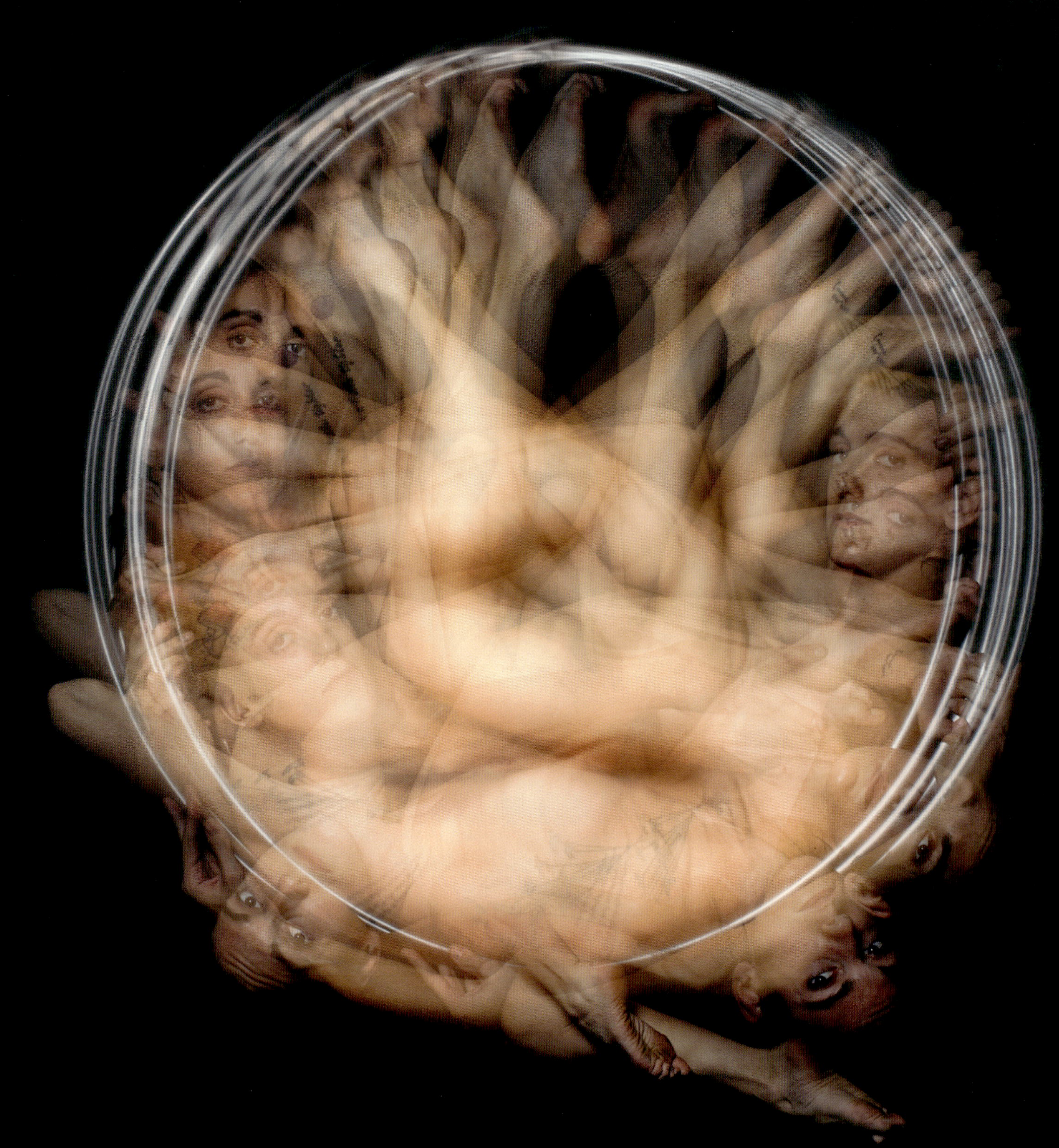

CIRCLE

1 : a round plane figure whose boundary (the circumference) consists of points equidistant from a fixed point (the center)

2 : a circle is a round-shaped figure that has no corners or edges; in geometry, a circle can be defined as a closed, two-dimensional curved shape

Wheel of Life—Creating an in-camera multiple-exposure image like this one can require a great deal of collaboration between the model and the photographer. For this image, the model and I planned where she would be for each exposure. Then, when she was in position, I made the exposure using studio strobes. The camera was set to combine these multiple exposures. This is a modern take on an in-camera technique almost as old as photography itself.

In this image, the model worked with a hanging hoop called a *lyre*. Our plan was for her to work her way around the circle to create a wheel of humanity for the entire composition. Each time she moved into a new position, I pressed the remote shutter release and fired the strobes.

Nikon D800, 55mm Zeiss Otus, single in-camera multiple exposure with eight exposures, each exposure 1/160 of a second at f/9 and ISO 100, tripod mounted.

Circles—and I use the term loosely to include ellipses and ovals—are compositionally powerful. But beware: relying on circles in your compositions can be dangerous.

Think of the way the language is used: A *virtuous* circle is a great thing, indicative of circular changes leading to improvement. In contrast, a *vicious* circle refers to a situation that just gets worse and worse.

Using a circle can be a visual trap. Once you are in the circle, how do you get out? What else is there to look at in the composition besides the circle?

These are true compositional dangers. But if you take the circle "by the horns" (so to speak) and embrace the peril along with the potentiality, circles can become an important part of the scaffolding that makes for compelling photography.

Backing up for a second, what exactly is the power of the circle?

Part of the power is that the eye is drawn to a circle in an image, particularly when the circle dominates the image. When you see a circle playing an important role in a photograph, it's hard to look beyond the circle.

What are the other "power" characteristics of circles?

I've already mentioned that a circle can represent a closed system. In a closed system, the trends can be either good (virtuous) or bad (vicious).

Also keep in mind that a circle has no beginning and no end. This continuous nature of a circle is what makes virtuous and vicious feedback loops possible. Circularity also has other important consequences.

While there are sometimes exceptions, a circle often seems the same everywhere. Unlike shapes that are different when you rotate them, a circle rotated around its center point can still be just the same circle. This depends upon how symmetrical the circle is.

Another way of looking at circular geometry is that you can go around a circle forever. Think of the circle as a cosmic contribution to a virtual merry-go-round. Using circles in your photographic compositions adds a *frisson* of the amusement-park experience to your images.

When you make it back to the starting point of a circle, it's time to begin again. Therefore, a circle can seem infinite. One way of thinking of this is to remember the classical motif of a serpent swallowing its own tail. There is no beginning, there is no end, and it goes on forever.

The idea of infinity is compelling enough. However, keep in mind that a circle can "drown out" all other shapes. When the eye sees a circle, nothing else may matter. The circle used in its broadest sense is such a compelling shape that it may preempt all other compositional gambits.

The danger in a composition involving a circle comes from the very potency of the shape (see "The Circle as Visual Archetype" on page 41). When a circle is present, who will think about, or look at, anything else?

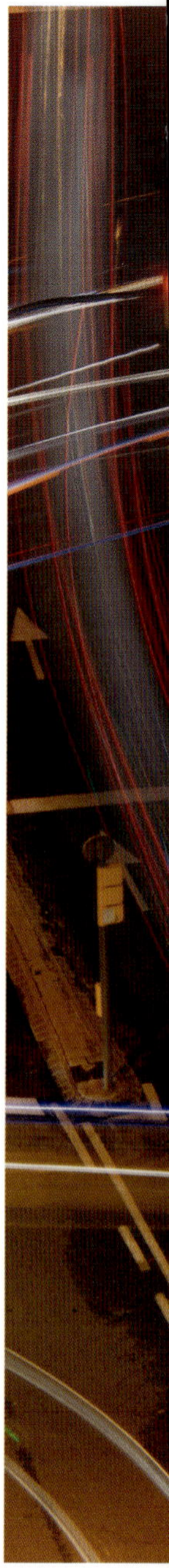

Gran Via, Barcelona—To create this image, I made my way past a "do not enter" sign and onto the roof of an art deco hotel in Barcelona, Spain. It was nighttime in the autumn and the air was crisp.

I went to the edge of the roof and peered down on the traffic circle below. The fountain in the middle of the circle seemed to be changing colors. I thought the blue was the most interesting contrast with car taillights going by.

With this kind of photography, truly you have to "overshoot," meaning it won't be clear which exposure is best, or even if it works at all until you are able to evaluate after-the-fact. In this frame, I was happy with the way the patterns of car lights and arrows on the pavement balanced the power of the central circle in the composition. (Also, see discussion of this image on page 49.)

Nikon D810, 28-300mm Nikkor Zoom at 100mm, 5 seconds at f/13 and ISO 64, tripod mounted.

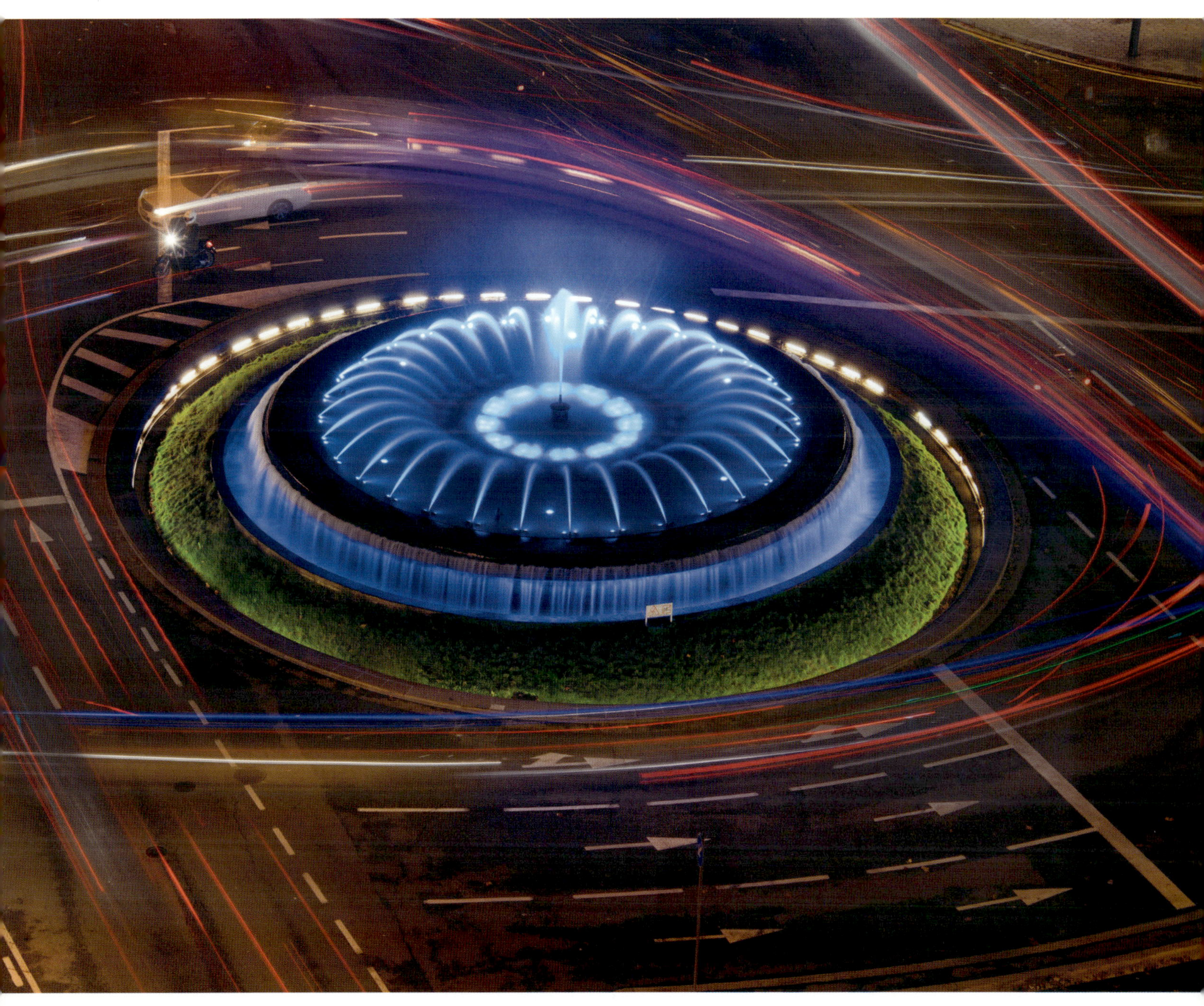

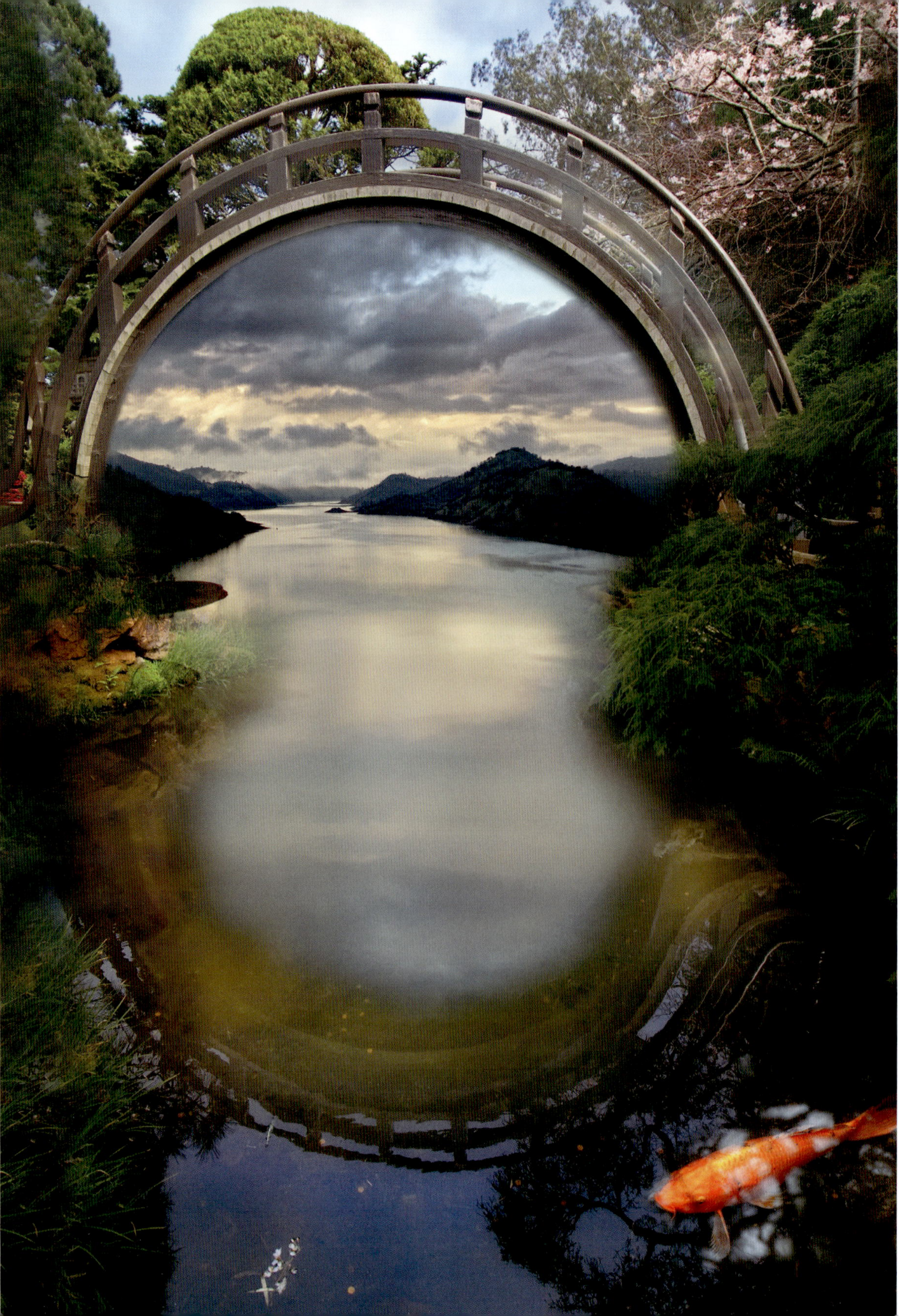

A circle, as in a mandala, can represent the entire world. Indeed, as you can see when you look closely at mandalas that go back into the deepest antiquity, a circle can also represent the entire universe. (To find out more about the mandala shape, turn to page 49.) So circles as shapes come with great symbolic meaning. Use a circle, use it well, but don't use it heedlessly.

The trick in making successful imagery that includes a circular shape is to use the power of the circle as strength without falling for the pitfalls of circular entrapment.

It's worth making the effort to learn how to accomplish compositional goals with circles. Some successful compositions that use circles do so by:

- Understanding the role of the circle as a visual archetype.

- Making the entire a composition about the circle, perhaps by creating an image where the circle performs as a complete and integral whole—for example, in a mandala.

- Playing with the viewer's likely preconception about circles, and placing the circle off to one side.

- Making sure the circle is smaller than and balanced by other elements in the composition.

- Using the circle as a compositional doorway into another aspect of the composition, or indeed into an entire new world or universe.

The Circle as Visual Archetype

Carl Jung (1875–1961) was a Swiss psychiatrist whose multi-disciplinary work spanned psychology, anthropology, archaeology, literature, philosophy, and religion. One of Jung's contributions involves understanding the importance of the *archetype*.

The idea of the archetype goes back to the beginnings of humanity's ability to tell stories, and in visual art, perhaps as far back as the paintings on the walls of the caves at Lascaux (roughly 20,000 years ago). Jung's ideas about archetypes were based in part on Plato's conceptualization of the universal (or primordial) pattern (circa 400 BCE).

The Jungian archetype is a universal theme or symbol that resonates generally. People respond to the archetype, whether or not they recognize it consciously, in some cases across culture and time.

Archetypes at the level of the collective unconscious can be found in religious art, fairy tales, and mythology from around the world. Jung thought that archetypes existed independently of world events, current politics, and even the specifics of culture. In addition, the true archetype has influence throughout the stages of each individual's unique development, although the way the archetype is perceived might vary from culture to culture, and between different individuals.

The study of archetypes is a large subject. However, it's well worth the attention of any artist, because "plugging into" archetypes makes for images that tap into the collective unconscious, which is one of the broader and most important goals of art.

To the extent that an archetype is visually referenced, the composition will have greater resonance with the viewer. This is true whether or not the archetype is consciously recognized, and in fact, may be more effective when there is no conscious awareness of the reference to the archetype.

Entrance to Sơn Đoòng Cave—Sơn Đoòng Cave is located in the impenetrable mountainous jungles along the old Ho Chi Minh trail on the Vietnamese side of the Vietnam–Laos border. To get to the cave, you have to slog down a jungle mountainside, up a river bed, and through another vast cave into a hidden jungle valley. This is a difficult place to get to and is rarely visited.

To make this image, I used multiple-exposure HDR techniques to show both the inside of the cave and the jungle landscape outside. This is indeed a portal to a different world showing never-scaled heights, shafts of bright light, unusual flora, and perhaps the occasional jungle monkey descending on vines.

Nikon D810, 15mm Zeiss Distagon, eight exposures total: seven exposures with shutter speeds ranging from 0.6 of a second to 30 seconds, at f/22 and ISO 200; one exposure at 30 seconds at f/22 and ISO 500; tripod mounted.

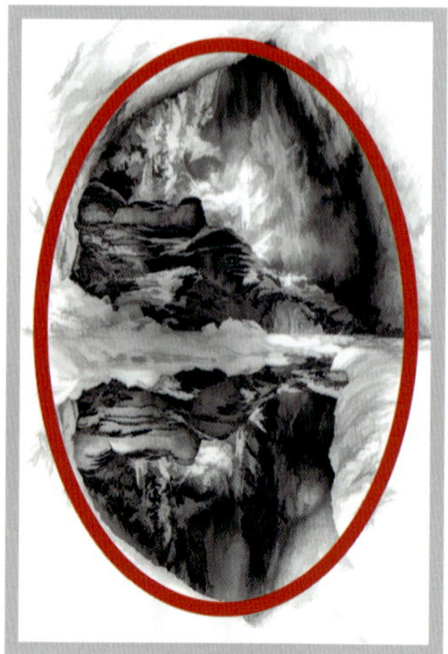

While this simplifies the composition (because there are additional horizontal lines), the cave entrance from within and its reflection form an ovoid. This oval shape matches the subject matter and evokes a portal to the sunlit world through the opening.

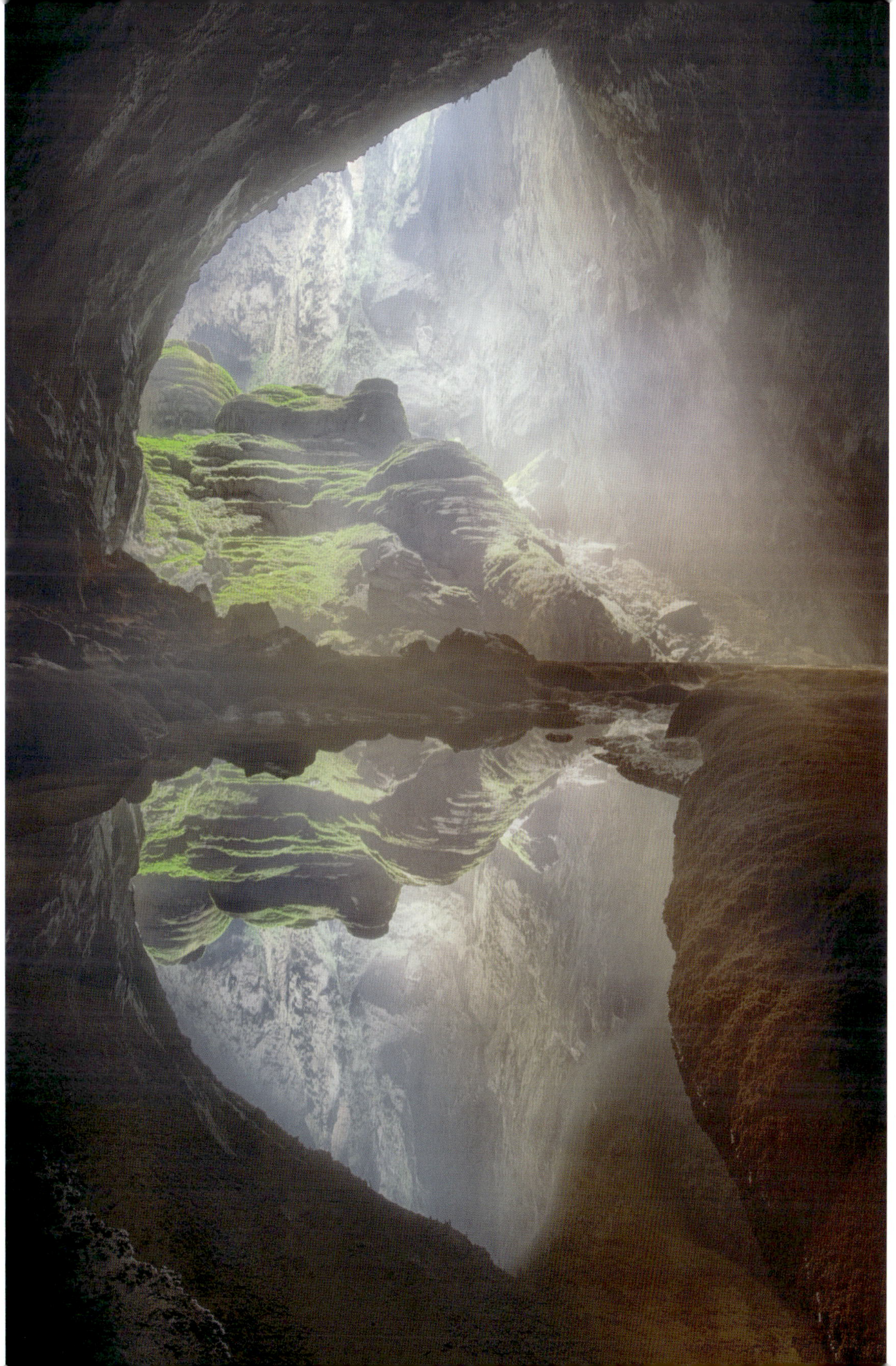

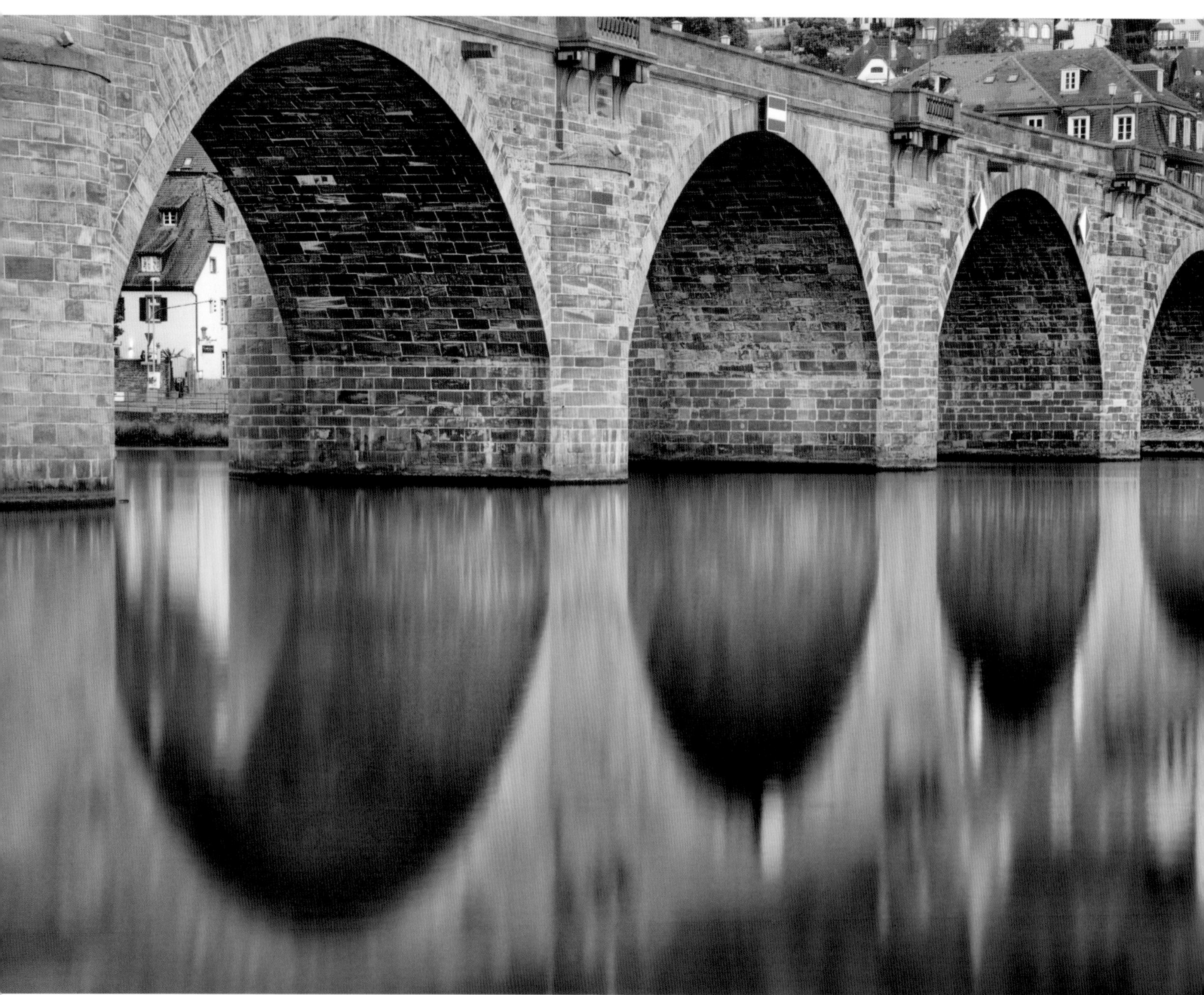

Regardless of the theoretical Jungian framework of archetypes, when I look at a photograph that includes deep shadows I am aware at some level that the "dark side" of human nature is being referenced.

Keep in mind that archetypes usually work in a subliminal way. In other words, this can be a secret between the photographer and the viewer, and in some cases neither the photographer nor the viewer is actually aware of what is really going on with the archetype, even if they know that something is being touched at a deep level.

The viewer of your photo should not be saying to themselves, "Hey! That artist has tapped into an archetype!" Often the association of an image to the archetype is perceived unconsciously.

Art presents projective opportunities for adding personal assumptions to a universal symbol, in much the same way that a deck of Tarot cards provides symbolic characters and attributes that can be read in light of a personal situation.

Jung was himself a visual artist. Leaving aside the general validity of many of Jung's ideas about the way the mind works, the concept of the visual archetype is important in photographic composition.

When it comes to visual archetypes, it is hard to think of any shape that is more fundamental than the circle. Indeed, if a

Alte Brücke, Heidelberg—One of Germany's great rivers, the Neckar, flows through the university city of Heidelberg to its confluence with the Rhine River in Mannheim. The Romans built a bridge on the site of the Alte Brücke ("Old Bridge"). When floods swept the Roman bridge away, there was no crossing of the Neckar for over a millennia until the Alte Brücke was constructed in 1788.

I photographed the Alte Brücke at dusk, and used a neutral density filter. That way, I could make an exposure long enough (60 seconds) so the circles formed by the bridge arches and their reflections became a striking composition.

If you diagram the shapes in this composition, you'll find successively smaller ovals. The converging perspective lines of the bridge and its reflection are almost tangent to the ovals. This is an attractive but somewhat complex composition taking advantage of the circularity of the bridge and reflections.

Nikon D800, 28-300 Nikkor Zoom at 90mm, +4 neutral density filter, 60 seconds at f/32 and ISO 50, tripod mounted.

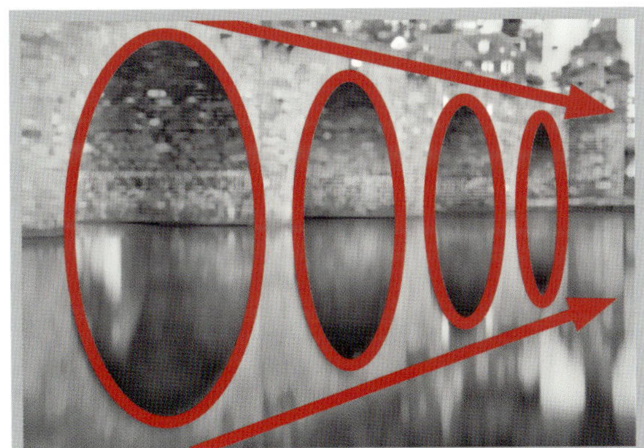

composition strongly involves a circle, it is probably referencing an archetype. The circle as "world without end," the circle as portal, the circle as wheel—one of the earliest, most important human inventions—and the mandala are some of the visual archetypes that are based on the circle.

Compositions That Are About the Circle

In its simplest form, the circle dominates the composition. In this kind of photograph, the composition is about the circle. Something is happening within the circle. A dancer moves around a ring or a flower gone to seed forms a bud. All, or most, of the action takes place within the circle.

For the photographer, it's important to recognize a composition that is "about the circle" when it appears. Recognition of a composition that is about a circle will help you clear the frame of distractions and make the circle big, bold, and evident to the viewer.

Note that compositions that are about the circle often involve "squaring the circle." In other words, a composition that is about the circle is usually bounded by a square, and may often be presented in a square crop.

The opposite can also be true. If a circular composition cannot be framed as a square, but fits better as a rectangle, then maybe you should put the circle aside and emphasize other aspects of your composition.

Putting the Circle Aside

What happens when you have a round composition that is almost circular? And what if other things besides the circle are going on?

Papaver Pod from Above—This photograph shows the dried pod of a *Papaver somniferum*, also known as the opium poppy. I mounted the poppy pod on a black velvet background using a straightened paper clip to keep it above the cloth.

To get as close to the poppy as you can see here, I used a macro lens and an extension tube.

To me, this botanical image looks a lot like a living creature, perhaps some form of starfish surrounded by a circle.

Nikon D850, 50mm Zeiss Makro-Planar, 24mm extension tube, five exposures with shutter speeds ranging from 1 to 15 seconds, each exposure at f/22 and ISO 64, tripod mounted.

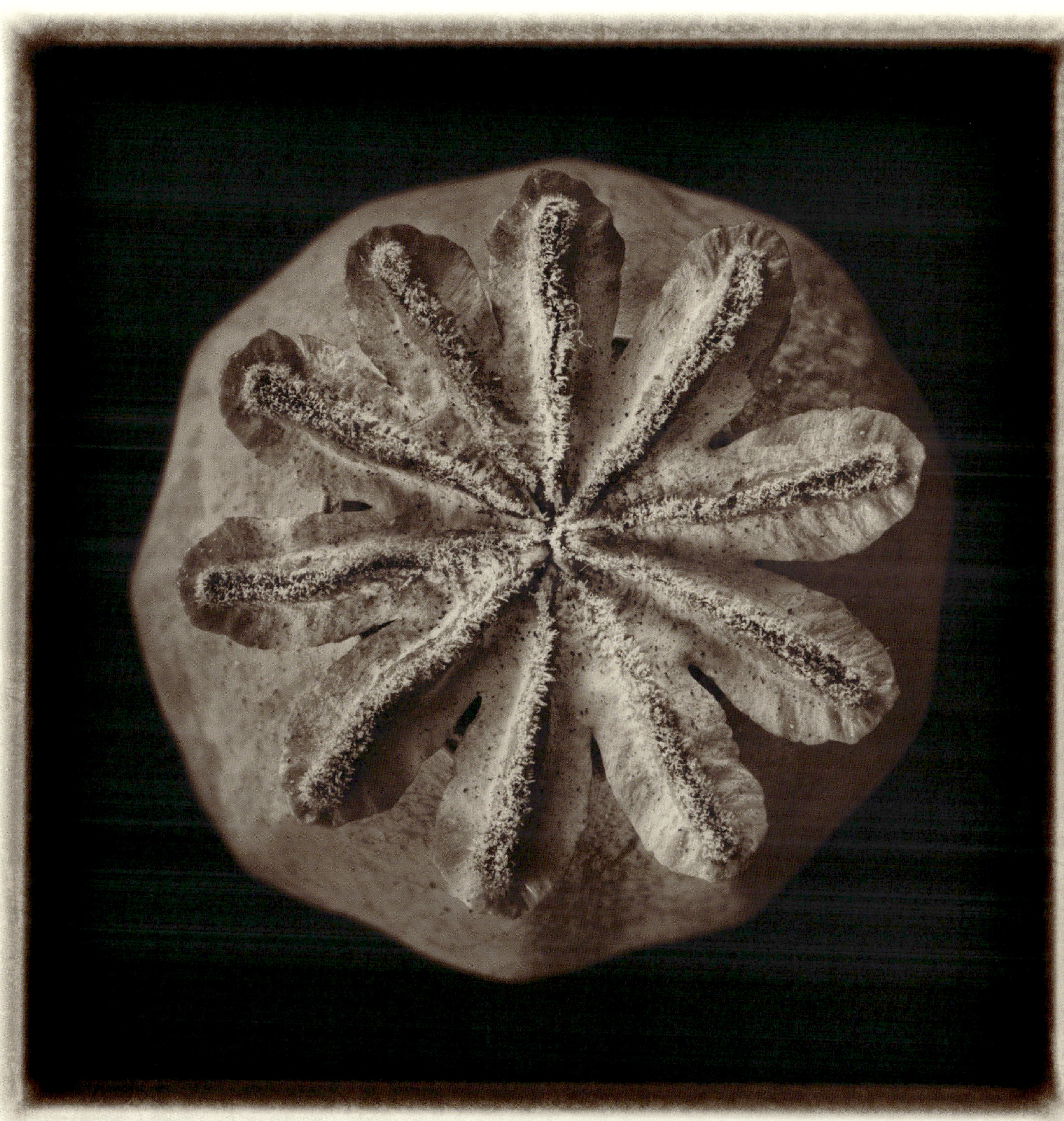

It's important to be able to step aside from the power of the circle and make the flourishes, lines, and shapes that are outside the circle important in their own right. A circle doesn't always need to dominate!

An example of this kind of composition is the photograph of a traffic circle in Barcelona, shown on pages 38–39. This image was photographed from above at night. Certainly, the oval shape in the center of the composition—the fountain—is important. But that element could not stand on its own in the composition. Therefore, the cars in motion creating lighted swooshes "outside the circle" were significant and needed to be treated with care. When making the image, getting the balance of the car taillights was far more time consuming and difficult than centering the circular fountain.

Making the Most of Portals

A doorway into a different world—or a *portal*—is magical. Creating portals is one of the things I strive for in my photographic compositions.

While portals are not necessarily circular, many are composed of circles or ellipses (for example, check out the cave entrance in the photo on page 43).

It's important when working with composition to take advantage of the suggestion of a magical portal. Other worlds can be good or bad, happy or sad, calm or apocalyptic. Whatever they are, alternate universes are fascinating and different. We look to portals to guide us in our lives in this world through their differences from our world, and to suggest what might possibly happen here in the future.

If the artist is a magician revealing what lies behind the shadows—and this is an important aspect of being an artist—showing portals is one of the most important tools of the trade. Emphasizing the presence of spiritual gateways in a photo is an easy and great way to show the possibility, as Leonard Cohen said, of a "crack where the light gets in."

The Mandala Shape and the Magic of the Universe

In Eastern religions, a mandala may represent paradise, deities, or sacred spaces, or simply be used as an aid for meditation. The hallmark of a mandala is its circularity. Mandalas are always based on a circular shape. This helps explain why the mandala (and the circle) is one of the oldest shapes used for human artistic expression. The shape stands alone as a symbolic beginning without end, an end without a beginning.

Once you've embarked on a mandala, it's often hard to integrate the circle of the mandala with an ordinary non-circular composition. Conversely, a rectilinear composition, such as a landscape, doesn't usually merge easily or neatly into the infinite and endless possibilities conveyed by the swirling mandala.

So mandalas tend to be part of their own genre, and a thing unto themselves. It's worth taking a hard look at the mandala for the purity of the circular shapes involved.

I'm not saying it is easy to construct mandalas using photography. In fact, this is a hard shape to integrate photographically; however, it is worth doing for the compositional exercise, and for the occasional extraordinary result.

My own mandalas are primarily created using flower petals on a light box (you can see one opposite), although of course I have used other materials as well. I've also experimented with cropping, and using a circular fisheye lens to create a mandala-like effect.

Your challenge is double-barreled: Try to learn about the power of the mandala so that this shape can be integrated into your own compositions. Then, practice creating images that consist entirely of a mandala.

It is worth learning about mandalas both in their art-historical context and in their usefulness as an adjunct to modern photographic composition. Creating successful photographic mandalas can be quite pleasing, and they will likely find an enthusiastic audience.

A Matter of Balance

In face of the overwhelming power of the circle as a compositional symbol, how do we find balance?

The answer, as in many things in life, involves clear communication. As a photographic artist, if you know that you have invoked the power of the circle, you should do so consciously. The fact that you are doing so with forethought by no means

Chasing Tails on Black—This image was constructed by placing alstroemeria ("Peruvian Lily") petals on a light box. As I pieced together the composition, my idea was to echo the circular nature of a mandala. But it seemed to me that I could do something more by creating an echo of its infinite form. The title, *Chasing Tails*, refers to the idea that you can "enter" this composition from several different directions. (For more about entering and exiting composition, turn to page 139.) But whatever way you choose to enter, you will soon be tangled in the endless loop of the mandala.

To finish the composition, I converted the white background to black in post-production using an LAB color inversion.

Nikon D850, 55mm Zeiss Otus, six exposures with shutter speeds ranging from 1/13 of a second to 2.5 seconds, each exposure at f/16 and ISO 64, tripod mounted.

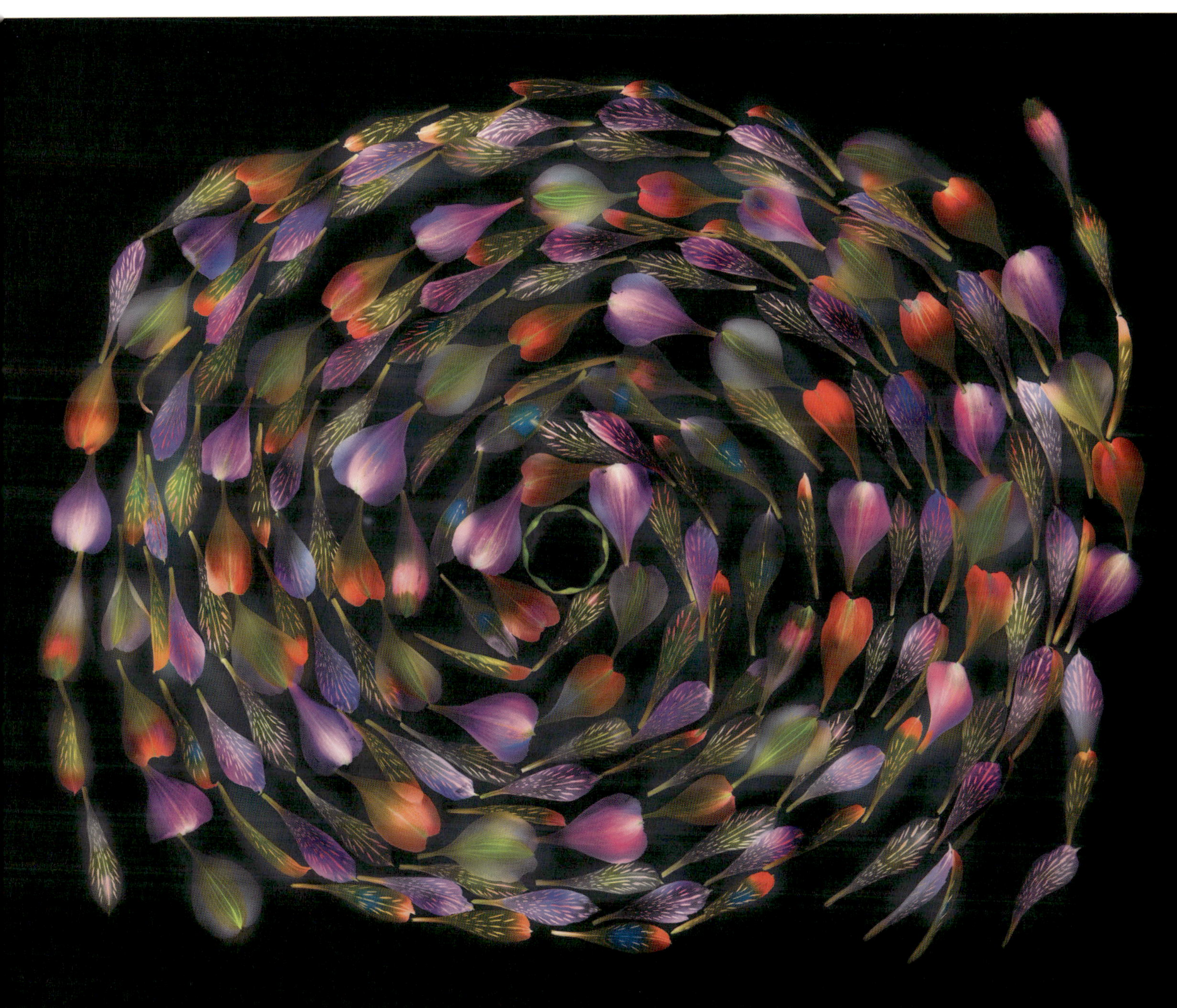

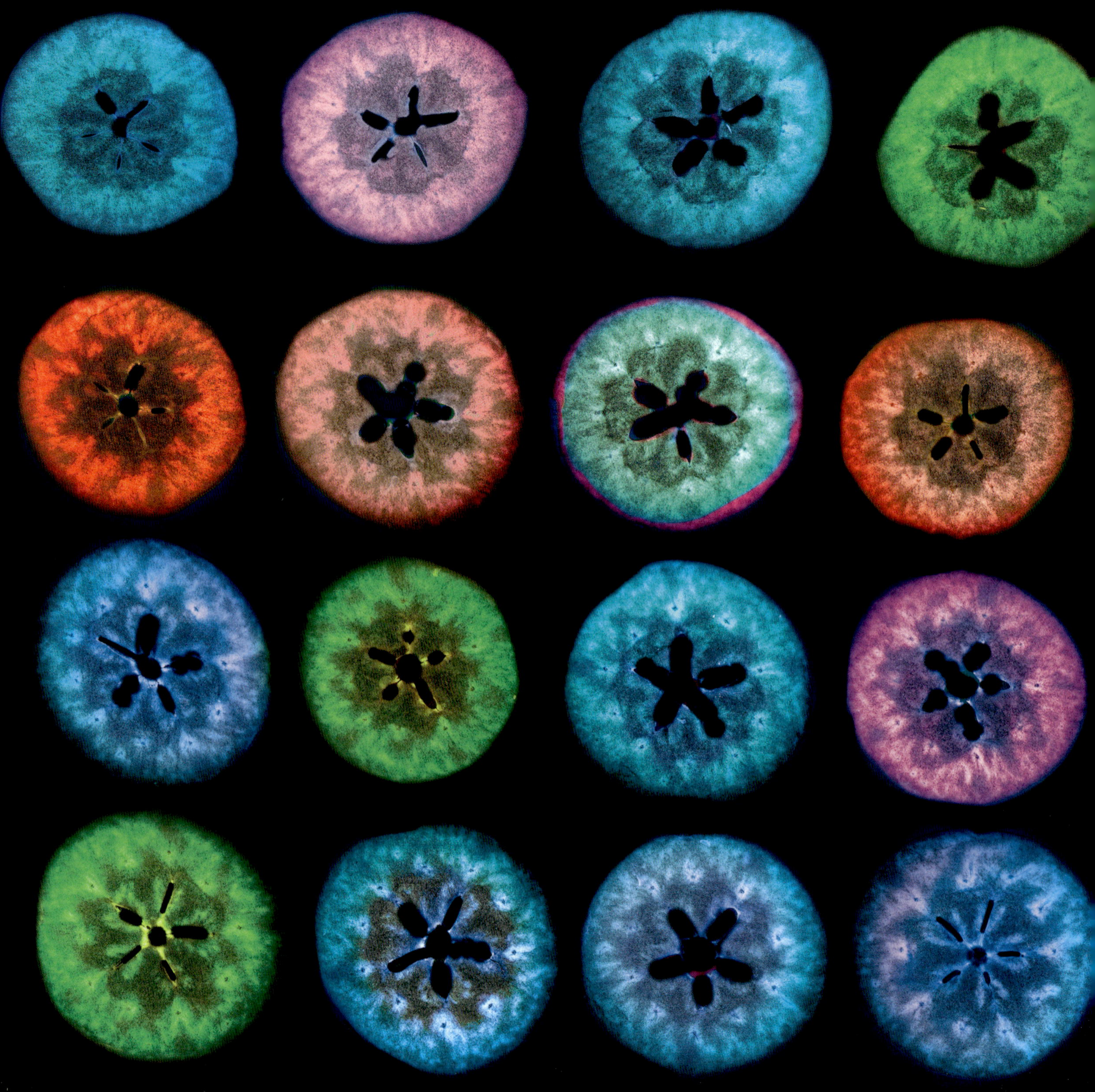

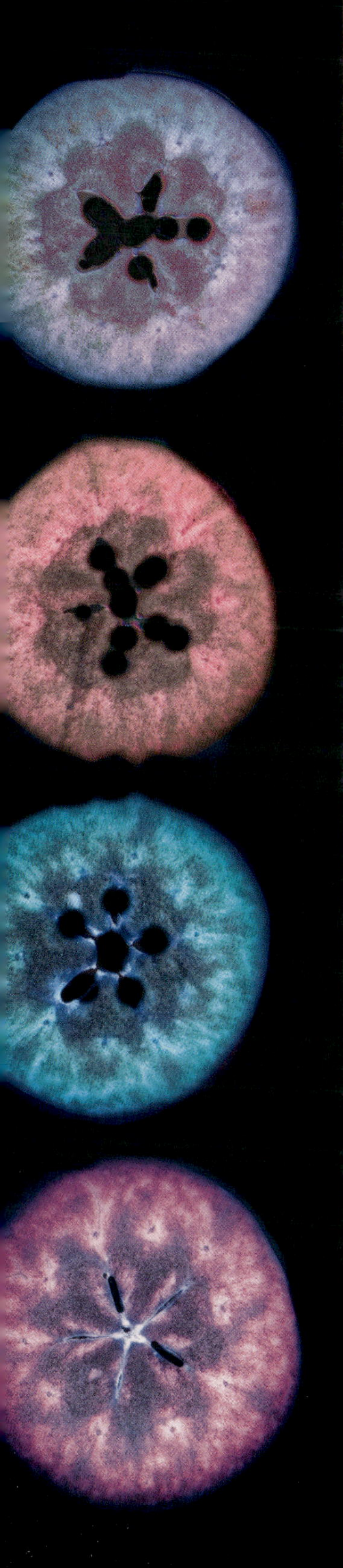

Colored Apple Slices—To photograph apple slices on a light box, the first challenge is to slice the apple thinly. Very thinly! This is more of a challenge than may be at first apparent. The best tool is a mandolin, which is a vegetable slicer used in kitchens around the world. But the mandolin must be used with great delicacy; otherwise, the center of the apple will collapse.

Apples, in particular, appealed to my photographic eye because their slices can be almost perfect circles.

I liked the idea of creating a grid of evenly-spaced apple slices. This visual effect could be punctuation dots, botanical art, and wheels on a grander scale.

Looking at the slices on the white background of the light box, I realized that I had a great opportunity to play in post-production. Manipulating colors using the LAB color space and Photoshop's Blending Modes is one of my favorite pastimes.

To create this version of the image, I started by inverting the Lightness channel from white to black, so the apple slices would appear on a black background. Next, I created layer stacks with color manipulations using LAB channel variations.

This image shows an example of integrating circular shapes into a rectangular form using a grid as an organizational principle.

Nikon D850, 50mm Zeiss Makro-Planar, six exposures with shutter speeds ranging from 1/30 of a second to 1 second, each exposure at f/13 and ISO 64, tripod mounted.

implies that the viewer of your image is aware of this.

Balance in circle compositions means either surrendering to the circle—acknowledging the circle as the key component of the composition—or complementing the circle with additional flourishes and swooshes that defy the centric nature of the circle.

KEY IDEAS

- Circles are powerful shapes that can enhance a composition (the virtuous circle). But circles can be a visual trap and overwhelm a composition (the vicious circle).

- A circle goes on forever. It has no beginning and it has no end.

- When a circle is used as a portal, it can open a door to another magical world.

- Circles are often used in visual archetypes.

- A circle is the key element in a mandala where it represents spirituality and the entire universe.

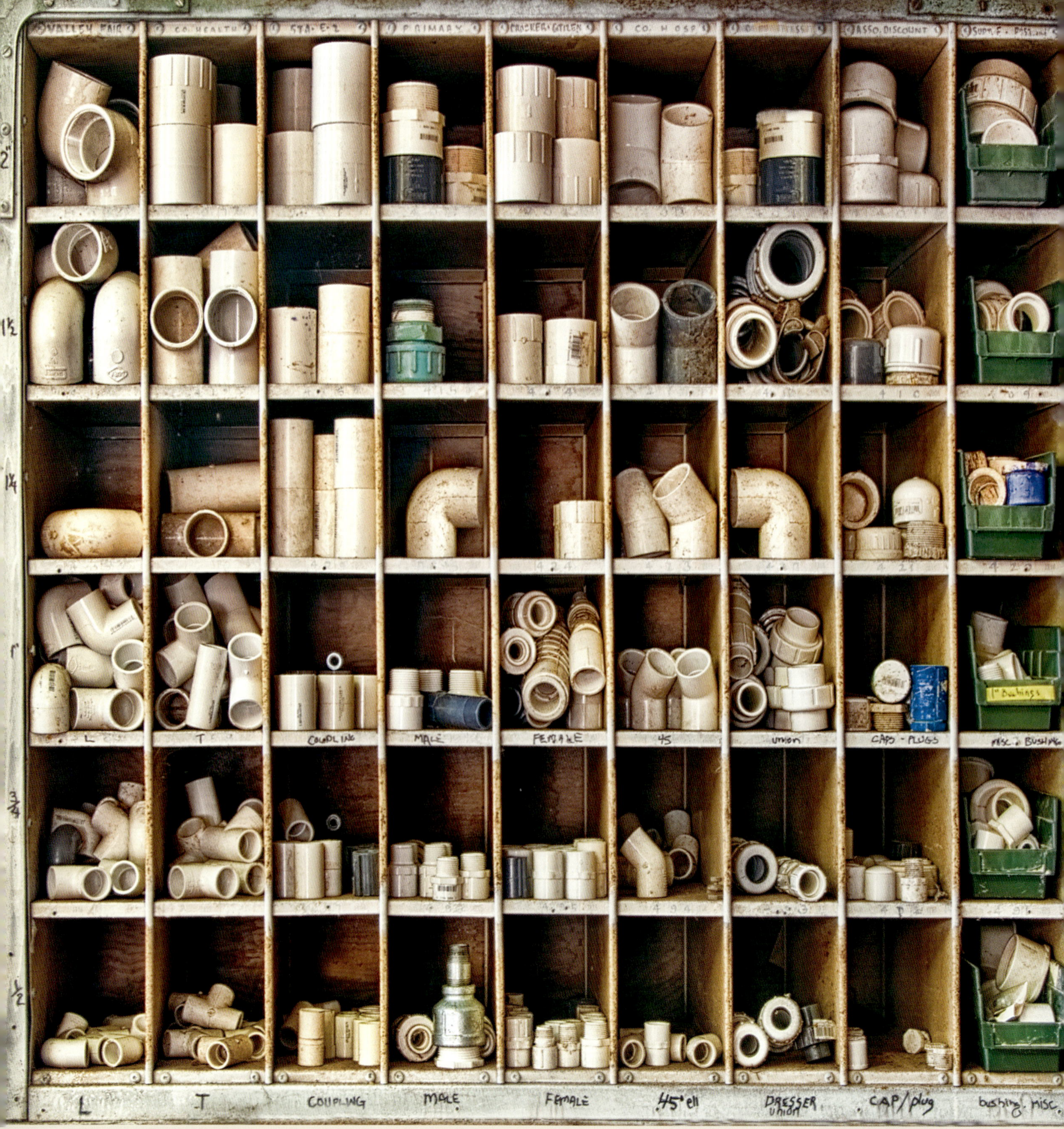
VALLEY FAIR
CO. HEALTH
STA-E-Z
PRIMARY
CRACKER-GTILEN
CO. HOSP
MISC
ASSO. DISCOUNT
SUPT F. PSS
2"
1½
1¼
1"
¾
½
L
T
COUPLING
MALE
FEMALE
45
UNION
CAPS - PLUGS
MISC. BUSHING
1" Bushings
L
T
COUPLING
MALE
FEMALE
45° ell
DRESSER
union
CAP/plug
bushing misc.

RECTANGLE & FRAME

All Squared Away—This grid of plumbing parts, found in a farming toolshed at a Zen monastery near San Francisco, yammered for my attention because of its obvious regularity. There are a lot of rectangles and squares in this composition!

If you're dealing with a lot of squares in a composition, it's a good idea to put them into a square boundary. That's why this image is presented as a square. Looking at the overall composition, it is a grid of rectangles. What's the one thing that should happen with a grid of rectangular shapes? It is important that the right angles appear as 90° angles; the shapes can't be distorted. This should not be a problem if the camera is positioned smack-dab in the middle of the height of the grid with the focal plane exactly parallel to the grid (see "Moving the Camera Slightly Makes a Big Difference" on page 61).

The sad fact of photographic life is that things are never perfect or ideal. The reality was that when I inspected this image on my studio monitor, some of the rectangles in the grid were bowed and no longer perfectly square. This took some work to correct in Photoshop, but eventually everything was "all squared away."

Why go to so much trouble with a grid of rectangles full of plumbing supplies? Because the entire visual point of this composition is to relate the outer framing square to the inner grid.

Nikon D300, 18-200mm Nikkor at 38mm, five exposures with shutter speeds ranging from 1/10 of a second to 2 seconds, each exposure at f/10 and ISO 200, tripod mounted.

Combine lines and some right angles, and pretty quickly you get to rectangles and squares. (For the record, a square is just a rectangle where all the sides are the same.)

I know! We're bypassing the humble—but mighty—triangle. But, don't worry! The triangle gets its due on page 75.

Rectangles play an especially important role in composition. It's hard to overstate. With few exceptions, every photographic composition is bounded by a rectangle.

Being bounded by a rectangle has extremely important implications; of course, the rectilinear spaces within a composition have important considerations on their own. Taking this all together—the bounding rectangle, internal rectangles, and the relationships of the internal and bounding rectangles to one another—there is a considerable and valuable tangle of compositional opportunities and considerations involving rectangles in almost every image.

Furthermore, in addition to the bounding rectangle and rectangles internal to an image, there is one other rectangle we need to consider: the rectangle made by the camera's focal plane.

Just a bit ago, I mentioned exceptions to the rectangular framing. One exception is the *tondo,* a piece of round art, which you can read about further starting on page 70. In regard to unusual framing and proportions, you might also check out the discussion on "Busting Into and Out of the Frame" starting on page 66.

Understanding Borders and Frames

As a generalization, the camera captures an image in a rectangular shape and most digital sensors are rectangular or square. However, a print or reproduction of a photograph—while often rectilinear—is sometimes manipulated into a variety of shapes.

Most often, the rectangular shape that was captured by the camera becomes the rectangular frame bounding the image both in its native capture and in a reproduction or print rendering.

When making a photograph, the precise geometric relationship of the camera's focal plane to the subject matter of your photo is not fixed until the shutter is released. The way you decide to establish this visual relationship has important consequences (see "Moving the Camera Slightly Makes a Big Difference" on page 61).

A study of rectangles starts with acknowledging the crucial, but often understated, role of "framing." What do I mean by framing? Framing is a word that can mean many things, and the concept causes considerable confusion, so it is important to proceed with clarity.

In this spirit, yes, a picture frame—like the one that sits around a print on the wall—is indeed a frame. But a picture frame made of wood or metal is not what we are talking about here in the context of a photographic image.

A real-world picture frame is a frame only in the most literal sense, although some art does play with the motif of the external frame, perhaps by incorporating it into the image.

Under the Yaquina Bay Bridge—The Yaquina Bay Bridge is a wonderful and massive Art Deco structure that was built in the 1930s along the Oregon coast.

On a chill autumn morning, exploring around the Yaquina Bay Bridge, I walked through an underpass with my camera and tripod. There I found this marvelous structure, framed through the internal peaked arches.

I do often find myself under things such as bridges. A partial explanation for this propensity is that observing scaffolding, structure, and underpinnings allows one to implement visual framing. I like understanding how things are built and this adds to my sense of the poetry of the place.

In the context of the Yaquina Bay Bridge photo, the image is anchored by the outer frame or border of the image itself. Within this outer frame are a series of receding arches. The most distant arch opens a window on the mechanics that support the cantilevered portion of the bridge.

Photographing through the arches allows a pleasing sense of symmetry and framing that uses the power of the outer border to its best compositional advantage.

Nikon D850, 21mm Zeiss Distagon, six exposures with shutter speeds ranging from 1/125 of a second to 1 second, each exposure at f/22 and ISO 64, tripod mounted.

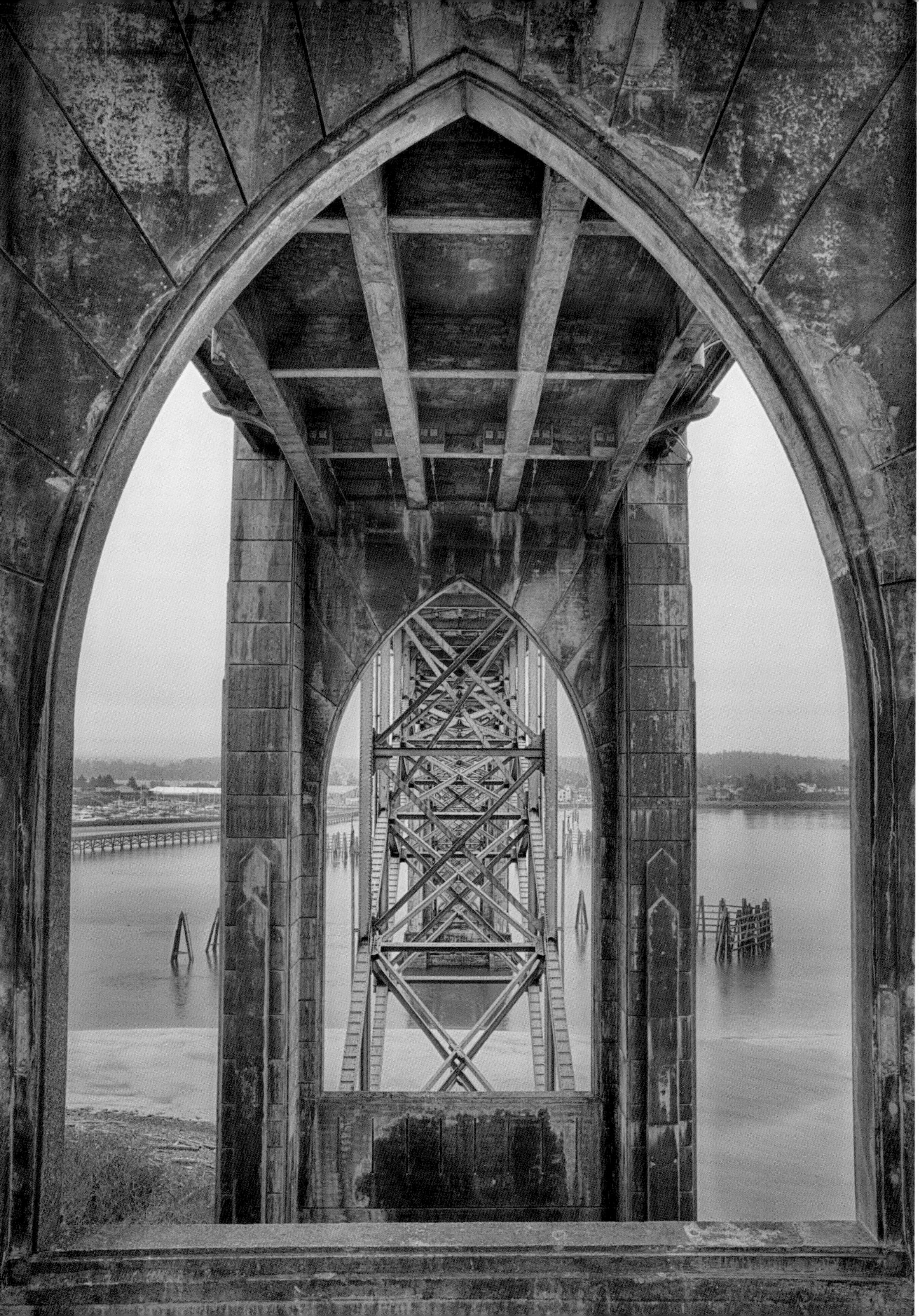

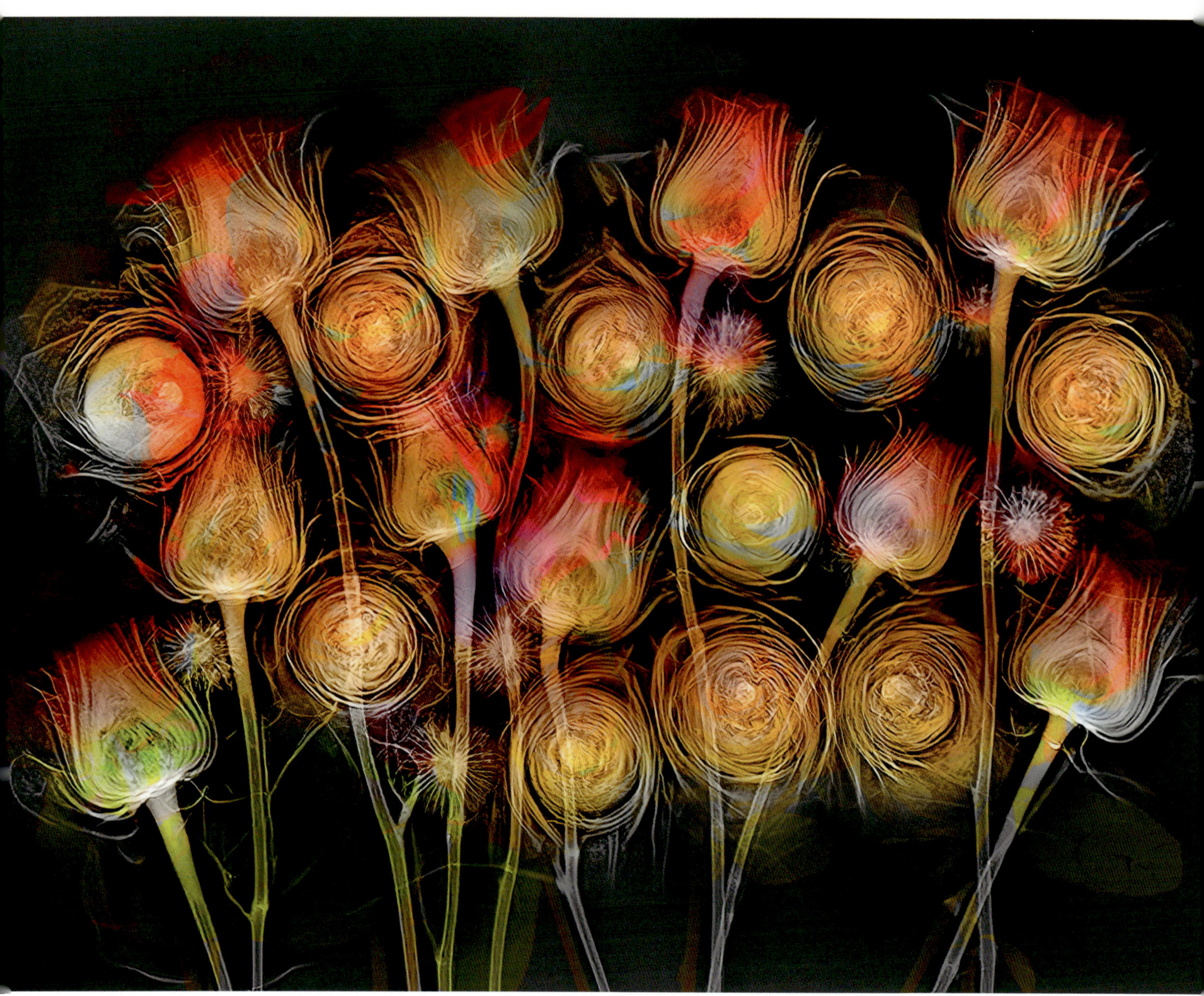

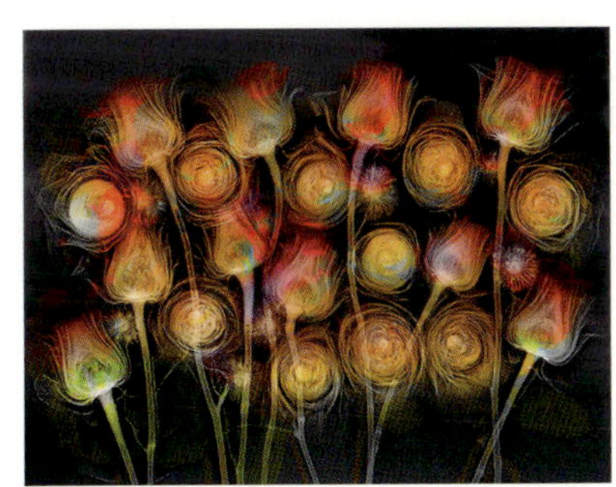

The most important part of framing in relationship to photographic composition concerns the boundaries of your image within and surrounding the image itself and does *not* involve the external picture frame.

All images have compositional boundaries, starting with the perimeter dimensions of the photo. In the case of a print on paper, this compositional boundary is expressed by the edge of the piece of paper, as well as the edges of the photo. In addition, most compositions of any complexity also have a variety of internal borders, boundaries, and frames.

The single most significant frame is that of the image itself. You don't need to print an image to see this frame. It is perfectly apparent when you look at an image on a monitor or the internet.

One challenge taken on by *Composition & Photography* is to position photography in relationship to two-dimensional design. Looking at photography from the perspective of two-dimensional design, essentially all photographs must interact in their composition with their own edges.

Let me re-emphasize that the word "frame" can mean a number of different things, including:

- The monitor on which you look at an image.

- The paper border of a print.

- The boundary and edges of the photo itself.

All of these are frames, with the boundaries and edges of the photo being the most universal and useful. Let's start by looking at how your internal composition can interact well with this photographic frame.

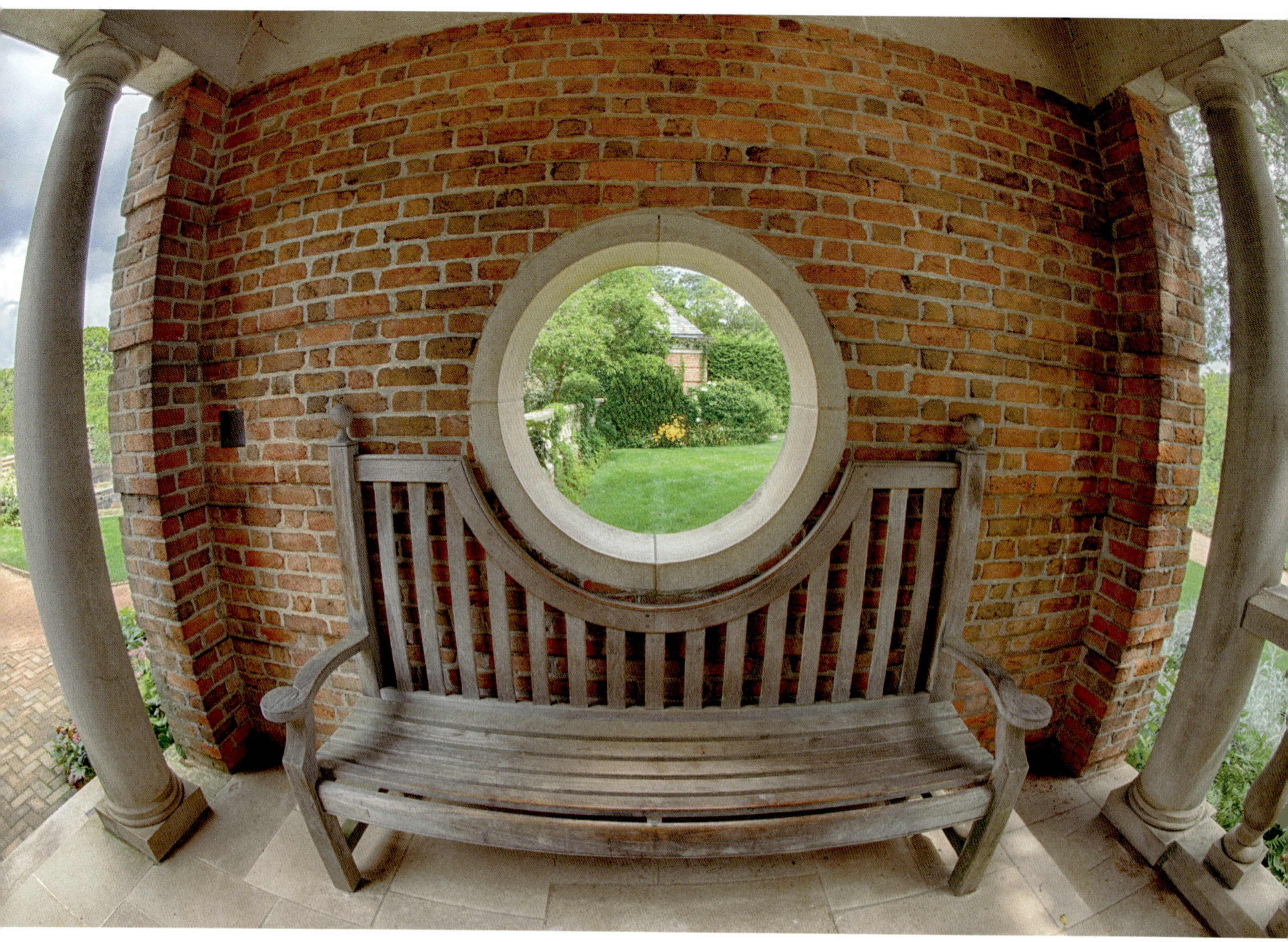

Tondo—In the English Walled Garden area of the Chicago Botanic Garden, a stylized gazebo sports a round porthole to the "outside" world.

I used a rectangular fisheye lens to capture this porthole window in a visual play with the borders of the photo. The circular shape, or tondo, in the center of the image is presented without distortion while the border areas of the image show the kind of bending distortion you would expect from a fisheye lens. This is a reversal of the normal order of things and adds to the interest of the composition.

Nikon D850, 8-15mm Nikkor fisheye at 15mm, five exposures with shutter speeds ranging from 1/13 of a second to 4 seconds, each exposure at f/29 and ISO 64, tripod mounted.

MOVING THE CAMERA SLIGHTLY MAKES A BIG DIFFERENCE

Slight changes in the position of the camera can make a huge difference in your final composition. Let's take a look at some of the details involved.

The focal plane of a camera is the rectangle of the capture medium. In a film camera this would be the film, and in a digital camera this is the sensor. The focal plane is flat, and it is where the capture takes place in the camera.

Almost every camera indicates the focal plane on its exterior, with a small symbol that looks like a circle with a line through it ($\ominus$), as shown in the magnified camera inset at the right. The line indicates the focal plane if you extend it from the symbol out toward the edges of the camera.

The geometric relationship between the focal plane and the subject has important optical consequences that relate to composition. When the focal plane of the camera is parallel to the plane of the subject, if focus is correctly set, all points of the composition will be in focus at any aperture. However, once the focal plane of the camera is no longer parallel to the subject at a wide-open aperture, not all points of the subject will be in focus, as you can see in the diagram on the lower right.

The important relationship between your focal plane and the plane of the subject is one that needs to be explored by moving the camera position around to find the relationship that works best given the specifics of the composition you are working on. You can think of this process as "scootching" with the focal plane!

Focus is impacted by the geometrical relationship between your focal plane and the plane of the subject. In addition, this geometry affects many other aspects of your composition in subtle but powerful ways. It's definitely a great idea to use your feet and move your camera to experiment with altering the focal-plane-to-subject relationship.

Moving the camera position slightly can also have a huge impact on the vanishing point in your image. Turn to page 162 to find out more about this.

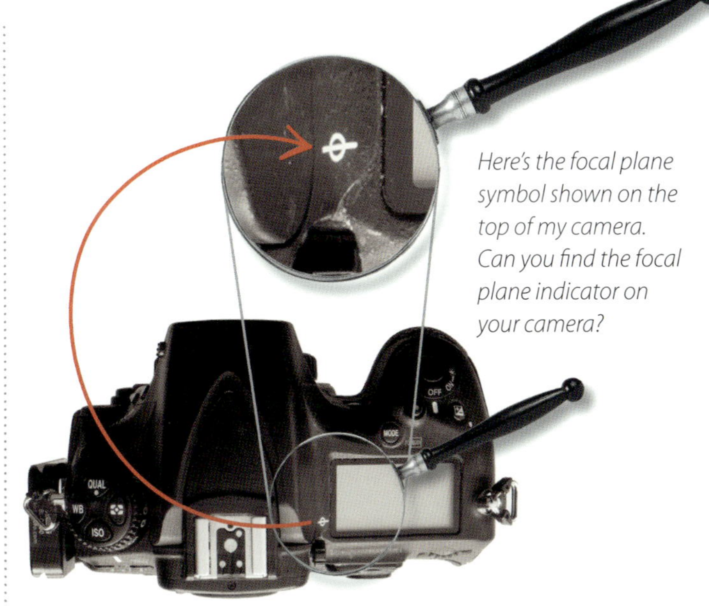

Here's the focal plane symbol shown on the top of my camera. Can you find the focal plane indicator on your camera?

*For an In-Focus Subject,
Keep the Camera and Subject Parallel!*

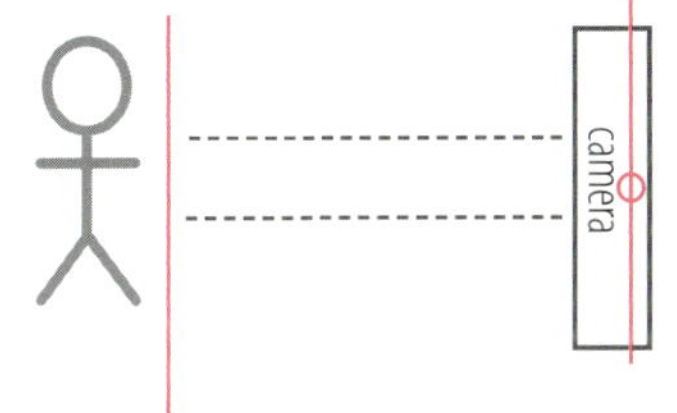

This camera is parallel to the plane of the subject. At any aperture, including wide open, all points in the parallel plane will be in focus.

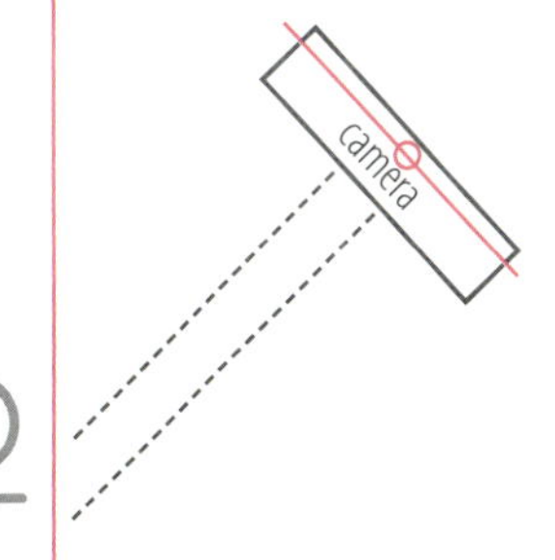

Here the camera is not parallel to the plane of the subject. Note that the dashed distance lines from the camera to the subject are not equal. At a wide-open aperture, not all points of the subject will be in focus.

This pink line is the subjects' plane. It should be parallel to the camera's focal plane.

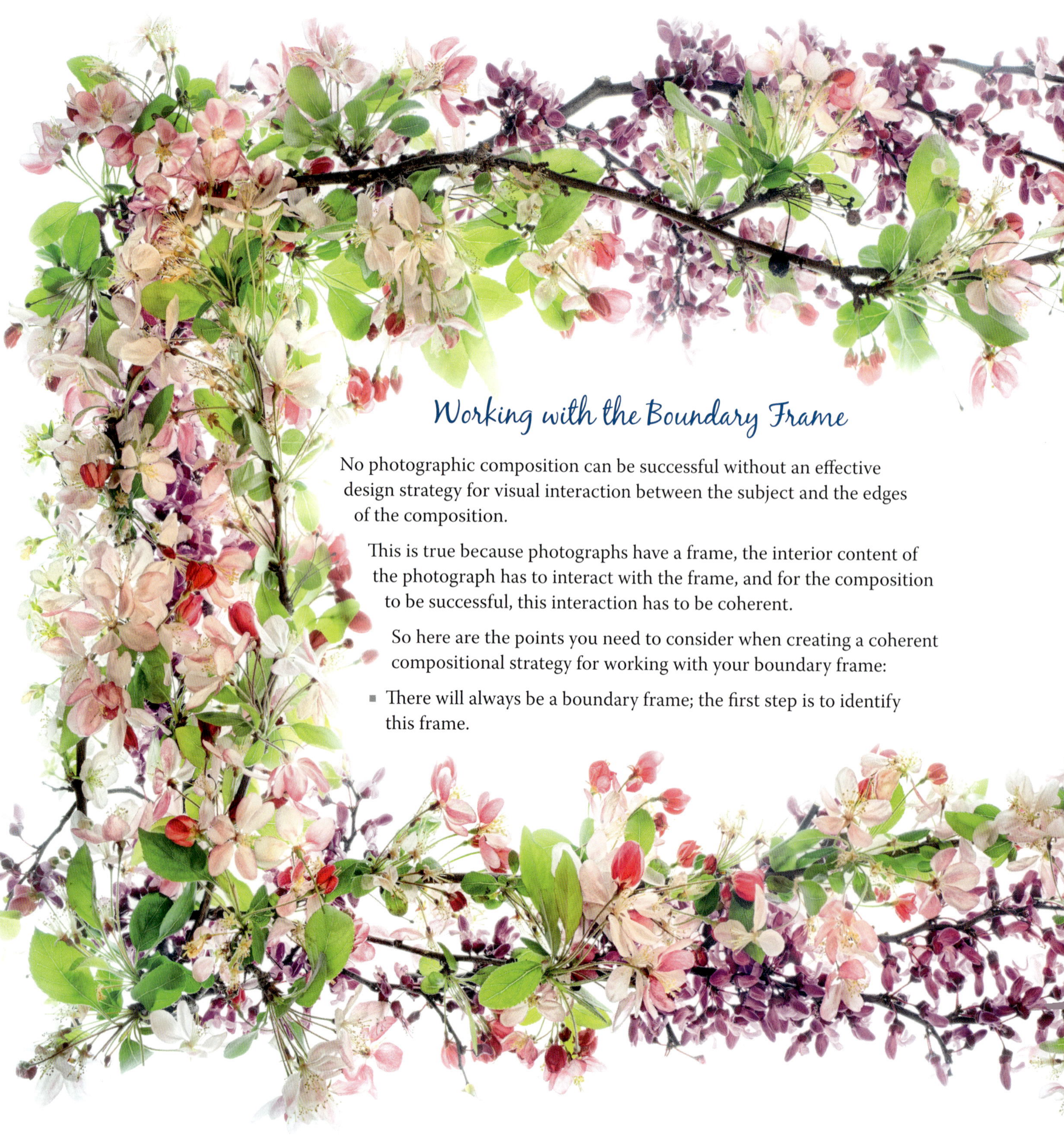

Working with the Boundary Frame

No photographic composition can be successful without an effective design strategy for visual interaction between the subject and the edges of the composition.

This is true because photographs have a frame, the interior content of the photograph has to interact with the frame, and for the composition to be successful, this interaction has to be coherent.

So here are the points you need to consider when creating a coherent compositional strategy for working with your boundary frame:

- There will always be a boundary frame; the first step is to identify this frame.

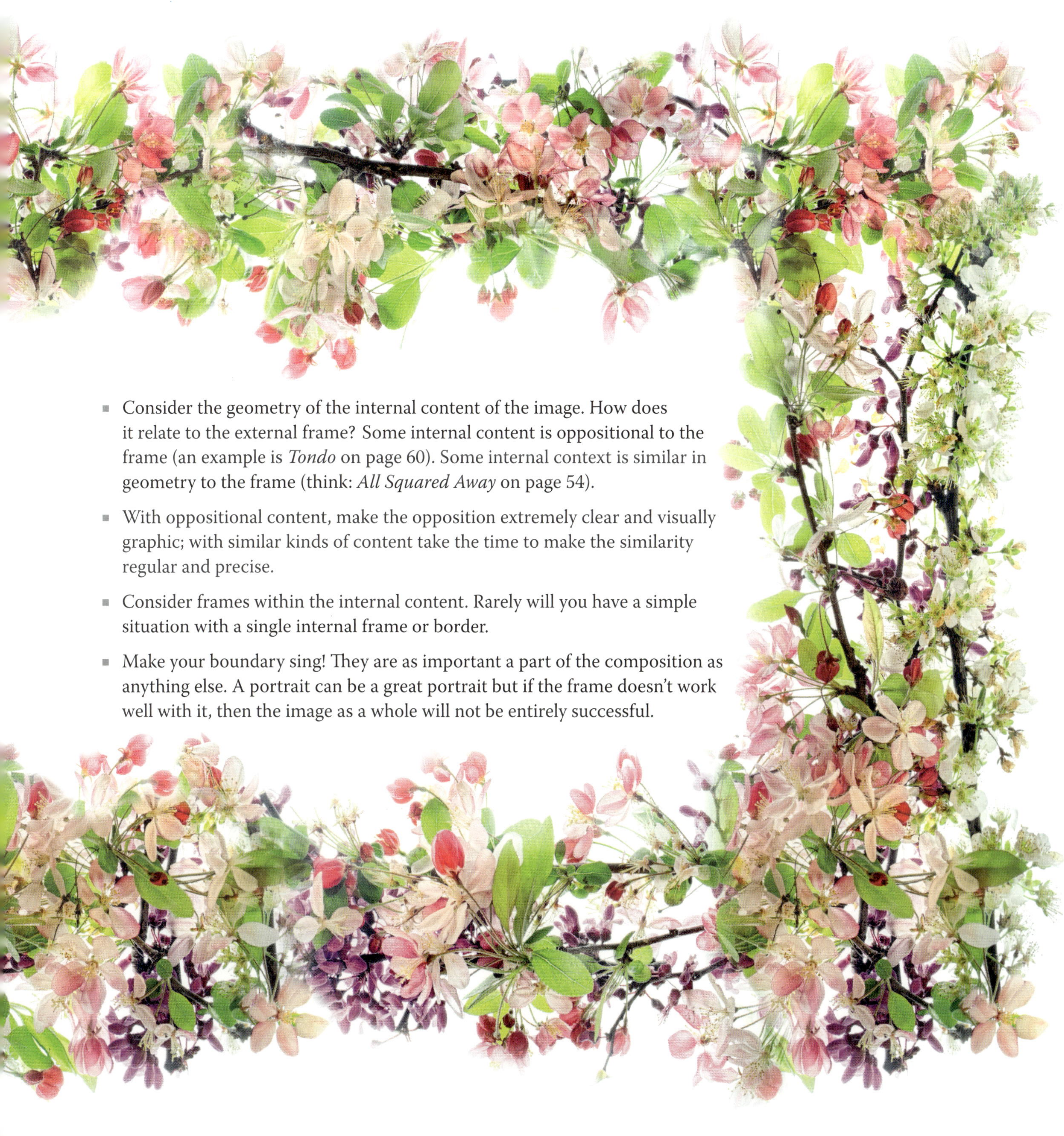

- Consider the geometry of the internal content of the image. How does it relate to the external frame? Some internal content is oppositional to the frame (an example is *Tondo* on page 60). Some internal context is similar in geometry to the frame (think: *All Squared Away* on page 54).

- With oppositional content, make the opposition extremely clear and visually graphic; with similar kinds of content take the time to make the similarity regular and precise.

- Consider frames within the internal content. Rarely will you have a simple situation with a single internal frame or border.

- Make your boundary sing! They are as important a part of the composition as anything else. A portrait can be a great portrait but if the frame doesn't work well with it, then the image as a whole will not be entirely successful.

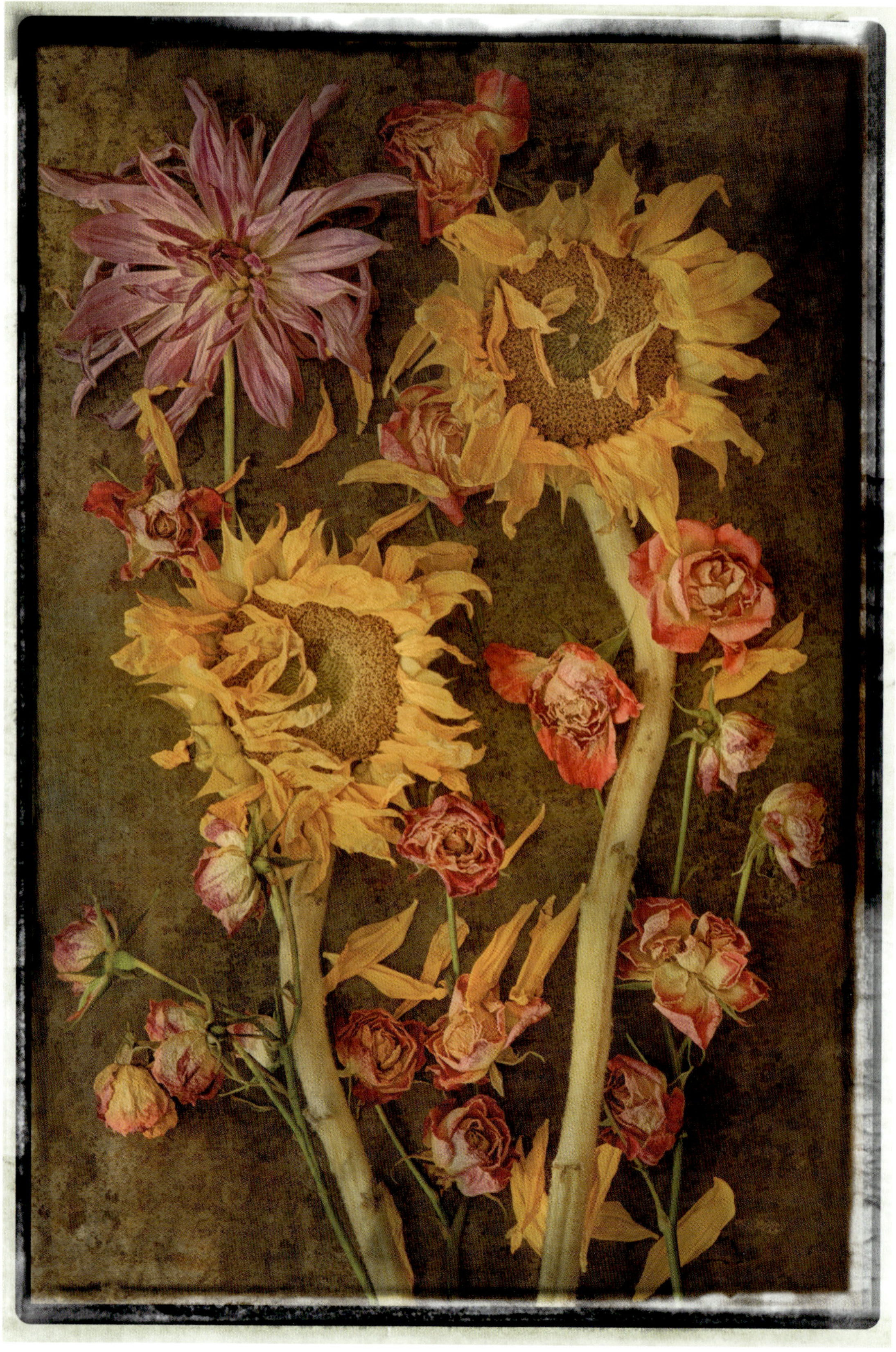

Pages 62–63: *Flowering Branches Frame*—It was high springtime near where I live and the branches of flowering trees were magnificent. I brought in a few apple and cherry branches, and I placed them on my light box. My idea was to create a lush floral frame with interior white space. The interior white space could be used eventually to add other design elements, or simply kept as an elegant "picture" frame.

Nikon D850, 55mm Zeiss Otus, seven exposures with shutter speeds ranging from 1/30 of a second to 10 seconds, each exposure at f/16 and ISO 64, tripod mounted.

Left: *Metamorphosis*—I photographed these beautiful sunflowers, dahlia, and roses—all a little past their prime in the way of *wabi-sabi*—using an old baking sheet as the background. The title of the image, *Metamorphosis*, represents the change that comes in life when flowers inevitably fade from their glory. They are beautiful as they age. There will be more flowers. Autumn may tend to winter, but warmth and life will come again in the spring.

When it came time to crop and print *Metamorphosis*, I noted that the baking sheet acted as an internal frame. With a strong internal frame like this, one does not want to fight the visual dynamics of the image.

It would have been a mistake to use the essentially arbitrary proportions of the digital capture to add another inelegant frame around the baking sheet. So I simply cropped the image closely to the baking sheet's dimensions. This is slightly off from the original proportions of the capture, but not so much as to be upsetting or alarming, and it creates a visually harmonious image.

Nikon D850, 55mm Zeiss Otus, six exposures with shutter speeds ranging from 1/10 of a second to 6 seconds, each exposure at f/11 and ISO 64, tripod mounted.

Controversy about Proportions

In 1726, Jonathan Swift published his satire *Gulliver's Travels*. In this book, the surgeon Lemuel Gulliver traveled to a variety of exotic lands, including Lilliput where the inhabitants were engaged in endless war over which end of an egg was the best to open, the big end or the little end. All this is by way of saying that folks will argue and fight fervently about almost anything.

So it may not surprise you to learn that there is an active and ongoing controversy about cropping proportions of a photograph. "Originalists" maintain that all crops must be in the same proportions as was captured in the camera. On the other hand, hard-core "visualists" just want what serves the image best, and are less concerned about the "authenticity" of any crop.

Well, this is a pretty silly thing to get agitated about. Let me be clear that my sympathies generally fall with the visualists: I want what is best for the image.

Thought Experiment

- Can you make or construct a photo that does not have a border or a frame?

- What would this look like?

- How would you create this "image without borders" in the real world?

- Does everything have an edge, a beginning, and an end?

However, the originalists do also have a point. If you are someone who views a lot of photographs—as most folk do in our society—or who works with photography, your compositional eye will have become accustomed to certain proportions, such as 1.5:1. Most post-production software specifically allows you to crop in the original proportions. There's a kind of internal alarm bell that rings when a photograph is presented outside of these original proportions.

You can almost always get away with a square crop, and an original-proportion crop is, of course, expected. But any other crop may tend to make the viewer think consciously or unconsciously that something is awry.

This isn't to say that you shouldn't crop out of proportion. Sometimes an unusual crop is fully warranted. What you should know is that an out-of-proportion or non-square crop will often draw a second glance—for better or for worse.

Busting Into and Out of the Frame

So the frame's the thing. It will be with every photo. But personally, I always get antsy when there are constraints on creative freedom. The frame is a constraint on my creative freedom and I don't like it one bit!

So what are you going to do when the two-dimensional design constraints take a bite out of your personal creative freedom? You can ignore the situation and go on making great images in a conventional frame. As they say, "where ignorance is bliss, 'tis folly to be wise."

That's fine. But, why be conventional? If you have to have a frame, and you're feeling antsy, you can either move toward the frame or move away from the frame. "Moving toward the frame" (busting into the frame) means intentionally adding

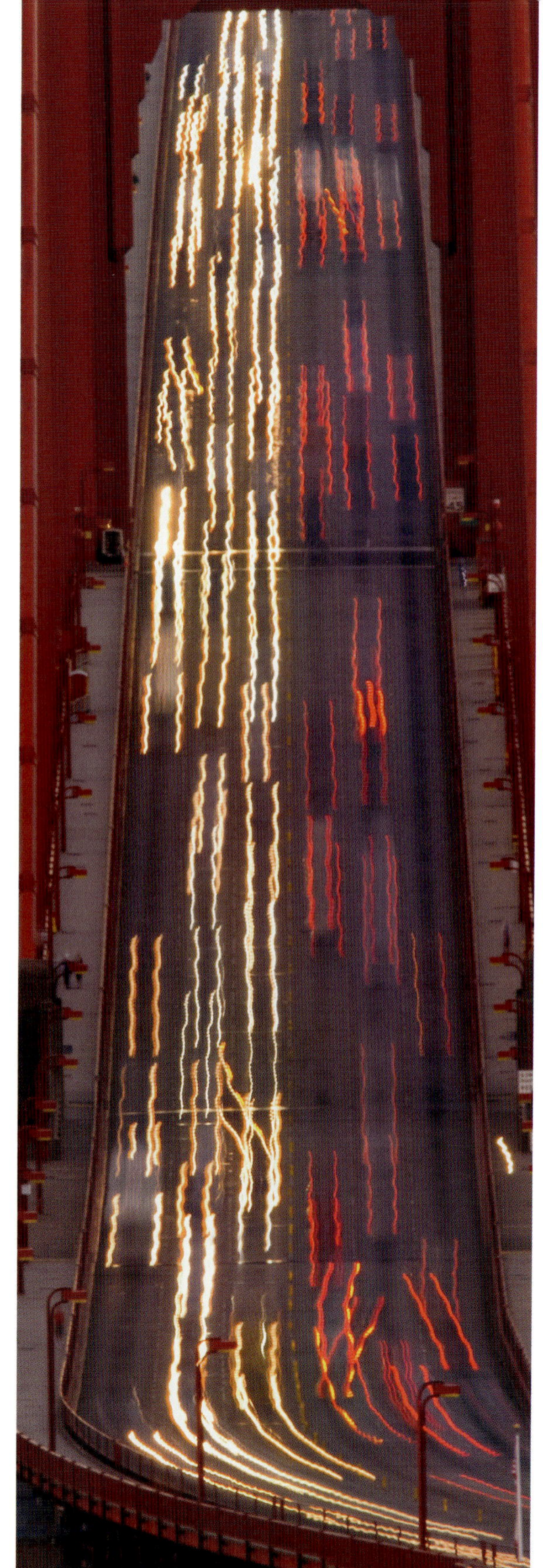

Cars—As late afternoon turned to twilight, I positioned myself on a battlement of the Presidio Battery West in San Francisco. Looking down on the Golden Gate Bridge, I decided to create an image focusing on the traffic on the bridge, so I chose a long telephoto lens (400mm, the equivalent of 600mm in full-frame terms).

With this photograph of traffic, I realized that the important part of the image was the traffic itself. The only way to present this traffic as the essential ingredient of the image was to use an unconventional, thin and long vertical crop.

Nikon D200, 400mm, 3 seconds at f/22 and ISO 100, tripod mounted.

Page 68: *Trouble on the Tracks*—My inspiration for this collage was the surrealist paintings of René Magritte. In Magritte's paintings, strange things relating to the framing often happen: snow-capped mountains appear on broken shards of glass; trains tunnel through the sky. So in this image, I used Photoshop to composite an example of a frame within an image showing train tracks that rise through an apparent fold in the landscape; this folds to another portion of the framed image. The idea was to combine apparent plausibility with surreal impossibility.

Landscape: Nikon D810, 28-300mm Nikkor zoom at 150mm, 1/125 of a second at f/8 and ISO 64, tripod mounted; Train tracks: iPhone 6s; images composited in Photoshop.

Page 69: *Dark Angel*—When making this image, I asked the model to stand still but move her arms up a step between each exposure. With in-camera multiple exposures, this created a pattern similar to wings. Looking at the image on my studio monitor, it seemed to me that it was closed in and constrained by its visual frame. I decided to go with this effect rather than fighting it, and added a simulated tintype border around the image.

Nikon D850, 50mm Zeiss Otus, in-camera multiple exposure with eight exposures at 1/160 of a second at f/8 and ISO 200, tripod mounted; exposures on a black background using radio-fired strobes; tintype frame added in Photoshop.

your own frames to photographs in a potentially highly artificial way.

"Busting out of the frame" means placing your image in a context that is not usually thought of as a frame: circles, ovals, spirals, diamonds, having the image ooze out of the rectangle of its frame, adding protrusions to the frame, and so on.

In some cases, such as with journalistic photography, photographers intentionally frame an image so that important parts of the subject are cut off by the frame. This can be used to show busyness, confusion, movement at top speed, or incompleteness. Cutting off a body part or other important element can be a visual indication that something is wrong in the scene. The world is a messy place and using the frame in this way can show it.

There are no rules! Just as what we think of as a "circle" can actually be ovoid or elliptical, a "rectangle" isn't necessarily a precise and rigid figure with right angles. The concept here is of a generally rectilinear space, but the corners can have some curves, and the lines can have character and be a bit wavy.

Here, we're not looking for the precision of a geometrician. The key issue when it comes to framing is the relationship of a closed internal space with the outer boundaries of the image. Look for the overall sense and feeling that the shapes and their relationships within the frame convey to the viewer.

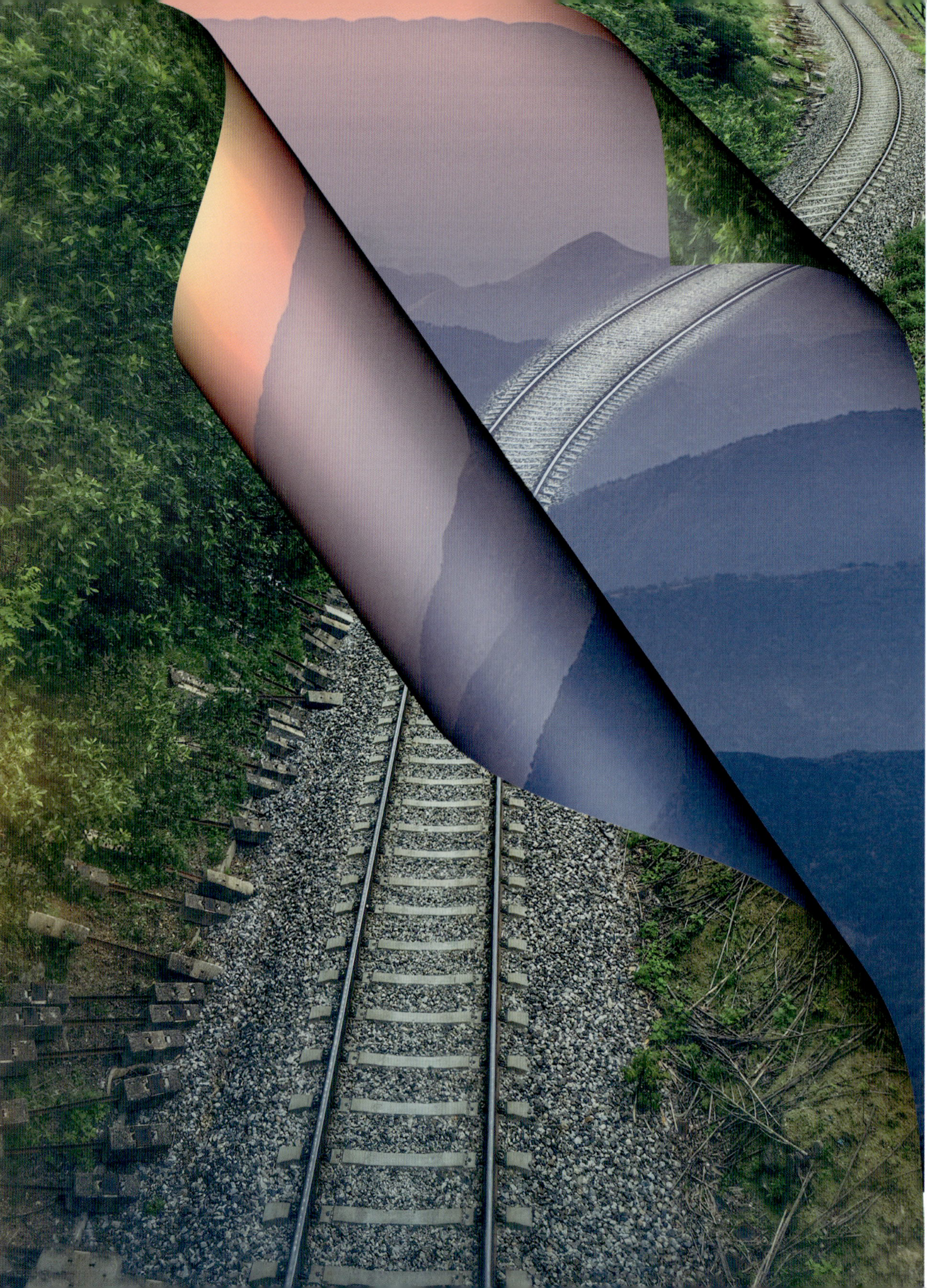

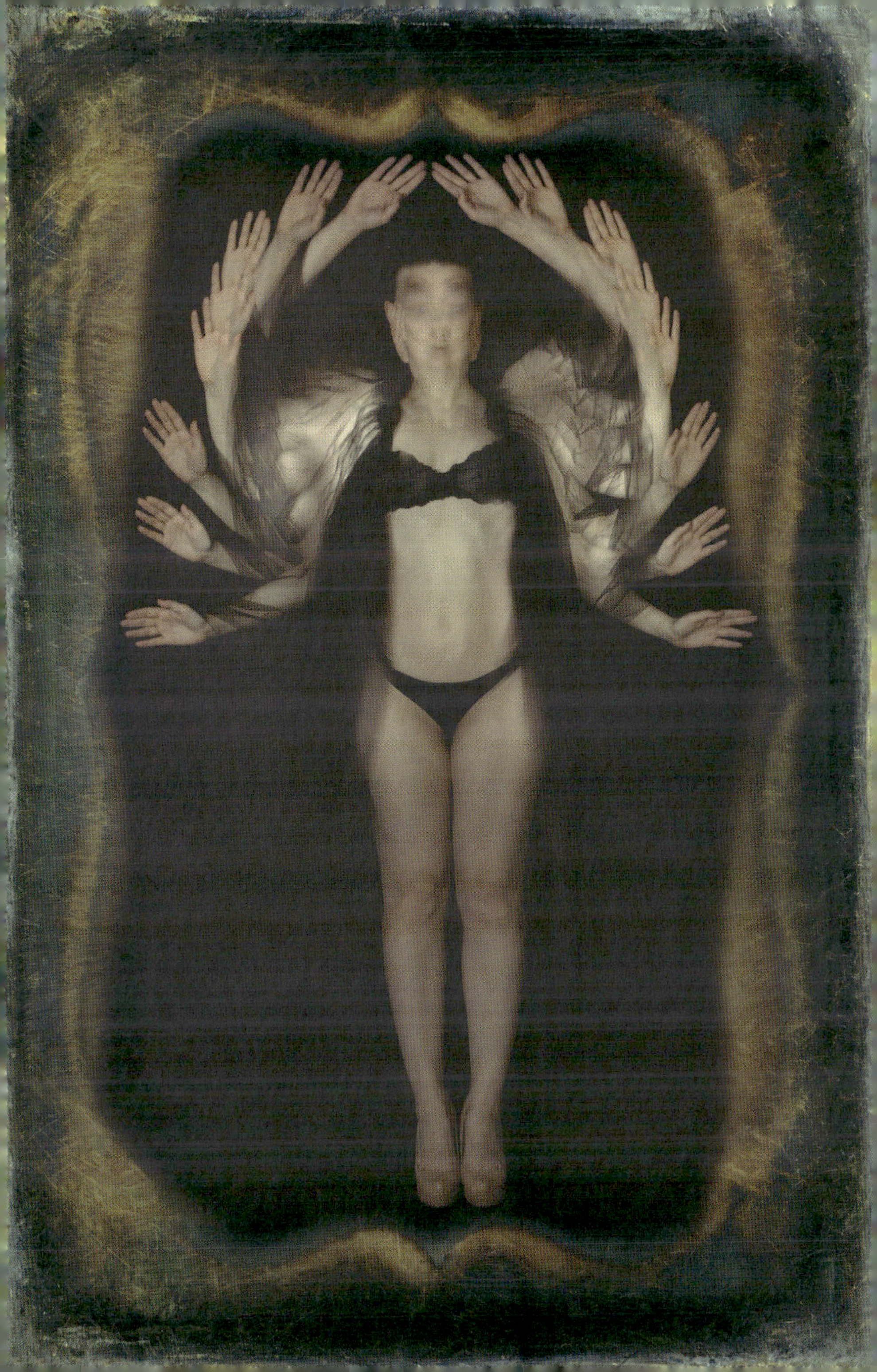

Tondos and Circles

An uncommon framing shape that you occasionally see is the circle, or as it is called in the painting world, the *tondo*.

There are several approaches to creating a tondo photographically. One is to use a circular fisheye lens (like the image of Mosta Dome shown on page 24 and the photo opposite).

Another approach is to construct a round image that is tondo-shaped on a solid background, usually bright white, as in a light box, or black. A third way to create a circular image is to use a selection and mask in Photoshop.

When creating a circular image optically, the name of the game is distortion. Whether you like it or not, your image will show distortion and curvature at the edges. The photo shown on page 60 is a good example of a fisheye—in this case horizontal rather than circular—where the center of the image has almost no distortion, but there is a great deal of bending at the edges.

Effective fisheye images embrace this distortion. They also acknowledge the height and inherent depth of field in an extreme wide-angle lens, and balance this compositionally using near-foreground elements as well as more distant subject matter.

Whether the round image is generated with the lens, as a construction, or in Photoshop, the circularity of a round image calls attention to its framing and to the borders of the image.

This means that compositionally it's important to create structural bridges between the circular inner image and its frame. For example, the blue flowers at the edges of the tondos shown on pages 72–73 touch the round edges.

This kind of structural bridge serves as a visual path to bring the viewer into the core of the image. Without the connection between the outer and inner portions of a round image, a tondo appears disconnected in space and will struggle to supply emotional meaning.

Crystal Ball—This photograph of a decorative pond at Blake Garden in Kensington, California, reminded me of a crystal ball. I decided to handle the framing issues inherent in a fisheye photograph by adding a black border around the circular area, enhancing the sense that this garden pond is floating in space.

Nikon D850, 8-15mm Nikkor fisheye zoom lens at 8mm, 2 seconds at f/22 and ISO 64, tripod mounted.

Pages 72–73: *Flower Tondo* and *Flower Tondo Inversion*— To create these circular images, I began by making a patterned, circular array of alstroemeria (Peruvian Lily), roses, and agapanthus (Lily of the Nile) on the light box. The main organizing principle was a single rose blossom at the center of the image.

I used a high-key layer stack to capture the composition and then reduced it to the version on white shown on page 72, using a black mask to emphasize the circularity. The inversion on page 73 was created using an LAB L-channel color adjustment.

Nikon D850, 85mm Zeiss Otus, six exposures with shutter speeds ranging from 1/30 of a second to 2 seconds, each exposure at f/13 and ISO 64, tripod mounted.

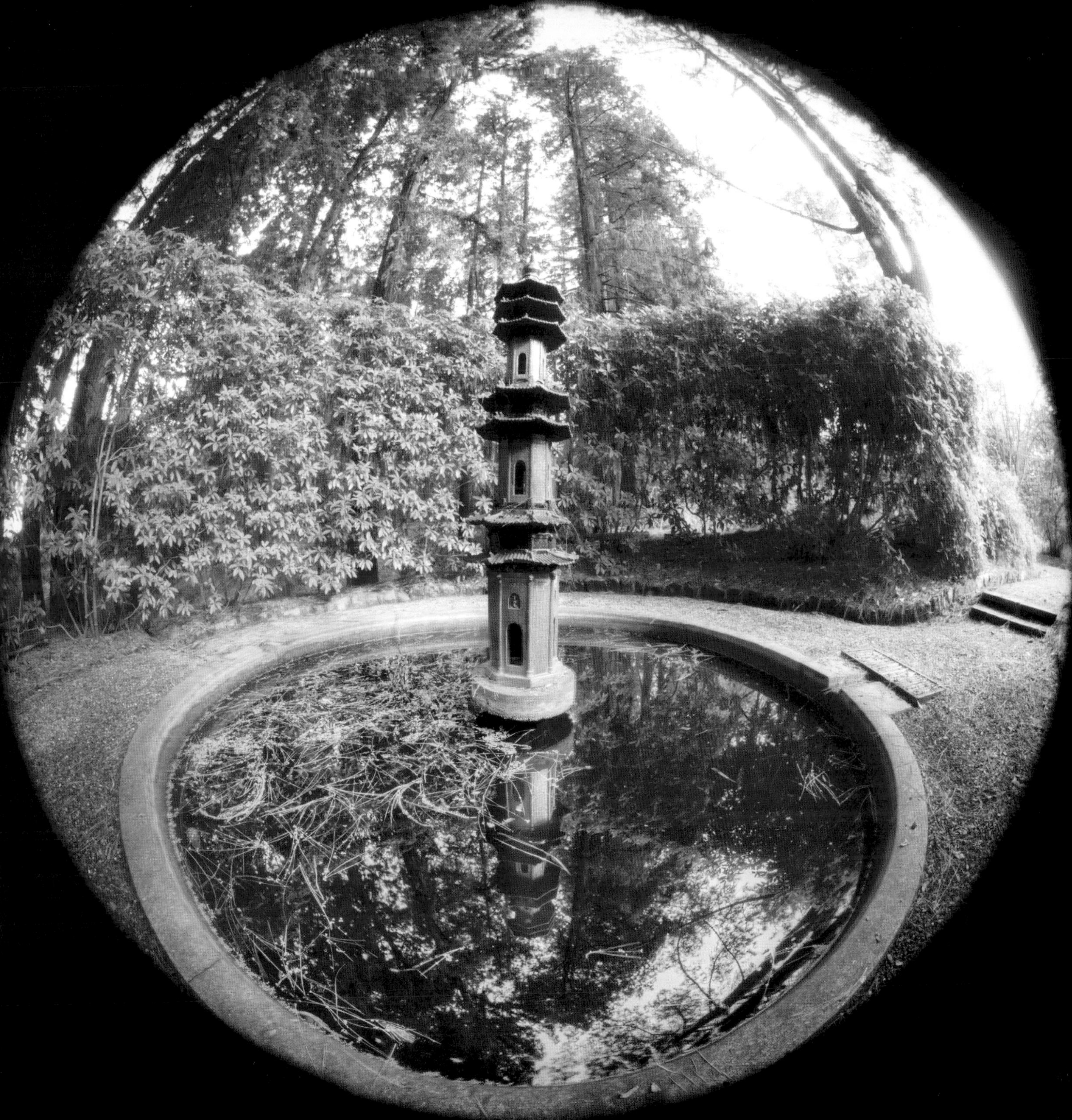

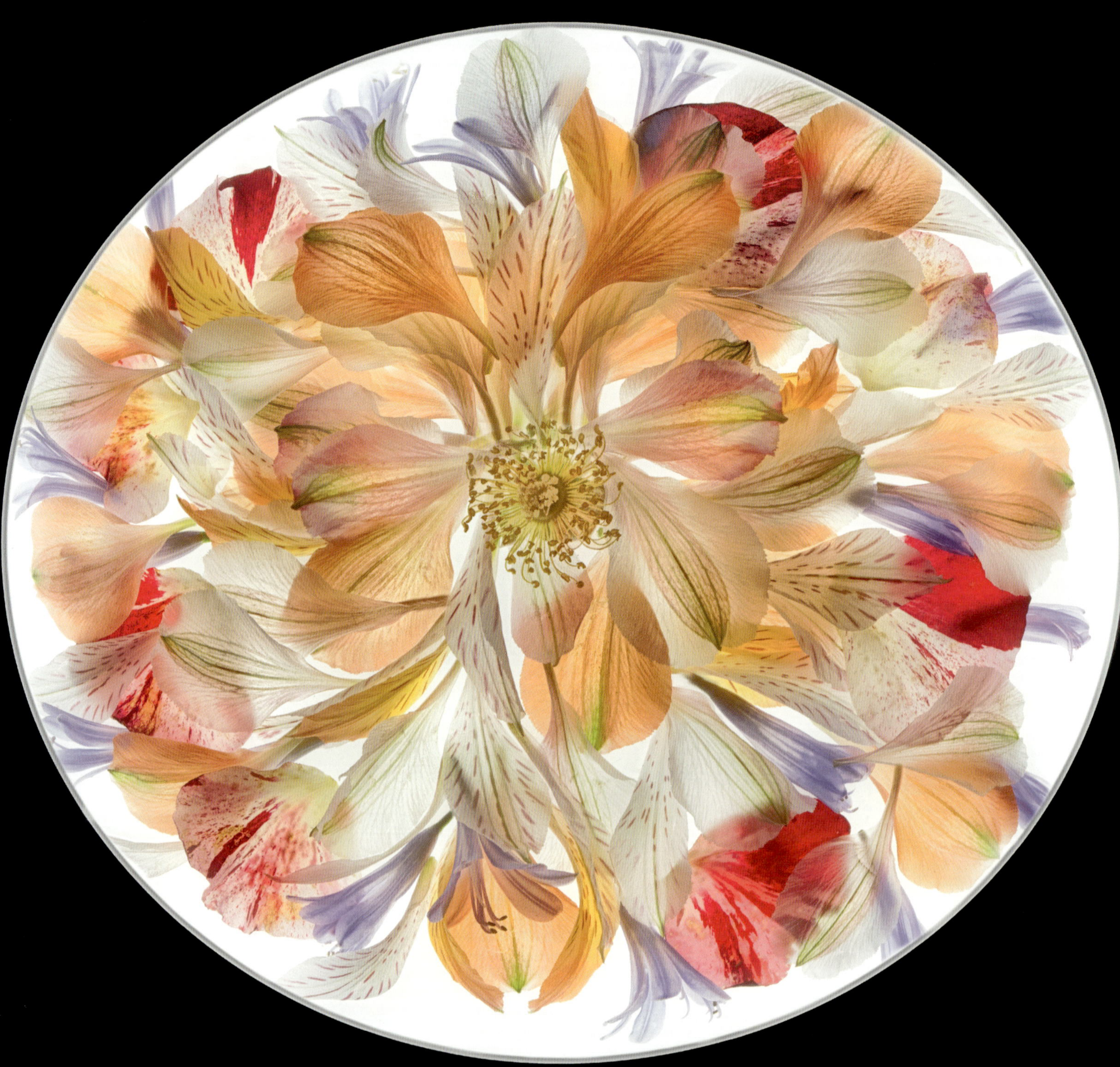

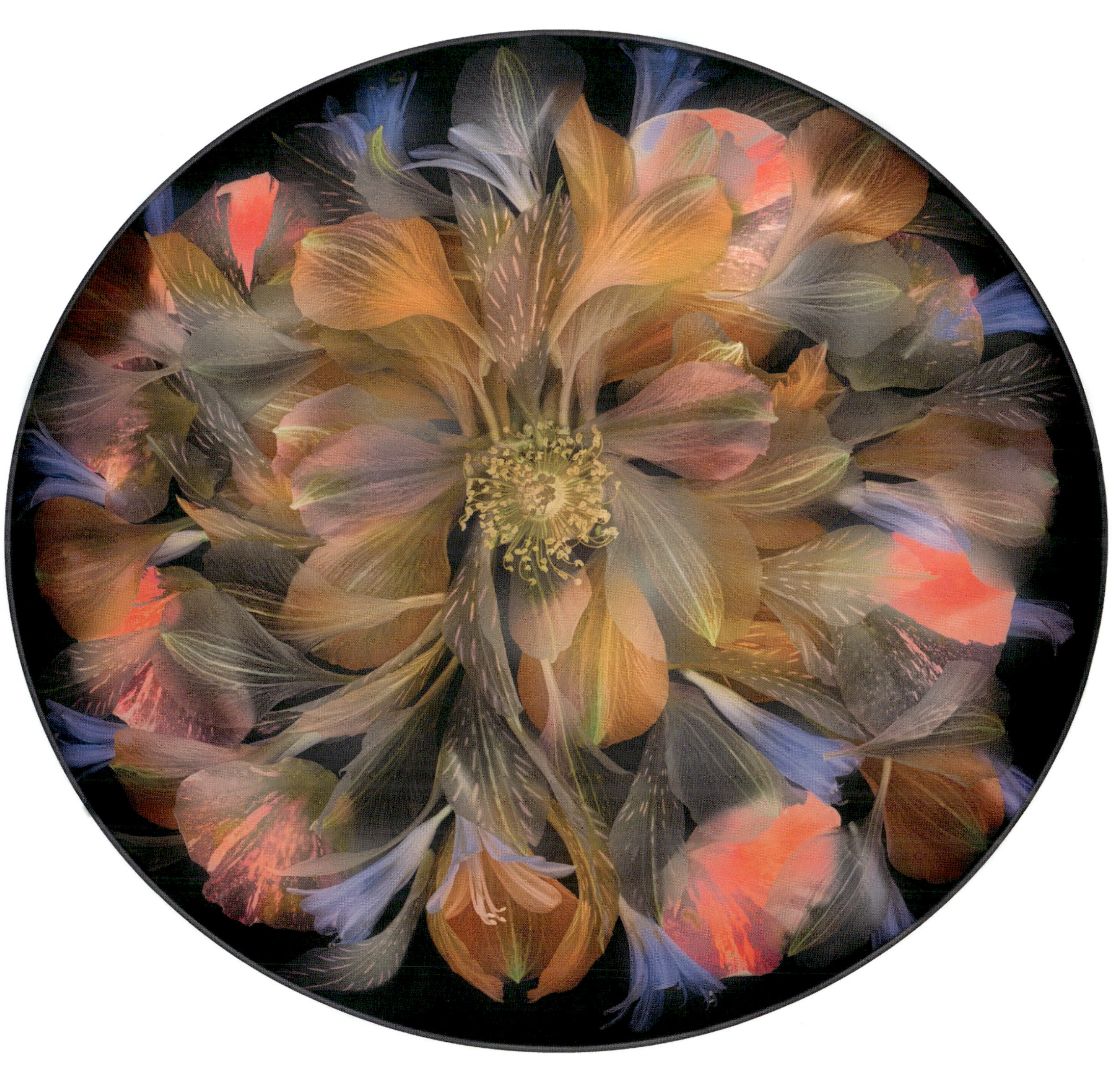

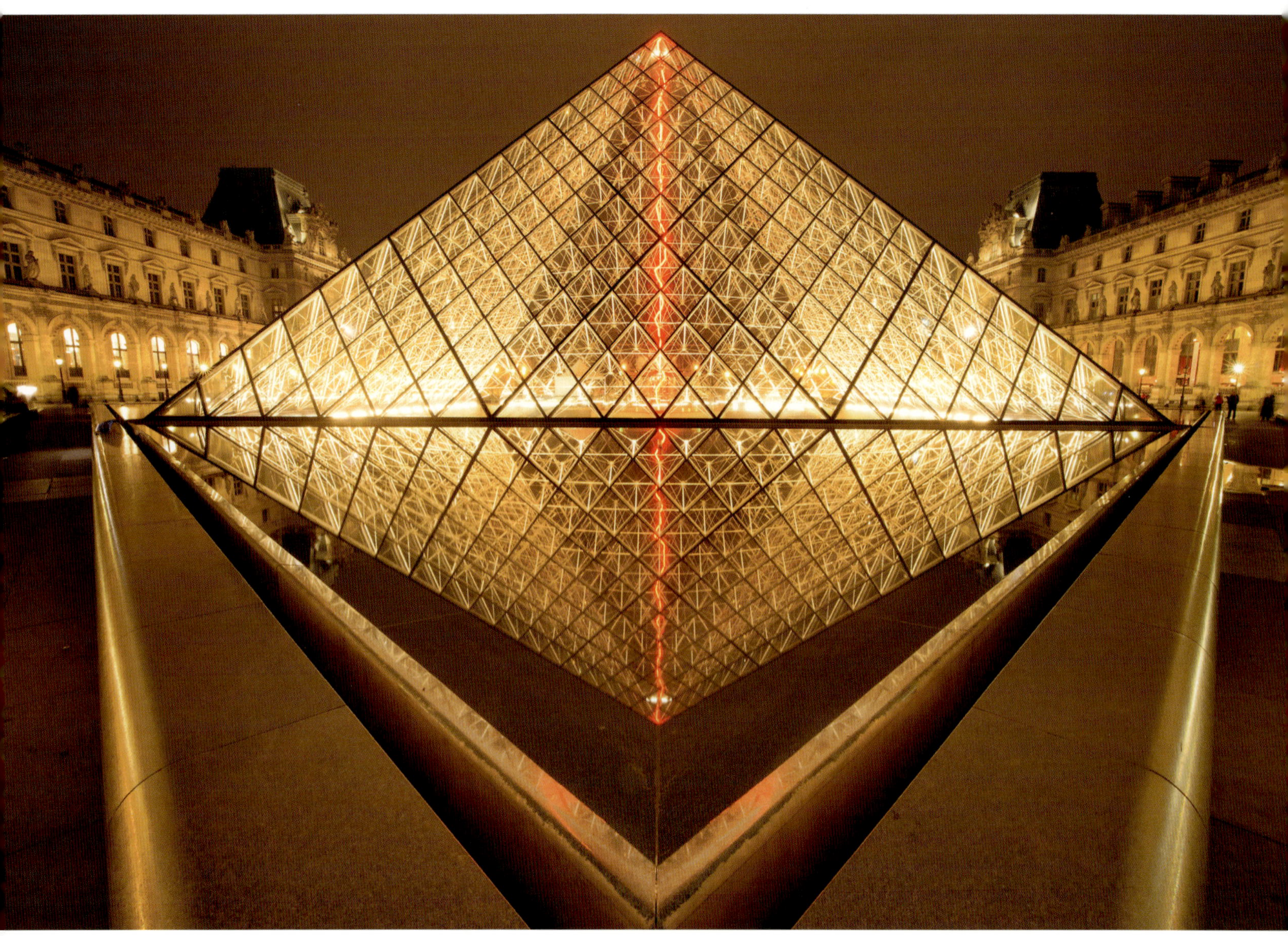

Opposite: *Pyramide*—Photographing after dark in the grand courtyard of the Louvre in Paris, France, is great fun! The Pyramide du Louvre, designed by I. M. Pei, becomes an abstraction of triangles and the reflecting pond itself shows triangular shapes.

When making this composition, I used an extreme wide-angle lens (15mm). My idea was to locate the structure of the Pyramide between the earth and sky so that the top of the Pyramide triangle rested against the upper frame of the image and the bottom vertex of the reflected triangle sat toward the bottom of the frame in the pond. The overall visual impact was to create a diamond of lights.

Nikon D800, 15mm Zeiss Distagon, 30 seconds at f/20 and ISO 200, tripod mounted.

Right: *Stair Knot*—High up in the belfry of an abandoned church in the Cuban city of Trinidad, I laid down on my back and photographed the stairs looking straight up. The resulting image had an almost impossible Escher-like effect with the staircase folding in upon itself. Years after I made the image, I decided to shape the *Stair Knot* into a triangle. I sent the photo to my iPhone, and used the Fragment app to convert the image into a triangular shape.

Nikon D300, 10.5mm fisheye, 2 seconds at f/22 and ISO 100, tripod mounted; geometric triangular folding added using Fragment on the iPhone.

The Humble but Mighty Triangle

A tripod holds your camera up and the tripod is humble but mighty. From an engineering viewpoint, the tripod and structures made from tripods provide great tensile strength.

But where's the tripod when it comes to photographic composition?

Pretty much absent except as part of a rectangular composition, and in architectural photography. Maybe we should do something about this—start a trend!

If you want to join the CTU (Club of Triangle Users), consider that a triangle has three sides and three points. Each side and point must relate to and anchor with the surrounding rectangular framing. The only exception to this is when the triangular shape itself has been cut out, as in the image shown on this page.

Let's emphasize: explicit triangles are fairly rare in compositions. Triangles can be powerful in photos and convey a sense of muscular compositional strength. Within a rectangular framing, triangles need to be clearly anchored at their vertices to the framework of the photo.

Working with Internal Rectangles

An image with internal rectangles is essentially presenting a frame within a frame. This may sound simple, but there is actually no end to the possibilities and complications of internal framing created with rectangles inside an image.

When the internal frames in an image are one after the other in a receding progression—as in *Endless Doors* on page 15 or *Train Bridge, Maine* shown opposite—this creates a unique sense of order as well as a visual approach to the infinite. For more about patterns and progressions, see pages 82–107.

Alternatively, an internal frame can represent a simple shape such as a window or a door, as shown in *Golden Gate Window* on page 78, or even a reflection in a puddle, as in *Framed* on page 79.

As you can see, one of the most common and effective motifs in photographic composition is the frame-within-a-frame, whether the inner frame is a literal window, a door, a reflection in a puddle, or sticks in a forest on the edge of a marsh.

The point is that internal framing creates a connection between the viewers' world outside the image and the more subjective material within the image. Yes, a frame bounds the image, but it is also a frame of regard and connotes passages and transitions.

When you are working with internal rectangles and frames-within-frames, pay special attention to the relationship of these internal frames to the external frame of the image. Your viewers will be scrutinizing this relationship whether they consciously know it or not.

Regularity—or irregularity—matters. A composition where the inner rectangles are lined up in an orderly way presents a very different world view from a composition where the rectangles seem askew or at an angle. In the first case, you have a progression that doesn't seem to end and represents a reasoned universe. In the second, you have something quirky, unusual, and potentially interesting.

I suggest that you consider the role of internal rectangles and frames-within-frames in any image where you are paying attention to the composition.

Train Bridge, Maine—Exploring the old ship-building town of Bath, Maine, I was surprised to find this almost abandoned train bridge crossing the Kennebec River. Climbing onto the trestle, I hoped not to encounter one of the remaining trains. In the meantime, I could see through my lens an alternating pattern of light and dark rectangles, receding to the infinite vanishing point.

It is interesting that from a compositional point of view, I was not really concerned with the engineering of steel girders when I made this image. The relationship of the internal frames and how they work together is what inspired the image, rather than the idea of a train bridge.

Nikon D810, 28-300mm Nikkor zoom at 250mm, eight exposures with shutter speeds ranging from 1/250 of a second to 1 second, each exposure at f/22 and ISO 64, tripod mounted.

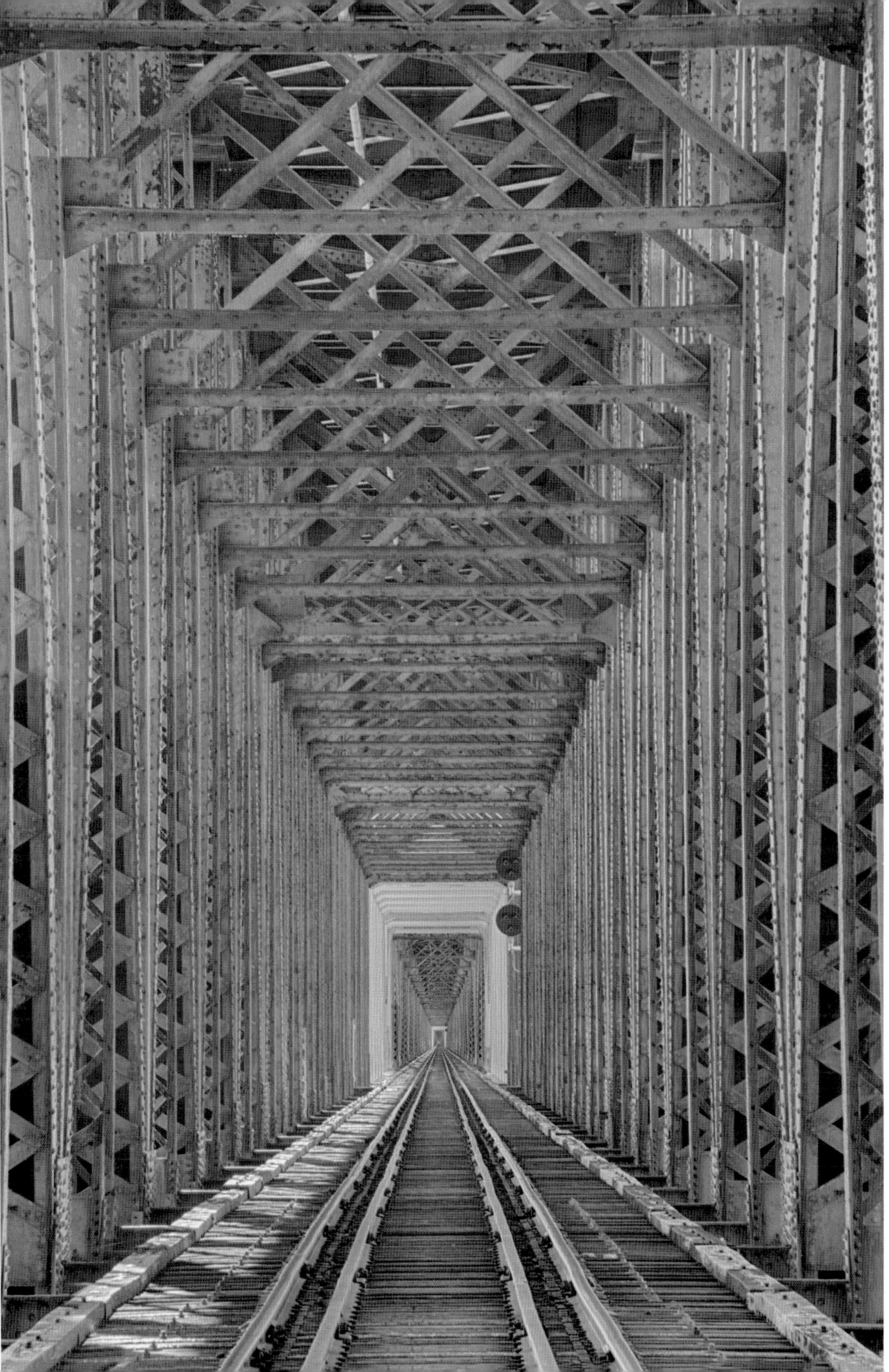

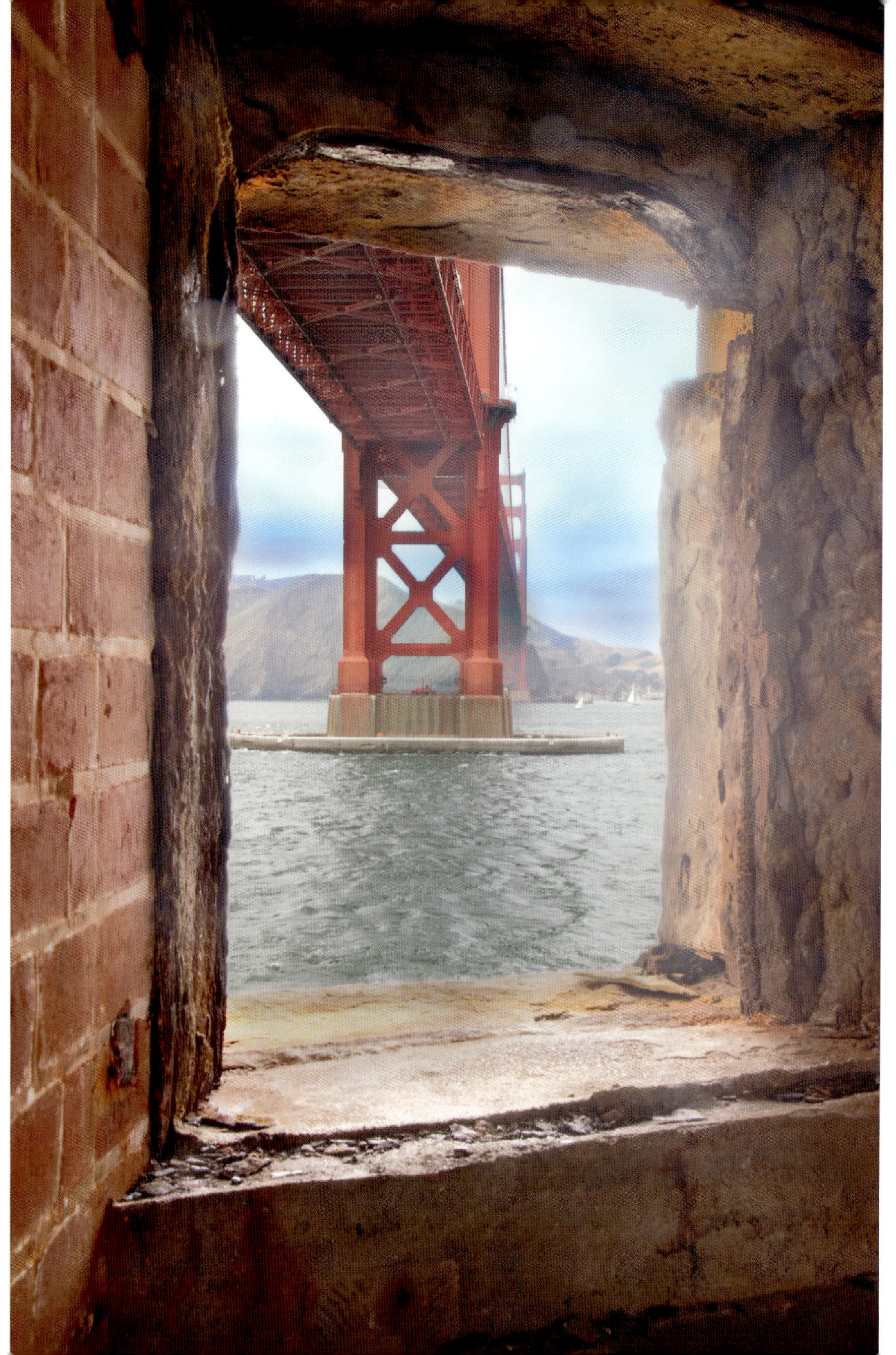

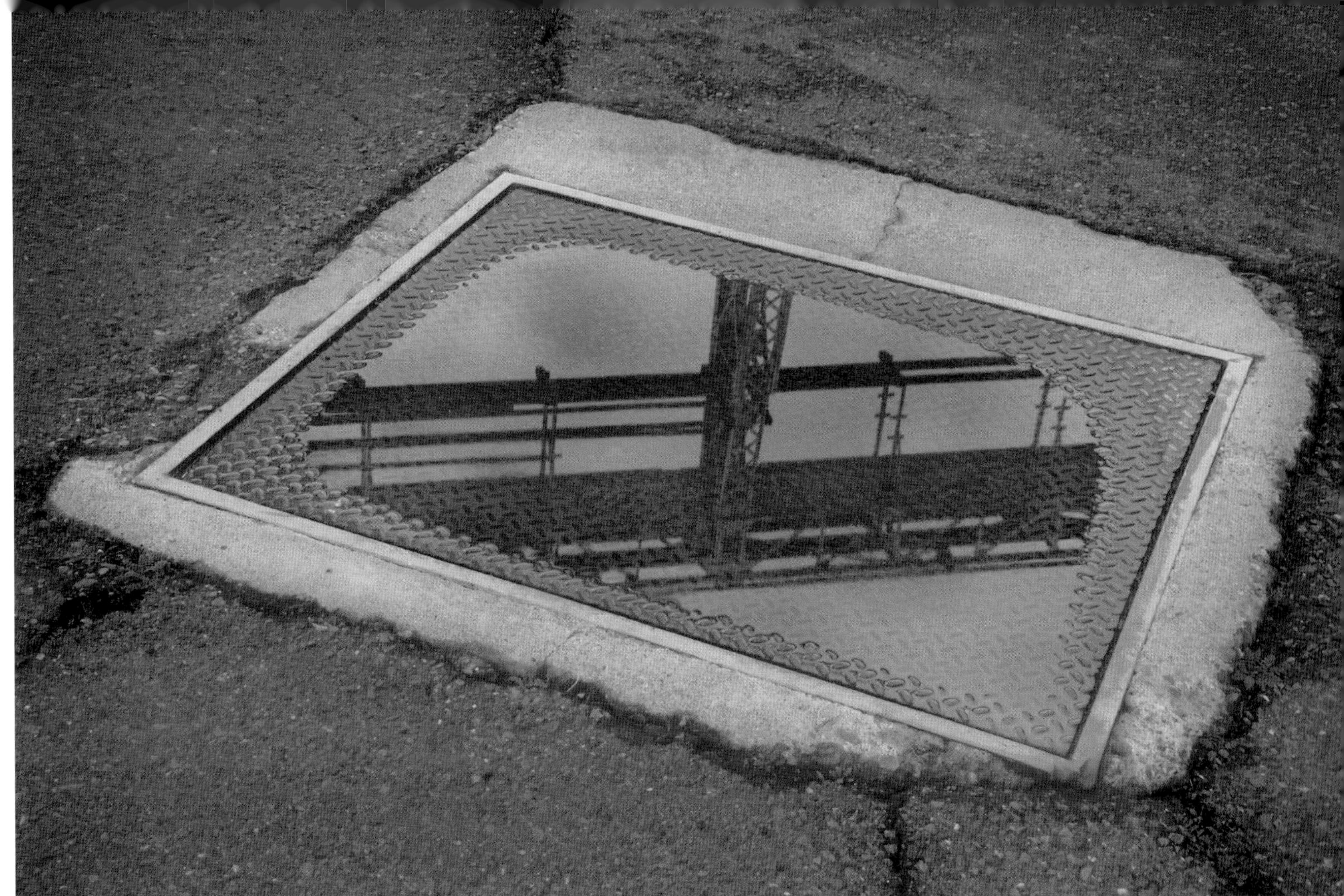

A Process of Framing

I'm excited by borders, frames, and boundaries! After all, the real magic happens when one slips from one domain to another—often in shadows, elusively, without being aware of the frame.

By slightly altering a frame, giving it a twist or a tweak, one can change the perception of the viewer and enter the realm of visual sorcery.

At the same time, there is certainly no formula for placing a frame within a frame. Once again, the only rule is that there are no rules. *So what I am preaching is mindfulness:*

- All images have an outer frame.

- Most images have an inner frame or frames.

- The relationship between the frames in an image, and particularly the inner and outer frames, is very important.

- Sometimes images with internal frames that appear simple are actually quite visually complex. This complexity is often "under the covers."

- Where does one frame end and another frame begin?

- Can you tell the subject matter that is framed from the content that is doing the framing?

Frames provide the underlying structure for much of creative photography and its compositions. Without the basic frame, there is no content. Without internal frames, there is no dialog between the interior composition and the external world of the frame. So pay particular attention to the questions involving boundaries and borders when you work through the process of framing in your images.

KEY IDEAS

- A compositional frame is *not* a picture frame!

- The most important boundary frame is that of the image itself.

- Camera position in relationship to the subject greatly impacts framing and composition, so "scootch" around to see what's best.

- Internal framing plays off the boundary frame either as an echo or as a contrast.

- Image proportions are important, but depending on the situation, you might find a crop that works better than the original proportions.

Door, Trapani—Wandering the dusty and decaying Sicilian seaport of Trapani, I enjoyed photographing the ancient architecture of this old city. Along the central avenue, Via Garibaldi, I came across this ornate door with the internal door open to the garden in the courtyard. In the context of a photographic frame, you have the oval door, and within that an inner frame.

Nikon D850, 28-300 Nikkor zoom at 50mm, nine exposures with shutter speeds ranging from 1/15 of a second to 8 seconds, each exposure at f/22 and ISO 64, tripod mounted.

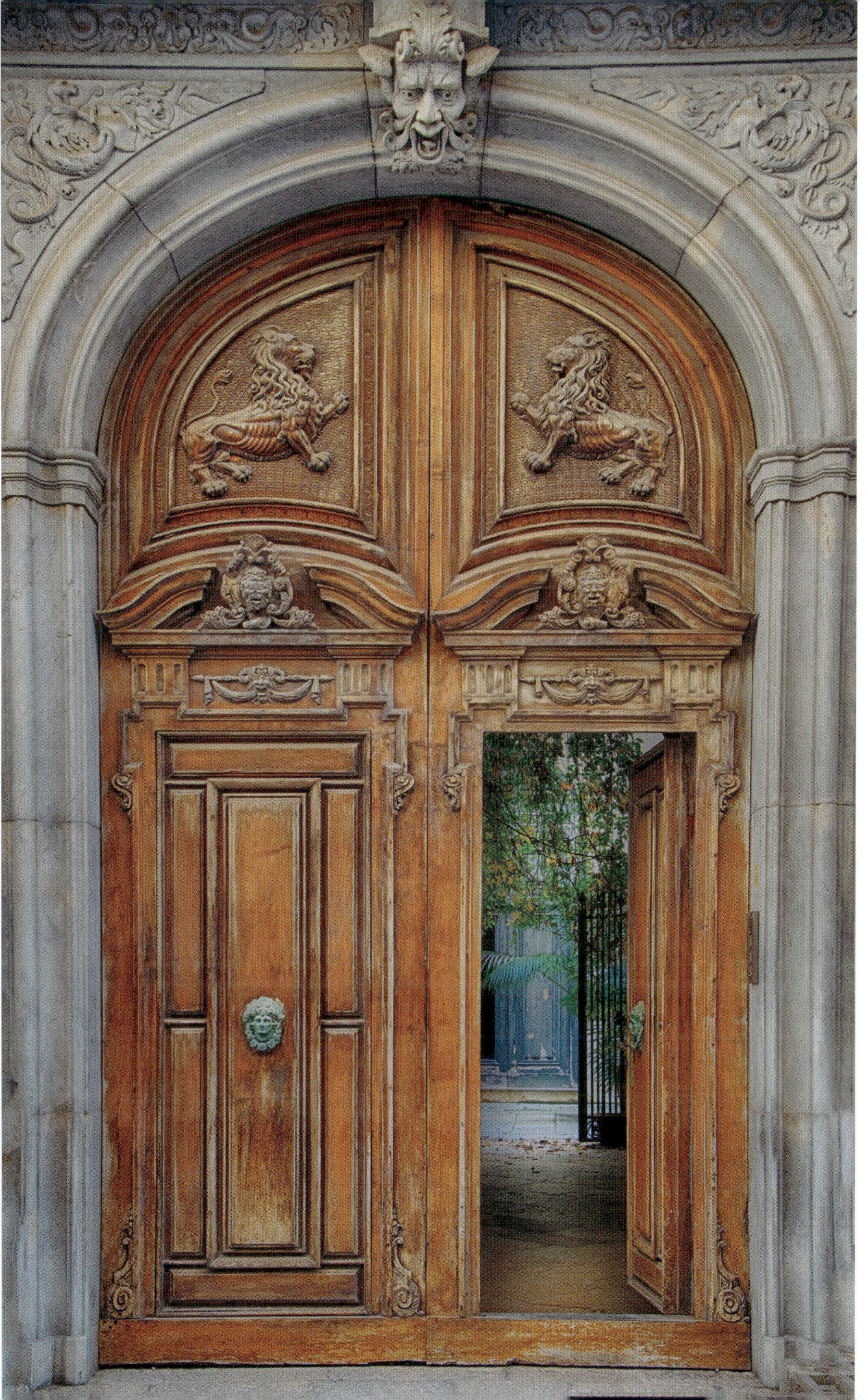

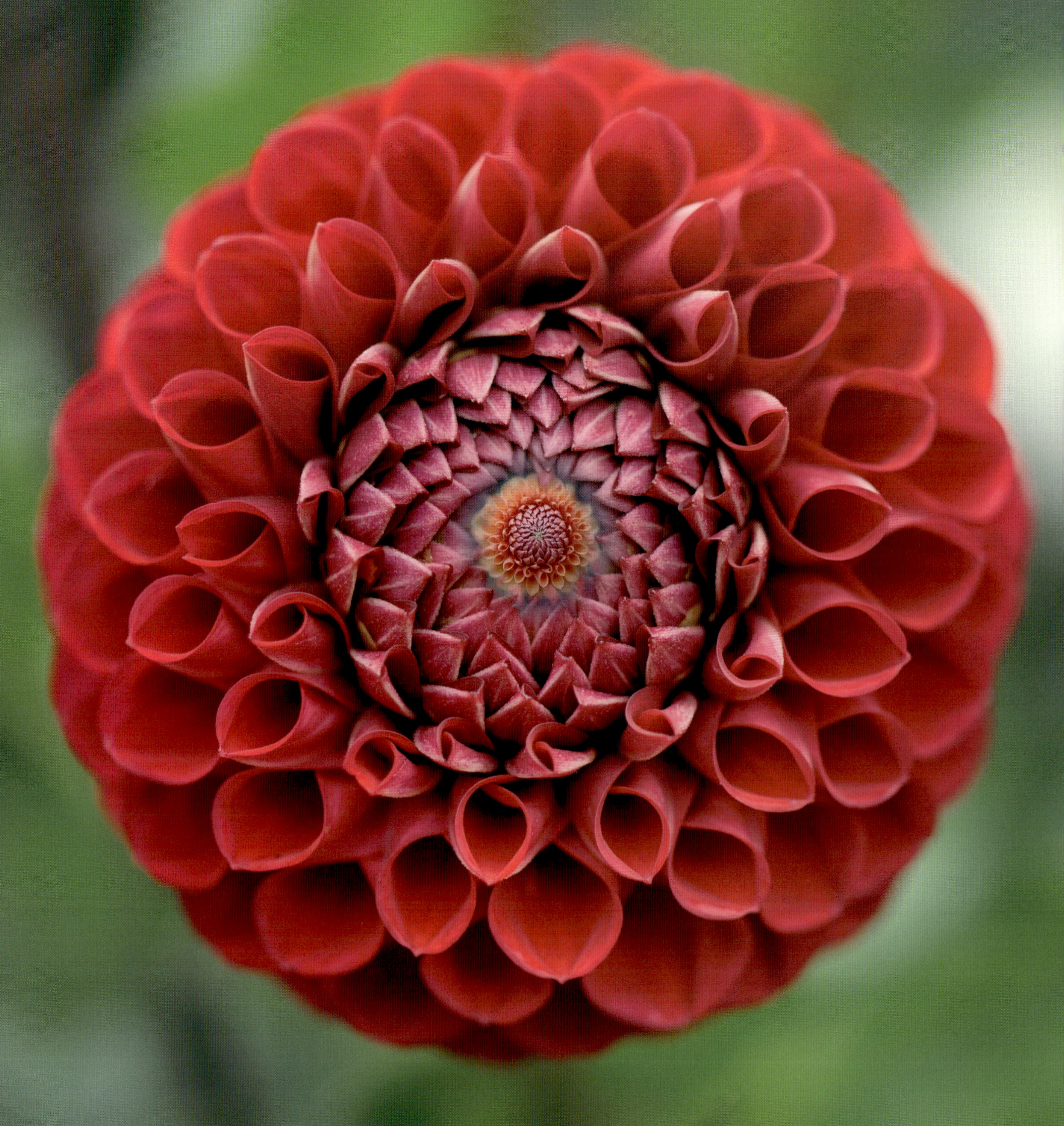

PATTERNS & REPETITION

What is a pattern? Patterns can mean many things and our daily lives are full of them. In visual art, put simply, a pattern is repetition with visual meaning. Let's unpack this a bit and clarify the relationship of patterns to repetition.

Repetition often involves easily recognizable similar or matching shapes. These shapes can be amorphous but are usually recognized as lines,

Mandahlia—On a field trip with a flower photography workshop at Maine Media in Rockport, Maine, we visited the Endless Summer Dahlia Farm. The farm sells tubers to "dahlia addicts" across the country.

This particular dahlia caught my eye because of the regularity of several aspects of its pattern: not only the concentric circles, but also the repetition in the larger petals surrounding the center of the image.

Nikon D810, 50mm Zeiss Makro Planar, 1/800 of a second at f/2 and ISO 200, hand held.

rectangles, and circles—which is one of the reasons the earlier chapters in this book discuss these simple shapes. While it is possible to literally repeat shapes, repetition often involves a progression: a shape gets bigger or smaller, or is replicated across the frame with some variations (some examples are on pages 15, 85, and 105).

Human beings are wired to respond to patterns and repetition. We recognize patterns when we encounter them, look for patterns, and are encouraged in our lives when we find patterns.

Our recognition of patterns falls across fields of human endeavor well beyond the visual arts. The underlying structure of music is made up of patterns, as is mathematics. In fact, our lives in their entirety are largely made up of patterns.

Thus, it behooves the artistic creator to recognize and use patterns in our compositions. The key point for artistic creators is that the patterns you use must be *recognizable* and *recognized* by your viewers.

The point of this chapter is to help you master tools that will allow you to capture and manifest patterns in your work. As noted, these patterns must be recognizable to the viewer.

What's important is to create patterns that your viewers feel an instant connection with, even if they don't understand the subject matter that is used to embody the pattern, the pattern as a whole, or why they feel the connection.

Sometimes the unconscious mind is better at grasping the entirety of a pattern that has only been partially presented. When we manipulate the viewer's response to patterns, we are manipulating the viewer's unconscious mind and not necessarily their conscious grasp of the details of the patterns. Perhaps understanding comes later in an "aha!" moment when the viewer internalizes and makes a connection with a larger pattern.

Kinds of Patterns

A good starting place for learning the tools you need to master patterns in your work is to become familiar with common types of patterns found in photography and visual art.

The simplest patterns involve repetition. The element that is repeated can be circular, rectilinear, a person, flower shapes, little bears, water drops, spirals—indeed, anything you would like.

The simplest patterns merely repeat without variation of the element sizing or spacing, but most patterns add some kind of change or shift as the elements repeat.

One simple way to add a little interest to pure repetition is to change the size of the elements that are repeated; for example, from small to large or large to small. This kind of pattern is often called a progression. To see some examples of a visual progression, check out pages 150 and 182, and *Chorus of One* to the right.

There are many possible variations in almost any pattern. For example, in a pattern involving repetitions and progressions, the distances between the elements as well as the elements themselves can vary.

It is important to understand that the viewer must recognize the pattern as a pattern at a

Chorus of One—This model, whose modeling name is Jin N Tonic, was very amenable to trying something new. I explained the in-camera multiple-exposure process to her and the idea that I wanted to realize. My idea was to create a pattern that looks like an entire chorus line using a single model.

We worked together on positioning and placement, and Jin was able to precisely move and place her body to create a sense of pattern using her body position, hat, red stockings, and facial expression each of the eight times that the strobes fired.

Nikon D850, 28-300mm Nikkor zoom at 38mm, in-camera multiple exposure with eight exposures at 1/160 of a second at f/8 and ISO 400, tripod mounted; exposures on a black background using radio-fired strobes.

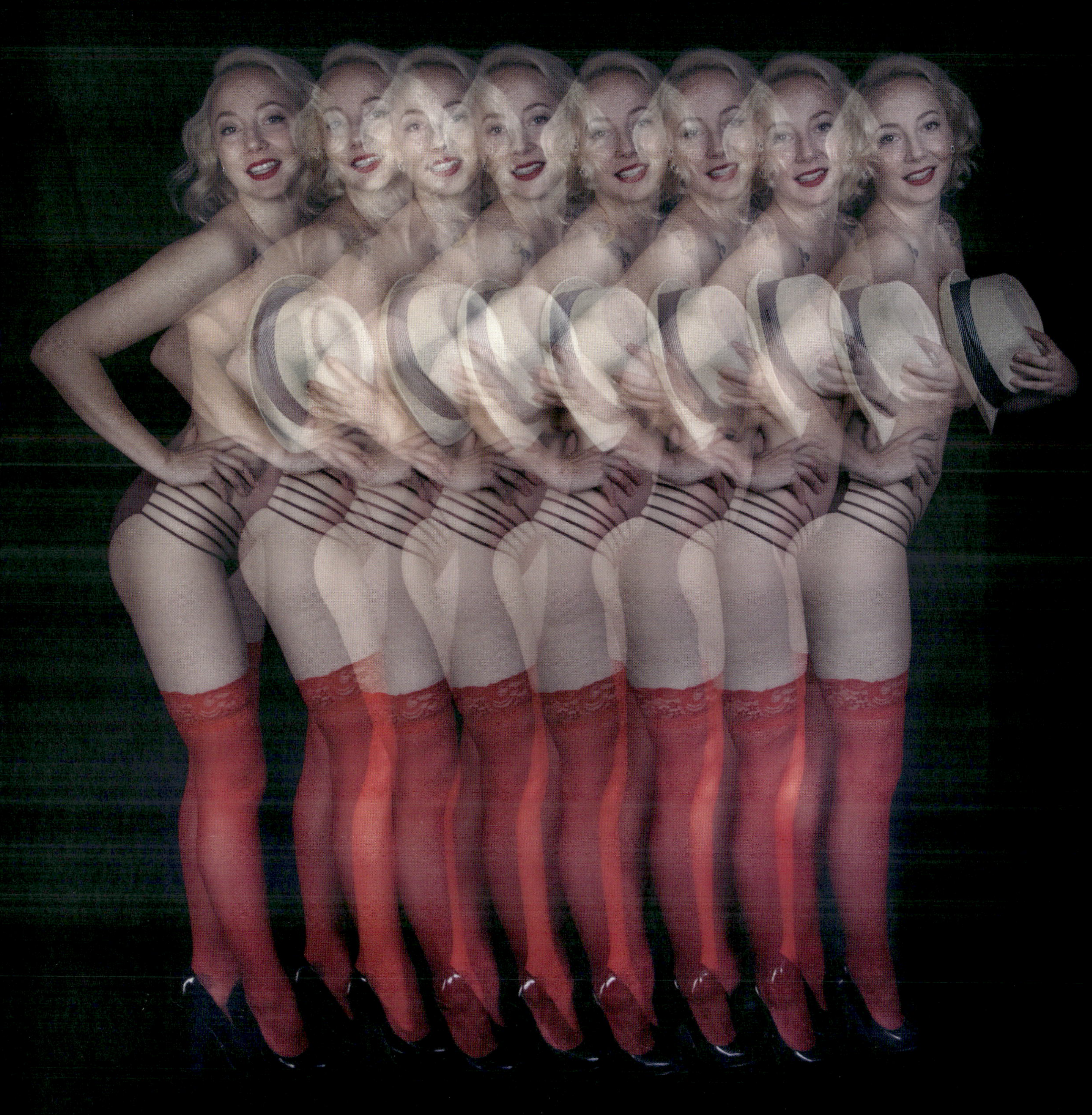

conscious or unconscious level. This implies *regularity* and order: completely random splatterings do not a pattern make. Actually, the human propensity toward pattern making is so strong that it is quite difficult to create random imagery without patterns. For example, some people think of the famous Jackson Pollack paint-splatter canvases as random. In fact, if you take a close look at these paintings, they are highly structured and involve a variety of complex patterns.

As an artist, the question becomes, how does this ordered regularity manifest itself? In other words, in a world that largely seems random, how can an image be presented that is both apparently "real" and also contains structured patterns?

Receptivity to patterns is largely a function of the viewer's unconscious. Their unconscious will let them know when they are seeing a pattern, and when the use of the pattern seems to create a complete whole and "works." Likewise, a viewer will often know, perhaps without being able to put it into words, when the depiction of a pattern seems incomplete and unsatisfying. Basically, their brains will stop processing the image and shut down on it.

Besides simple repetition or progression, patterns can involve:

- *Alternation*, as in one-on and one-off, long and short—for example, Morse code where there are long stashes and short dots. The star trails in *Death Valley Campsite* on pages 106–107 are an example of this.

- *Series* and *sequences*, such as the Fibonacci numbers, where each element is the sum of the preceding two elements. In the visual arts, series and sequences are often represented by objects in the composition. The thing about a series or sequence is that it can be almost arbitrarily complex. In the face of this complexity, the canvas size for a photograph is limited. The trick is not to get so complex that the series or sequence is unrecognizable. As an example, look at *Chorus of One* on page 85.

- *Irregularity*, where the pattern takes elements of regular patterns and combines them in a more complex way. In other words, there is nothing to stop someone from recognizing or creating patterns that are made up of sub-patterns. An example is *Blind Shadow*, right.

As I've noted, pattern recognition is one of the most important aspects of human creativity across the arts, sciences, and life itself.

Blind Shadow—On a late afternoon the sun streamed in through my office window. It was a warm day and I had opened the window. I had a Venetian blind hanging behind a cream linen curtain, both to block the sun so I could see my studio monitor. The lines of the shadow created by the Venetian blind curved on the linen curtain as the curtain itself moved in the breeze.

Making this photo, I was intrigued by the way the curved lines caused by the curvature of the curtain met the straight lines of the Venetian blind on the right of the image.

Nikon D200, 18-200mm Nikkor zoom at 112mm, 1/125 of a second at f/5.6 and ISO 100, hand held.

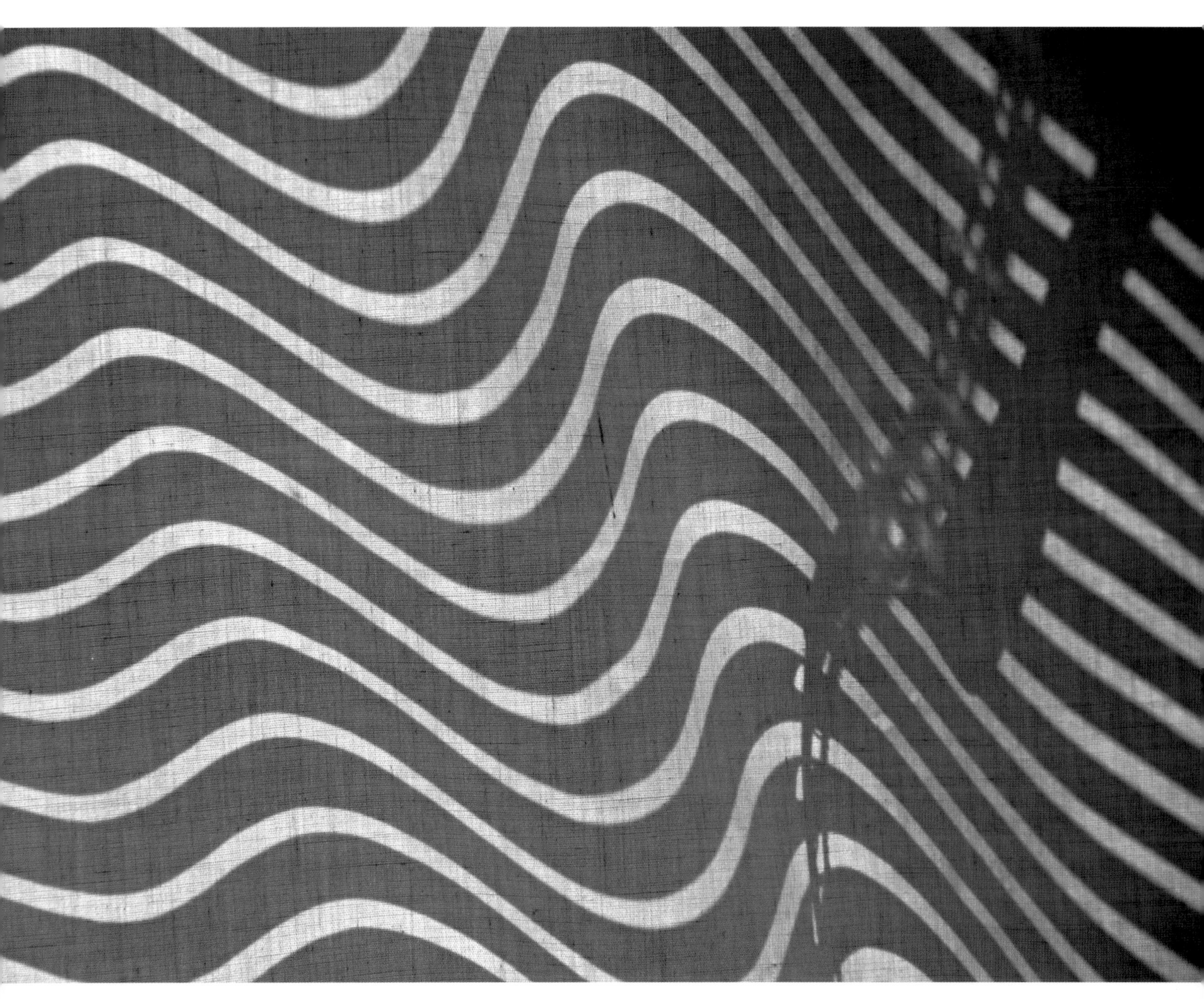

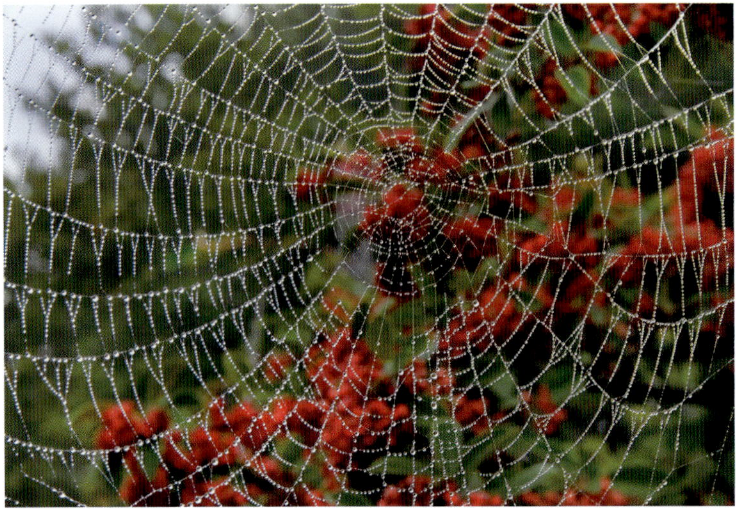

Thought Experiment

How do you recognize a pattern? Is everything a pattern? Some folks think that all of life is made up of patterns.

So try this: Find a subject that absolutely does not appear to have a pattern. Now, make a photo of this "patternless subject" that makes sense of the subject and presents a pattern that helps organize the image for the viewer.

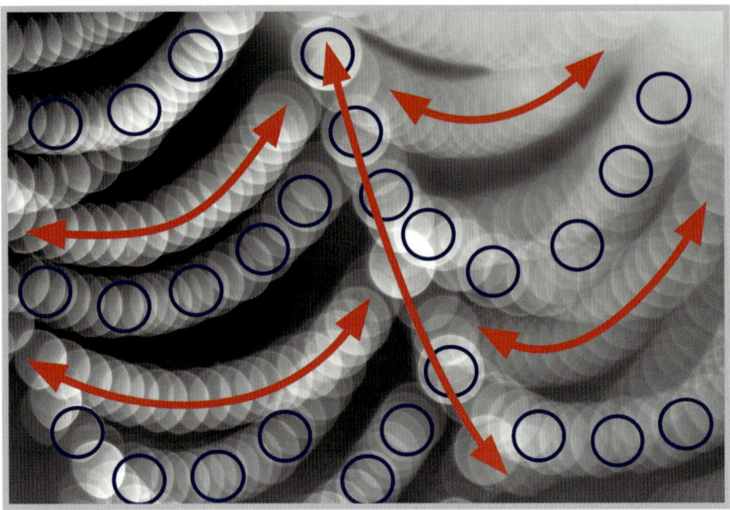

Spider Web Bokeh—To the right is a photograph of a spider web covered with dew in the early morning of a foggy day. To create the sense of a pattern consisting of the round rings of light made by the water drops on the spider web, I threw the composition way out of focus and concentrated on the underlying shapes made by the refractions of the lens diaphragm.

The *Wet Web* image shown at upper left gives a sense of the radial pattern of a spider web in its entirety. This is a more literal capture of the web and, therefore, the pattern shown looks more like the spider web we expect to see. Note that the more abstract the image content is (as in the version on the right), the more there needs to be a strong composition with recognizable patterns.

With both images, the important thing for me was to capture the water drops on the web. This involved underexposing each image in relation to the light meter reading by about 2 EV. Without this −2 EV adjustment, the water drops would have been blown out.

Taking the *Spider Web Bokeh* image on the right, there are really two kinds of patterns that the creative focus technique reveals. As you can see in the diagram at bottom left, there is the repetition of circular light refractions (the blue circles). Next, you also have a pattern of arcs that meet in a central line (the red arrows). The arcs draw the eye upward and into the composition.

Right: *Nikon D810, 50mm Zeiss Makro-Planar, 1/4000 of a second at f/2 and ISO 200, hand held.*

Upper Left: *Nikon D300, 18-200mm Nikkor zoom at 65mm, 1/100 of a second at f/14 and ISO 500, hand held.*

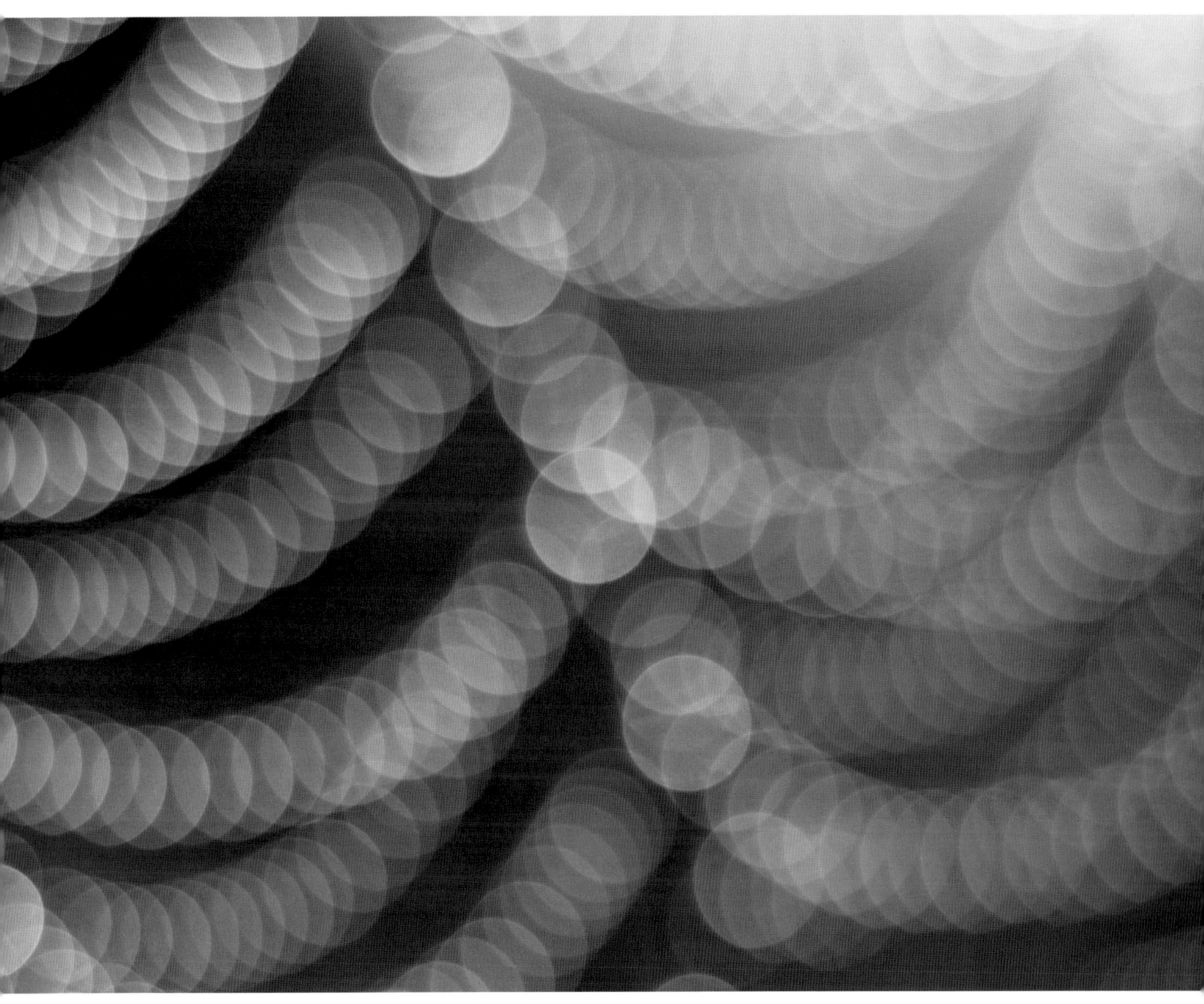

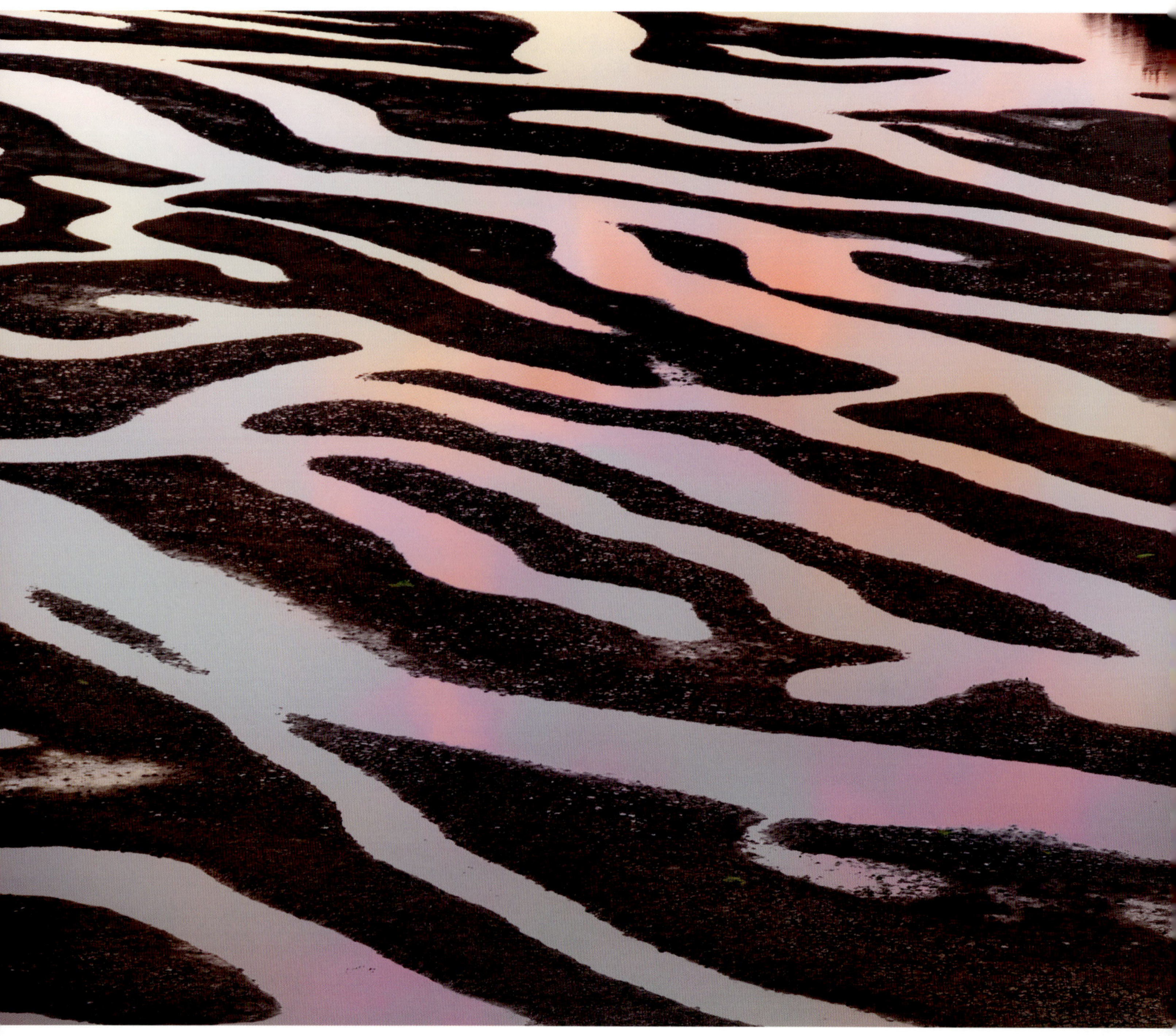

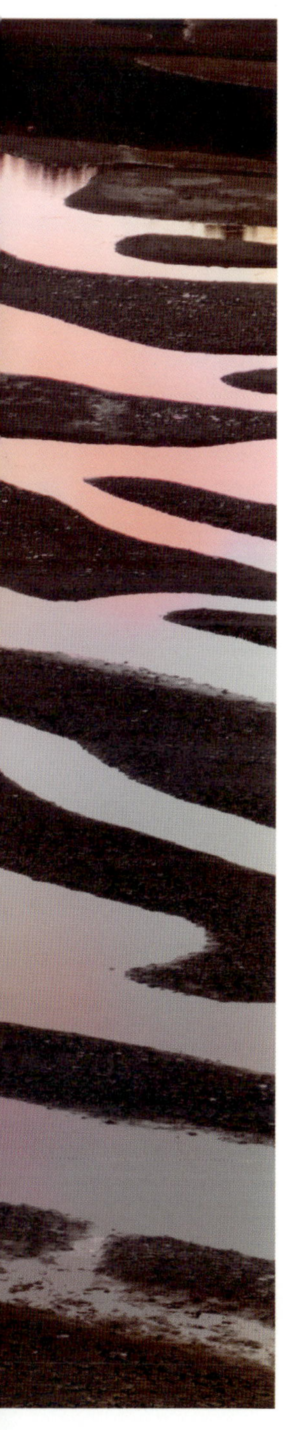

Patterns with Circles

Circles and curves are all around us. Curved and circular shapes can be found in nature and in our everyday lives—for example, the wheels of our cars and the curvature of the Earth. On a broader level, we can think of our lives as arcs and circles, and position our art within the larger arc of living.

Circle patterns generally come in some basic varieties:

- A single large circle that monopolizes the composition. This could be a large circular flower like the one on page 82, taking up the entire frame, or a circular image like the one from a fisheye lens on page 71. Another possibility

Estero at Low Tide—Hiking in the backcountry of Point Reyes National Seashore in California, I crossed Drakes Estero at a narrow point on a bridge and followed the trail up a steep hill.

Drakes Estero is an estuary complex made up of branching bays that drain into the Pacific Ocean. It is the most probable landing spot of Sir Francis Drake on the coast of North America in his 1579 circumnavigation of the world.

From the top of the bluff, I looked back to see sunset reflected in the patterns of the channels in Drakes Estero at low tide.

Nikon D200, 18-200 Nikkor zoom at 90mm, circular polarizer, 1/6 of a second at f/10 and ISO 100, tripod mounted.

is the mandala. For more about this, take a look at the mandala discussion starting on page 49.

- A grid composition with many smaller circles arranged in a regular pattern. This involves fitting smaller circles into the larger rectangle of the frame. An example of this is *Colored Apple Slices* on pages 52–53.

- Concentric circles that involve a composition with a general large circular shape and additional arcs or curved or circular shapes. *Spider Web Bokeh* on pages 88–89 is a good example of this kind of pattern.

For a detailed discussion of working with circles in your compositions, see the "Circle" chapter, starting on page 36. As that chapter notes, a circle has no beginning and no end. This leads to the question of entry and exit points, which are always an issue with images that involve circular patterns. You'll find a detailed discussion of entry and exit points, and how to use them in your compositions, starting on page 136.

It is both a pitfall and a power of the circular pattern that frames are almost universally rectangular (the exception to this, the tondo, is discussed on page 70). This is a pitfall because the circular shape works in opposition to its rectangular boundaries, and for the viewer to be satisfied with this visual contradiction, there needs to be some mechanism for its resolution. It's like trying to fit the proverbial round peg into a square hole.

The power of the circular pattern comes paradoxically from this very contradiction. Since there is already a differential between the circular pattern and its rectangular boundary, a conflict has been set up. Conflicts are good for narrative! But narrative only works when there is some kind of resolution.

So circular patterns call out for acknowledgement of their nature and for a visual bridge to the rectangular. Two common ways to bridge the gap between the circular pattern and the rectangular frame are:

- Putting the circular pattern in the context of a grid.

- "Squaring the circle," meaning connecting the circle to the corners of the composition.

Putting the circular pattern in the context of a grid works to resolve the conflict between the circles and the rectangular frame because the underlying structure of the pattern is rectangular, even if the manifestation of the underlying pattern involves circular elements.

By "squaring the circle," I mean paying attention to all four corners of the composition. There needs to be a visual bridge in each of these four corners between the right angle of the compositional frame and the arc of the internal circle. When this is accomplished, the viewer no longer feels inordinate tension between the internal circle in the composition and the rectangular (or square) frame of the image.

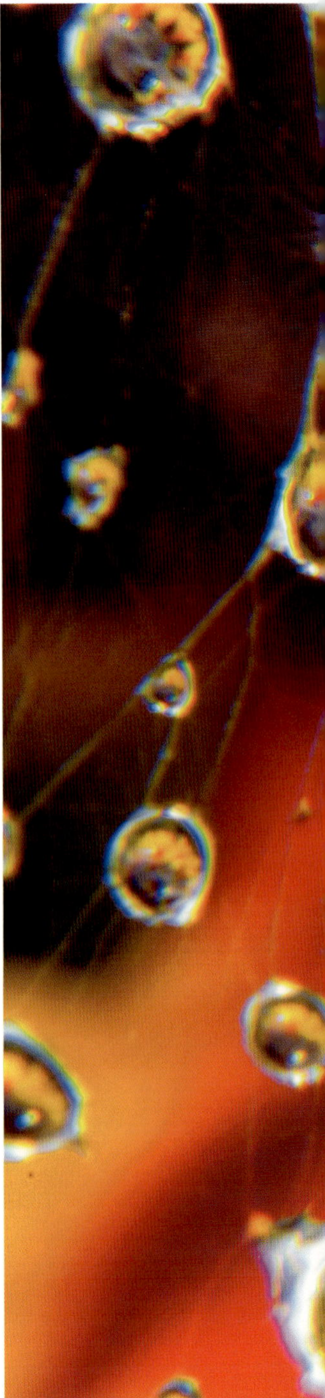

Falling Flowers—In my experience, the best time to photograph water drops is right after a rain storm. With this image, we had a late spring shower and then the sun came out. I went chasing water drops with my camera, tripod, and macro-telephoto lens. A macro-telephoto lens is ideal for water drops because you can get close, but at the same time are not creating "selfies" by being reflected in the drops.

Looking around, I saw light glistening on a spider web. Each drop of water on the web reflected a flower, a gaillardia, also known as a Blanket Flower, a species native to North America.

The web looked to me like it was "raining flowers," and in fact, there was an obvious pattern of circular repetition.

I photographed straight down but arranged my composition as much as possible to show the mass of water drops, each containing a refracted flower, with the idea of conveying my image of a rain of falling flowers.

Nikon D300, 200mm Nikkor macro, 36mm extension tube, +4 close-up filter, 1/20 of a second at f/32 and ISO 200, tripod mounted.

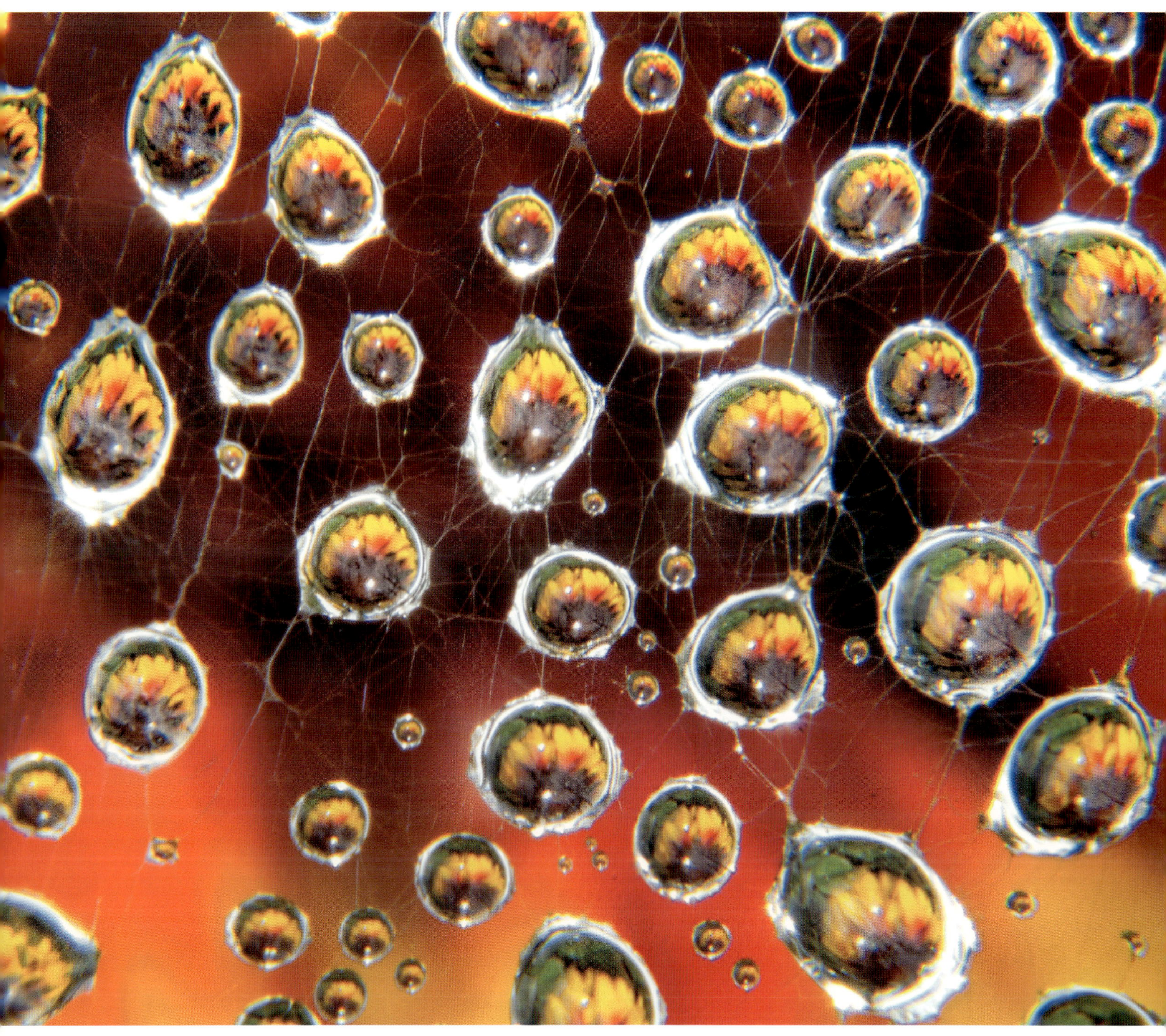

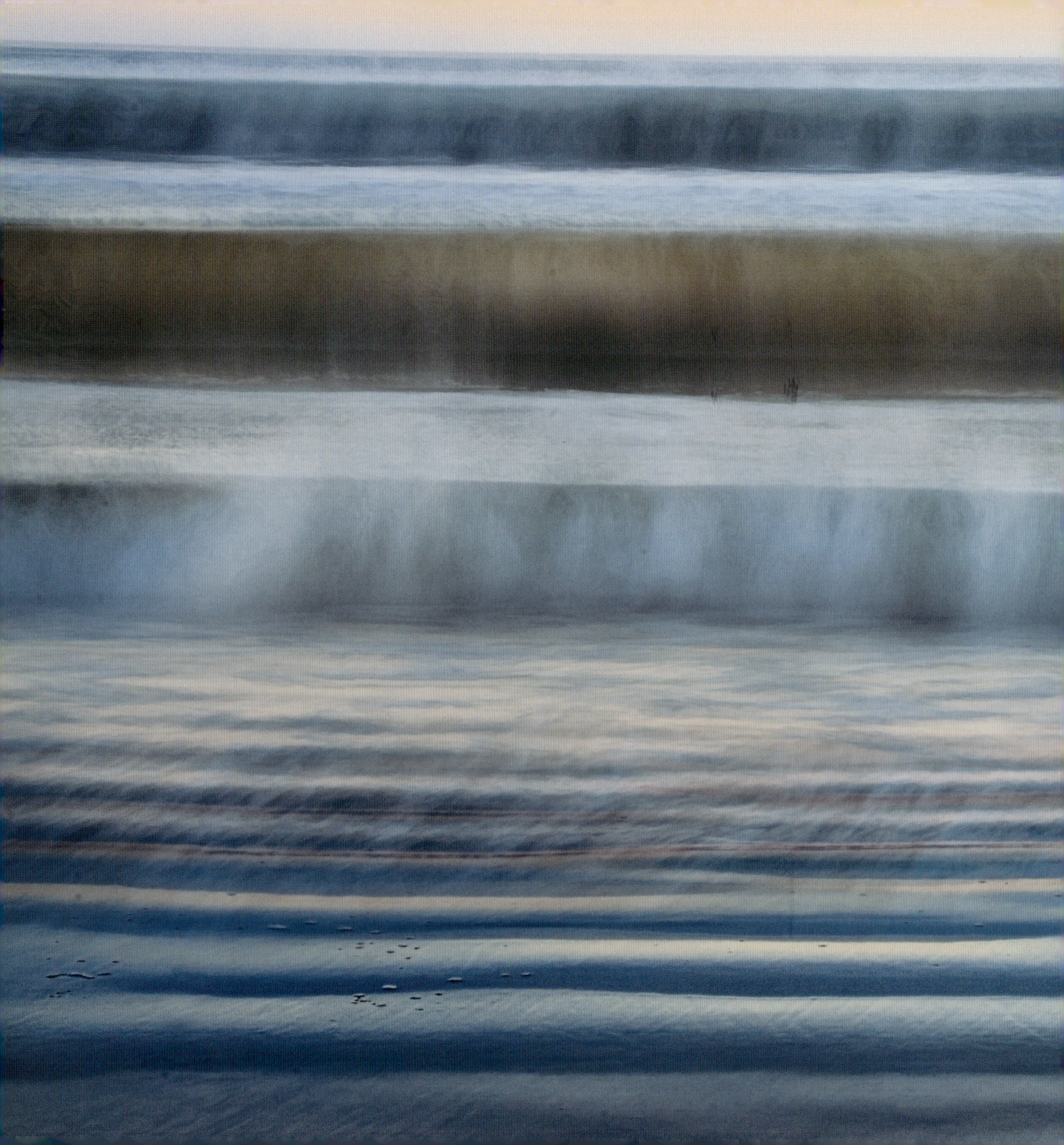

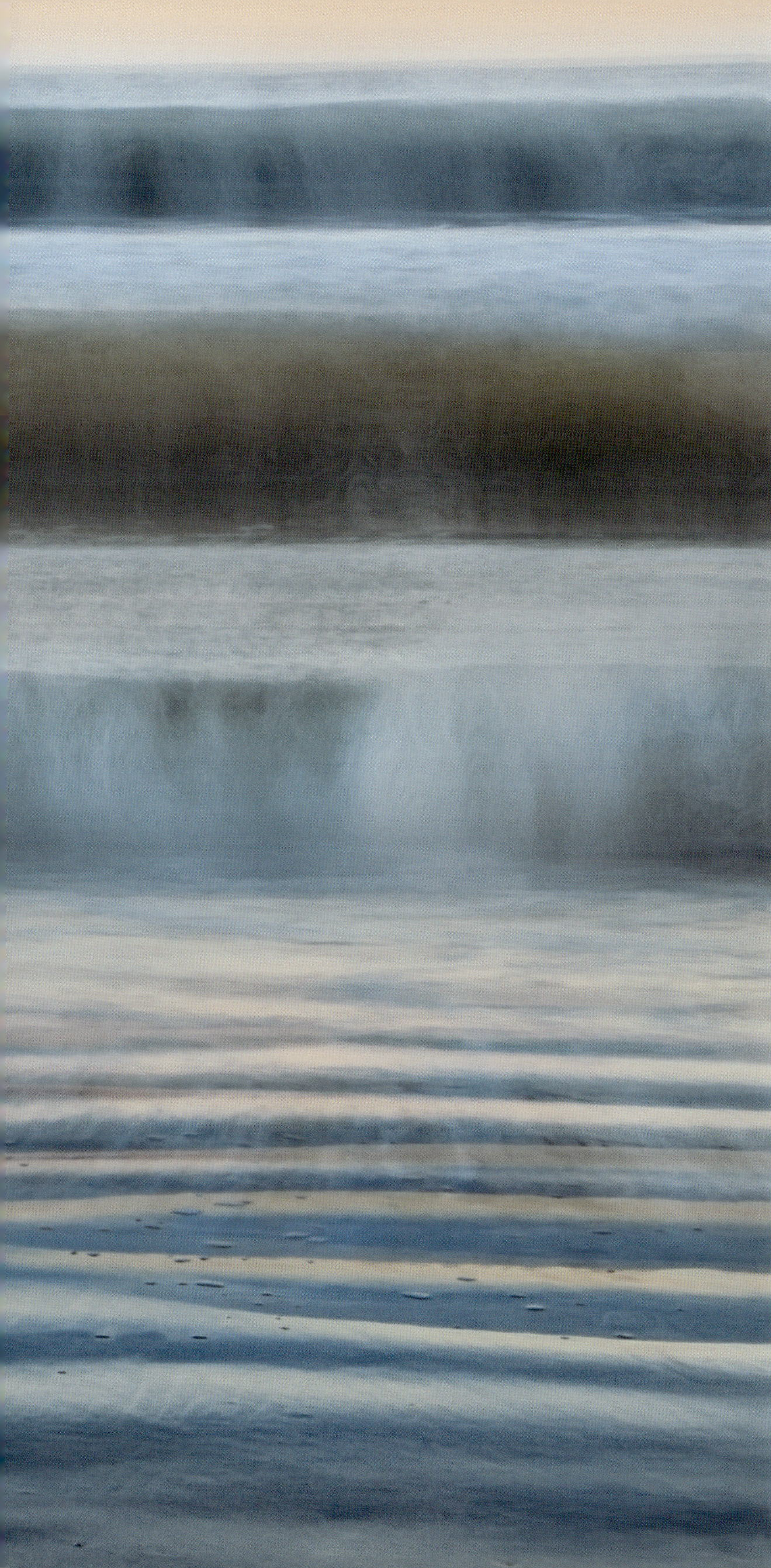

Waves on Drakes Beach—One Thanksgiving weekend I drove out with my boys to Point Reyes National Seashore. It was a balmy summer-like day. We decided to explore Drakes Beach and walked along the beach under towering bluffs at extreme low tide until we reached the Drakes Estero inlet to the Pacific (see the photo on pages 90–91).

On the way back along the beach, I let the kids play while I stopped to make some sunset images of waves with my camera on the tripod for long, slow exposures. I kept a weather-eye out for "sneaker" waves, and also to make sure that the kids didn't whack each other too hard with the driftwood at hand.

Drakes Beach often presents an interesting photographic opportunity because the prevailing wind blows in the opposite direction against the tide. So, the waves come in but the wind blows out.

While incoming surf can always be thought of as a wave pattern, this interplay of elemental forces creates an especially interesting pattern where the smaller waves, closer to shore, are more regular than the larger waves farther out in the Pacific. The larger waves are subject to interference from the strong prevailing winds and create a blurred line in addition to the normal shape of the wave.

Wave photography involves capturing the repetition of wave motion. What is particularly interesting about the conditions at this beach is that there are two different kinds of repetition: the larger waves and the smaller waves.

Nikon D300, 18-200mm Nikkor zoom at 95mm, 1 second at f/36 and ISO 100, tripod mounted.

Above: *Bus Window 1*—As I was riding in a bus in Iceland watching the beautiful landscape go by, I decided to experiment with in-camera motion (ICM) using my iPhone. I used the Slow Shutter Cam app, which let me choose a long-duration shutter speed by pressing a button to start and stop the exposure.

An ICM image uses motion—both of the subject in relation to the camera, and the camera itself—to create an abstraction. Much of the time, ICM images come out incoherent without a clear pattern. But when an ICM image gets things right, the resulting abstraction can show the underlying pattern and "bones" of the subject.

In the case of *Bus Window 1*, the underlying pattern involves a relationship between the lighter and darker fields, and the lines of both fields against the lighter gray of the sky. This pattern of lights and darks becomes very clear in the ICM rendering of the Icelandic landscape.

iPhone 12 Pro Max using Slow Shutter Cam app.

Right: *Tyre*—Traveling in Iceland with a group of photographers, we were assigned a large, red, 4-wheel drive "monster" of a truck converted to a bus. This thing was a behemoth! It was capable of crossing rivers in Iceland's Highlands, traversing glaciers, and much more. We dubbed it "the Beast." So patterns, of course, are everywhere—last but not least on the tire treads of your "run-of-the-mill" red monster Beast.

iPhone 12 Pro Max.

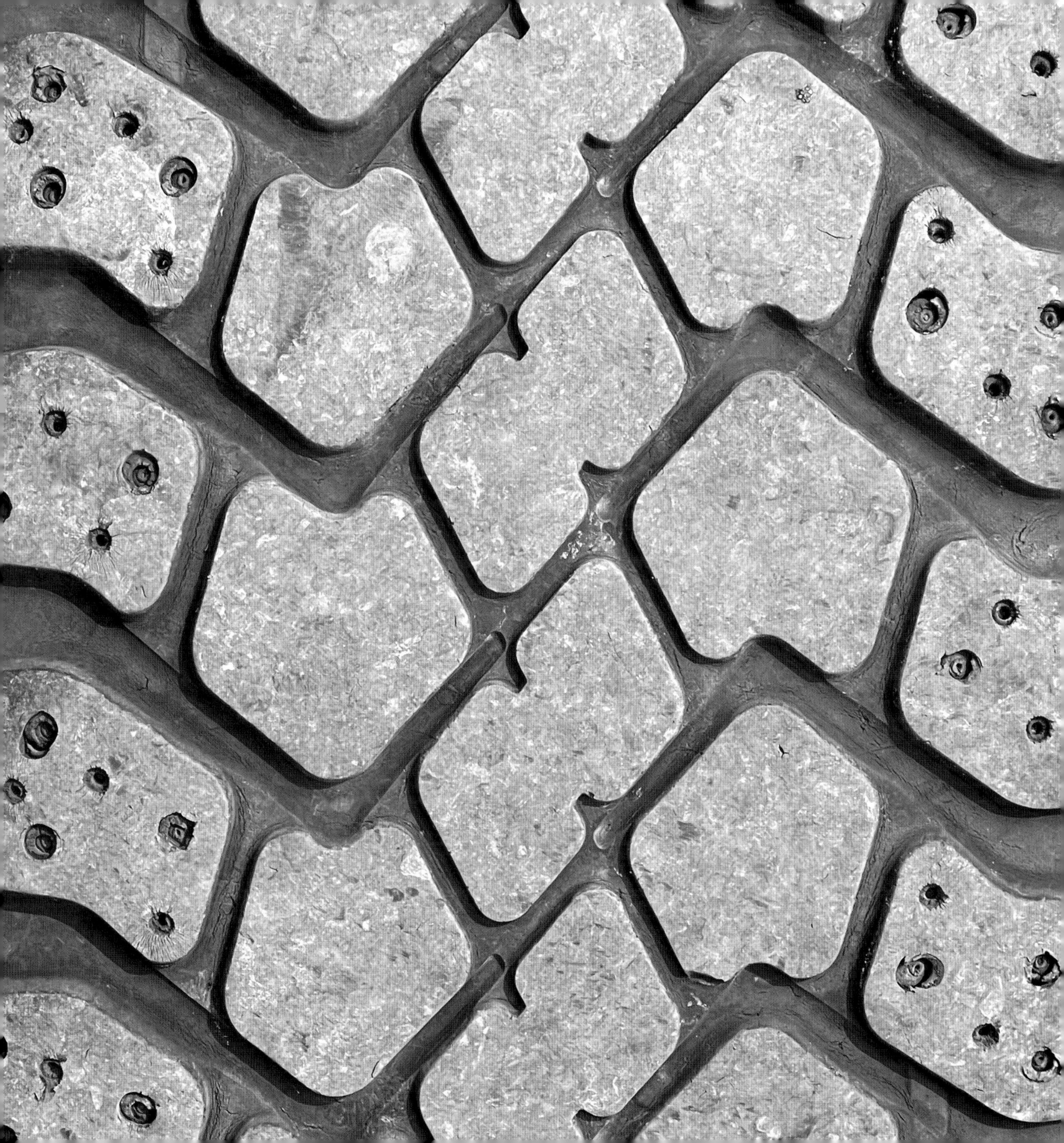

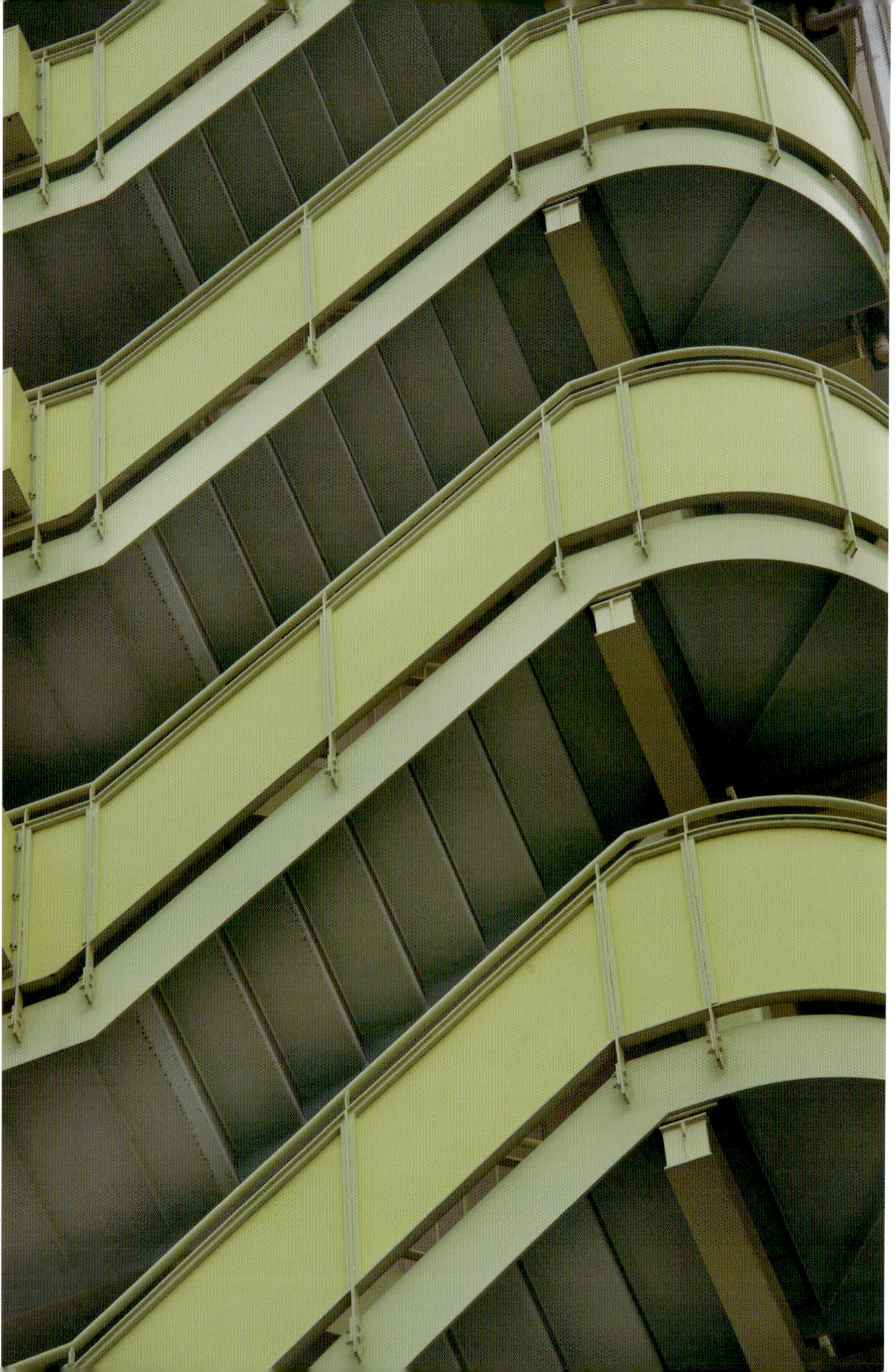

Patterns with Squares

When you embark on a pattern involving squares or square shapes, it is important to understand that the basic shapes of your pattern are in sympathy with the rectangular frame bordering the image. This sounds good but can lead to a serious danger of too much regularity, tending toward boredom.

A pattern that looks programmatic and is filled with right angles will make the viewer's eye go to sleep. Because there is no deep tension in this kind of composition, the viewer's brain makes a quick assumption, scans the image superficially, and tucks the image away as uninteresting or unremarkable.

The technique for dealing with this eye glazing is to add variation. In real life, most things are imperfect and most shapes are not really perfect rectangles or really even rectangular at all. Even the tire treads shown in *Tyre* on page 97, which seem like they should be in a regular grid-like pattern, are, in fact, not square.

You can vary the regularity of a pattern with squares by altering some of the elements so they are slightly off square. This can be accomplished by moving an element off a grid or slightly changing its shape. The same goal can be achieved by varying the outer shape of a large square so that it is more like a trapezoid.

Undoubtedly, patterns involving rectangular shapes have their place. For example, take a look at *Railroad Bridge, Maine* on page 77. As a creator, you need to understand that rectangular shapes will always lead to patterns that have an apparent mechanical aspect. This can be apt when the subject matter is machinery, engineering, or the like. However, if you are striving for a more humanistic effect and you start with a pattern of rectangular objects, you should definitely try to break things up.

Using Irregular Patterns

As I noted in the previous section, there's a great possibility of boredom with too much visual regularity. Fortunately, life is neither boring nor regular. In fact, it's messy and in the infinitude of patterns presented by life, the world, and the universe, you'll find complexity, diversity, and very little regularity. That said, some of the very best patterns come precisely from this very messy and irregular world that is all around us.

As an example, consider waves crashing on a beach or tidal pools in an estuarial mud flat. These are never the same twice, and they are never precisely regular, but they do follow a pattern and they often present visually compelling subject matter. You can see what I mean by taking a look at *Estero at Low Tide* on pages 90–91 and *Waves on Drakes Beach* on pages 94–95.

It is manifestly true that patterns of waves and on the beach are created by forces beyond our control: sun, moon, tide, wind, and so on. Continuing with the waves example, what is a poor, lonesome photographer to do when faced with these primordial forces?

The set of tools available to the photographer is limited. Observation is the most important. You can recognize an interesting irregular pattern when you see it. This involves understanding regular patterns, noting the deviation from regularity, and making sure that your irregular pattern has some degree of symmetry and closure. The pattern can't be so "out there" that it's unrecognizable.

Once an irregular pattern is recognized, you have the tools of the photographer's trade, such as exposure and framing, to work with. Often an irregular pattern becomes more interesting when you work with exposure to focus attention on the elements of the pattern. For example, you might want to expose for the reflected sunset in the pools of water like in the *Estero at Low Tide* image, emphasizing the nature of this pattern without regard for the rest of the image.

The most important aspect of the photographer's ability to respond to an irregular pattern is framing. The choice of how you frame the image is crucial to how the viewer will perceive the pattern and whether they will see it as a pattern at all.

When you make the image, your choice of focal length, and whether you choose to be close to the pattern or farther away, will establish the framing. Of course, in a given situation, you may not be able to change your focal length, in which case it is well said that the best zoom lens is your feet.

In other words, the way you use your positioning in relation to the subject and the focal length of the lens you use largely determine the framing of your image.

Flower Made from Radish Slices—The purple daikon radish is native to Asia where daikons have been cultivated for thousands of years. When you slice a daikon, it has a beautiful bicolored pattern showing purple lines on a white background.

To create this image, I used a light box and thin slices of purple daikon radish. The radish slices were arranged in two concentric circles with both circles using the radish slices in their long direction. The overall effect was to create a flower made up of the pattern of daikon radish slices.

Note that each slice in this image has its own internal, irregular pattern. As I made this image, I thought that the lines within each slice looked like calligraphy, quite appropriate for the Asian heritage of the daikon radish.

Nikon D850, 50mm Zeiss Makro-Planar, four exposures with shutter speeds ranging from 1/13 of a second to 1 second at f/11 and ISO 64, tripod mounted.

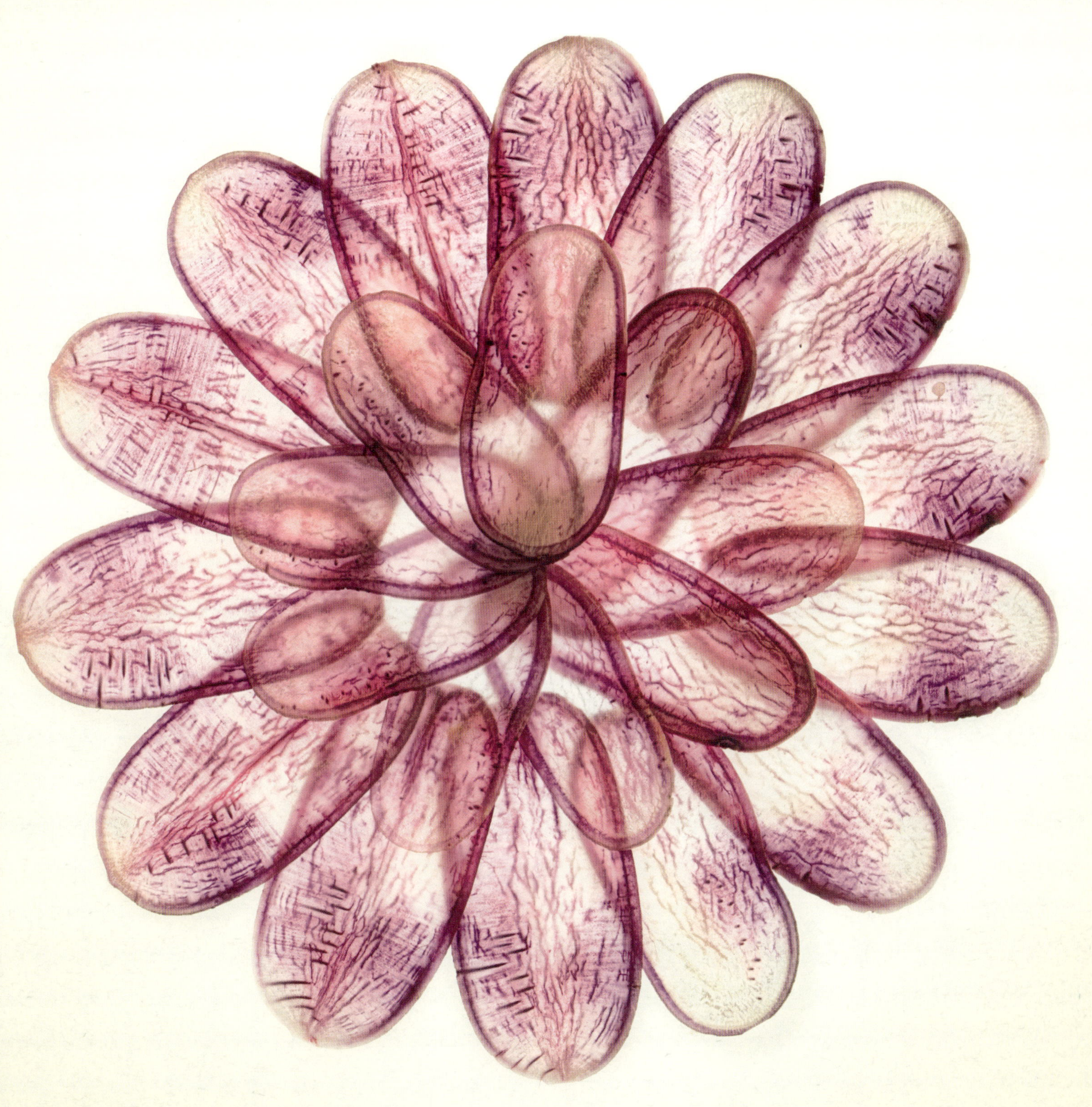

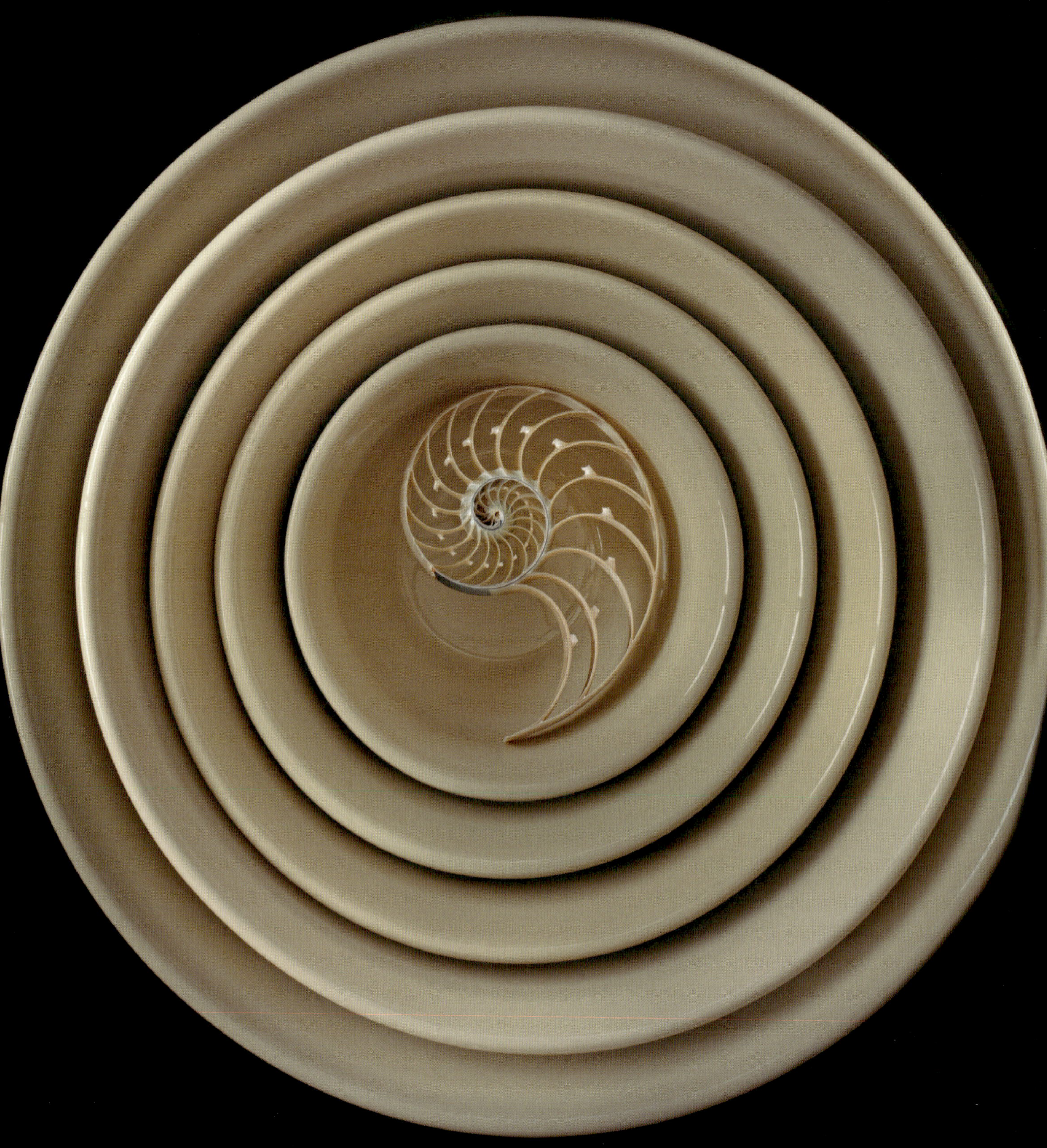

Working with Repetition

Here's an amazing thing about patterns: simply duplicating an element automatically gives you a pattern. Depending upon the element and how many times it has been duplicated, repetition in and of itself can make an interesting pattern.

You can find all kinds of repetition in photographic imagery whether the photos involve capturing nature at large or are renderings of studio compositions.

The following kinds of repetition can be kept in mind:

Progression, where the element gets successively larger or smaller. See the *Nesting Bowls*, opposite.

Rotation, where the element is rotated across the canvas, such as the *Flower Made from Radish Slices* on page 101.

Grid, where the elements are arranged in a regular rectangular scheme. *Apple Slices* on pages 52–53 is an example of this.

Patterns that repeat. This kind of pattern can move from left to right, right to left, top to bottom, or vice versa. It is possible to design a repeating pattern that repeats in all four directions. However, a four-way repeating pattern, while potentially useful for applications such as textiles, is unusual and may seem overly artificial in a photograph.

Keep in mind that repetition in a pattern is easy but often not satisfying. You can think of a repeating pattern as a bit like junk food: it may go down easy but it won't nourish your body or soul for long.

The main problem with repetition in a pattern is where the pattern begins and ends. Sometimes with a circular composition, such as *Mandahlia* on page 82 or *Flower Made from Radish* Slices on page 101, the repetition works regardless of its unending nature. This often depends on the kind of subject matter. If you consider a subject like the *Nesting Bowls*, shown at left, this didn't work as a repeating pattern until I added the nautilus-slice element in the very center.

Design Patterns

In the 1977 book *A Pattern Language: Towns, Buildings, Construction*, architect Christopher Alexander coined the concept of the *design pattern*. In architecture, a design pattern solves a general problem once; that way, a solution doesn't have to be reworked. Each implementation of the design pattern can contain variations suitable to its context.

As an example, Alexander cites the Place des Vosges in Paris, France. It's a town square surrounded by covered arcades. This is a template that can be used and reused in many geographic locations with minor variations.

The concept of the design pattern has been fruitfully applied to many fields besides architecture, with perhaps the best-known results related to software design.

The proverb, "give a man a fish and you feed him for a day, teach a man to fish and you feed him for a lifetime," says that it is more important to teach generally how to do something than to provide the solution to a specific problem.

In this spirit, rather than pinpointing and analyzing specific visual patterns, I'd like to share a technique to help you with a general approach to using patterns and repetition in your work.

Here I'm borrowing the concept of the design pattern from Christopher Alexander and the disciplines of architecture and software development. A design pattern is a kind of template. You can use these templates to repeat specific patterns across a wide variety of imagery.

May I propose that you begin a notebook with the specific design patterns that you like to use in your imagery? If you look through this chapter and peruse the rest of *Composition & Photography*, you'll find many patterns in the imagery and described in the text.

Patterns and Living

Human beings are creatures of habit. We brush our teeth in the morning, have a pattern of meals, commuting to work, and so on. Some of us, of course, are more creatures of habit than others.

A habit is a pattern of living. And our patterns help define us. How does this relate to your photography?

Bike Rack—Repetition can be found in some unlikely places. When I saw this empty bike rack on the University of California at Berkeley campus, I knew I had to make a photo emphasizing the repetition of the arches. Picking my spot carefully, I got down in the middle of the structure and focused about a third of the way to the distance. This strategy was intended to maximize the depth of field and the range of arches that would be in focus.

As I looked down the aisle of repeating arches it seemed to me that the space at the end of the rack was like a portal, and that the entire image from its mundane origins as a simple bike rack evoked the possibility of travel to another dimension.

Nikon D850, 28-300 Nikkor zoom at 68mm, seven exposures with shutter speeds ranging from 1/60 of a second to 1 second at f/32 and ISO 64, tripod mounted.

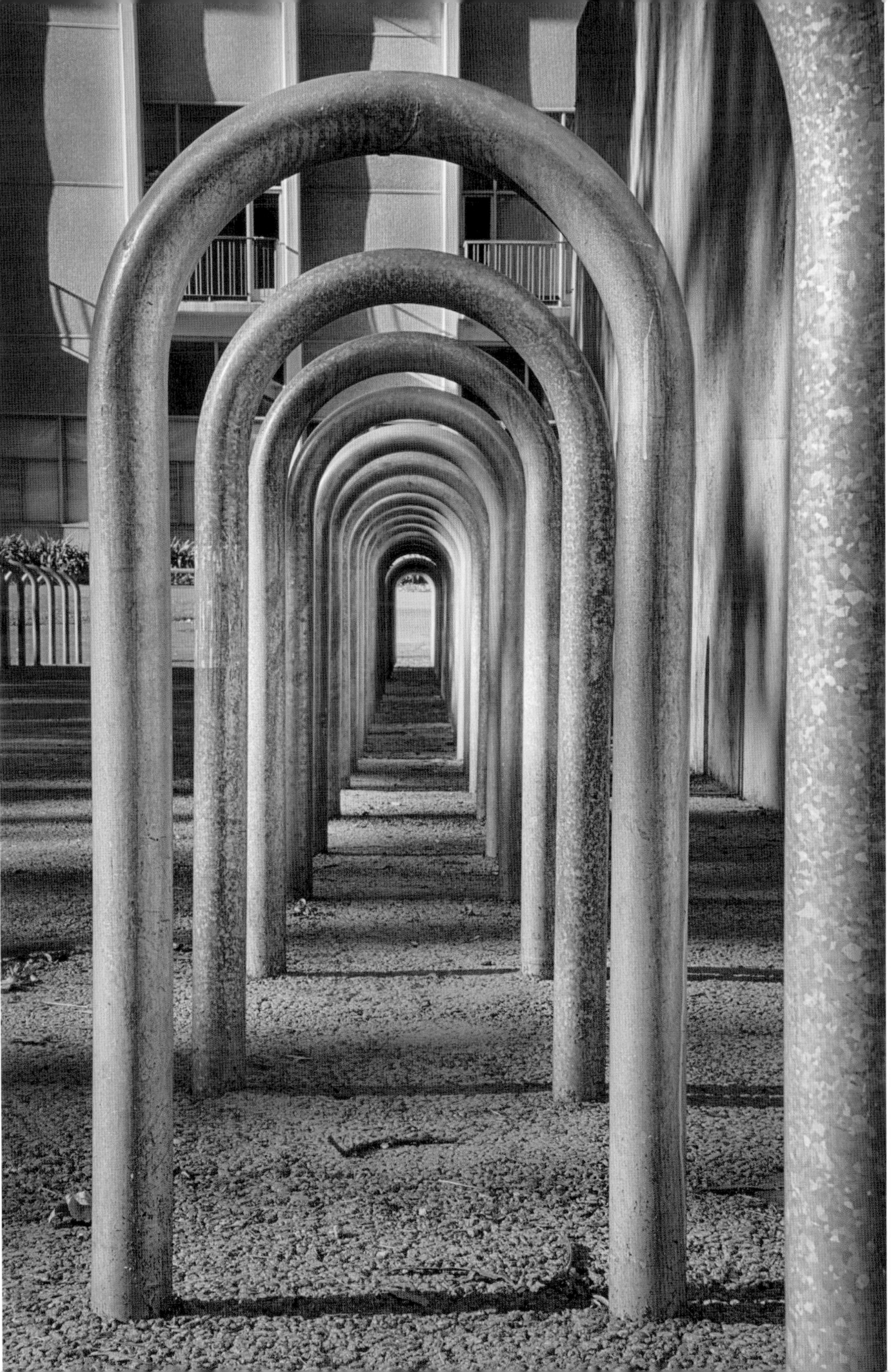

It's well said that if you want to take better pictures, stand in front of more interesting things. But, if you *really* want to make better pictures, become a more interesting person.

If our patterns of living help define us, and if the subtlety, quality, and beauty of the underlying pattern makes the photo, then we should work to implement life patterns that are meaningful to us. Eventually, these improved life patterns will be reflected in your photography.

Integrating improved patterns into our lives means different things for different people. I know that I am living the life I want to live and creating the patterns I want to create for my life and my art when I achieve a measure of serenity. It's important to me not to be owned by my possessions, and to express the love I feel for those around me, as well as caring for the Earth that nurtures us.

It's not always an easy thing to hold to the values that are important to me in my life patterns. But when I do, the patterns that emerge from my photographs appear naturally on their own. These life patterns resonate more with viewers of my images than when I try to artificially impose patterns on my imagery without integrating them with my life.

KEY IDEAS

- Patterns are organized repetition of elements within a design.

- Patterns create order out of chaos.

- The pattern or patterns within an image need to work well with the border frame of the image.

- Creating templates for patterns—sometimes called "design patterns"—helps you work with patterns without reinventing the wheel each time.

- Our patterns for living are reflected in our art.

Death Valley Campsite—If you look at the tent in the foreground of this photo, you'll see a shadowy figure inside. That's me! I was reading a book using my headlamp, until I went to sleep about half an hour into the four-hours worth of exposures.

As astronomical photographers know, to make a long-duration image of the night sky, you are better off making a sequence of shorter exposures rather than one long exposure. So for this image, instead of a single four-hour exposure, I made sixty exposures at four minutes each. The short exposures were combined using Photoshop (there are a variety of other programs that will also combine night images).

The pattern in the sky was created by star trails, specifically the apparent movement in the stars created by the Earth's rotation on its axis. In some sense, this is an ancient pattern that has accompanied humanity since the dawn on time, at least at night where there is limited light pollution.

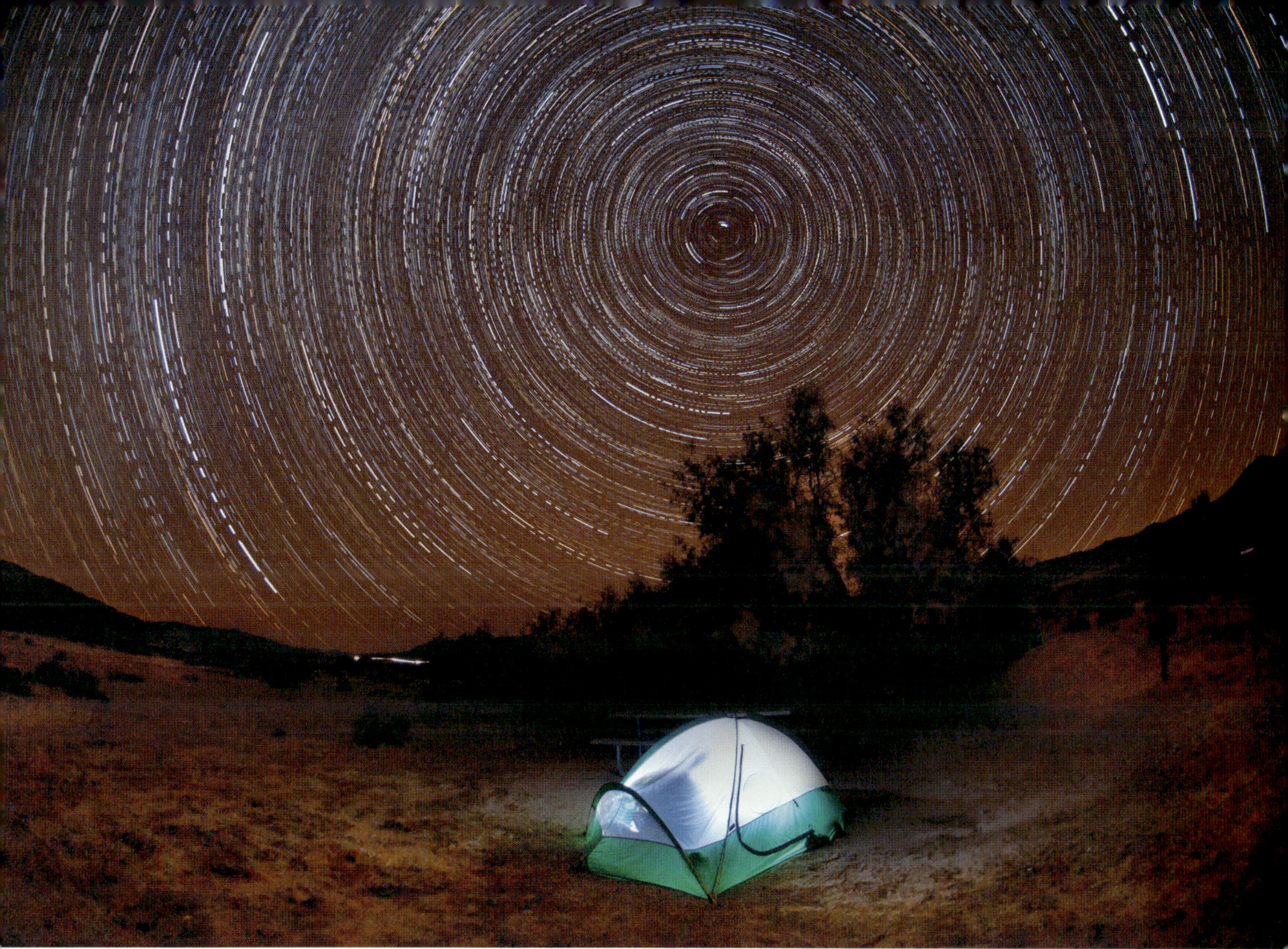

With this particular image, the radial pattern of the stars shows some solid lines and some dashed lines. The dashed lines represent gaps where my *intervalometer*, a program-mable exposure timer, was set not to expose.

When I am camping in dark night-sky locations, I often fol-low this routine: setting the camera up on a programmed timer for a long set of night exposures, and going to bed while the camera works. This represents one of my pat-terns for life with the heavens rotating above me as I enjoy my time in the wilderness.

Nikon D300, 10.5mm Nikkor horizontal fisheye, sixty exposures, each exposure 4 minutes at f/2.8 and ISO 320, tripod mounted (total exposure time about 4 hours); exposures stacked in Photoshop.

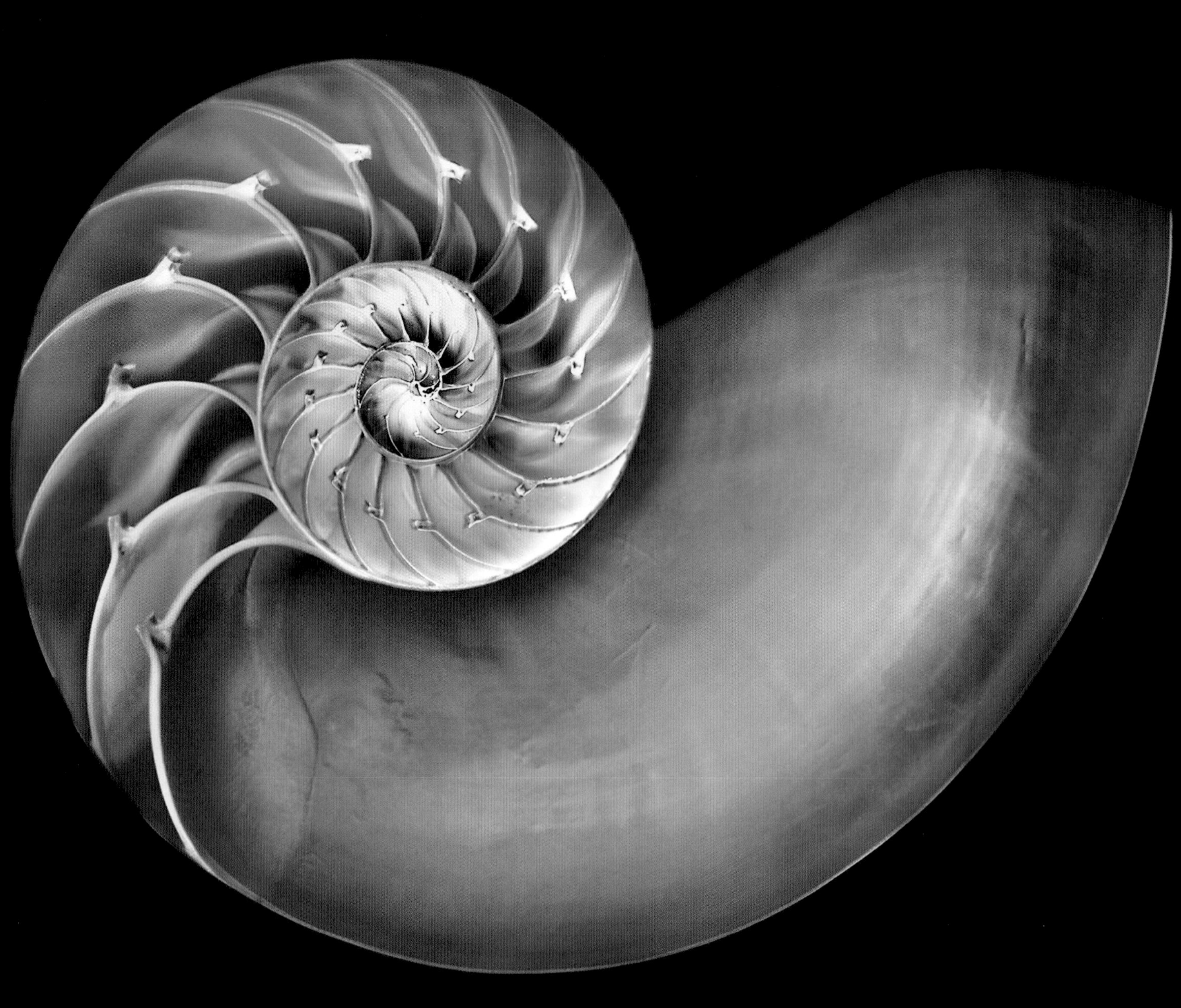

SPIRALS & FRACTALS  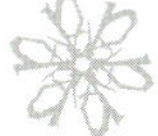 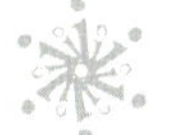 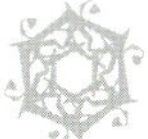 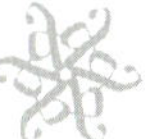 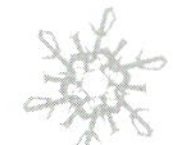

> "The spiral represents the unfolding of our hidden creative powers and symbolizes both self-realization and boundless expansion. Its secret is beautifully dramatized by the chambered nautilus whose in-dwelling life unfolds cyclically and periodically, mirroring in itself the expanding spirals and eternal patterns of the evolving cosmos." —Finley Eversole, *Art and Spiritual Transformation*

Nautilus in Black and White— The interior of the nautilus shell is roughly logarithmic. Each nautilus shell maintains the same proportions in the spiral throughout the lifetime of the cephalopod that creates the chambers within the shell.

In the wild, no scientist has ever documented a nautilus from hatching to maturity. So a great deal is unknown about these wondrous animals.

What is known is that they can live for 15 to 20 years and reach maturity when they are about 12 years old. Nautilus eggs are huge and are among the biggest eggs relative to adult size of any animal. As a cephalopod, the nautilus is a member of the same family as octopi and squid.

I photographed this cross-section of a chambered nautilus shell on a black background and paid special attention to lighting to bring out the luminescent quality of the internal shell.

Nikon D200, 50mm Zeiss macro, 8 seconds at f/32 and ISO 100, tripod mounted.

A *spiral* is a three-dimensional curve rotating around a fixed position that is receding or approaching the viewer—think of a spiral staircase or the spiral arms of a galaxy. Spirals range in size from the tiny spiral in a flower to the vast reaches of intergalactic space; the spiral is a universal shape that occurs over and over again.

A *fractal* image is an image where small areas of the image are replicated across the larger image in its entirety.

There a number of different kinds of fractal images, ranging from those generated mathematically (take a look at the note on page 126 about fractal art) to photographs of fractals in nature. With natural fractals, examples include the pattern of an ice crystal that mimics the pattern of a frozen pond (page 121), branches in a complex tree that resemble the tree itself (page 123), and portions of a landscape that look like the landscape as a whole (page 174–175).

Keep in mind that visual uses of spirals and fractals are not intended to be precisely mathematical in many images. Most representations of spirals and fractals are not exact: a spiral staircase is often irregular to fit the needs of the architecture, and a portion of a fractal image can be reminiscent of the image as a whole without precisely duplicating the image. Outside of the world of pure mathematics, precise fractal replication is aspirational rather than exact.

A spiral is a shape—think of a chambered nautilus shell such as the one on page 108—and also a template for a pattern within an image. For more about working with pattern templates, turn to "Design Patterns" on page 104.

A fractal is not a shape in and of itself, but represents a family of shapes. Since each fractal contains information about how the fractal was created and about the fractal as a whole, a fractal can also be thought of as a kind of blueprint for life and a way of creation.

SPIRAL spi·ral | \ˈspī-rəl \

adjective : winding around a center or pole and gradually receding from or approaching it

noun   *1 a : the path of a point in a plane moving around a central point while continuously receding from or approaching it*

b : a three-dimensional curve (such as a helix) with one or more turns about an axis

2 : something having a spiral form as a spiral galaxy

Inside a Red Vein Indian Mallow Blossom—The Red Vein Indian Mallow blossom of the species *Abutilon striatum* is beloved by hummingbirds. The flower is veined and shaped like a calyx that dangles off branches. If you look inside a blossom, you'll see a deep cup with the petals swirling in a spiral around the sigma, ova, and anthers, which itself appears spiral.

When I looked inside this hummingbird magnet, it seemed like a great place to try out my Laowa Macro Probe lens. This lens is a unique macro wide-angle lens on a stalk that is over a foot long. You might think it is an ideal lens for photographing venomous small critters without getting too close to them, and you'd be right! It's also a great lens for getting inside an *Abutilon striatum* and other concave blossoms.

The macro probe lens includes an LED ring light at the end of the stalk. The wide-open aperture for this lens is f/14, but I found that it needs to be stopped down all the way to its smallest aperture of f/45 to get even minimally adequate depth of field. Focus stacking is not an option here due to the ergonomics of the lens because it is constantly slightly vibrating and slipping.

I started with the camera and probe on a tripod and the probe lens inserted into the flower blossom. I wanted to photograph the flower stopped down at f/45 and use the natural backlighting to create an attractive image. But at f/45, using natural light, nothing can be seen through this lens. What to do?

My workaround technique was to turn on the LCD ring light and focus with the aperture wide open at f/14. When everything looked good to me, I turned the ring light off and stopped the lens all the way down to f/45, and created the image.

Nikon D850, 24mm Laowa Macro Probe, 24mm extension tube, 2 minutes at f/40 and ISO 64, tripod mounted.

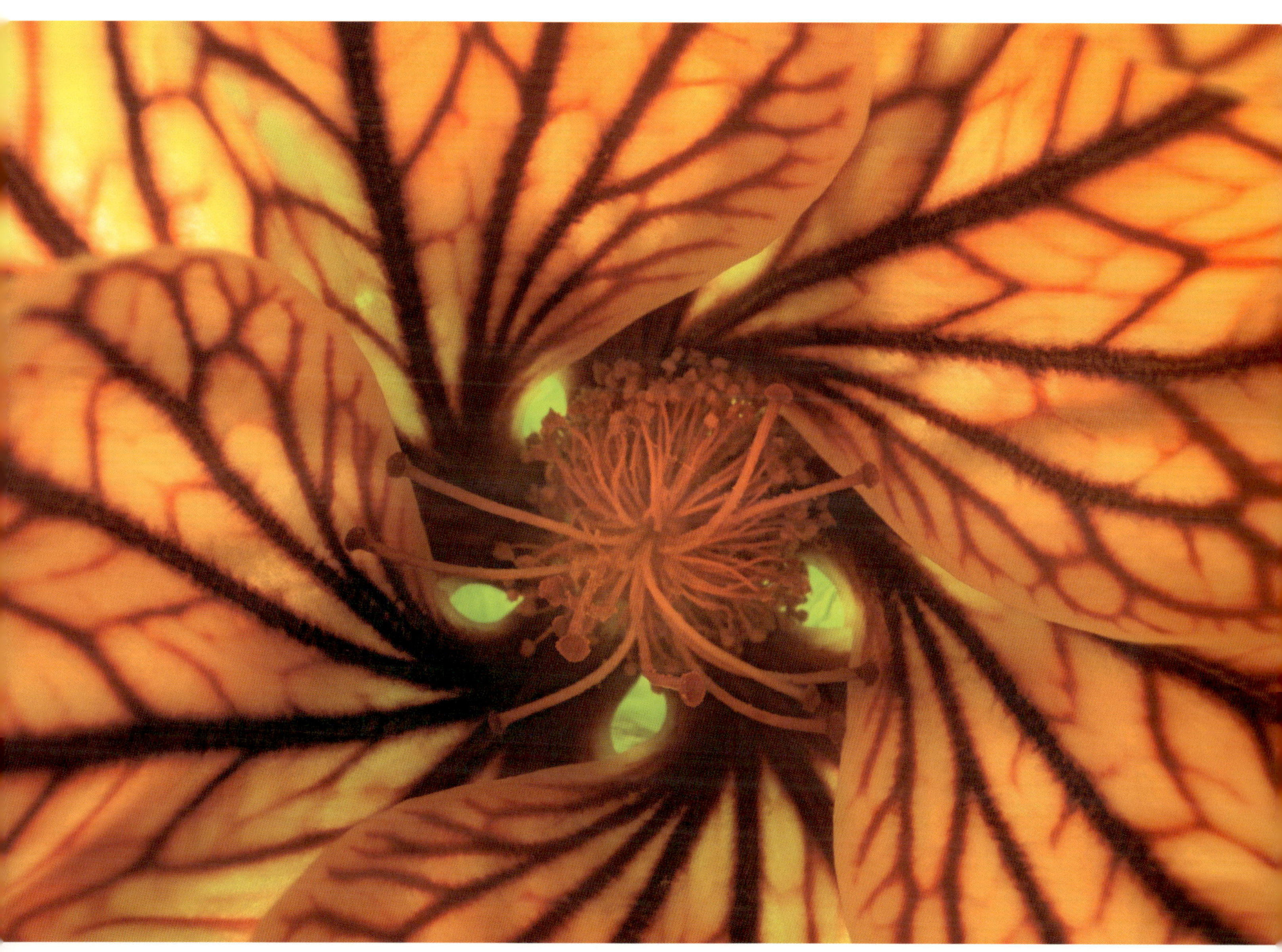

Both fractals and spirals are often found in nature. A spiral can be a fractal, and a fractal image often contains spirals; the two shapes are related.

Fractals are "cousins" of the spiral, often accompany spirals, and are a design pattern that is invaluable to learn to work with. The fractal way of life, which is closely related to our sense of the infinite, is always significant.

Spirals are, themselves, powerful shapes with emotional and spiritual connotations.

In this chapter, we'll explore how to use spirals and fractals in your compositions and how to take advantage of their power.

Working with Spirals

When working photographically with spirals, there are three common points of view. These refer to the camera and focal plane position in relationship to the spiral subject matter. The spatial relationship of camera position to subject is discussed on page 61.

- Perhaps the most common configuration is a head-on photo of a spiral that is in front of the camera; for example, the photo of the nautilus shown on page 108.

- Another common camera-subject relationship involving spirals is to look down at the spiral. Examples include the mallow blossom shown on page 111 and the shell on page 114.

- Looking up and through the spiral (for example, the staircase shown opposite) is somewhat less common. But gazing up a spiral is quite powerful because seeing to the end of the spiral brings a sense of completion and viewing the infinite.

It is important to identify which of these three scenarios your image will use before you undertake a detailed setup, as they are quite different in implication, meaning, and how you want to position the camera.

The first configuration, a frontal, head-on spiral, leads to a relatively flat composition that does not require much depth of field. The key point here is to position the focal plane of the camera as parallel as possible to the subject.

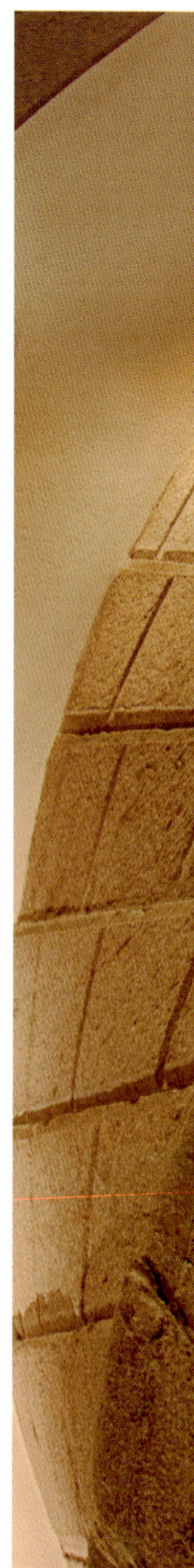

Twisted—The city of Santiago de Compostela in Galicia, Spain, is where the main route of the Camino de Santiago pilgrimage trail ends. It is a city of many wonders and a World Heritage Site. Not least among these wonders is the triple-spiral staircase in the Convent of Santo Domingo de Bonaval. Built by Domingo de Andrade in the 1700s, this is one of the very few triple-spiral staircases in the world.

To photograph this incredible triple spiral, I laid down on the cold stone floor beneath my tripod and used an extreme wide-angle lens (a 15mm rectilinear fisheye) to photograph straight up the spiral.

Nikon D850, 8-15mm Nikkor fisheye zoom at 15mm, six exposures with shutter speeds ranging from 0.5 of a second to 13 seconds, each exposure at f/22 and ISO 200, tripod mounted.

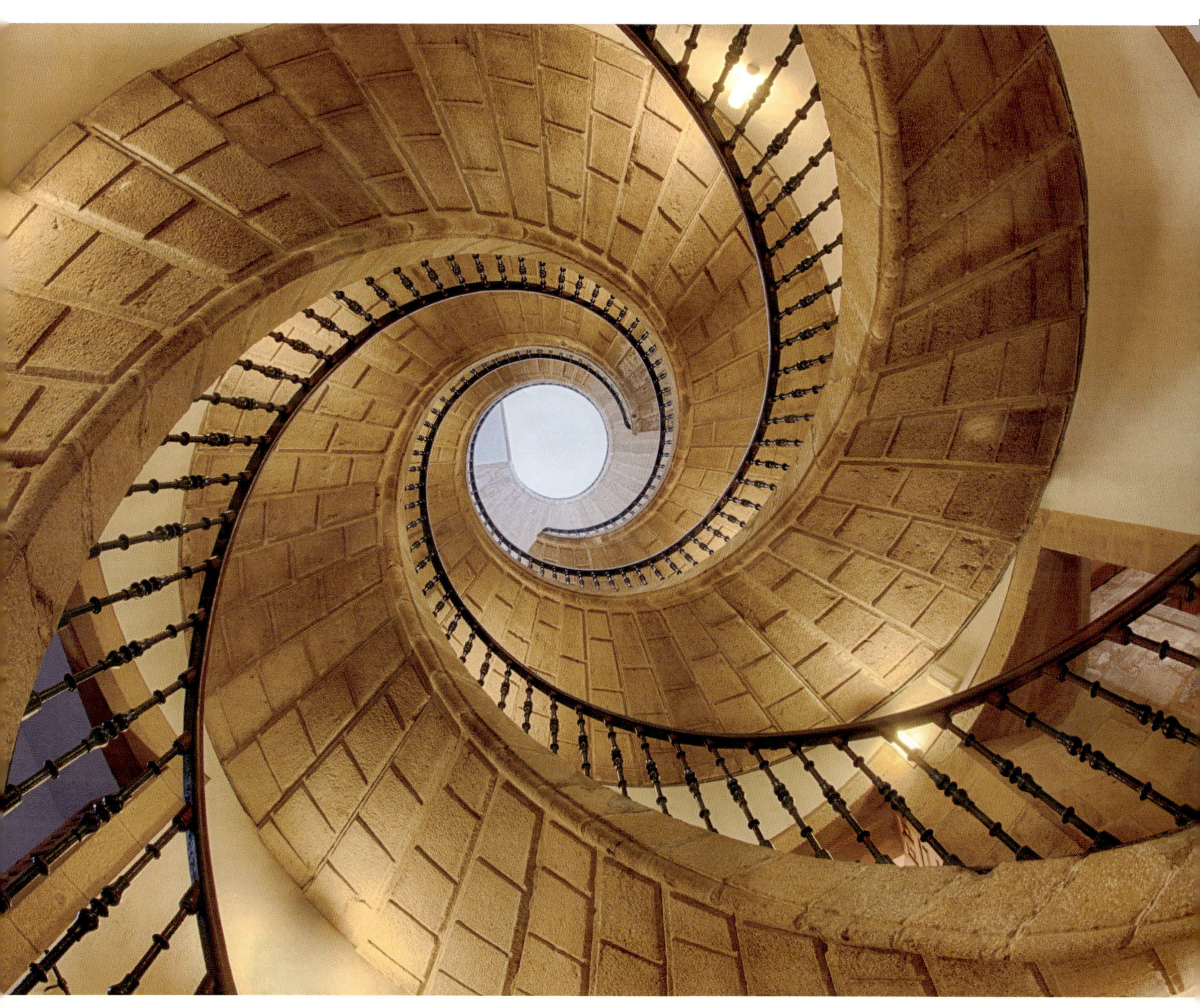

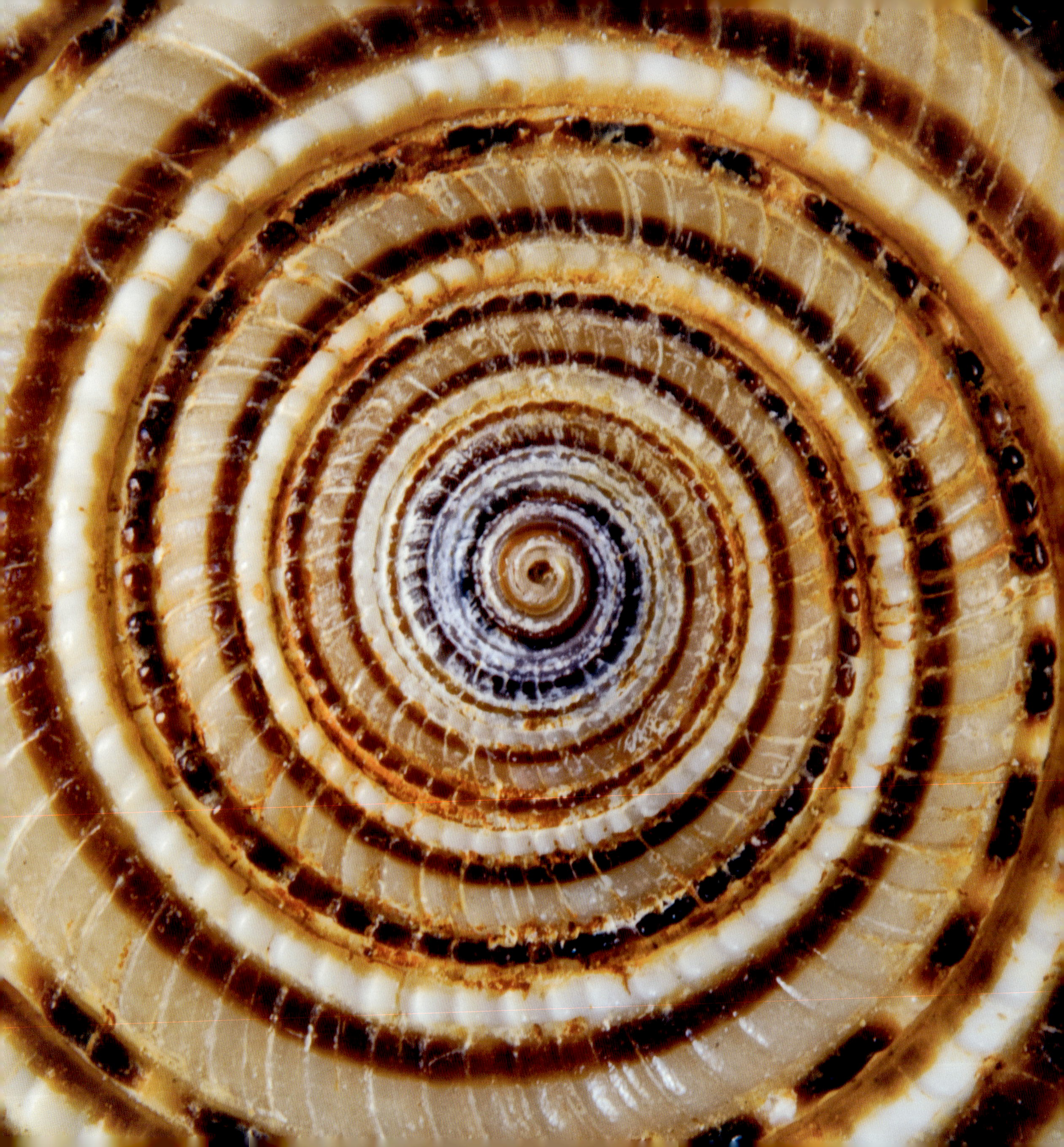

When you are looking down on a spiral, it's important to think about how far down the tunnel of the spiral you are going to go to frame the image. There are always compositional choices and options, starting with changing your position.

Depending upon your equipment, you can also change the focal length of the lens. Particularly with spirals photographed close up (such as the shell, opposite), your point of focus and aperture can make a great deal of difference to the composition. Changing the point of focus when you are up close can actually alter the framing of the image. (If you don't believe me, give it a try!)

As a result of these choices, you can frame the spiral at a distance or close up.

Peering through the camera down a spiral, there is always a center point. A compositional question becomes how much of a spiral around the center point will your image show?

The closer to the center point you are optically, the less your image will reveal of the spiral. However, if you pull back to show more of the spiral, then the spiral can become "tunnel-like" and you lose the sense of grandeur inherent in the spiral.

There's a balance in this decision about whether to get close or capture more of the spiral from far away, and often an optimum point. This choice largely determines the kind of image you make.

The key thing to think about is symmetrical closure. In other words, the composition should be attractive at the edges of the spiral as well as in the center, regardless of where you choose to crop the composition.

Architectonica perspectiva —The common name for this shell is the "perspective sundial" shell. It is a kind of sea snail, a marine gastropod mollusk of the genus *Architectonica*. This shell is also sometimes called a staircase shell. The snail is found in Asian coral reefs mostly near the Indian subcontinent.

Looking at this shell, I saw an almost perfect spiral. An issue was that the center of the shell rose like a cone toward the lens. It was clear that depth of field was going to be an issue. To resolve this, I captured a number of exposures using different focal points and combined them in Photoshop, creating the final composition.

Nikon D810, 100mm Zeiss Makro-Planar, 15 seconds at f/2 and ISO 64, tripod mounted; twelve exposures, stacked for extended depth of field.

Thought Experiment

Go out and take a walk and see how many spirals and fractals you can find. Look up at tree branches and look for shadows with a curl. Maybe there's a farmer's market nearby selling fiddlehead ferns (only in the spring!), Romanesco broccoli, or some other great fractal vegetable.

Explore your world! Look up, look sideways, look at things from the corner of your eye. Is there a dandelion seedpod ready for close inspection?

Try to get out of your normal pattern, and see how many spirals and fractals you can find along the way.

When choosing to photograph a spiral looking up from underneath, the key thing to keep in mind is that you are *looking up*. Most upward spiral photos are captured with a very wide-angle lens, because there is no other way to capture the full extent of a widening spiral. Therefore, as a matter of geometry, you will need to be below your camera (unless you want a body part to appear in the image). This means lying or crouching on the ground under your tripod.

Whether you're looking at your subject head on, up, or down, a spiral, like any other subject, needs to fit into the frame boundary of your image (framing is discussed in more detail starting on page 54). This means that as you previsualize a spiral composition, you should consider how the outer edges of the spiral interact with the frame to create an interesting composition.

Positioning the Center

In addition to the interaction between the spiral and the frame, the positioning of the spiral's center is extremely significant. The most common compositional approach is to position the spiral's center at or near the center of the photographic composition. You'll find that roughly 99 percent of spiral photos take this approach.

The advantage of centering is that it leads to a sense of completeness and allows the viewer to see the whole spiral. A possible disadvantage is that placing the spiral center in the center of the composition can lead to an unexciting, static image.

If you decide to break the normal pattern either by omitting the spiral center—as in *Caixa Forum Stairs* on page 118—or by skewing the composition so the spiral center is close to one edge—as in *Wright Stairs* on page 119—do so carefully.

If you play visual games with the location of the center of the spiral, you need to know that you are doing so. You should provide clues so the viewer can clearly extrapolate the location of the spiral center, as well as visualize the completion of the spiral.

Spirals are everywhere and are a universally recognized shape and pattern. It's great to internalize the use of the spiral as a design pattern in your work, and to understand that when you encounter a spiral there's a good chance of making an exciting composition.

Gem of the Drakensberg—Aloe polyphylla, commonly called the "Gem of the Drakensberg," is native to the higher elevations of the Drakensberg mountains in the landlocked southern African Kingdom of Lesotho. While many succulents exhibit fractal-spiral patterns, the Drakensberg is unusual in its regularity and obvious spiral.

The plant will grow its spiral in only one direction, either clockwise or counterclockwise. When fully mature there will be at least five fractal-spiralling rows.

While the Drakensberg is considered rare, it has become a popular succulent in the gardens near where I live, so it is possible to find great specimens to photograph like this one!

Nikon D810, 85mm Nikkor macro, 2.5 seconds at an effective aperture of f/51 and ISO 64, tripod mounted.

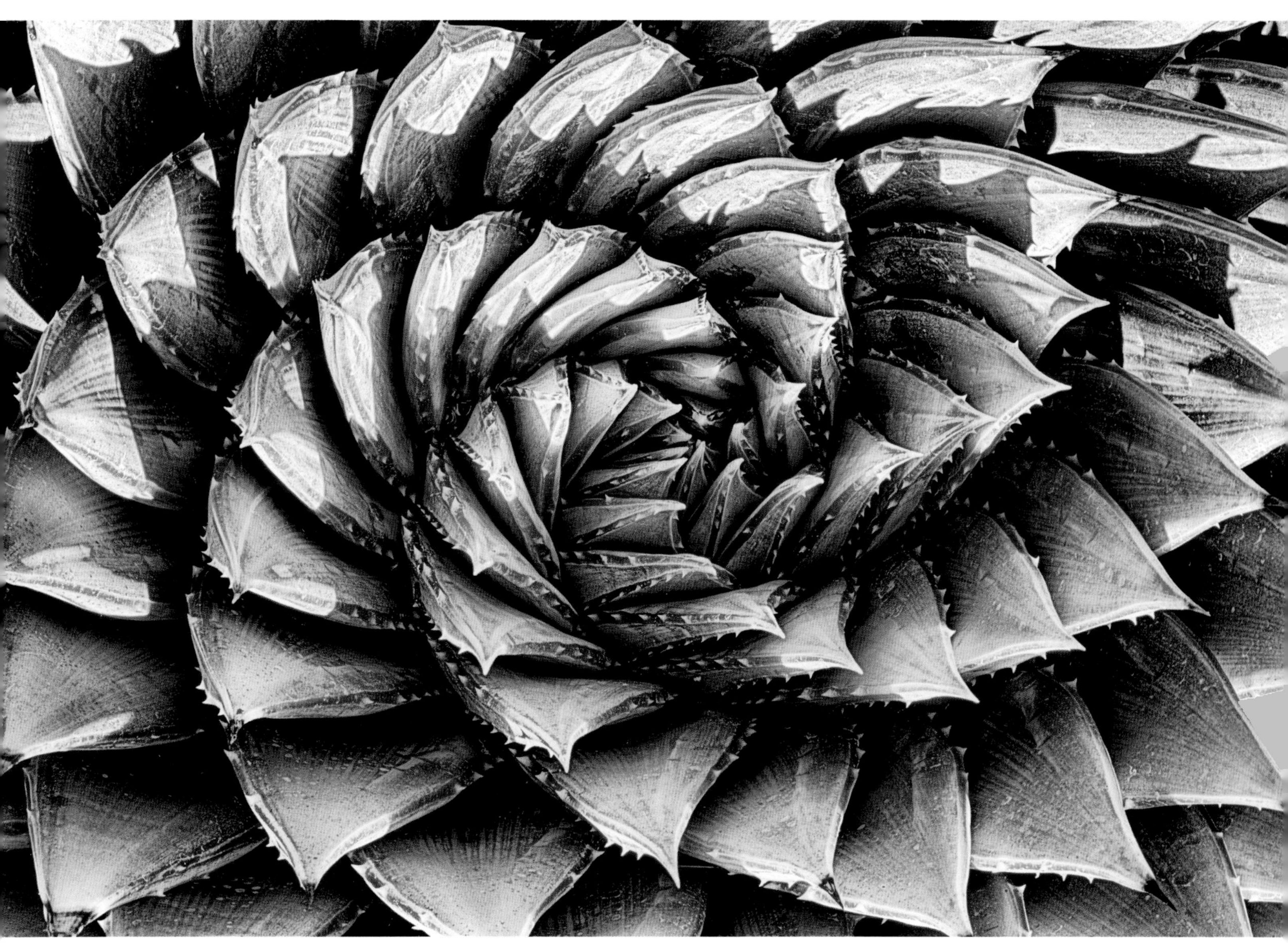

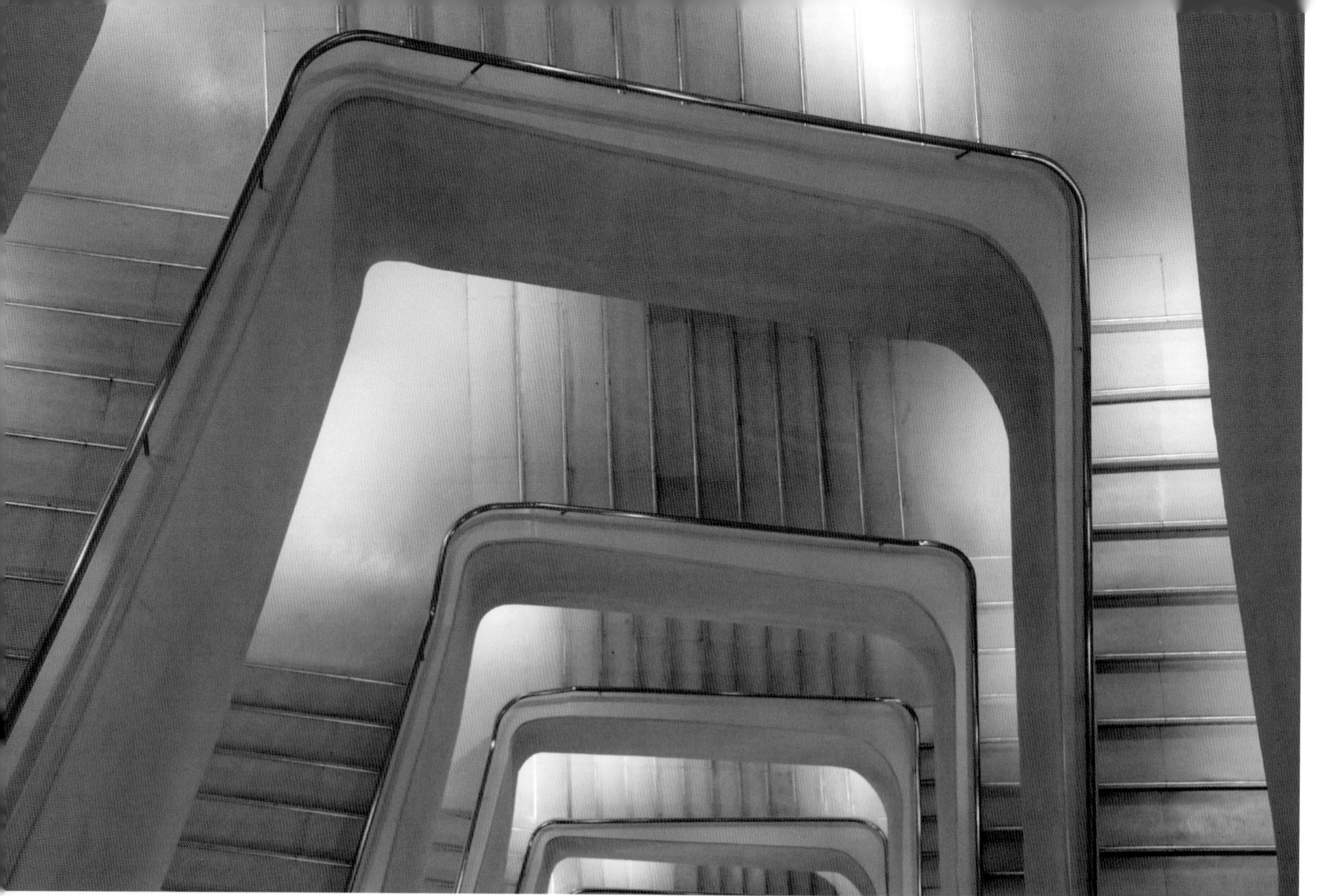

Above: *CaixaForum Stairs*—The CaixaForum in Madrid, Spain, an art center on Madrid's "museum row," boasts a spectacular, almost rectangular, internal spiral staircase. In this image looking down the CaixaForum stairs, I omitted the center of the spiral from the frame.

My idea was that the viewer of this image would complete the pattern unconsciously—and mentally finish the spiral—even though it's not fully shown in the image.

Nikon D850, 28-300mm Nikkor zoom at 68mm, 1/20 of a second at f/9 and ISO 1250, hand held.

Right: *Wright Stairs*—The vast Marin Center in San Rafael, California, is the largest public project designed by Frank Lloyd Wright. The building contains a number of Wright's distinctive spiral stairs, reminiscent of the shapes in the Guggenheim Museum.

This photo looking up a back stair at the Marin Center is intentionally framed off-kilter with the spiral center toward the top of the frame.

Nikon D300, 12-24mm Nikkor zoom at 15mm, 10 seconds at f/22 and ISO 100, tripod mounted.

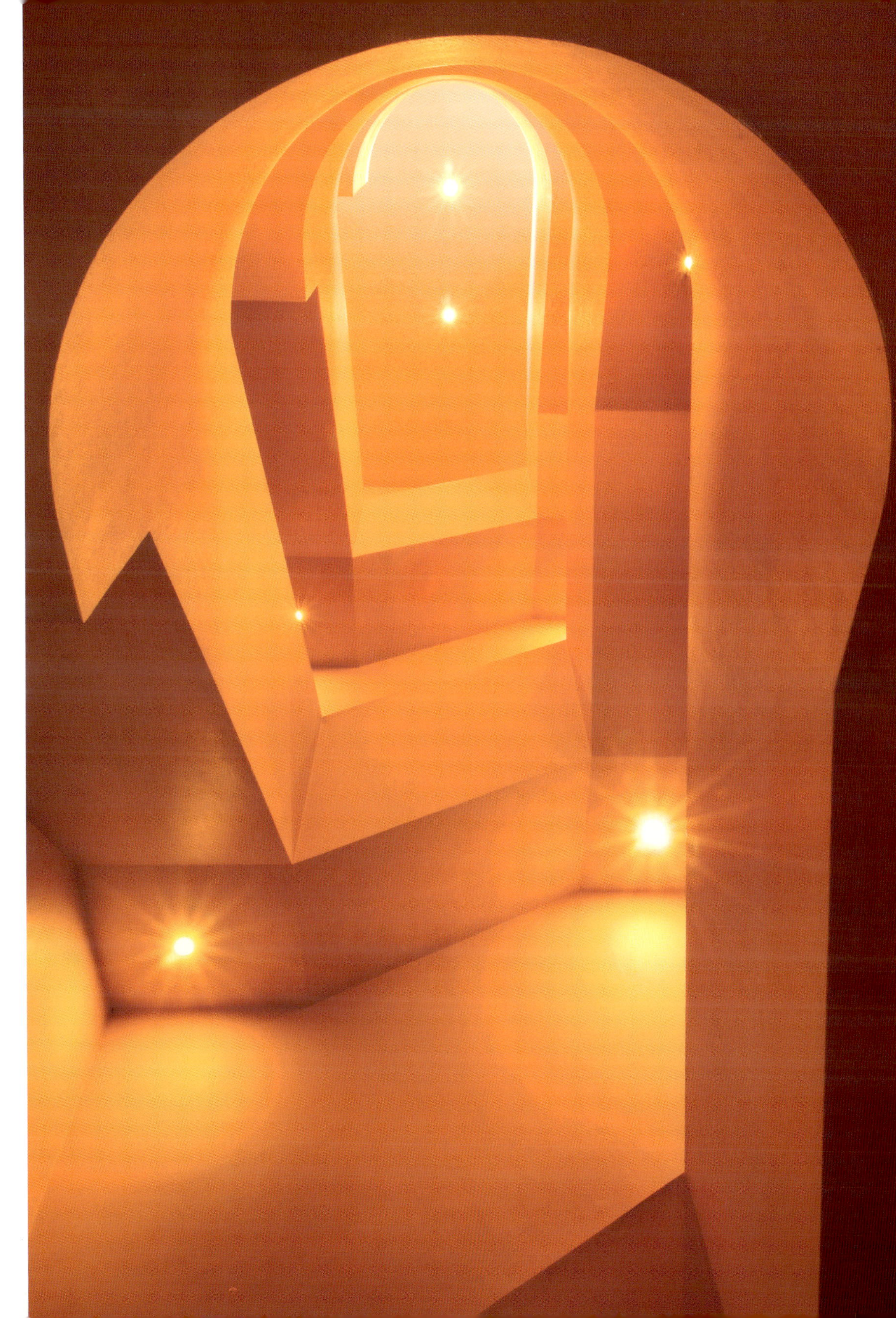

Fractals the Natural Way

The gist of the fractal—whether natural or mathematical—is to create complexity from simplicity. In other words, a simple transformation is used on a portion of the image to eventually create a highly complex overall image. In mathematics, this transformation is accomplished through recursion (repetition of a formula). Leaving math out of it, in the real world this transformation is accomplished primarily through a natural process that repeats itself.

In nature, fractals include all manner of branching patterns, such as trees, river deltas, lightning, and blood vessels, as well as spiral patterns like sea shells, hurricanes, and galaxies. In fact, the largest known fractal is a spiral galaxy.

Since all fractals are formed by simple repetition, if you combine repetition with rotation and resizing, it's easy to create your own spiral-shaped fractals. You can also create your own universes and images using fractal repetition whether or not spirals are involved.

Many fractals can be found in the plant family, with examples including pine cones, sunflowers, aloes, and the agave cactus. Aloes and agaves are typical and interesting because they form a spiral by rotating a fixed amount before growing each new piece. The angle of rotation is determined by each plant's best angle to the sun. So the angle of rotation of the fractal created by the plant's spiral growth depends on the sun's angle in the location where it is planted. Turn to page 117 to see a *Gem of the Drakensberg* aloe that grows in a spiral-fractal shape.

It is astounding and true that the incredible complexity of organic forms around us comes largely from simple repetition.

This is because most apparently complex fractal patterns start with a simple sub-element. The sub-element is modified slightly with rotations, resizing, mirroring, and so on. This modification occurs consistently and is repeated indefinitely, with the newly modified elements added to the original pattern.

So ultimately, a fractal is a larger pattern using repetition to create a complex and pleasing larger shape that is often symmetrical in part, and all based upon a simple element and method of growth.

Skim Ice—In early spring in Yosemite Valley, California, the surface of still water was covered with a thin layer of ice. The water beneath the ice was partially thickened from the frost and snow, and crystalline drops were embedded in this intermediate layer.

Snowflakes and ice crystals are ideal places to look for fractal-like compositions. If you take a detail of this close-up of skim ice on water, the detail itself could be the entire composition. Out of the simplicity of the ice formation comes incredibly complex patterns and compositions that can be repeated and enlarged as much as the artist would like.

Nikon D850, 28-300mm Nikkor at 300mm, 13 seconds at f/36 and ISO 64, tripod mounted.

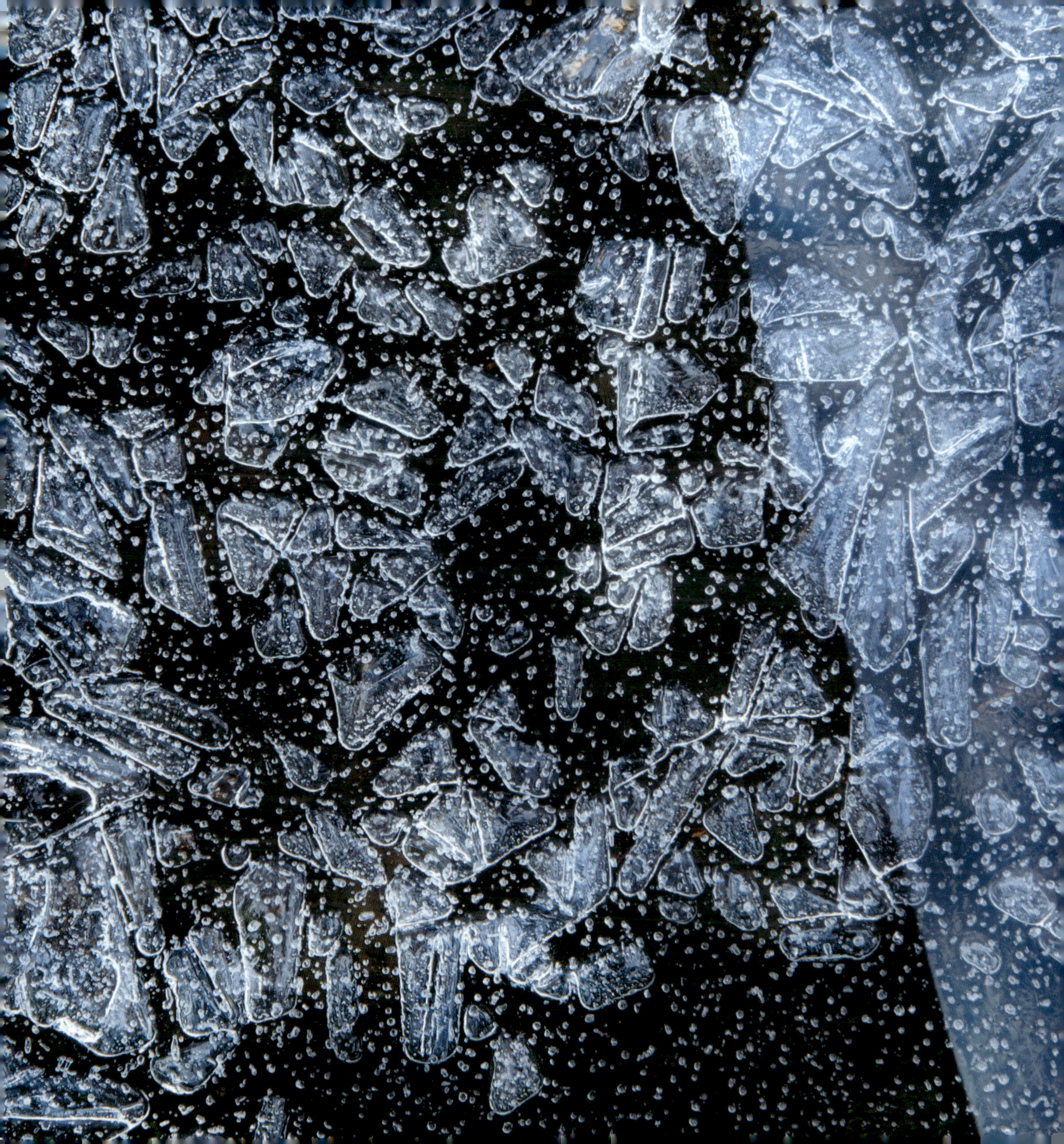

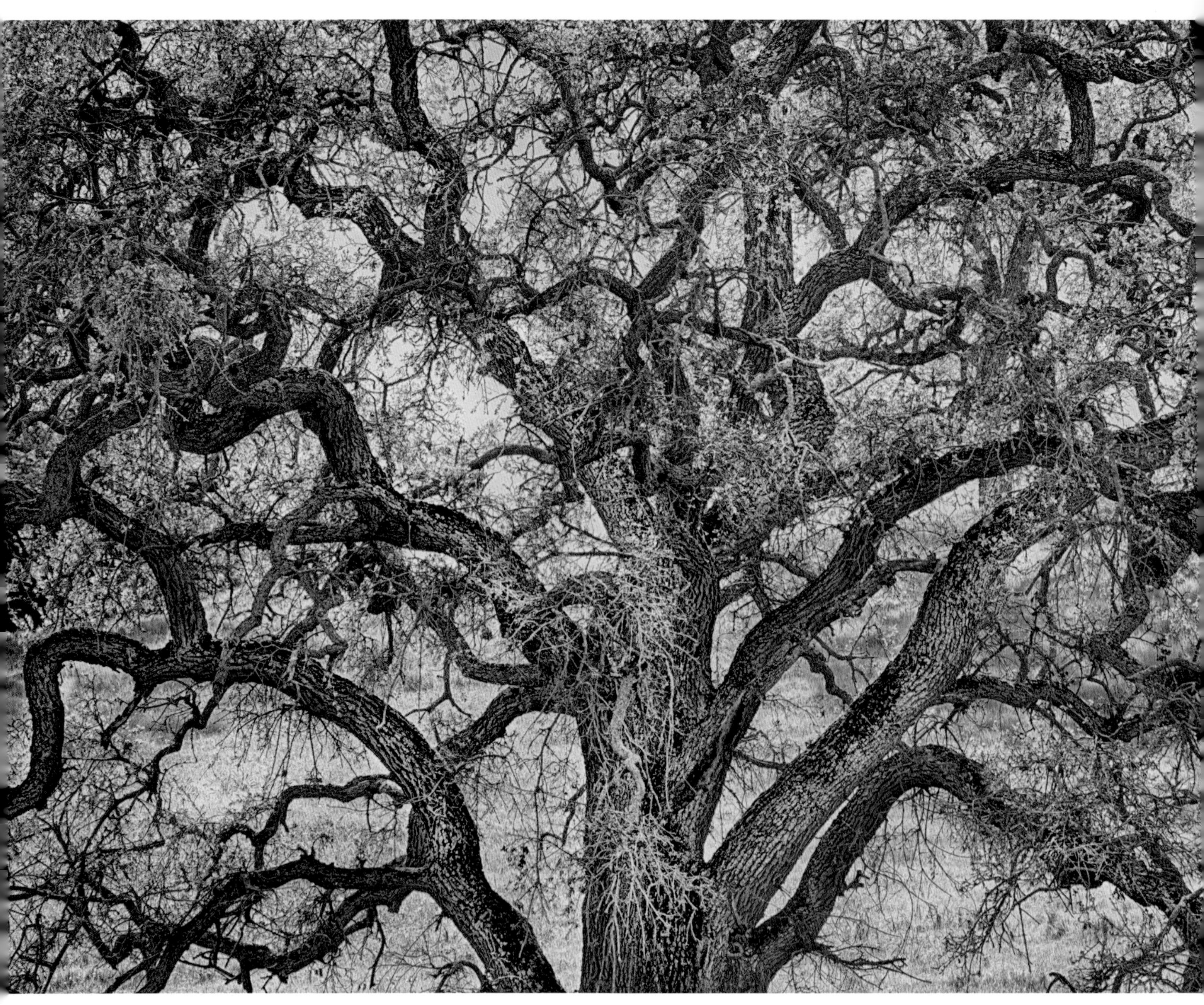

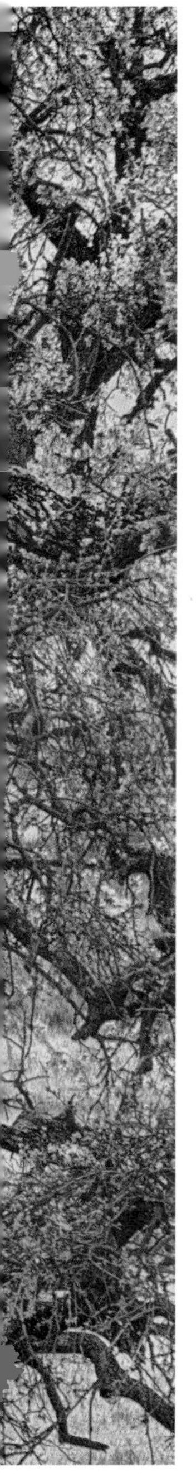

Left: *California Live Oak*—In the hidden nooks and valleys of California's Coastal Range, ancient gnarled and twisted California live oaks (*Quercus agrifolia*) thrive. When I photographed this imposing specimen near Walnut Creek, California, in early spring, the tree looked almost as if it might be dead. But it was merely dormant for the winter and would soon be putting forth ample greenery.

Before the foliage camouflaged things, it was very easy to see the fractal nature of the tree. Natural fractal patterns are formed by repeating a simple branching process. While the ultimate fractal can become unbelievably complex, the process of creation is simple and always tells the story of the pattern.

This magnificent tree grew by simple, repetitive branching that led quickly to complexity. The fractals tell the story of the processes that created it.

Right: While many of the tree branches can be taken as fractal pieces, one is shown here to give you an idea of how fractal-like branches from this old tree combine to form the fractal whole.

Can you see where the magnification on the right came from in the photo of the entire tree on the left?

Nikon D850, 28-300mm Nikkor at 210mm, five exposures with shutter speeds ranging from 1/100 to 1/8 of a second, each exposure at f/14 and ISO 64, tripod mounted.

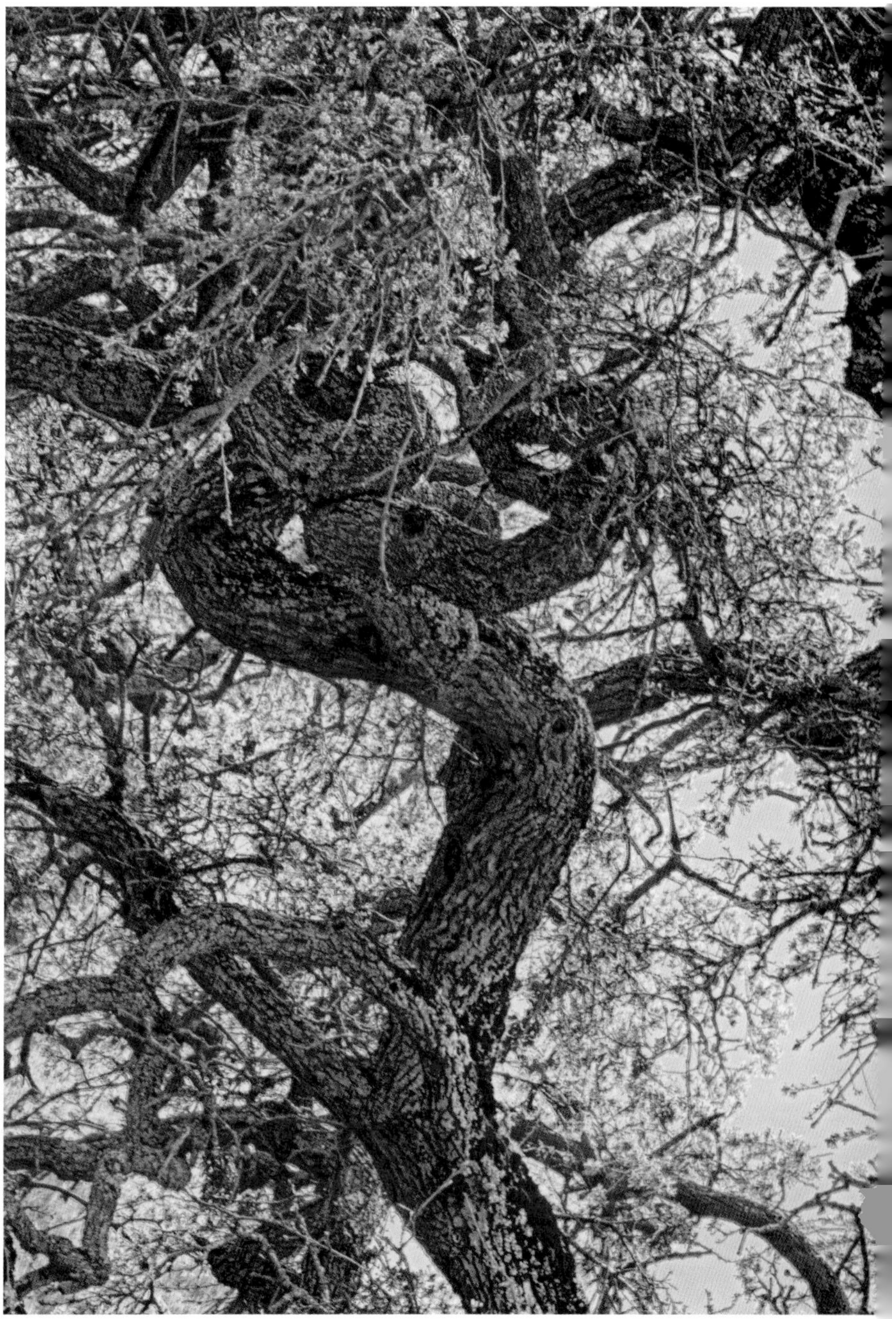

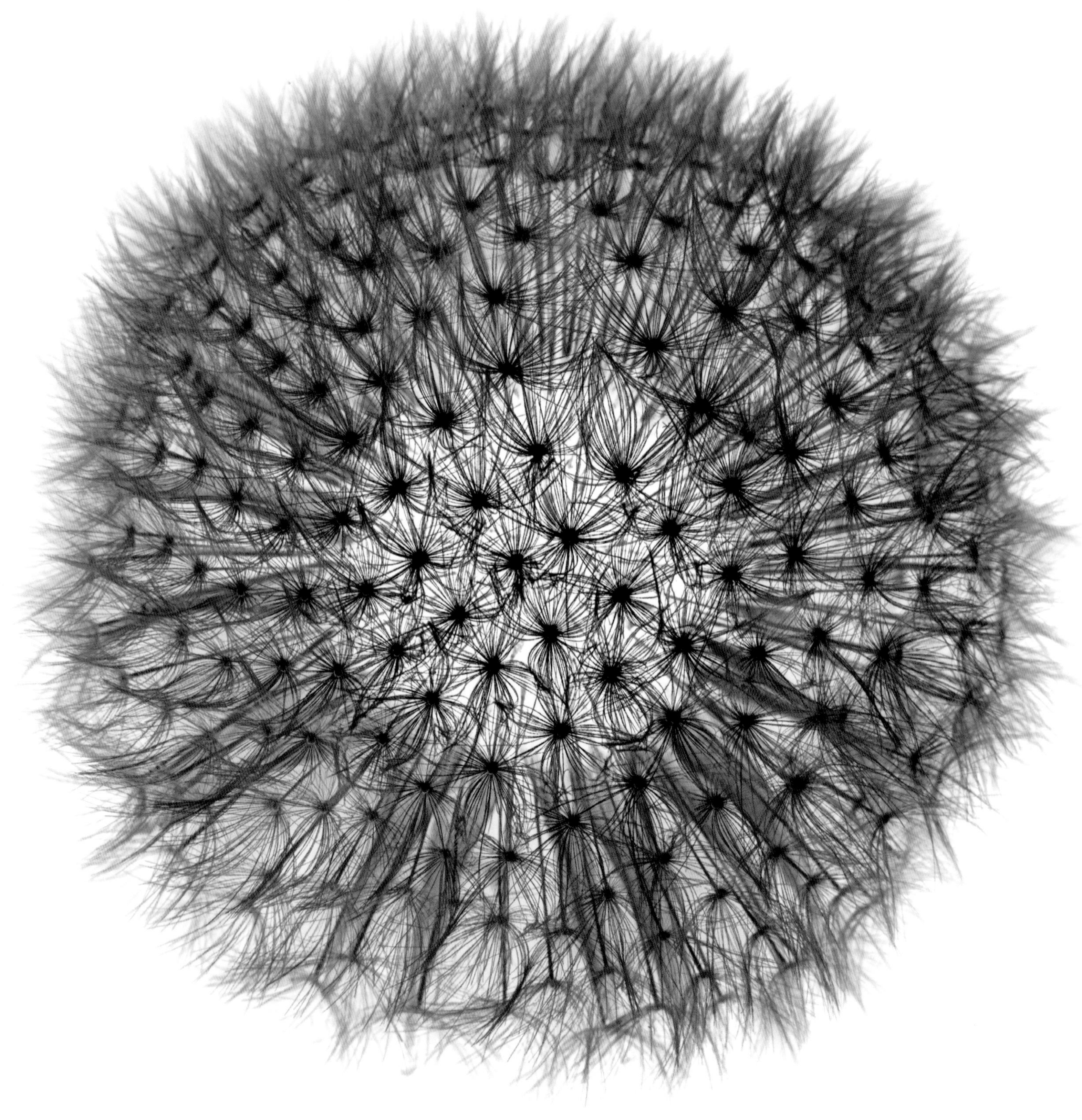

Left: *Dandelion Inversion*—A dandelion seedpod contains an entire universe within a small, puffy sphere. In this sense, it's a fractal image: when you look at each seed node within the pod at high magnification, the node itself becomes an entire pod.

When I photographed this image outside, the seedpod was white against a dark background in a field. Back in my studio, I used Photoshop to invert the dark background to white, and presented the design of the dandelion in black against a white background to create the image you see here.

It always fills me with awe and wonder to contemplate the beautiful symmetry and repetition in a modest dandelion seedpod.

Nikon D850, 50mm Zeiss macro, 1/13 of a second at f/20 and ISO 200, tripod mounted.

Right: *Romanesco Broccoli*—Browsing in the produce section of a local green market, I was transfixed by the spiral nature of Romanesco broccoli, an edible flower in the broccoli family. The flower's form approximates a natural fractal because each flower is composed of a series of smaller flowers, each one arranged in a logarithmic spiral.

This pattern is repeated in smaller sizes at different levels on the Romanesco broccoli flower. The pattern only approximates a fractal because the pattern eventually ends when the flower size becomes really small—in contrast, a mathematically-generated fractal would go on forever. Incidentally, the number of rotations in a spiral found on a head of Romanesco broccoli is always a Fibonacci number. Fascinating!

Nikon D810, 85mm Nikkor macro, 24mm extension tube, five exposures with shutter speeds ranging from 2.5 to 25 seconds, each exposure at an effective aperture of f/64 and ISO 64, tripod mounted.

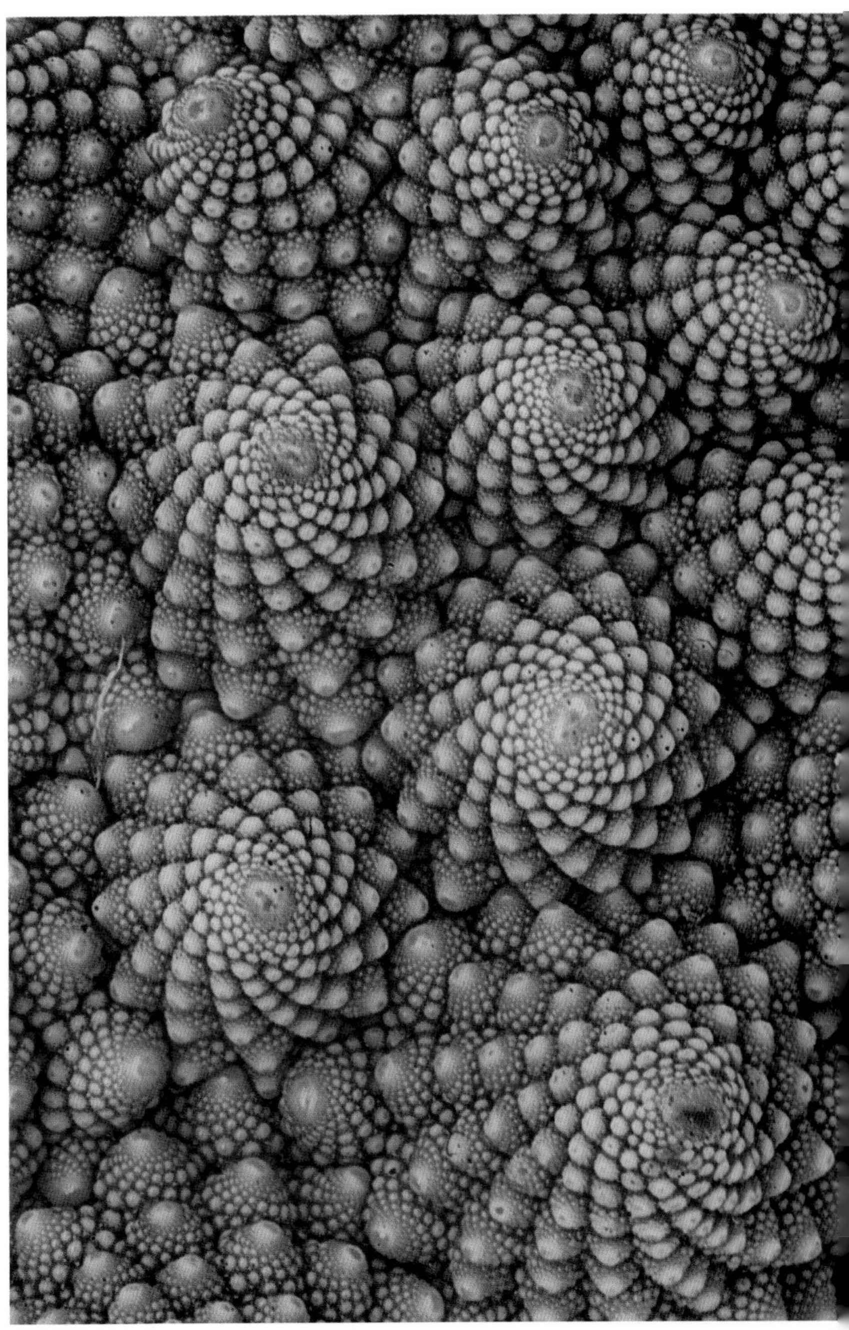

Mathematical Fractal Art

Mathematical fractal art uses software for algorithmic generation of images by iterating through specific fractal sets or equations, such as the "Julia set" and the "Mandelbrot set." This kind of repetitive mathematical action is called *recursion*.

Creating visual art this way leads to a diversity of images from synthetic landscapes to kaleidoscopic. This work is not photographic and—depending on the math equations and data sets used—is fully fractal, meaning it is replicated identically *ad infinitum*, and goes on forever.

Just to be clear, the photographs shown in *Composition & Photography* don't show fractals in this mathematical sense. Fractals found in nature, as well as my images, are "fractal-like"—they resemble fractals.

Like natural fractals, my images show selective fractal replication, but are not always exact mathematical fractals. Most likely, natural fractals, such as the ones I have photographed, do not go on forever. They do share the fractal characteristic of self-replication, and in appearance definitely resemble fractals.

Zabriskie View—One of the world's great destinations for landscape photography is Death Valley National Park in California. Within Death Valley, no one should miss Zabriskie Point, a short distance from the parking lot and possessed of views that are always changing depending on the light. There is seldom a sunrise or sunset when photographers aren't lined up with their tripods on the viewing platform above Zabriskie Point.

In making this image, I was mindful of the way the folds in the land repeated, with slight variations in the angles of the bluffs. It seemed to me that to make the most visual sense of this landscape meant emphasizing the fractal nature of the scene in front of me.

Nikon D850, 28-300mm Nikkor at 78mm, six exposures with shutter speeds ranging from 1/8 of a second to 3 seconds, each exposure at f/22 and ISO 64, tripod mounted.

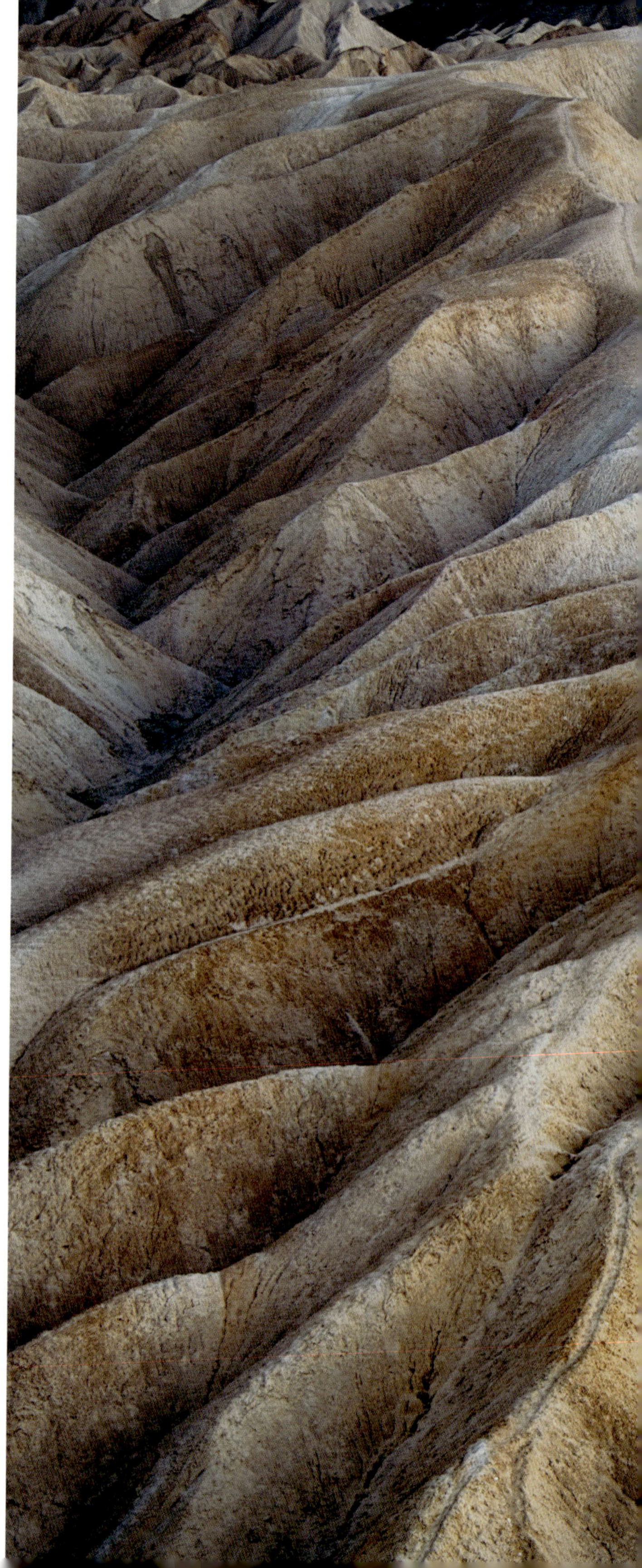

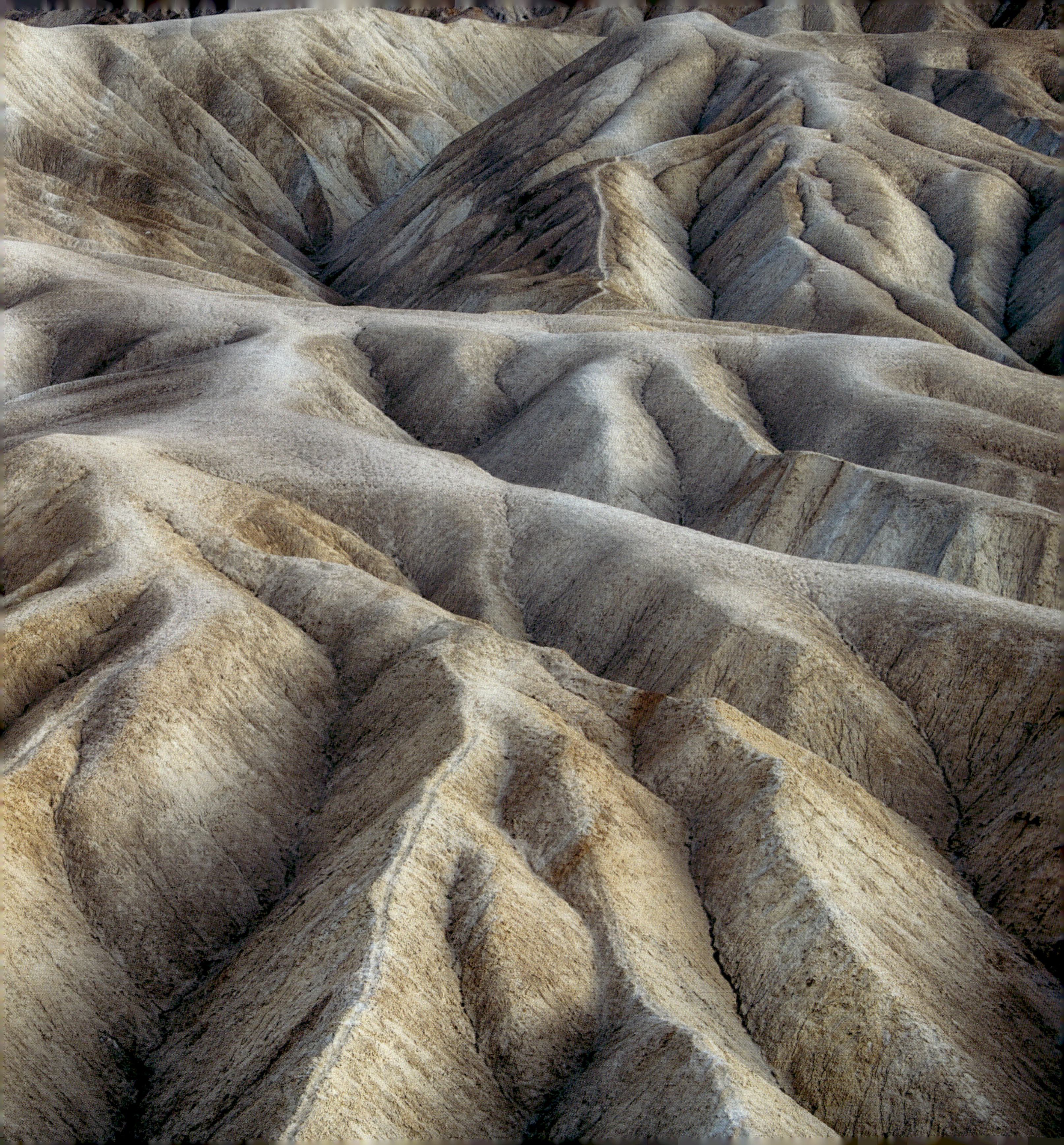

Kinds of Fractal Compositions

In my work as an artist, I have created fractal images in a number of ways. Like some other visual artists with a background in mathematics (M.C. Escher comes to mind), besides intuitive visual approaches, I am always interested in artistic methods that involve computation. Of course, the proof of the art is in the pudding, as it were. Good art transcends whatever technique may have been used to make it.

Using computers and mathematical formulas to create fractal art is a significant trend in and of itself. I've played with these possibilities over the years. For more about mathematical fractal art, turn to page 126.

Back in the film days early in my career, I played with prismatic auxiliary lenses to create fractal-like effects in-camera. Maybe you've seen this effect in 1930s films such as those created by Busby Berkeley. Back in the day, I bought my prismatic lens in New York at a camera-gadget store called Spiratone. These days, this type of special-purpose, auxiliary lens is sometimes referred to as a "fractal lens."

> # FRACTAL   frac·tal | \'frak-tᵊl\
>
> *noun : any of various extremely irregular curves or shapes for which any suitably chosen part is similar in shape to a given larger or smaller part when magnified or reduced to the same size*

My favorite approach is to photograph fractals in nature or create them in the studio using specialized photographic techniques. *Fractal Face 2*, opposite, is an example of a studio fractal creation using in-camera multiple exposures.

Many of the photographs that illustrate this chapter are of fractal-like subjects that I have found in nature. To photograph fractals in nature requires identifying fractal structures when you see them, and understanding a coherent way to relate the fractal composition to the edge of the image.

Fractal Face 2—I used multiple in-camera exposures to create a psychological portrait of a model with a fractal appearance. The multiple exposures lead to an interesting composition with the "fractal" hands around a face with a repeated gaze looking at the camera.

It is interesting that repeating elements in a figure study have such a profound effect on the way we view the portrait. It's almost as if by breaking up a person into a repetitive pattern, we are making a suggestion of a personality pattern or emotional state.

Consider the impact of the cubist painters such as Pablo Picasso and Juan Gris: largely the impact of their paintings was to break up subject matter into fractal-like pieces. This was most shocking when the subject was people, such as Picasso's famous *Portrait of Gertrude Stein* or *Les Demoiselles d'Avignon*. In fact, *Demoiselles* was so shocking at the time it was first exhibited in 1916 that it was considered bizarre and immoral and one critic exclaimed, "the end of the world is upon us!"

Nikon D810, 28-300mm Nikkor at 122mm, five images combined via in-camera multiple exposure, each exposure at 1/160 of a second at f/13 and ISO 400, tripod mounted, studio strobe lighting.

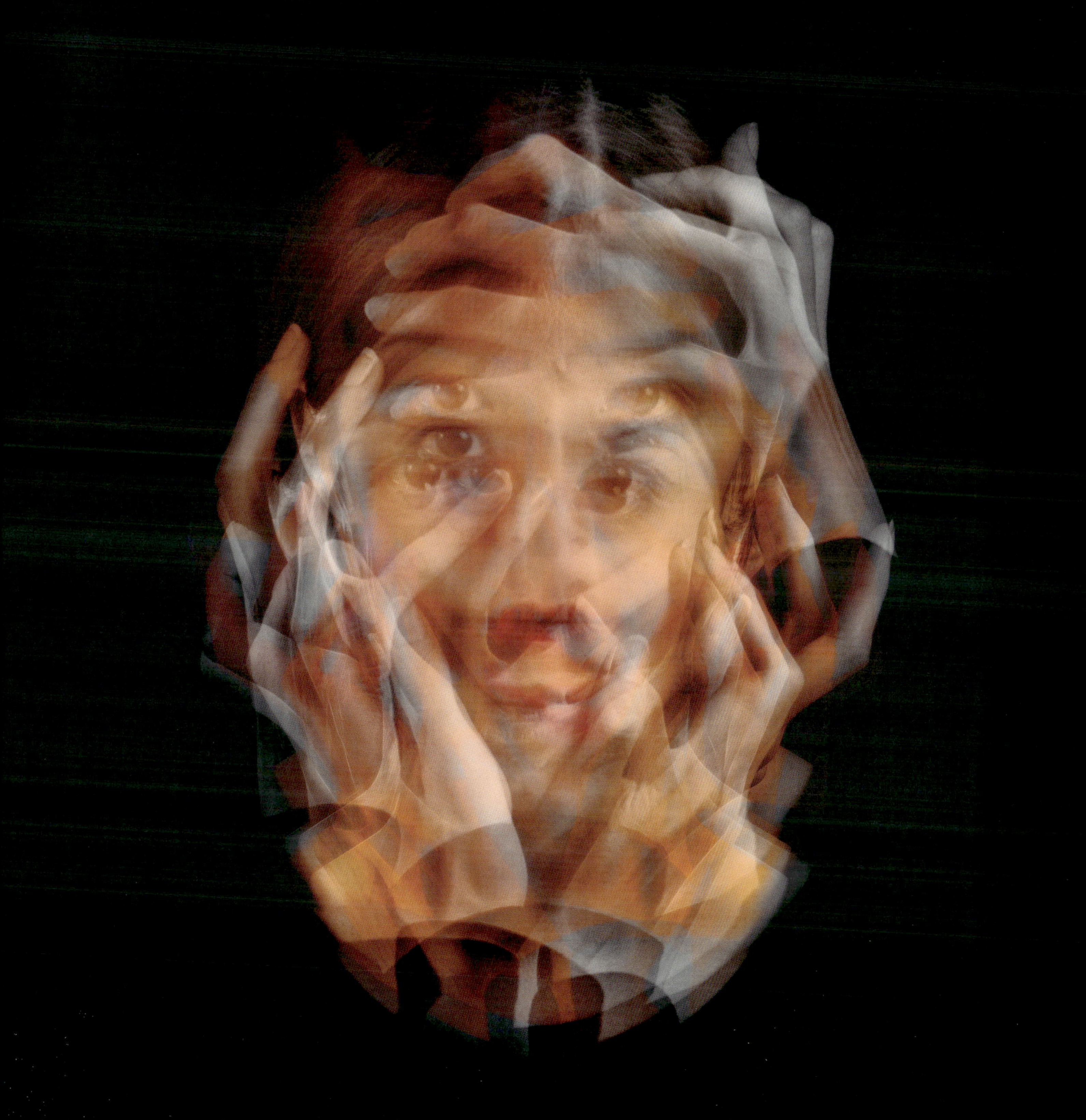

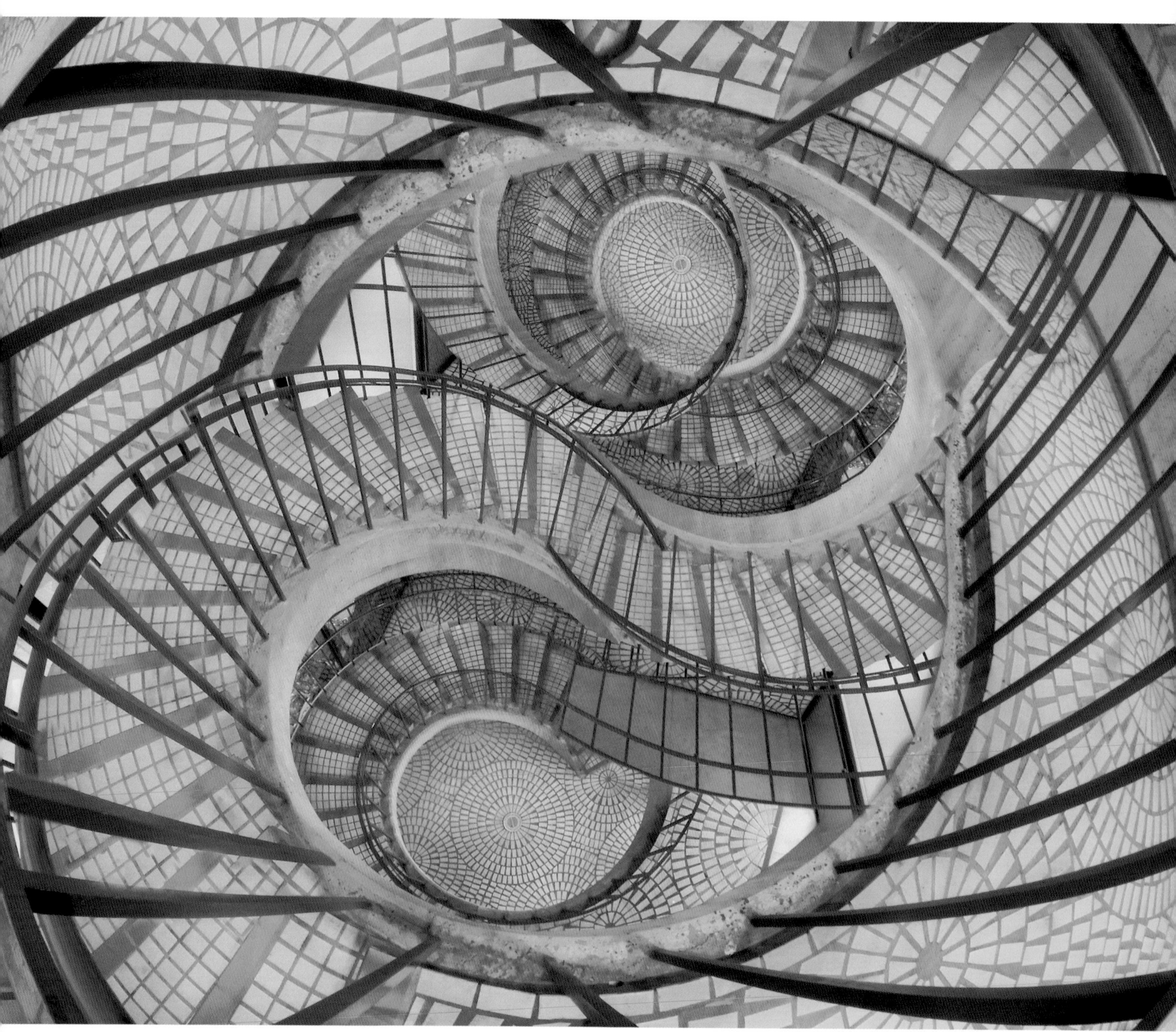

Framing Fractals

Many, if not most, spirals are also fractal. Generally, the framing issue with fractal-spirals is straightforward. Whatever your position in relation to the spiral (see page 112 regarding the camera's focal plane orientation to the spiral), the spiral should take up most of the space of the composition and have an apparent relationship to the boundary frame of the image. So this quickly becomes an issue of positioning the spiral.

Compositional challenges become more intriguing with a complex fractal such as *California Live Oak*, shown on pages 122–123. With a natural fractal, such as this tree, in some sense the composition has no beginning and no end. How do you put a border around a subject that is inherently border-less and constantly expanding?

I don't have a simple answer to this conundrum other than to say it is a little bit like Edward Weston's take on the study of composition and gravity. The response should be intuitive. Compositional framing of a large fractal can probably never be perfect, but it can be graceful. This kind of framing should not seem arbitrary. In other words, there should be a reason for drawing the boundary and border.

It's a good idea to plan to include enough of the subject matter so that its fractal nature becomes clear, but not so much that the viewer becomes lost in the details of the composition. As with any composition, there needs to be a guiding, underlying principle even if this principle isn't clear to the viewer. For example, the tree itself organizes the composition in *California Live Oak*.

With fractal compositions, considering how the viewer will enter the composition, the visual path the viewer will take, and how the viewer will exit the composition is particularly important. See "Entering & Exiting," starting on page 136.

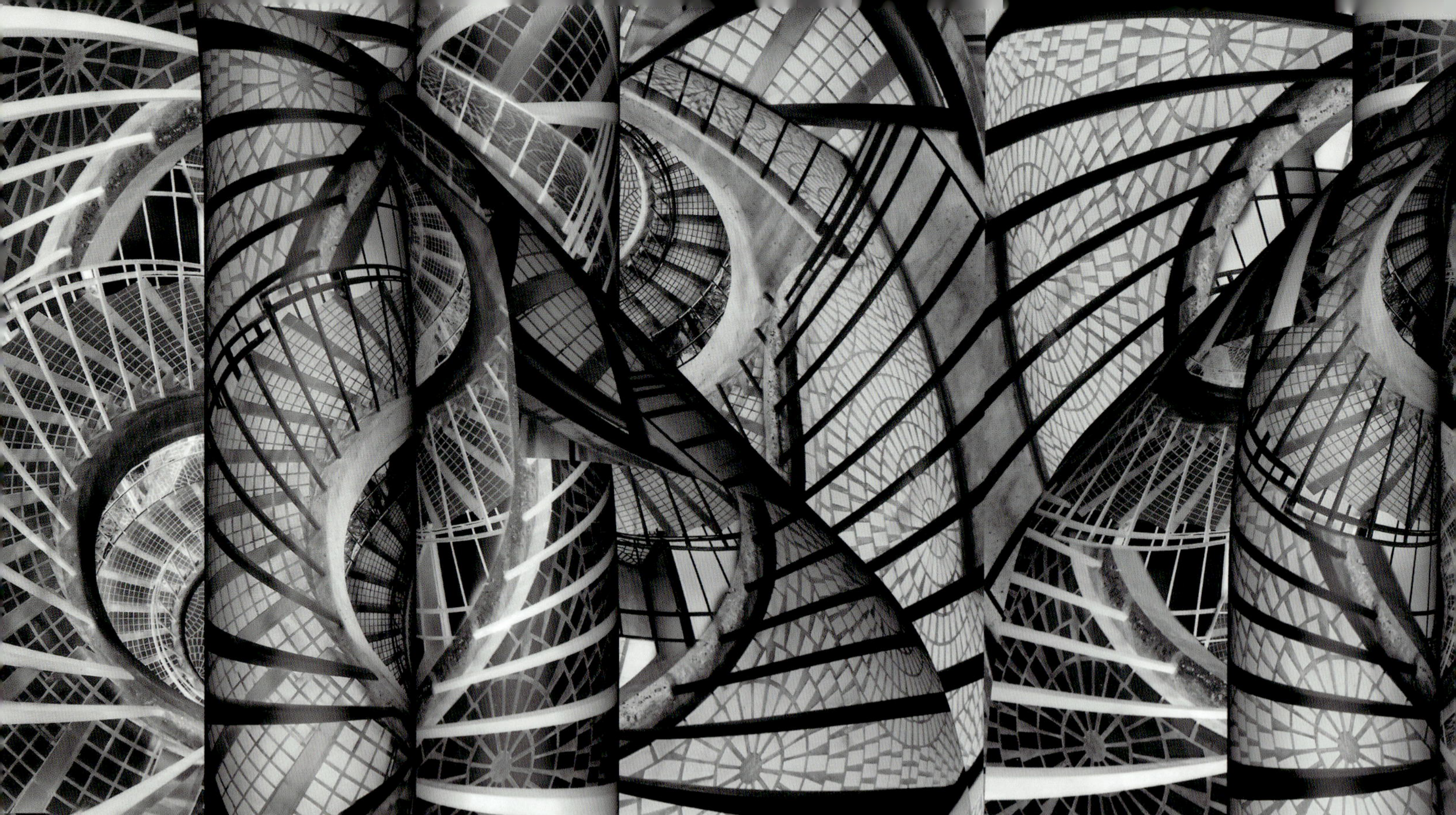

Creating Fractal Composites

Fractal compositions can be created in post-production using compositing with surprisingly interesting results. Post-production fractals created in Photoshop (or with other comparable software) use the techniques for their creation that mimic the mathematical or natural approaches to fractal formation. As in mathematics and nature, this is a process that creates complexity from simplicity.

If you are going to invoke complexity from simplicity, this can be accomplished by creating some simple rules for processing the component parts of your image. There's no magic formula for what these rules should be, and you most likely will need to find them using trial and error. Examples of the kinds of transformations that you can use to create an iterative rule include replication, rotation, inversion, and resizing.

You do want to consistently apply the rules once you have found them. Consistency is what gives a fractal-like composite the sense of being a regular pattern that is comprehensible.

To create the fractal-like image, you need to repeat the steps—meaning iterate your rules— many times. The way this works is that whatever

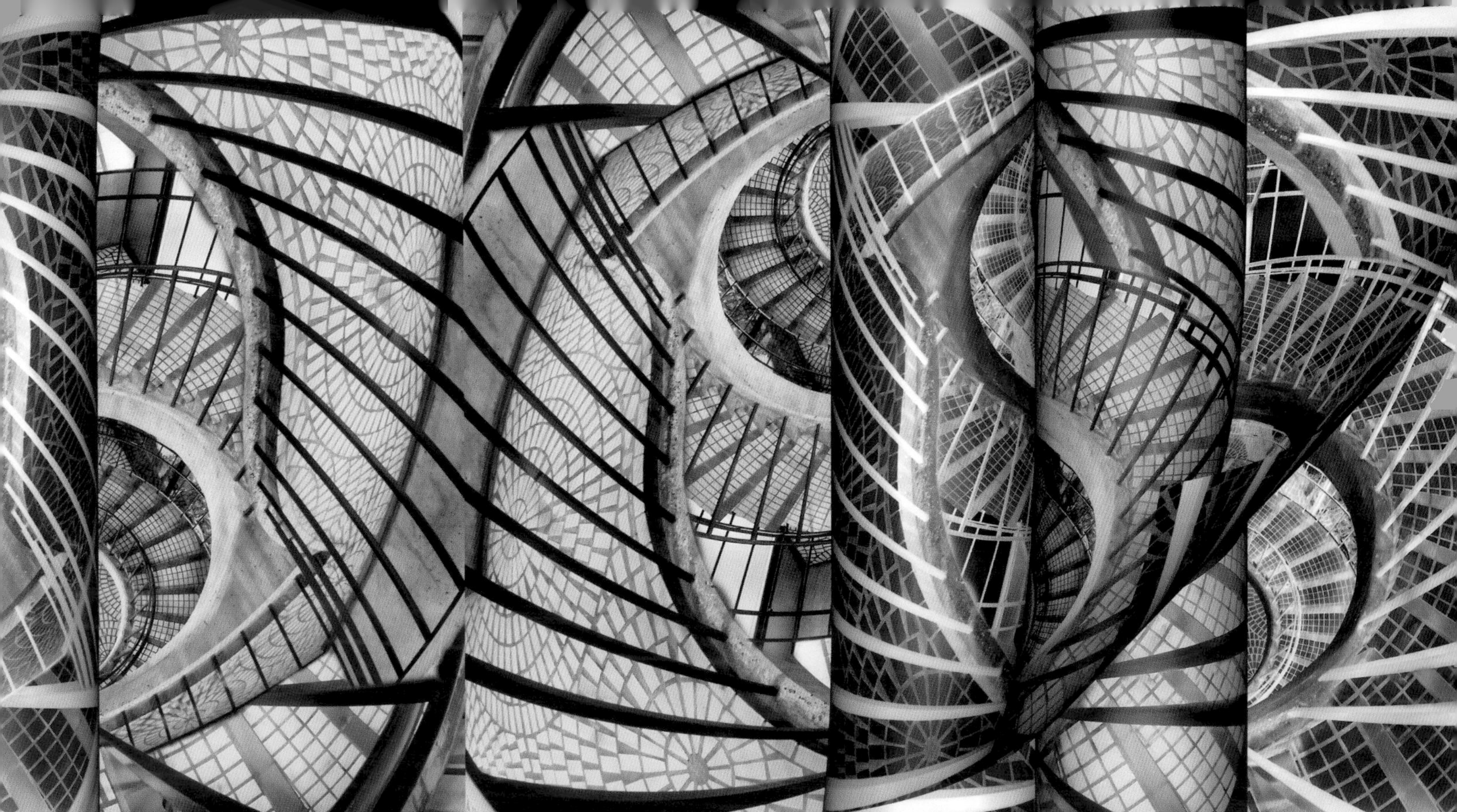

the rule is, it gets applied and reapplied to the work that has already been altered. It's this repeated reapplication that serves to create the fractal-like effect. The rule needs to be repeated regularly on the image that has already been modified with your rule.

For example, suppose I make a rule that a portion of the image will be resized smaller by 10 percent and rotated 90 degrees (most rules will be more complex). I apply this a first time, and now I have an image with a portion of itself that is smaller and rotated. Next, I could take the entire modified image with the changes and apply the rule once again to either the entire image or a portion of it.

Epic Stairs—To create this photo collage, I used post-production techniques that are essentially fractal-like (see text). *Calling Alice*, shown on page 130, was the base image.

I took a portion of *Calling Alice* and used it as my repeating element to create the fractal-like effect. The repetitions were modified in a regular way—meaning each repetition was modified using the same angle of rotation and the same proportional scaling. Eventually, I put together the various pieces that I had created, making this collage. The final image shows many elements that are themselves modified sub-pieces of the entire image.

Photo collage based on Calling Alice, *created using Photoshop LAB inversions, transformations, and compositing. As a final step, the image was converted to black and white.*

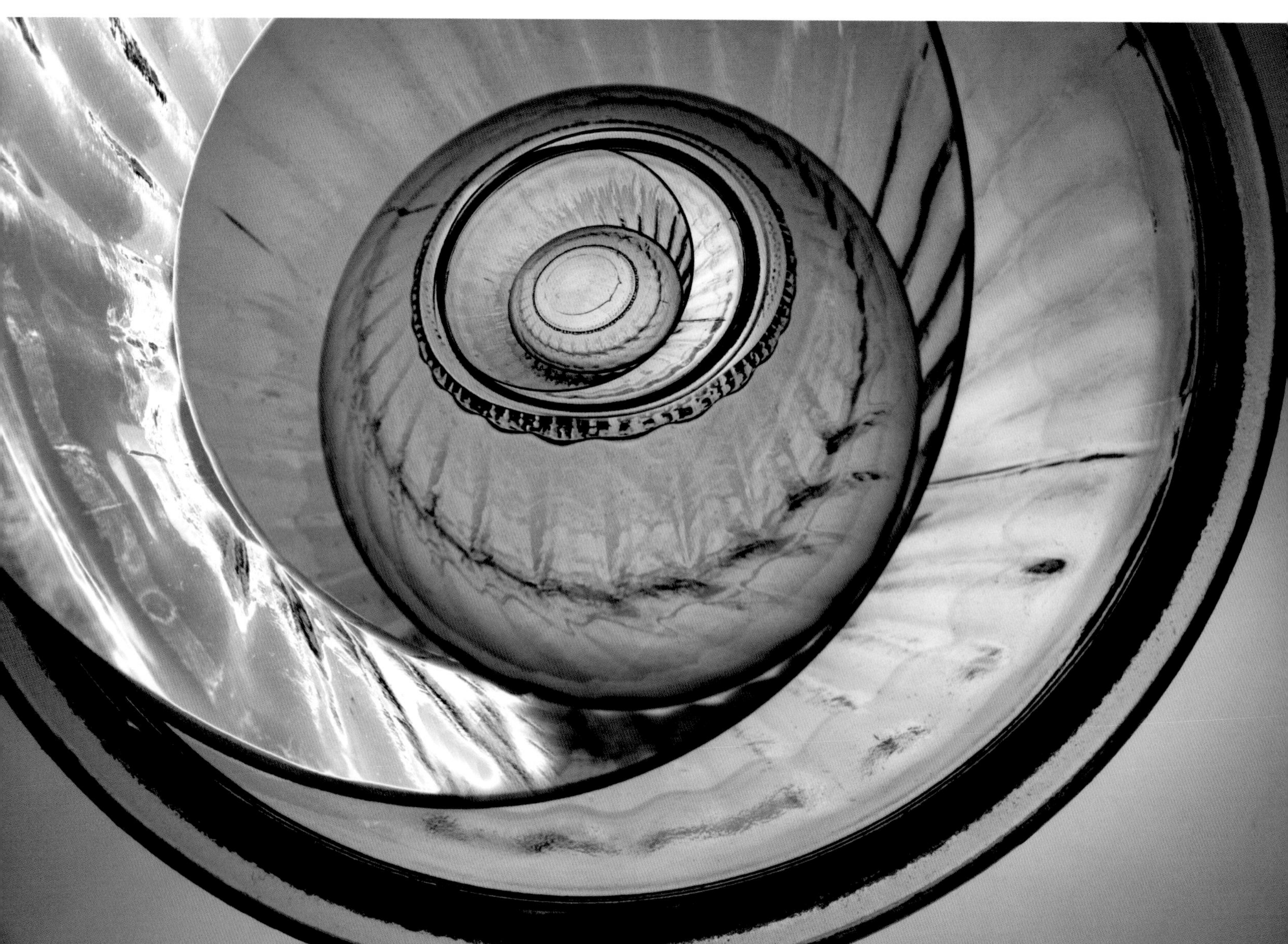

Rinse and repeat, then rinse and repeat!

A number of kinds of transformations can work as rules, but you will need to find these by experimentation. Also, the image that the rule operates on must be chosen carefully. Not every kind of image will work for fractal replication in post-production. Successful composite subject matter usually calls to mind architectural or natural fractal processes (for an example, take a look at *Epic Stairs* on pages 132–133).

Creative Use of Spirals and Fractals

If I only had two shapes or patterns in my artistic palette, I would likely choose the spiral and the fractal. For good reason, most folks love spirals. Fractals are best thought of as a pattern for creating patterns, rather than a pattern in and of themselves.

Images that make good use of spirals or fractals are always interesting, so I recommend that you look for these shapes and patterns in nature and in your work. The more you study spirals and fractals, the more likely you are to find creative approaches to working with them. The examples

Crystal Spiral—I spent the morning setting up parfait glasses on my light box. I tried various lenses and angles but nothing really came together. Then, I got really close with my wide-angle, macro-probe lens. Looking through the viewfinder, a very surprising spiral, fractal-like pattern was revealed.

Nikon D850, 24mm Laowa Macro Probe, 0.8 of a second at f/40 and ISO 64, tripod mounted.

in this chapter show some of the ways I have worked with fractals. I hope you find them helpful.

Spirals echo many of the fundamental shapes of the universe around us and are great representations for our life voyage. Fractals demonstrate the building blocks of life and show how complex forms, shapes, and ways of being can come together using simple mechanisms.

Together, spirals and fractals are well worth study and experimentation. Artists and photographers who work creatively with spiral and fractal shapes and patterns will find their work enhanced and enriched.

KEY IDEAS

- Pay attention as to whether you are photographing a spiral head on, from above, or from below.

- The center of the spiral is very important to spiral compositions; usually it will be in the center of the frame, but some off-beat and unusual positions for the center point can work.

- A fractal is an image that uses simplicity to achieve complexity; this can be in a mathematical or natural way.

- Putting the boundary frame on a fractal image involves careful thought about where you want to interrupt the expanding fractal.

- If you use your powers of observation, you will find many fractals around you.

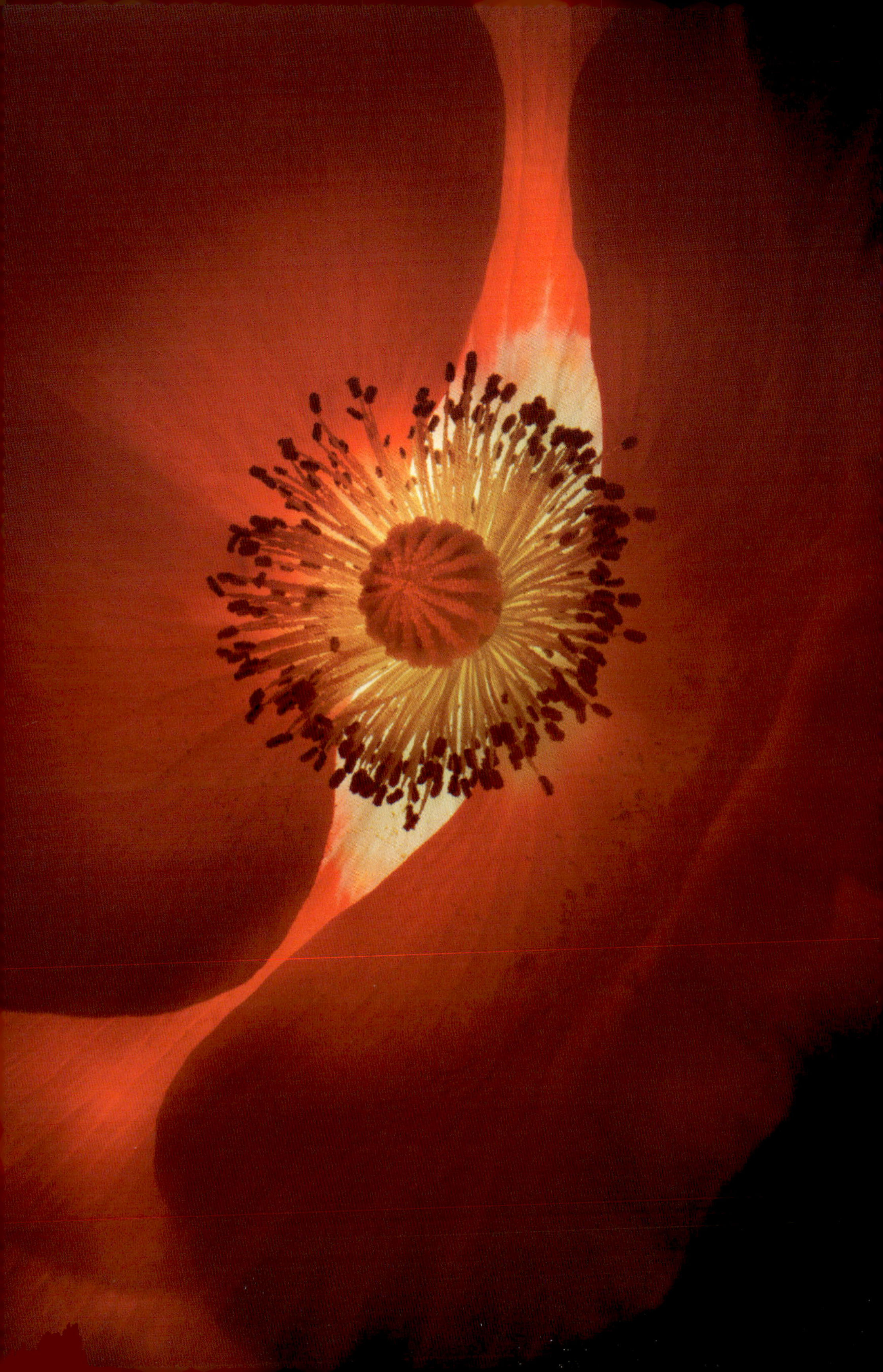

ENTERING & EXITING

"The photographer can guide the viewer's journey through his image with the distribution of the elements. The most frequent pattern in percentage terms starts from the lower left and travels up the image to the right." —José Benito Ruiz

Corn Poppy—The corn poppy, *Papaver rhoeas*, is one of my favorite flowers to photograph. It's a common flower that is pretty easy to grow and is spectacularly colored with many sentimental associations.

My corn poppy image was photographed on a light box with a wide-angle macro lens. It's pretty unusual to have a macro lens that is also wide angle because this out-of-the-ordinary combination makes for a seldom seen view of the flower.

Besides the optics, I used the exposure to emphasize the light channel going from the bottom of the image to the top by intentionally underexposing the image (by about 3 EV).

As the viewer's eye travels this channel, there's an intermission at the center of the poppy where the eye circles on the core for a while before continuing on the journey up and out of the image.

Nikon D850, 24mm Laowa Macro Probe, 3 seconds at f/40 and ISO 64, tripod mounted.

In the early chapters of *Composition & Photography*, I explained formal design issues beginning with points and lines. From these simple shapes came more complexity, with shapes that included rectangles, circles, and spirals.

In the real world context of the two-dimensional design of a photograph, these shapes have a border frame. In addition, repetition, as well as pattern building, can be used to construct designs of grace, beauty, and almost unlimited complexity. It's amazing that you can take something as simple as a line and repeat it so that it turns into a complex pattern that can grow fractal-like into its own visual world!

The design language of shapes and patterns, and how this vocabulary fits into the image boundary frame, is a great springboard for working with photographic composition. But one of the joys of being human is that there is always more than one way to think about anything!

Nowhere is that more true than when it comes to photographic composition. Almost everybody who is knowledgeable about art and photography has their own way of analyzing images, and tweaking composition. Many of these "competing" systems are equally valid, and it pays to look at all your alternatives.

It's not unusual to have alternate systems that coexist and work together. As one example, within the human brain the limbic system controls emotions and coexists with the nervous system that processes sensations.

This chapter presents a different system that coexists and often works *with* the system of shapes and patterns. You can think about this system as a complementary language of formal design in photography that gives you additional options.

In formal design, shapes such as leading lines and circles often work to direct the viewer's gaze and are complementary to the system of visual direction.

But understanding the underlying conceptual nature of the viewer's gaze and how that gaze will interact with your images is an important aspect of mastering composition in photography.

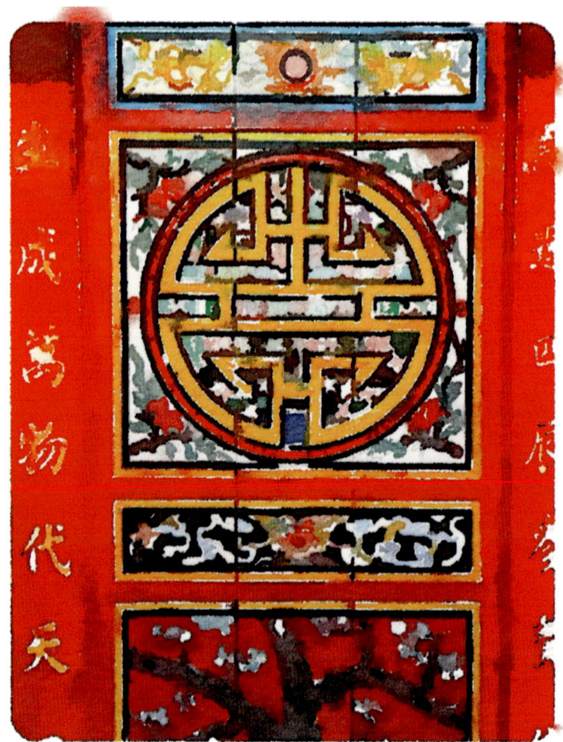

Left: *Warding Evil Away*—This painting, found on a door in Hue, Vietnam, is *apotropaic*—which means that it is designed to ward off curses, bad luck, and evil. The ancient symbolism creates a visual maze that has no exits. The menace is captured forever, going round and round, unable to pass through the door to enter the house.

iPhone 6s, using the Waterlogue app.

Right: *Havana Cross*—It's all in a day's work! This particular day found me lying on my back in a dark alley in central Havana, Cuba. Looking up, the open sky between the decaying buildings created a cross-like pattern above me.

From the viewpoint of the vocabulary of entering and exiting, the cross in the composition grabs the viewer's attention. The eye then traverses back-and-forth and up-and-down the cross shape, without having the urge to leave the composition until the viewer disengages.

Nikon D300, 12-24mm Nikkor zoom at 12mm, 1/400 of a second at f/10 and ISO 100, hand held.

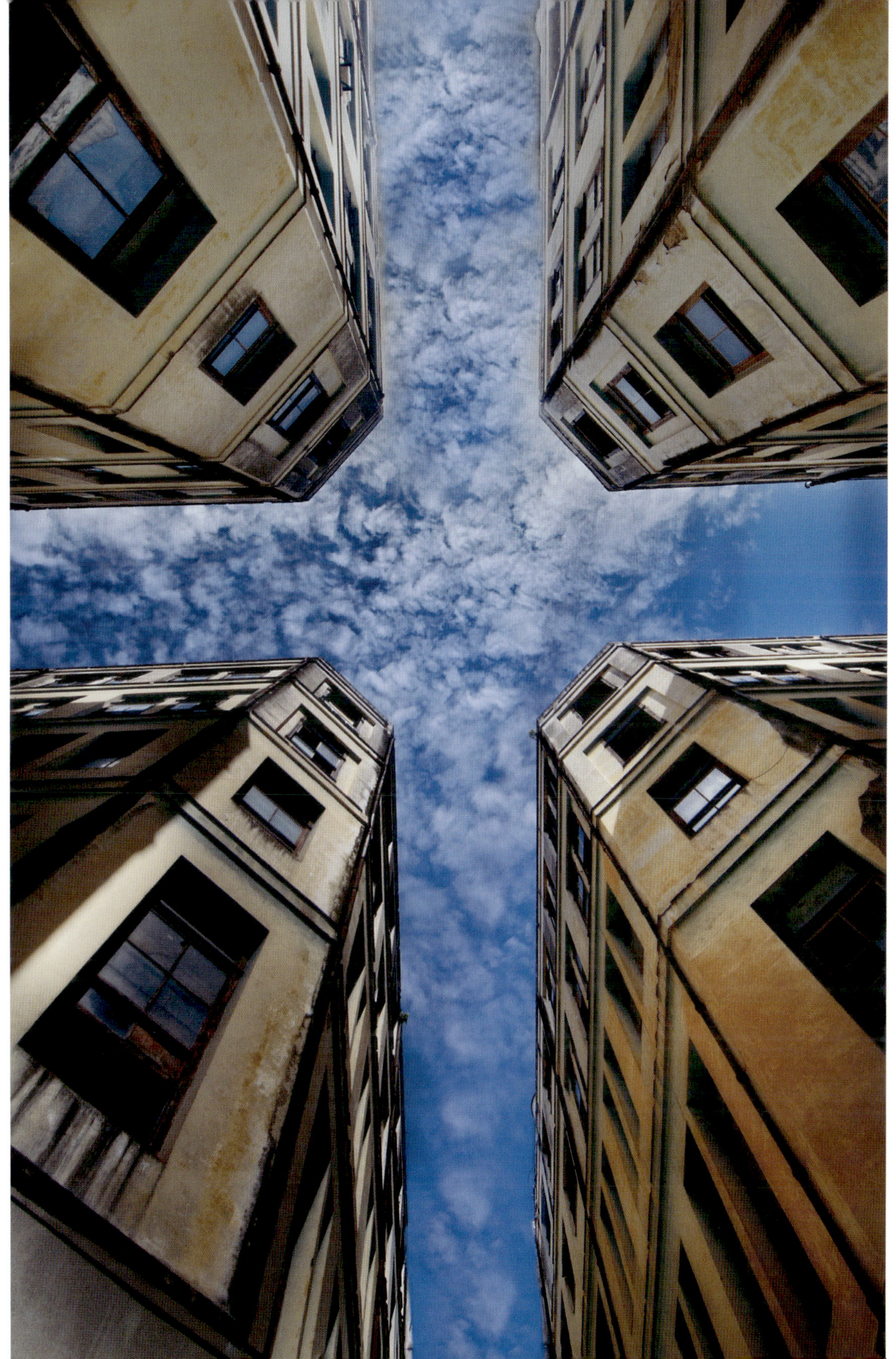

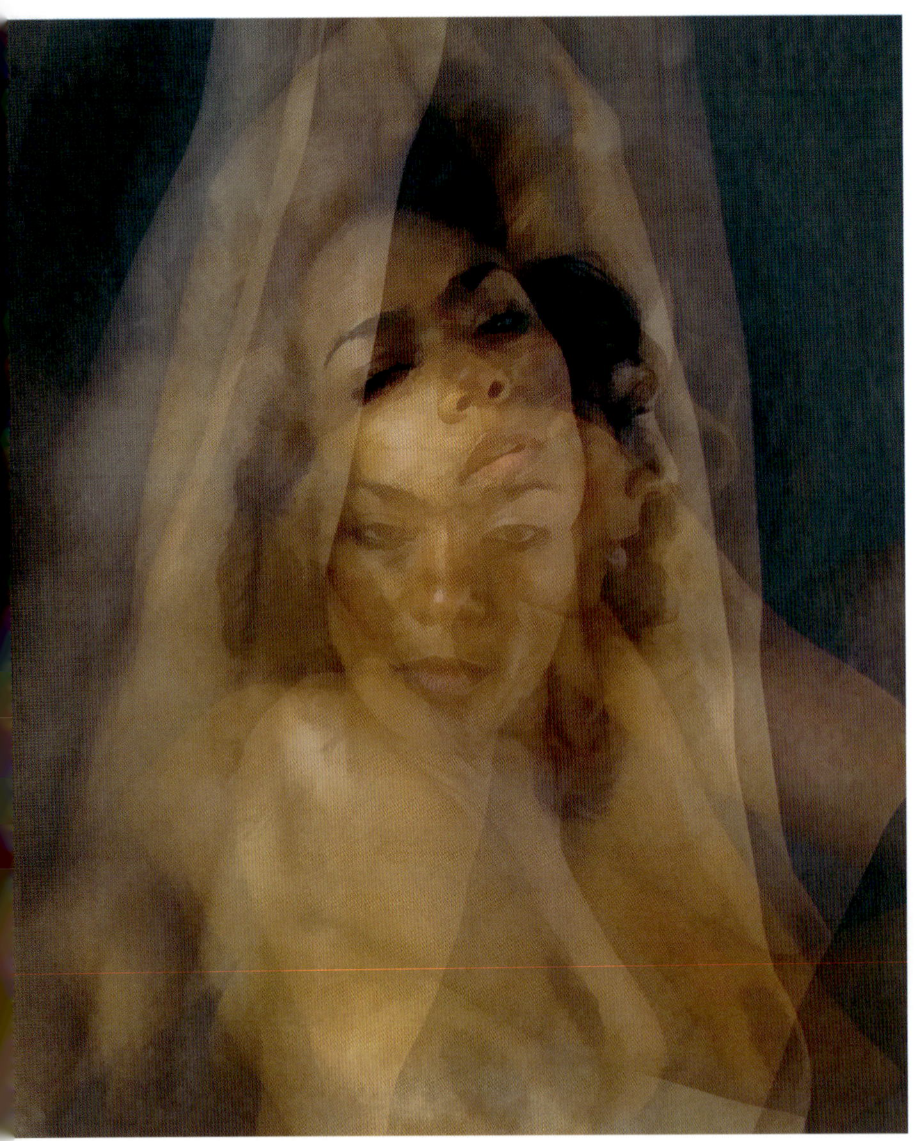

Left: *Passion*—Working with this beautiful model, I noticed the plasticity of her face. Her expression readily changed from staring mask-like directly at the camera to a more closed, languid look as she tilted her head. I took advantage of this variability, using in-camera multiple exposures.

The viewer enters the image by looking straight into the direct gaze of the model's open eyes at the center. Next, the eye travels up to the model's angled face in a kind of repose. Finally, the viewer's eye looks right to the model's profile, and then exits the image.

Within this overall visual journey, the eye lingers between the two faces turned toward the camera, going up and down between the two.

Nikon D800, 28-300mm Nikkor zoom at 52mm, single in-camera multiple exposure with three exposures, each exposure 1/160 of a second at f/9 and ISO 200, hand held.

Right: *Devotion*—This model was an experienced yoga practitioner. For one of my in-camera multiple exposures, I asked her to practice a series of yoga poses. For my conception of the image, this needed to be performed with precision so that the poses lined up in a single, devotional figure.

The entrance point is the image's center. This is followed with a circular arc to the left and right, and back again, following the geometry of the model's arms and eyes.

Nikon D850, 55mm Zeiss Otus, single in-camera multiple exposure with five exposures, each exposure 1/160 of a second at f/10 and ISO 200, tripod mounted.

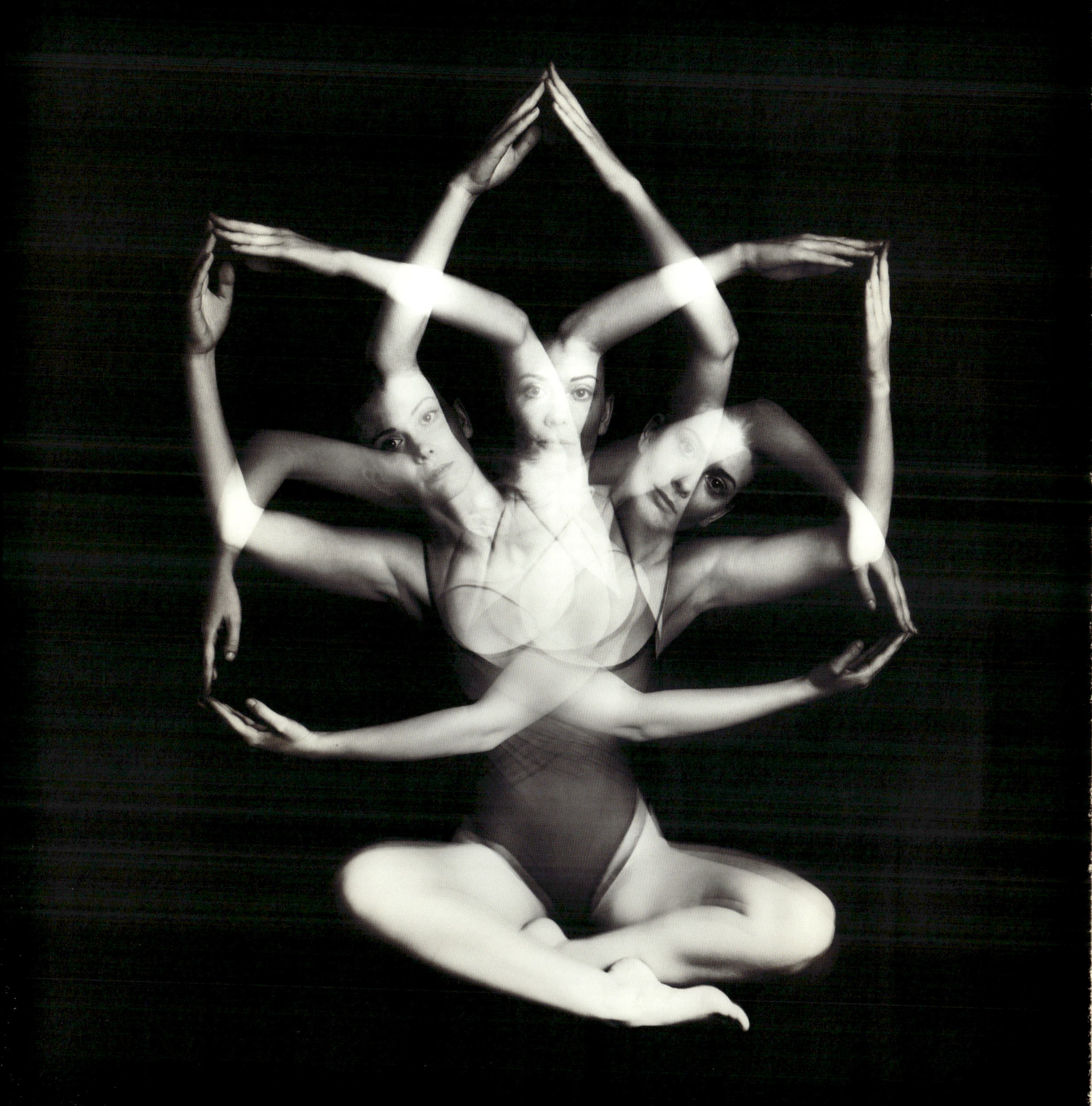

The Language of Direction

The language of direction primarily concerns the viewer's gaze. The visual journey through an image contains three components or stages of this gaze: the *entry point*, the *exit point*, and what happens in between, the *transitional passage* from entry to exit.

The *entry point* refers to where the viewer's gaze begins "going into" the image. For example, in *Cayucos Pier*, shown opposite, the entry point is at the lower left at the first pier piling, and the viewer's eye follows the line of the pier into the image.

Some images have no obvious entry point for the viewer. This kind of image might be uninteresting, and the viewer might have difficulties engaging. However, there are some images that are interesting but have no obvious entry points. Most of the time these images are visually scanned by the viewer from the lower left to the upper right. An example of this is *Wings of Man* on pages 32–33, where there is no apparent entry point.

It's important to be careful to design compositions that are, in fact, accessible to the viewer and their gaze, encourage a reason to linger, and present visual tracking that complements and underpins the story that your image is trying to convey.

One kind of image that can be quite interesting and can work without a definitive visual entry point is a collection of things. Two examples are the grid of plumbing supplies in *All Squared Away* on page 54, and the floral arrangement, *X-Ray Floral Medley Fusion*, shown on page 58. Neither of these have obvious explicit entry points.

Cayucos Pier—As late afternoon turned to twilight, I stood in the intertidal zone with my camera on the tripod and photographed this pier with a long exposure (3 minutes). The fog in the atmosphere seemed to combine with the rendition of the waves to create a seamless sense of the world.

For most viewers, this image starts on the lower left and proceeds up and out to the right, following the line of the pier. This is the most common directionality for an image. Here, the directionality combines the Zen sense that the image conveys with an optimistic and pleasing view of the world.

Nikon D300, 18-200mm Nikkor zoom at 120mm, 3 minutes at f/22 and ISO 100, tripod mounted.

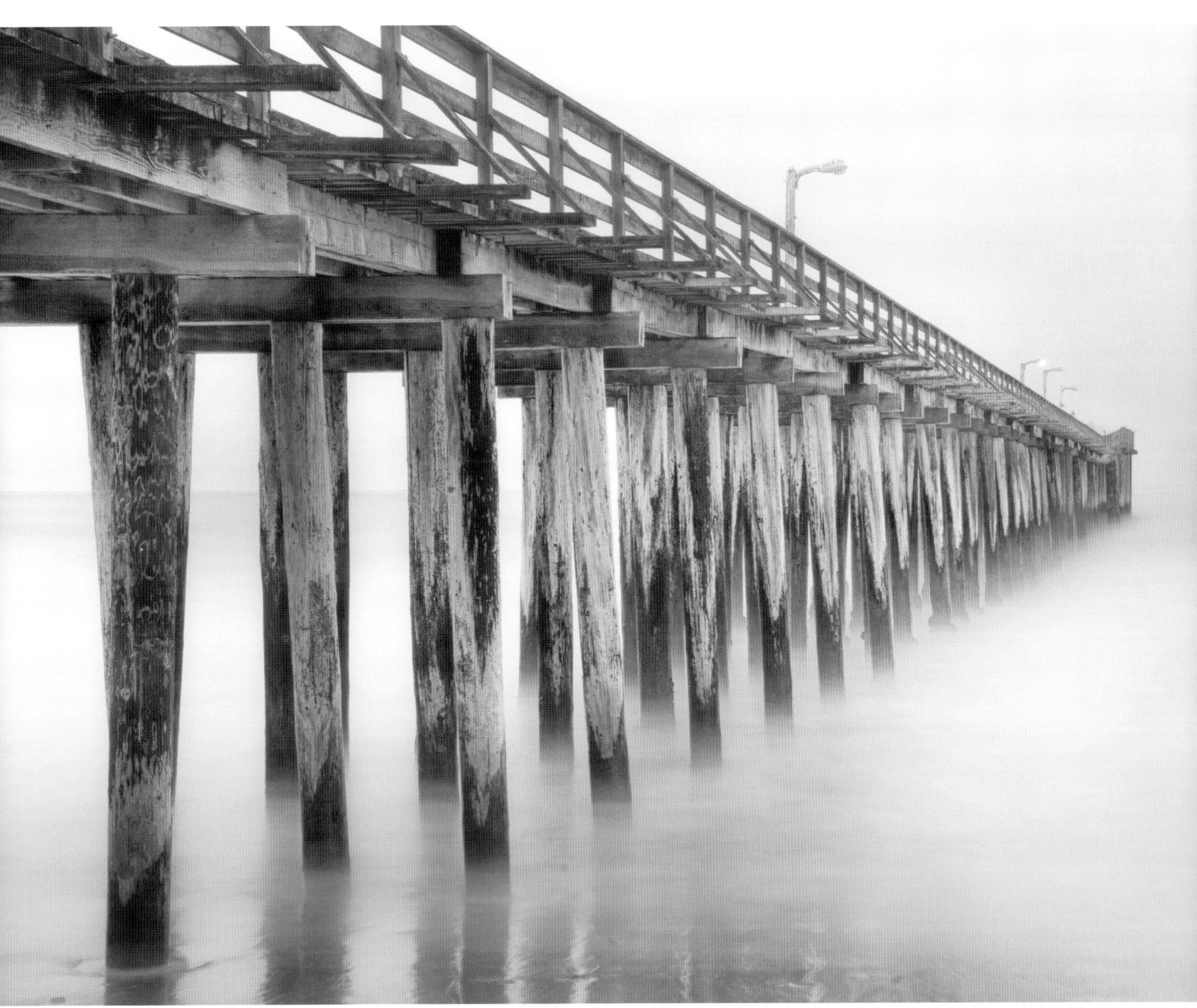

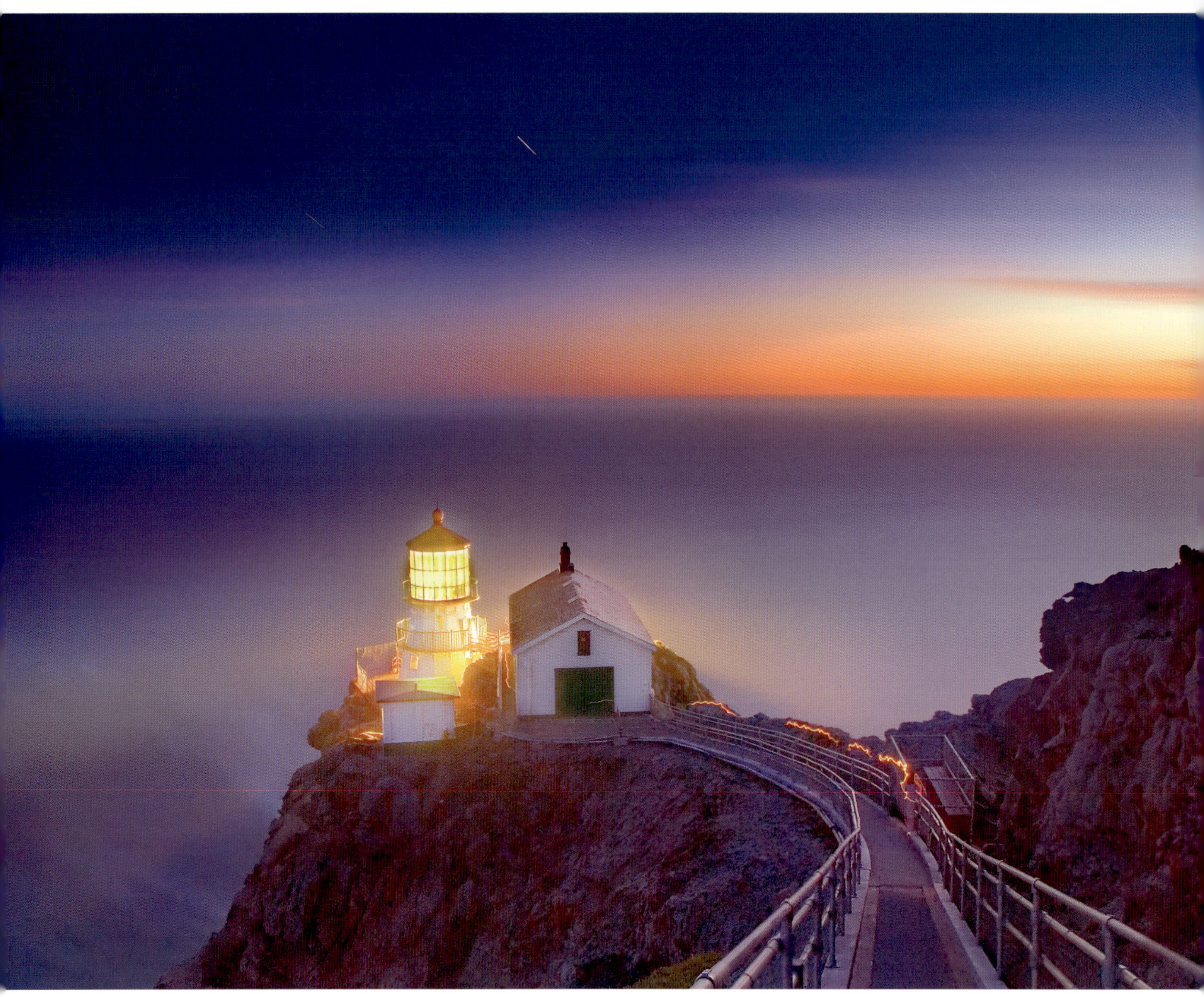

The *exit point* is where the viewer leaves the image after traveling on a visual journey through the image. For example, the exit point for *Corn Poppy* on page 136 is at the middle top of the image via the channel of light that roughly bisects the image horizontally as it curves up.

The *transitional passage*—what happens as the viewer's eye travels through the middle of the image—is an area with a great deal of possible variety. With some images, the viewer never leaves and gets stuck in the middle (for example, take a look at the two images on pages 138–139). This can be intentional on the part of the image creator or in some cases accidental.

If the viewer's gaze never leaves the middle area of an image, then there is no formal exit point. Theoretically, this means that the viewer keeps looking at the image forever. As a practical matter, nobody looks at an image forever! The real-world consequences of this image design choice is that the viewer stays with the image until their attention wanders elsewhere. You may think that holding the viewer hostage is a good thing, but actually it often leads to boredom.

When an image without an exit point does not convey narrative intent, the image can be amusing, but may feel gimmicky. This can be a little frustrating for the viewer.

While the language of direction is certainly not the only way to analyze formal composition, it is an important aspect of photographic composition. As an image creator, you should give serious thought to how the viewer's eye is going to approach your image, what the viewer's gaze will do within the image, and how that gaze will exit from the image.

The journey from entry point to exit point forms the language of direction and provides an important subtext in the narrative story that your image is telling.

Direction and Misdirection

The devious compositional creator, also known as a photographer, often thinks in terms of *open* versus *closed* compositions—whether there is or is not an exit path—and whether the act of composition is intended to "trap" the viewer. Every image represents a narrative and a journey. Some journeys are easy and joyful while others present inherently difficult or darker situations.

Directionality can lead the viewer into a trap when the entry point seems clear but there is no obvious exit point. How long do you want to keep the viewer bouncing around inside your image? Forever?

Endless Doors on page 15 and *Railway Bridge, Maine* on page 77 are examples of closed images that potentially suck the viewer down a long visual tunnel without an obvious exit.

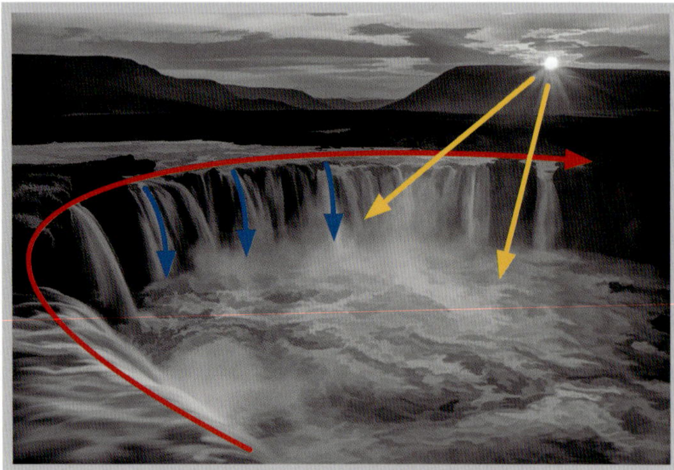

In this diagram, the red arrow shows the most important entry point to the image. The red arrow curves around to meet the solar rays (yellow arrows), which lead down to the churning water below.

Godafoss—Godafoss, meaning "Waterfall of the Gods" in Icelandic, is one of the largest and most beautiful waterfalls in Iceland, a land of many waterfalls. Godafoss gets its name from the Icelandic history of conversion to Christianity. Around 1000 CE, Iceland's parliament—the *Alþingi* ("Althing")—adopted Christianity by decree and pagan idols were thrown into Godafoss, although apparently the old religion was still practiced discreetly.

To make this photo, I visited Godafoss at midnight sunset during Iceland's brief summer.

There's a lot going on in this image, just as there is a great deal of water flowing, and the visual paths involved are complex. But clearly, the most important entry point is the great arc of the waterfall, which combines with the flowing motion of the water. The waterfall arc meets the rays of the setting sun, and the sun is a secondary entry point. Where the solar rays and the falling water meet, the water churns and froths, and holds the gaze of the viewer for a substantial beat.

As I made this image, I tried standing in various positions, all of them beyond the slender rope that was supposed to keep visitors safe. It became clear that even slight adjustments to the location of the camera made a huge difference in the effectiveness of the composition. If I had even been a foot to the left or right of where I was positioned at sunset, the entry and exit points would have changed and the photo would not have been as compelling.

Nikon D850, 28-300 Nikkor zoom at 28mm, five exposures with shutter speeds ranging from 1/20 to 0.8 of a second, each exposure at f/22 and ISO 64, tripod mounted.

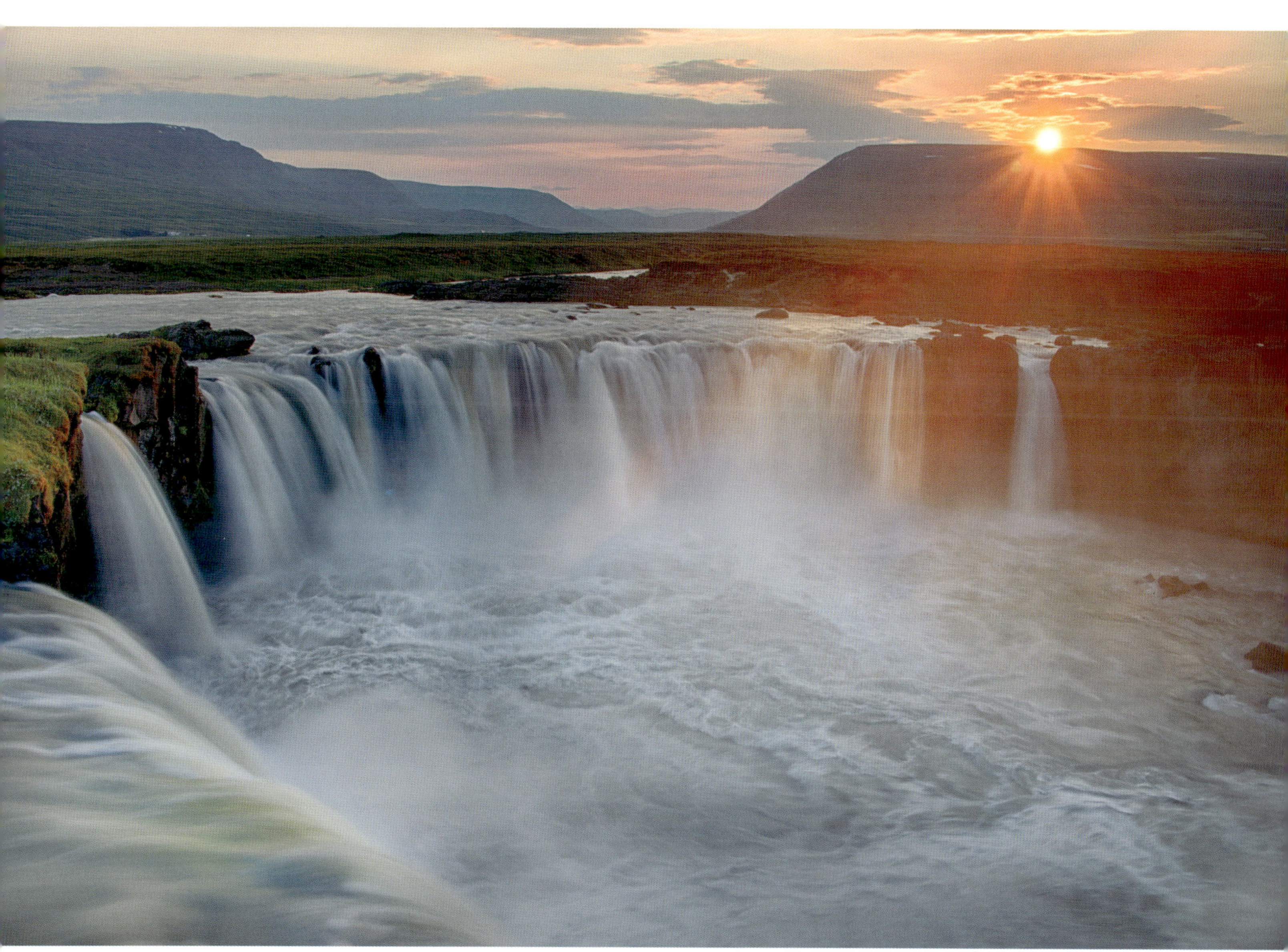

Calling Alice on page 130, is devious in a slightly different way. The viewer's gaze might simply "bounce" off this image. But if they engage with the image at almost any entry point, then their eyes will trace it around in infinite continuous loops.

Some images that are visual traps can use misdirection to seem anodyne, but are emotionally manipulative. A famous painting that uses this compositional gambit is *The Garden of Earthly Delights*, painted by Hieronymus Bosch around 1500. This triptych sucks you into heaven, which seems pleasant enough. Scanning left to right, it quickly becomes apparent that hell is a lot more visually interesting and colorful than heaven. After being captured, most viewers' gaze never leaves the nether regions, and remains trapped.

Tools of the Trade

If you look at the language of directionality as important to photographic composition, then as an image creator it becomes important to understand how to guide the viewer's gaze. How do we create entry points? What makes an exit point? How do we create an effective narrative for the transitional passage in the center of an image?

First, sometimes the entry point in an image is driven by the subject matter. A good example of this is in a portrait where the subject is looking directly at the camera. With this kind of image, the viewer almost always enters the image by looking at the subject's eyes. The eyes, as they say, are the window to the soul, so the subject's eyes as entry point in a portrait have a great deal of coherency.

Another subject matter example is an image that involves food. Most likely, the most scrumptious looking morsel will be the entry point for the image. This is just human nature: when we see something that strongly appeals to an appetite, we are likely to start there.

Besides inherent interest in the subject matter—such as a scintillating pair of smoky eyes or a delicious lemon poppy-seed muffin, hot from the oven—there are some technical tools that you can use as the image and visual-narrative creator to guide the viewer through your image. With appropriate use of visual formalism, you can attract the mind with no need to rely on appetite.

Lonely Forest—The most surprising thing about this image portraying a grove of trees along California's San Mateo coast is the apparent portal between one row of trees and the next. This grove nestles on a bluff high above the Pacific Ocean, and I made this image during the winter season when the trees are bare.

The issue in making this kind of photo is finding something distinctive so that the composition has more interest than the simple verticality of the trees. The "hook" that captures the viewer's imagination is supplied by the portal between the rows of trees. In addition to the portal, which is the first entry point to the image, the tree line also draws the eye into the photo.

The invitation to the inner grove is further extended by a branching tree limb, almost arm-shaped, above and immediately to the right of the opening.

Nikon D850, 28-300 Nikkor zoom at 68mm, five exposures with shutter speeds ranging from 1/4 of a second to 4 seconds, each exposure at f/22 and ISO 64, tripod mounted.

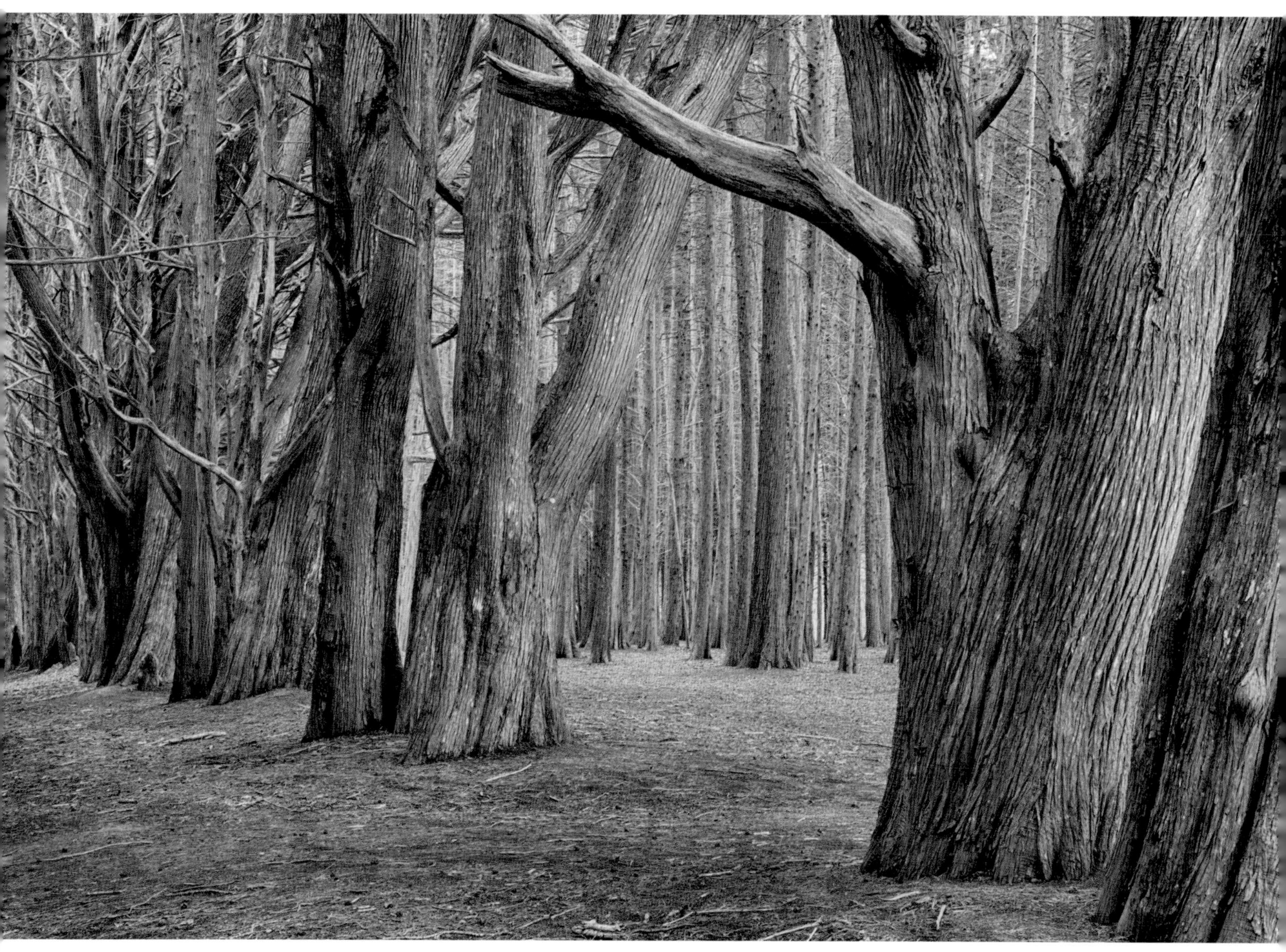

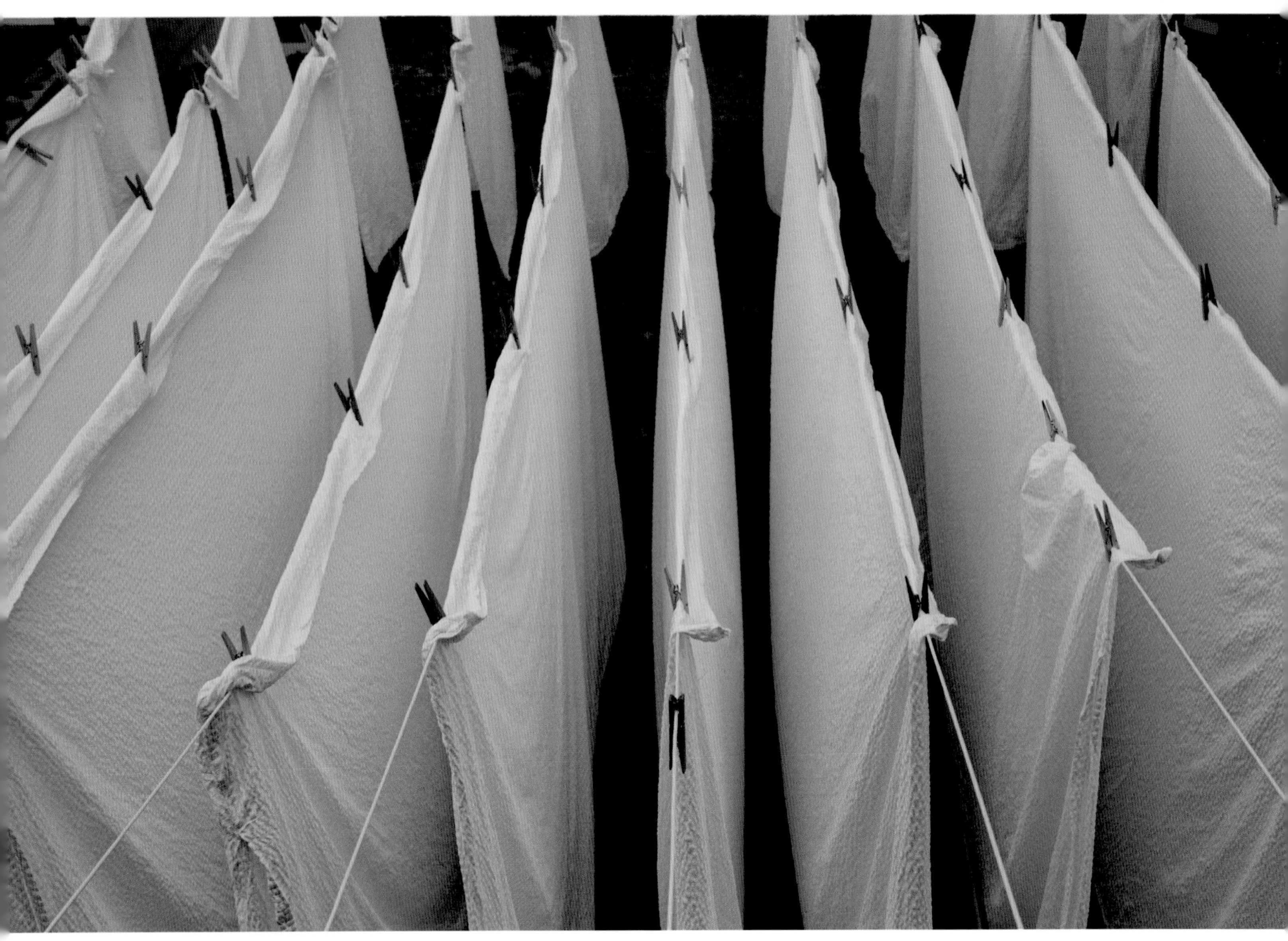

These formal narrative-enhancing tools include:

- Color

- Contrast and brightness

- Sharpness

- Focus

Colors draw the eye, so a shape that is brightly colored against a dark background is likely to be an entry point just because of its color. Take a look at *On the Brooklyn Bridge* on pages 154–155 to see an example of how the car lights stand out because of their bright color, creating a visual entry path.

In the absence of color in a monochrome image, contrast plays the role of color. Thus, contrast will compel the entry point. In *Lonely Forest* (on page 149) I worked hard in post-production to make sure that the portal opening was lighter than the row of trees. This increased contrast draws

Drying Sheets—Arriving at my bed and breakfast in Patreksfjörður in the Westfjords area of Iceland, I found these sheets drying outside. In the oncoming dusk, the white of the sheets contrasted with the dark background to make some interesting shapes. I walked around the sheets until a composition came into view from a vantage point slightly above the clotheslines.

The visual entry point for this image follows the clotheslines. The viewer is drawn in from the bottom via the parallel lines of the ropes and sheets, and then bounces back from the top of the image.

Nikon D850, 28-300 Nikkor zoom at 45mm, 1/320 of a second at f/11 and ISO 200, hand held.

the eye, helping to make the portal the visual entry point to the image. This was a conscious compositional choice on my part as I worked on the image in the Photoshop darkroom. You can make these kinds of choices as you consider how you are going to process an image.

If you cannot take advantage of color or contrast to draw attention, selective sharpness in an image can also be used to create entry points. Selective sharpening is one of the most important tools in the photographer's compositional quiver because it registers below the viewer's conscious level.

To put this differently, if you draw the viewer's attention to an entry point using selective sharpening, the viewer will probably not understand why their attention has been drawn to that portion of the image. This is distinct from grabbing the attention with a bright color, where the viewer will probably be able to consciously identify why their eye is being drawn. For example, I selectively sharpened the poppy centers in the *Bouquet of Poppies* on page 153.

As another example, in a portrait where both eyes are captured, if one eye is in focus and the other is not, the visual entry point will be the eye in focus rather than the comparatively blurry eye.

This becomes really apparent in figure studies or portraits where there are more than two eyes— for instance, *Passion* on page 140, *Fractal Face* on page 129, or for that matter, in a Picasso painting. The viewer's gaze starts with the dominant in-focus eye, and then surveys the surroundings, including the less distinct eyes.

The Pattern of Direction

As a 1960s television commercial for men's suits put it, "You never get a second chance to make a first impression." (This quote has also been attributed to Oscar Wilde and Will Rogers, though it is doubtful that either of them actually said it.)

So the visual entry point is probably the single most important part of the language of direction. The first impression that your image makes is what will resonate with the viewer and be important to the gist of their emotional takeaway.

The entry point is only the first impression, and the rest of the pattern of visual directionality matters as well. If you have a standard directional pattern of entering from the lower left and exiting at the upper right in a standard way, things are pretty clear. It's quite possible that reading an image from left to right is an issue of cultural relativism (see the "Thought Experiment" on page 142). Whether in fact this is culturally determined, statistically it seems to be true more often than not.

But often there's a great deal more complexity involved than a straightforward bottom-left entry.

With landscapes, the typical pattern of direction is to enter at the bottom heading up toward the horizon, then exit either left or right along the horizon line.

Many images have no obvious exit strategy. As an intentional strategy, this can be effective. You can keep the viewer's eye bouncing around within your image until they have had enough and leave the image entirely. This is also a place for finding ways to allow the viewer to explore the central areas of your image more deeply.

The key thing with the pattern of direction is to understand that your role, in part, is to drive the viewer's gaze. This is sometimes accomplished with absolutely no effort, simply based on the

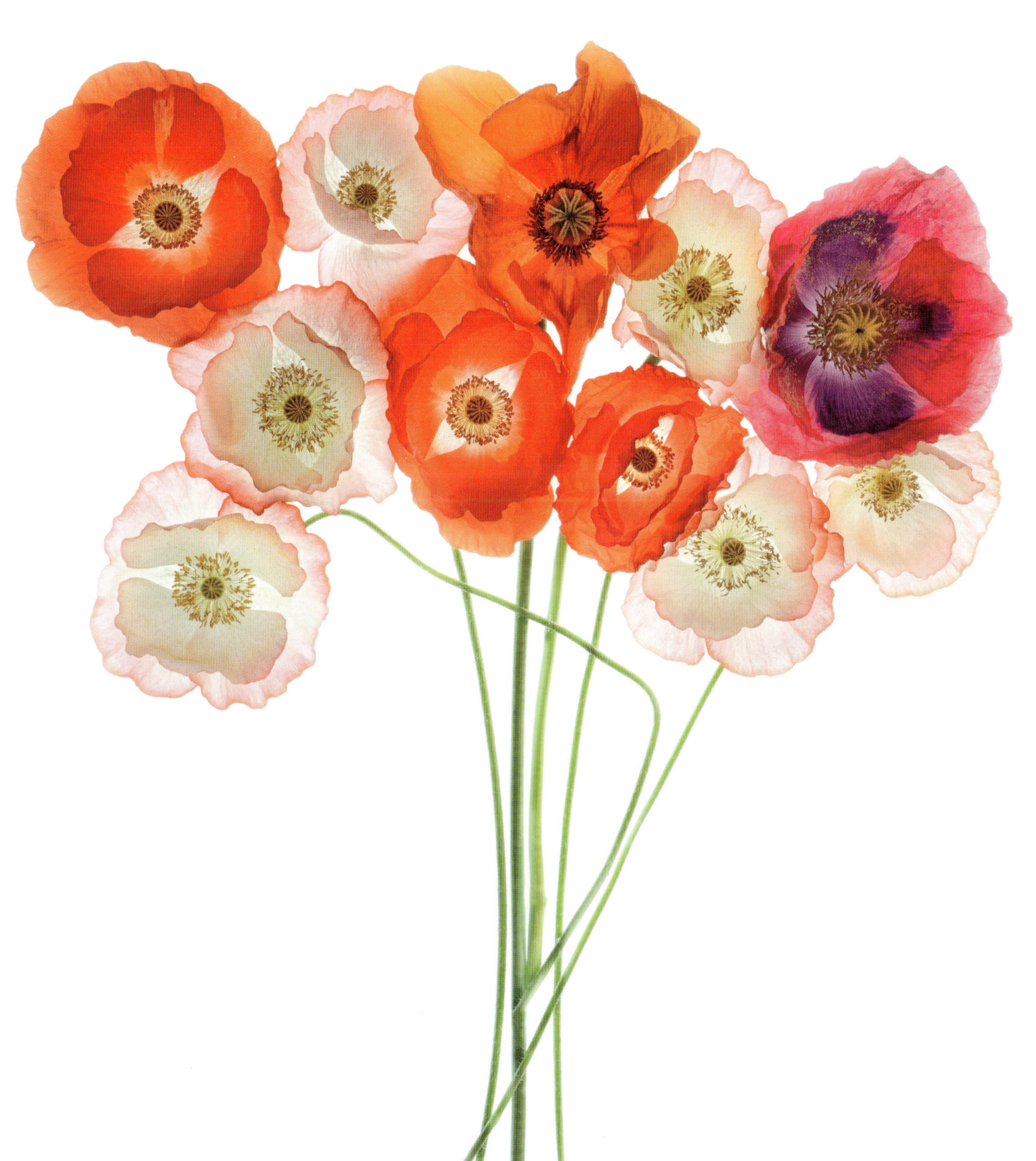

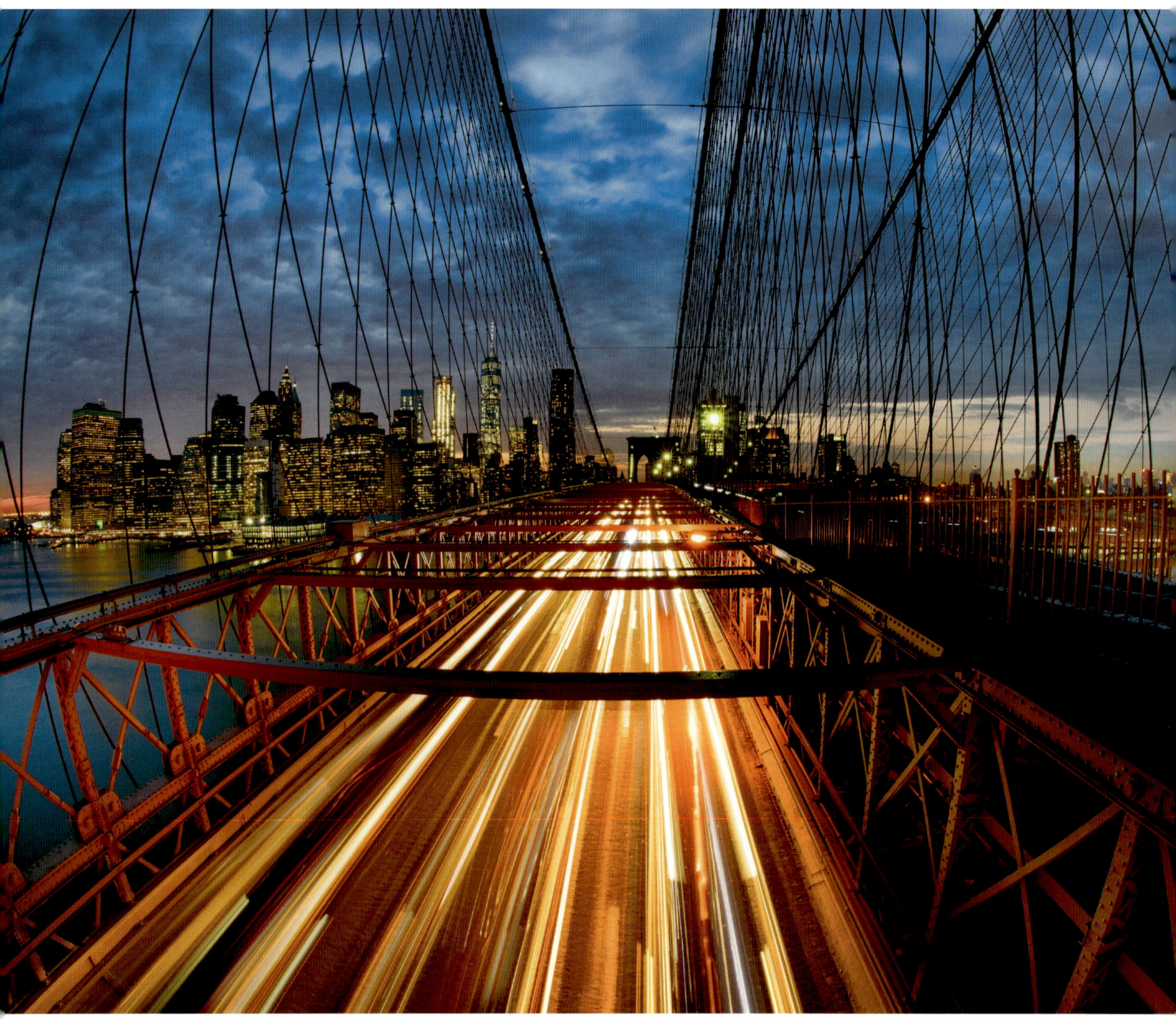

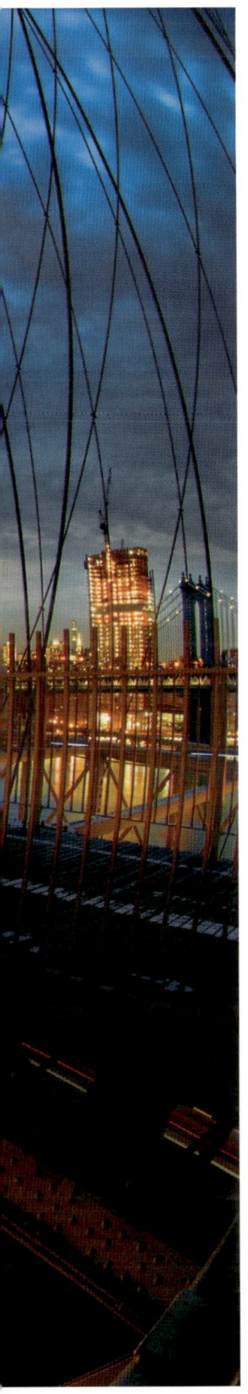

subject matter photographed without conscious effort on part of the photographer.

At other times, the directional pattern will need to be strategically planned. This can sometimes be accomplished as part of photography, but is also done in post-production. What I often find is that I have an idea about entry and exit points, as well as the internal flow of the image, but cannot fully realize this pattern in the camera, and need to work in the Photoshop darkroom to fully realize my thoughts about visual direction in my image.

It's important to use the tools of the trade, such as color, contrast, and sharpness, in addition to the emotional content of the image to guide the viewer. With this in mind, you can and should direct the complete narrative pattern within the image and toward the image exit.

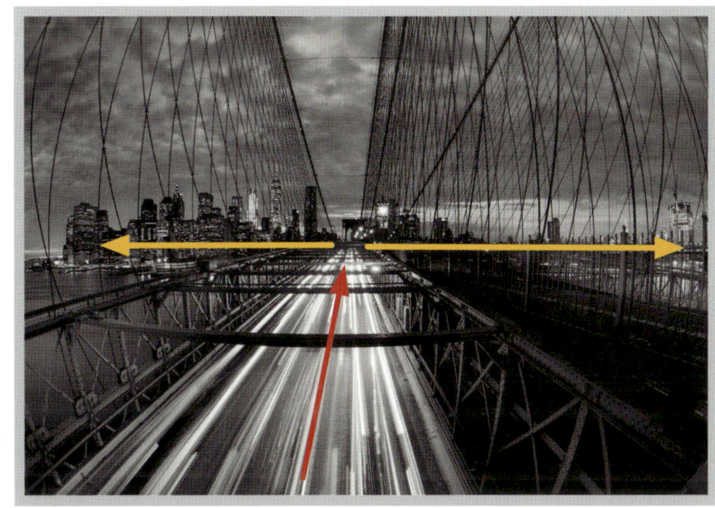

The viewer's gaze starts at the middle bottom of the image, and then follows the speeding traffic along the path of the red arrow to the city. From there, the gaze moves from left to right, and back again along the glowing Manhattan skyline in the direction of the yellow arrows.

Evoking Emotion with Direction

If you take the most typical entry and exit points—in other words, an image that starts at the lower left then swoops up to the upper right—all other things being equal, this image will give the viewer a happy, uplifted, and expansive feeling. Why? Nobody really knows—one theory is that it has to do with how memory and recall work—but you should take advantage of this in your compositions.

Challenge yourself to work with the general principles of entry-exit points and directionality:

- If you start looking at images with entry-exit points in mind, you will see lots of things differently. Check this out with photos and art you like, in books and in museums. What has the artist done regarding visual entry, visual exit, and the path through the image, and why? Does it work for you?

- Can you find any images that make you uneasy without being able to pinpoint why? Study them and figure what the entry-transition-exit strategy is, if any. Does this contribute to your unease?

- Visual entry-transit-exit paths are important, so plan to use them in your own work. Come up with a strategy for drawing the viewer's gaze into the narrative of your composition.

KEY IDEAS

- The design language of direction (and of visual gaze) is complementary to, but distinct from, working with shapes.

- The language of direction encompasses *entry* and *exit points*, and the *transitional passage* between entry and exit.

- The entry point is the most important part of directional language.

- Some images are caught in a central transitional portion—intentionally or otherwise—and never provide an exit point.

- Part of the job of the photographer in creating a composition is to plan the underlying directional structure of entry, transition, and then exit.

Poem of the Road—On a lonely stretch of US Route 6 in Nevada near the California border, smoke from vast wildfires to the west drifted inland. In the late afternoon, I stood in the middle of the road and captured a single car headed west into the gloom, following a line of utility poles.

Back in my studio, I added a texture to the sky to increase interest in the photo.

The clear visual entrance to the photo is heading down the road from the lower right, following the line of the road until the viewer's eye reaches the lone car and the road converges with the line of utility poles and the horizon line. Does the viewer's gaze ever leave the photo?

Nikon D810, 28-300mm Nikkor zoom at 300mm, 1/800 of a second at f/5.6 and ISO 200, hand held; texture added in post-production.

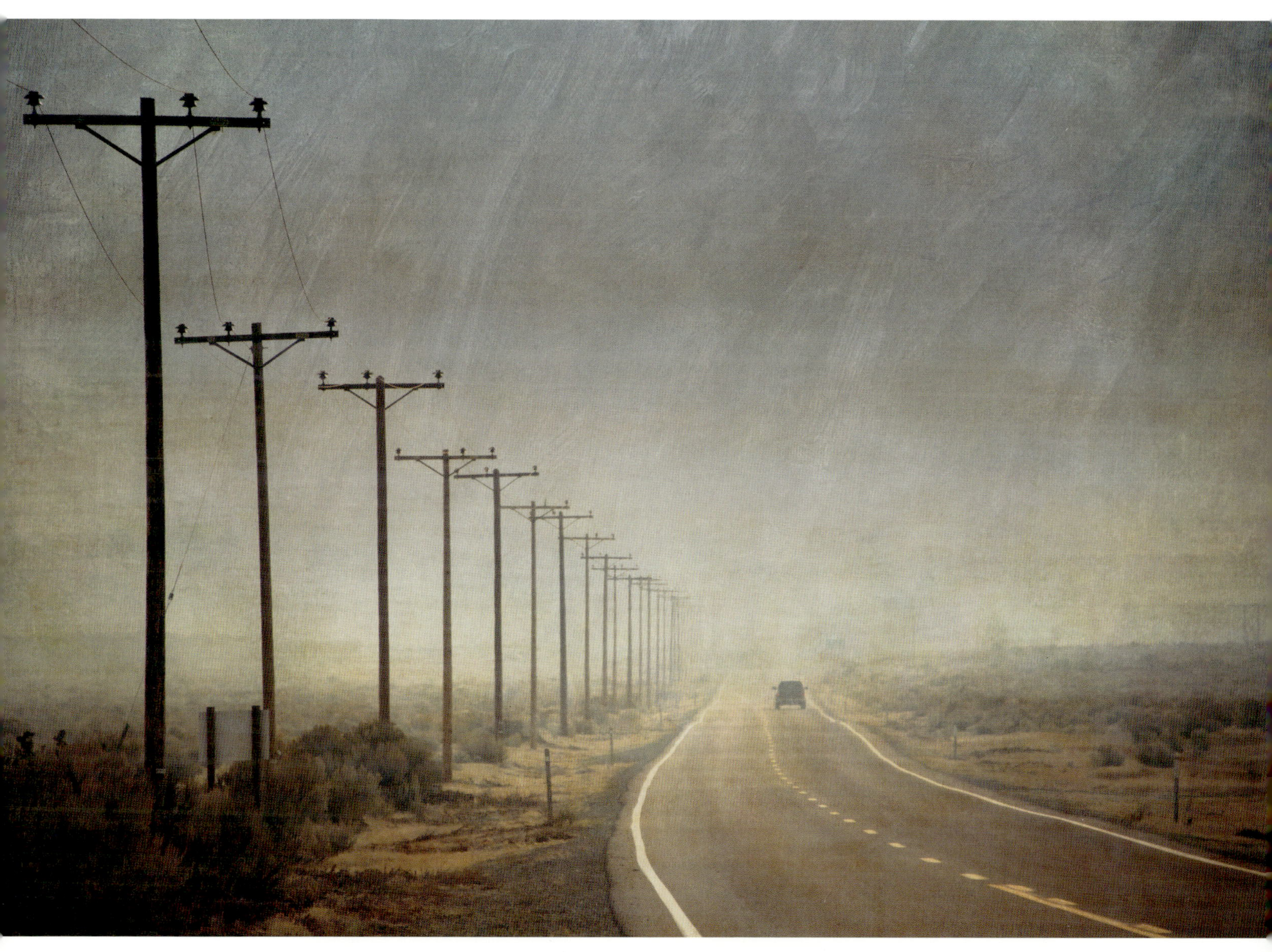

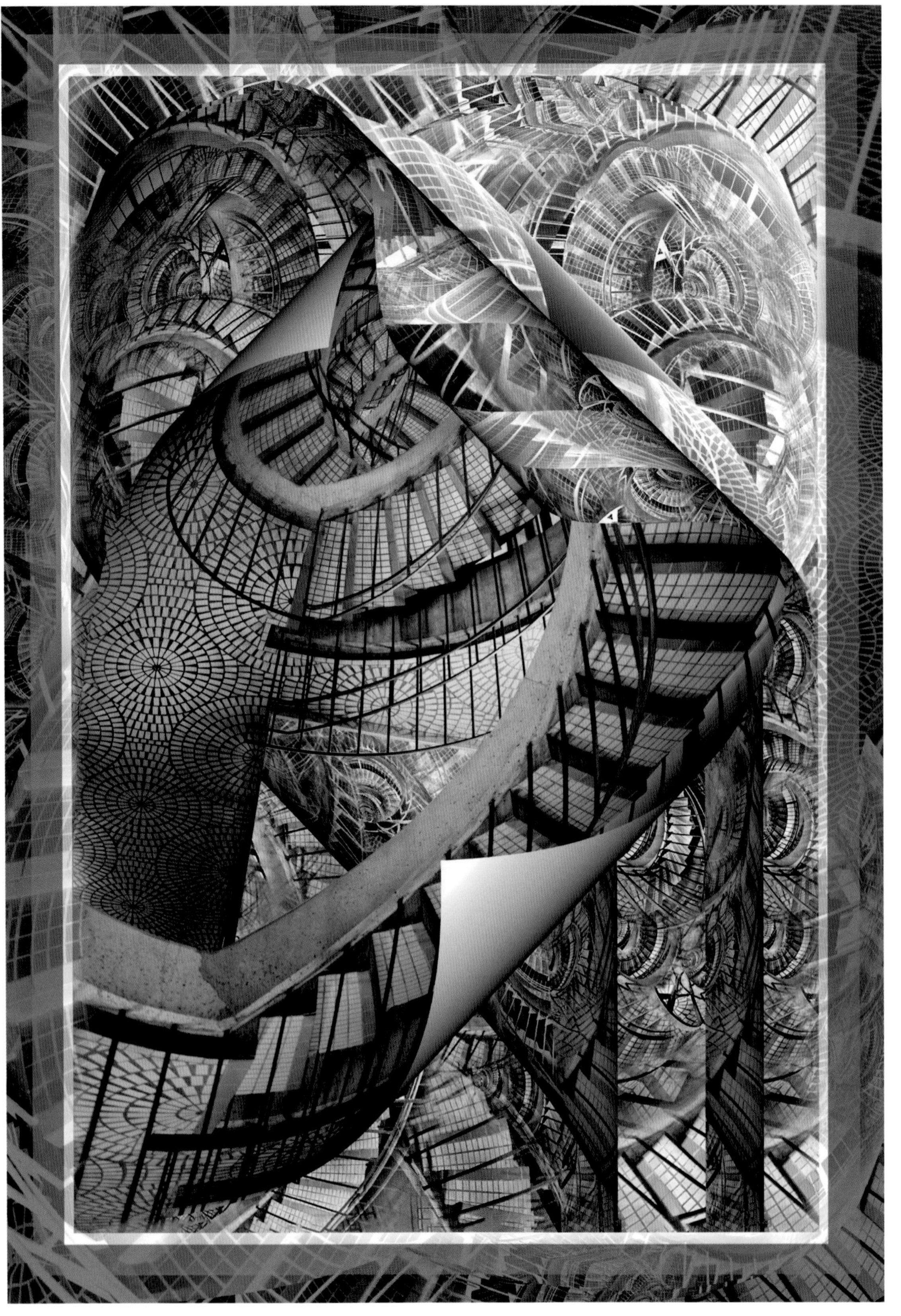

VANISHING POINTS & PERSPECTIVE
VANISHING POINTS & PERSPECTIVE
VANISHING POINTS & PERSPECTIVE
VANISHING POINTS & PERSPECTIVE

VANISHING POINTS & PERSPECTIVE

> "What we call reality in pictures, seems to be the optical projection, a European way of looking at the world, that accepts a world seen from a single point.…There is nothing wrong with photography, if you don't mind the perspective of a paralysed Cyclops." —David Hockney

Down the Rabbit Hole—In this wild and wacky composite, I intentionally used a number of different vanishing points. Take a look at the image and see if you can identify some!

The sense of depth in this image is partly enhanced by the variety of vanishing points. For example, the entry point to the image is the dark staircase that arcs up and around from the lower left. While this staircase starts out with a conventional vanishing point, the spirals in the other image quadrants are anything but straightforward, and each section of the image has its own vanishing point and perspective.

The compositional idea of *Down the Rabbit Hole* is to be both complicated yet remain cohesive. This is tough to pull off. If you look at an individual area, you'll see more and more detail as you magnify the area. At the same time, there's a broader architecture where pillars of light and dark support spirals that seem to go on forever.

Composite and self-composite of three images. Primary Staircase: Nikon D850, 25mm Zeiss Otus, 1/125 of a second at f/1.4 and ISO 1250, hand held; Background Images: Nikon D300, 10.5mm Nikkor fisheye, 10 and 13 seconds at f/22 and ISO 100, tripod mounted.

Of the great strands of human curiosity and experimentation that led to the development of photography, few inventions were more important than the *camera obscura*. A simple device, the camera obscura is a dark room or box with a hole on one side. The scene outside the camera obscura is projected onto a wall opposite the hole.

Starting in the early Renaissance, mathematicians and artists, such as Filippo Brunelleschi, rediscovered the principles of single-point perspective, which had been known to the Romans but lost in the Dark Ages.

As time went by, artists interested in painting realistic scenes began using portable camera obscura devices to project single-point perspective renderings so this could be incorporated into their work. For example, Johannes Vermeer enthusiastically used a portable camera obscura in creating the perspective projections in his paintings.

Before the invention of the camera obscura and widespread adoption of single-point perspective, most art was rendered as basically flat or following a cartoon-like map structure. Occasional elements, such as tables or chairs, were rendered in perspective, but there was no consistent method for achieving this.

Single-point perspective was so incredibly effective as a way to present the world that it has basically taken over our sense of visual reality. It has changed the way we collectively see the world.

Paintings with a single vanishing point appear absolutely real, and we sense them as accurate representations of three-dimensional reality. But, of course, this is an illusion. A painting, like a photograph, is a two-dimensional object that can appear to present three-dimensional reality based on a visual convention—but it can never be three-dimensional reality itself. It's odd—and ultimately delusional—that we have come to automatically accept single-point perspective as reality itself.

When it comes to photography, we have one-upped the camera obscura. There's no need to project the lines of perspective onto a wall for tracing and transfer. The vanishing point and related projections are captured optically using the pinhole effect, and can be saved for future use, either chemically or digitally. Perspective is already baked into the mechanics of photographic rendition, as well as into our consciousness.

Nonetheless, single-point perspective with a vanishing point remains a convention—a method of mapping three dimensions onto a two-dimensional space—and only one way of depicting three-dimensional reality. As a matter of photographic composition, one can use the absolute certainty of the viewer's belief in the veracity of perspective to shift the way the viewer sees reality.

If you are using single-point perspective in your image without considering how it is being used and, most importantly, what the alternatives are, it's time to change things up a bit. The results can be startling!

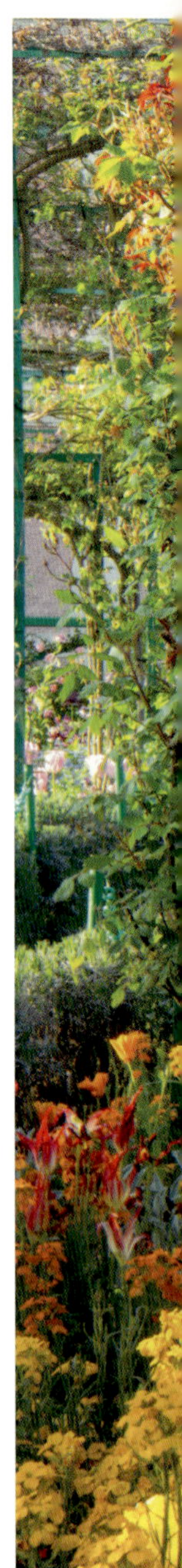

Flowers at Giverny—In the late-afternoon light in Monet's garden at Giverny, I was thrilled to see the beautiful assortment of radiant flowers under this arbor. The way the flower beds were planted looked like a living Impressionist painting.

As I was setting up my camera and tripod, I realized that I wanted to add a dash of Monet-type blur to the foreground of the image I was previsualizing. To do this, I used as low an ISO as possible to extend the length of the exposure.

The entry point of this composition is at roughly the lower middle third of the image where the flowers are mostly orange and yellow. From there, the viewer's gaze moves right down the center of the arbor, past the purple flowers, toward the vanishing point that falls in the center of the image, slightly above the horizontal axis.

Nikon D850, 28-300mm Nikkor at 122mm, 2 seconds at f/29 and ISO 31, tripod mounted.

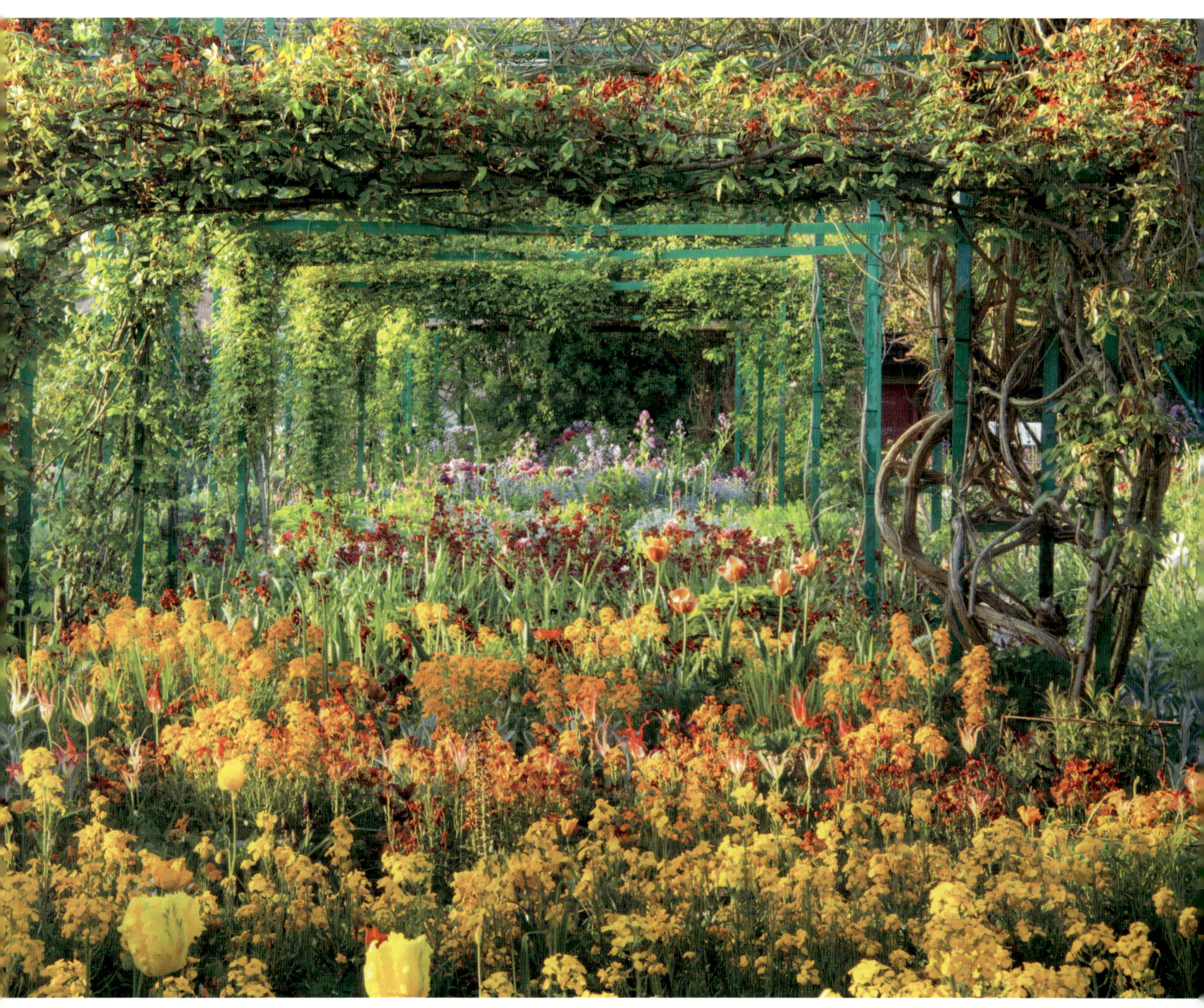

Working with the Vanishing Point

A good working definition of a *vanishing point* is the point at which receding parallel lines appear to meet when rendered in linear perspective. There is more to this definition than meets the eye. For one thing, the parallel lines in question only "appear," or seem, to meet. In many perspective renditions, the vanishing point is implied and does not actually appear anywhere in the image. The viewer's brain assigns a position to the vanishing point, even if it isn't seen, by following the perspective rendition.

As I've mentioned, one of the progenitors of today's camera is the camera obscura. The projective device of the pinhole in the camera obscura has been improved and enhanced using optical science and lenses. The projection of the camera obscura on the back wall of the box or room is now captured using a digital sensor (or film).

This literal one-to-one correspondence between the camera obscura and today's cameras has led artists and critics astray! The mistake that is made is to assume that because today's cameras have camera-obscura functionality, they can only render perspective the way a camera obscura does. David Hockney's quip that photography is like a "paralysed Cyclops"—or is seeing things with only one, fixed eye—comes from this misapprehension.

True, the easiest and default mode when photographing the kind of subject that responds well to perspective—such as landscapes and architecture—is to fall back on basic single-point perspective. But even within the realm of single-point perspective, the photographer has choices as to where the vanishing point is and how to apply that perspective. As I'll also discuss later in this chapter, multi-point perspective is possible photographically. Once refraction and curvature enter the picture, the vanishing point becomes a complex issue, and multiple vanishing points are possible. In addition, the Photoshop darkroom provides a number of very effective ways to alter the "rules" of perspective.

The simplest relationship to the vanishing point and single-point perspective is to have one vanishing point pretty much in the middle of the image. This central vanishing point is likely to be raised a bit above the midline of the image, just as

Black Sand Beach—Looking down on Reynisfjara Beach on Iceland's southern coast, I previsualized a composition where the white line of the surf operated as a border between the black sand of the beach and the dark patterns of the North Atlantic Ocean.

To accomplish this visual idea, I underexposed the image by 3 EV. This served to capture resolution in the white surf line while rendering the beach sand and ocean very dark.

My other goal was to sight the surf line as a diagonal across the frame from the lower-left corner to the upper right. To accomplish this, I needed to change the angle at which I held the camera so that the vanishing point for the entire image was near the upper-right corner of the frame.

Nikon D850, 28-300mm Nikkor at 70mm, 1/800 of a second at f/8 and ISO 64, hand held.

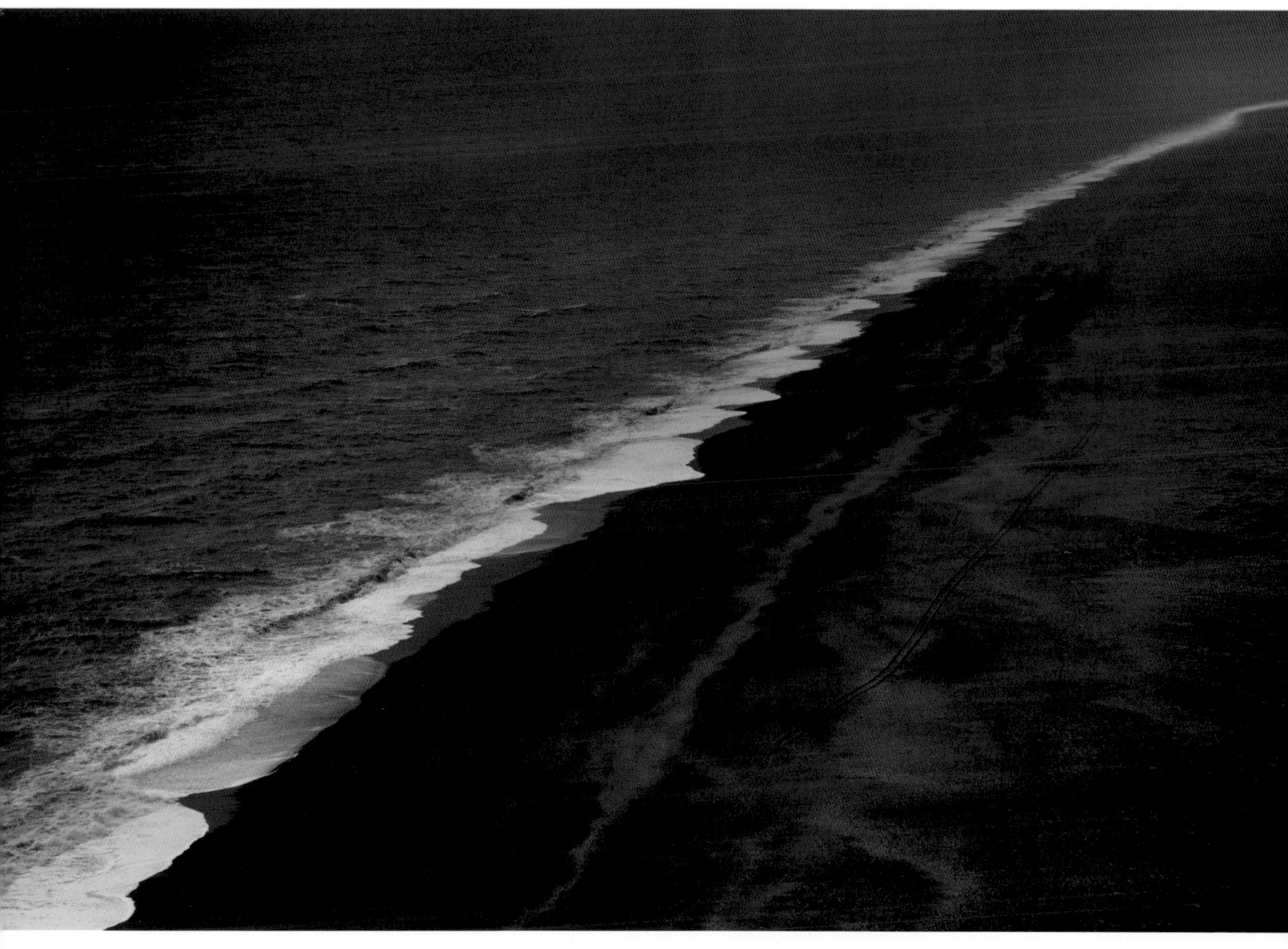

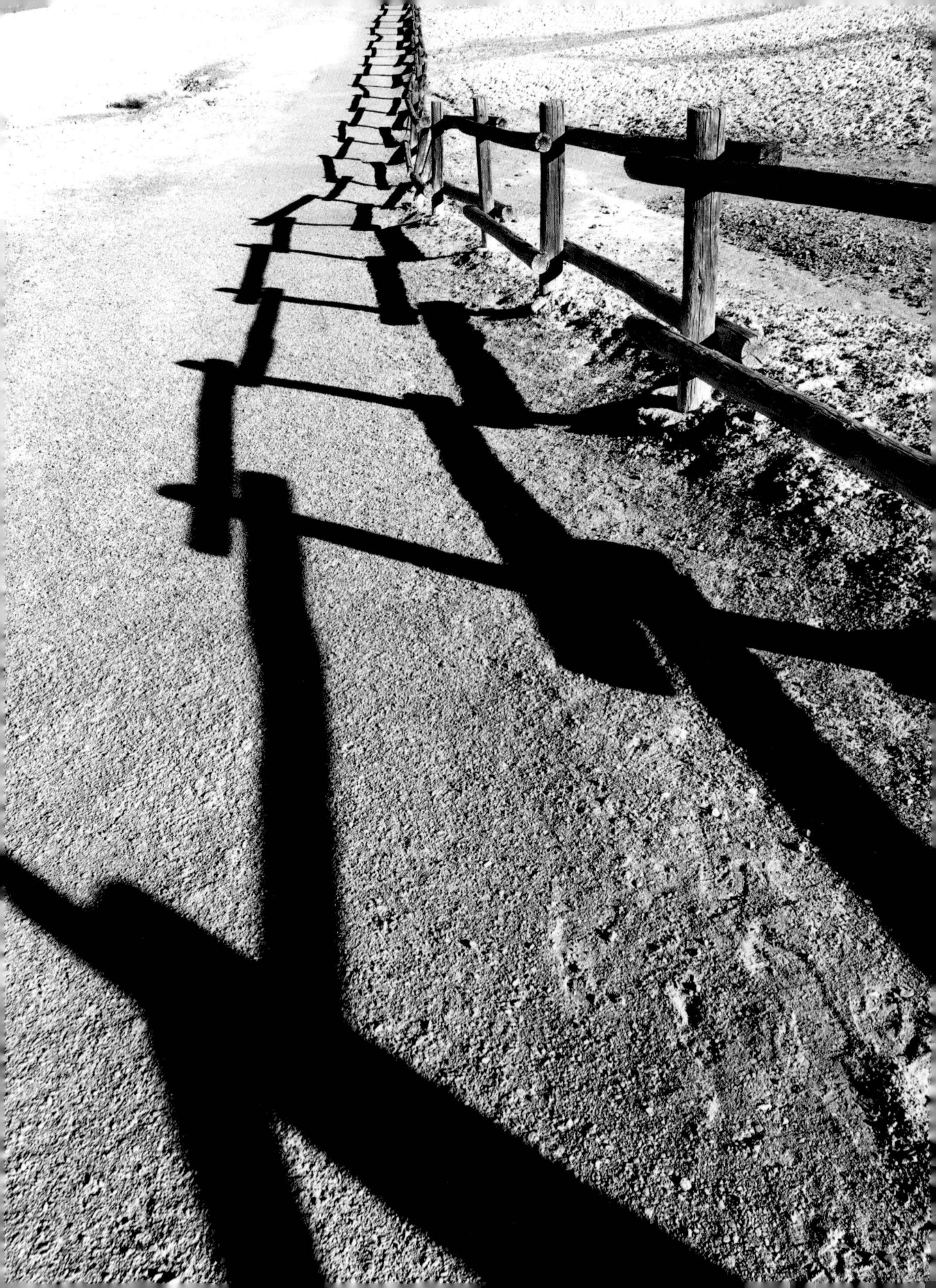

the horizon line tends to be raised when looking across the landscape, and in some cases tends toward the top of the image.

There's certainly no rule that says that even a single vanishing point needs to be in the middle of the image, and often it isn't.

Move your camera, and use your feet to "scootch" around and try different positions to experiment with changing the vanishing point (see page 61).

As with a number of photographic issues, very small changes in camera position can have a big impact on the final image. Even if the vanishing point doesn't itself change, its location in relationship to the boundary frame of the image will move as you shift your camera's position.

- If the camera's angle in relationship to the subject is shifted to the left, the vanishing point will probably move to the right.

- If the camera's angle in relationship to the subject is shifted to the right, the vanishing point will probably move to the left.

- If you move the angle of the camera up in relation to the subject, most likely the vanishing point will go downward.

- If you move the angle of the camera down in relation to the subject, most likely the vanishing point will go upward.

It's worth taking the time to get a feeling for how the camera angle in relationship to the subject can impact the location of the vanishing point. Even in the simplest images, location of the vanishing point plays a big role in how your viewers will perceive the "reality" that your image has captured.

Fence Shadow—In the middle of the day the shadows were strong near Furnace Creek in Death Valley National Park, California. I was intrigued by the fence and shadow line that you can see here.

To make this image, I got down low on my belly on the gravel path and placed the vanishing point at the upper center of the image. At first glance, this appears to be a pretty straightforward single-point perspective rendition. But if you look more closely, as the fence line approaches the vanishing point, it appears to curve upward. This portion of the fence and shadow combined can also be visually interpreted as a front-facing ladder that leads up and out of the image.

The initial entry point to this image is the strong, dark shadow at the bottom of the image. The eye then follows the shadow rails toward the vanishing point. What gives the image a visual kick is the curvature as the shadow approaches the vanishing point. This could almost be considered a visual pun.

iPhone 6s, converted to black and white in Snapseed.

Thought Experiment

Point your camera at a subject with a typical single-point perspective vanishing point in the center area of the image. With your camera on a tripod, try moving the camera's angle in relation to the subject. Does the vanishing point change? How? Can you control the location of the vanishing point in the image depending on how you position the camera?

The vast majority of images—particularly land-scape and architectural studies—show a world with a single vanishing point. Just because you only have one doesn't mean you are out of options!

Understand the importance of the vanishing point to your image, and to the way your viewers visually interpret the relationship of your image to the world, and to their overall sense of the reality of your work. Keeping this importance in mind, it is important to work with your camera when photographing to find compositions where the location of the vanishing point best comple-ments your compositional intent.

Multi-Point Perspective

If one vanishing point is good, then two should be better, and multiple vanishing points should be great—at least, so you'd think.

We have been trained since early childhood via almost all the media that we see—televisions, movie screens, books, our mobile phones—to view the world in a single-point rendition. Any image with more than one vanishing point auto-matically seems weird and feels uncomfortable.

If you look for them, out in the world there are many scenes that do have more than one van-ishing point. The most common scenario is when something splits our vision. This could be a building, a fence, maybe a post, a rock, or even a car. The key issue is that we see something dif-ferently on either side of the object that splits our vision. Any time we see something like this, the

The Alameda and El Dorado—If you stand at the corner of many streets and hold yourself in exactly the right position, it's fairly easy to encounter a scene with two vanishing points. It's a little harder than you might think to capture these two vanishing points photographically, but it can be done with the aid of a wide-angle lens.

At the meeting of these two streets in Berkeley, Califor-nia, the angle of intersection is particularly acute. The white picket fence comes together in a V-shape, making the two-point perspective particularly obvious. It also helps that the vanishing points of both perspectives are very similar.

I used a 21mm wide-angle lens to make this image showing a simple example of two vanishing points. My camera was on a tripod and it was tricky to find the right position so I could see both vanishing points equally. One inch to the left or right, or up or down, would have completely changed the whole image. Both paths are not exactly the same in terms of geome-try or what is at the vanishing point, but they are similar enough that at first glance they look the same.

What happens to the viewer looking at this photo? Initially, many people see the image as mirrored, and assume that it is manipulated and is not "real." Closer inspection shows that, in fact, this is a real street corner with two different paths that are not exactly the same. At this point, some degree of visual vertigo sets in. Depending on the viewer, the sense is that one is going to be "dumped" out of the image, or that one's eyes are going to continually focus back and forth between the two vanishing points.

Either scenario creates a visual "ping-pong" effect, which was my idea when I made this image of an apparently mundane street corner.

Nikon D850, 21mm Zeiss Distagon, five exposures with shutter speeds ranging from 1/13 of a second to 2 seconds at f/22 and ISO 64, tripod mounted.

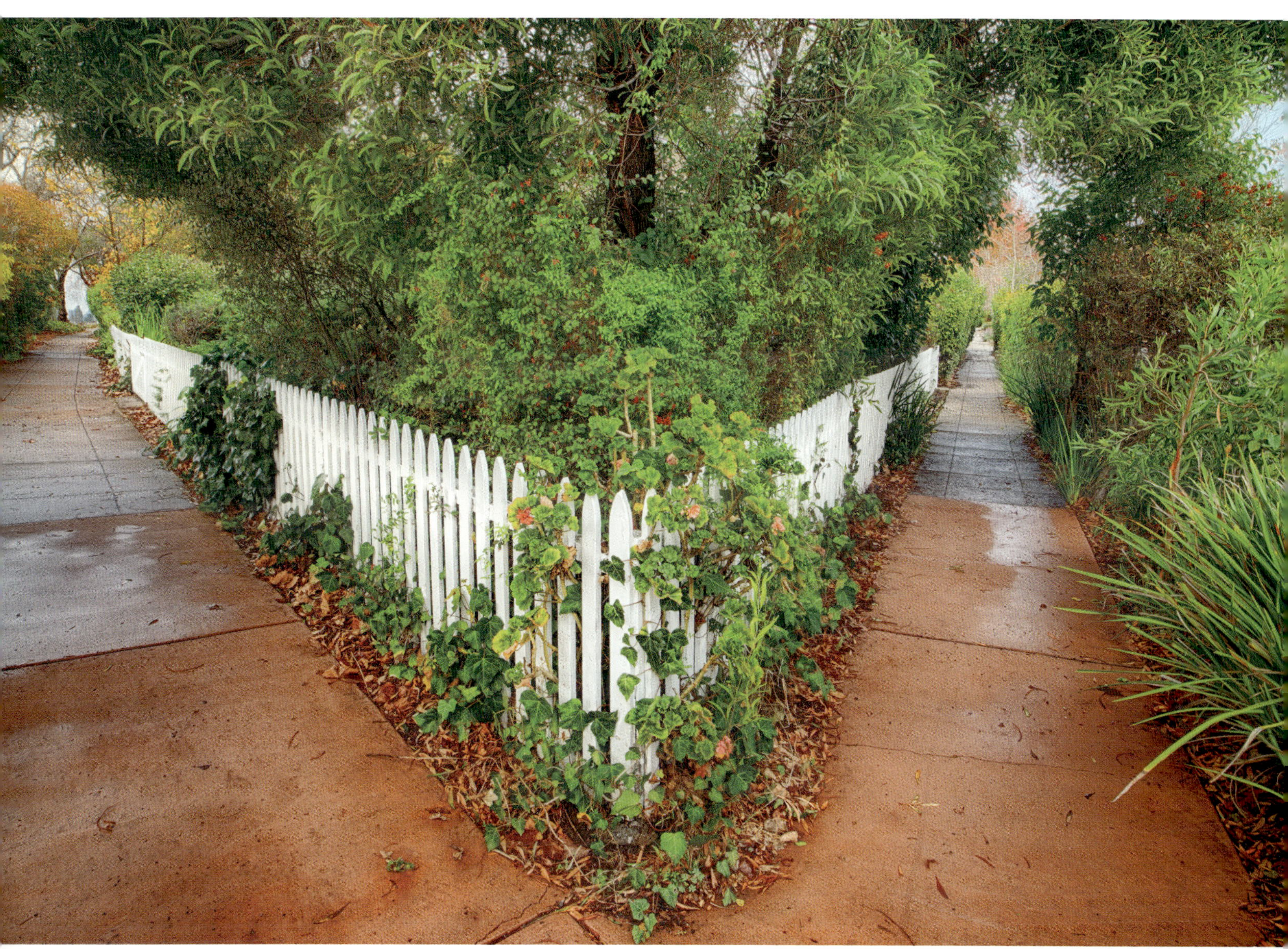

visual parts of our brains tend to work overtime, and it can be like decoding a visual puzzle.

To make an image that captures real-world, multi-point perspective, most likely you'll want to use a wide-angle lens. The best approach is to use a fairly wide-angle lens in the 21mm–28mm range. This moderate to extreme wide-angle lens will often work better than a wide-angle lens with distortion, such as a fisheye lens.

The problem with using a fisheye lens, and with curvature appearing at the edges of your image due to an extreme wide-angle lens, is that the viewer's eye notices this distortion immediately and assumes that the multiple vanishing points are related to this distortion rather than occurring naturally.

The idea of an image with more than one vanishing point is to create a sense of being off balance because the multiple perspective renditions contrast with the normality of the photo. The distortion inherent in a fisheye lens goes against this because the viewer expects things to be distorted, and they know right off the bat that they are not looking at a "normal" photo.

As with many aspects of composition, small movements in the camera position make all the difference with multi-point perspective images (for more about moving the camera to enhance composition, turn to pages 61 and 116).

For example, the photo on page 167 shows a street corner where a fence meets in a V-shape. This was photographed as two-point perspective as I pointed the camera directly at the area a little above the level of the fencing where the fence meets at the corner post. If I had moved the camera even a tiny bit in any direction, the image wouldn't have worked visually.

Wherever I am out and about in the world, I look for vistas that have multiple vanishing points. I believe that having more than one vanishing point adds interest and intrigue to an image. If there's an effective way to integrate multiple vanishing points into the purpose of a composition, then I know I am well on my way to making a compelling image.

Pont Neuf, Toulouse—The so-called "Pont Neuf," or "New Bridge," across the Garrone River in Toulouse, France, was finished in 1632. The bridge is shown here during spring with high water running through the arches.

The image has a very distinct vanishing point that the viewer's eye latches onto, following the line of the bridge from right to left. This vanishing point is reinforced by the geometrically diminishing circles of the bridge arches and their reflections. This is the kind of single-point perspective we are used to, except that it is less common to have it run from right to left—more typically, it goes from left to right.

There is also a second vanishing point in this image. Take a look through the largest arch under the bridge! Once the second vanishing point is seen, it is hard for the viewer not to split their attention between the vista through the arch and the vanishing point along the span of the bridge.

Nikon D810, 28-300mm Nikkor zoom at 28mm, seven exposures with shutter speeds ranging from 1/250 to 1/4 of a second at f/14 and ISO 64, tripod mounted.

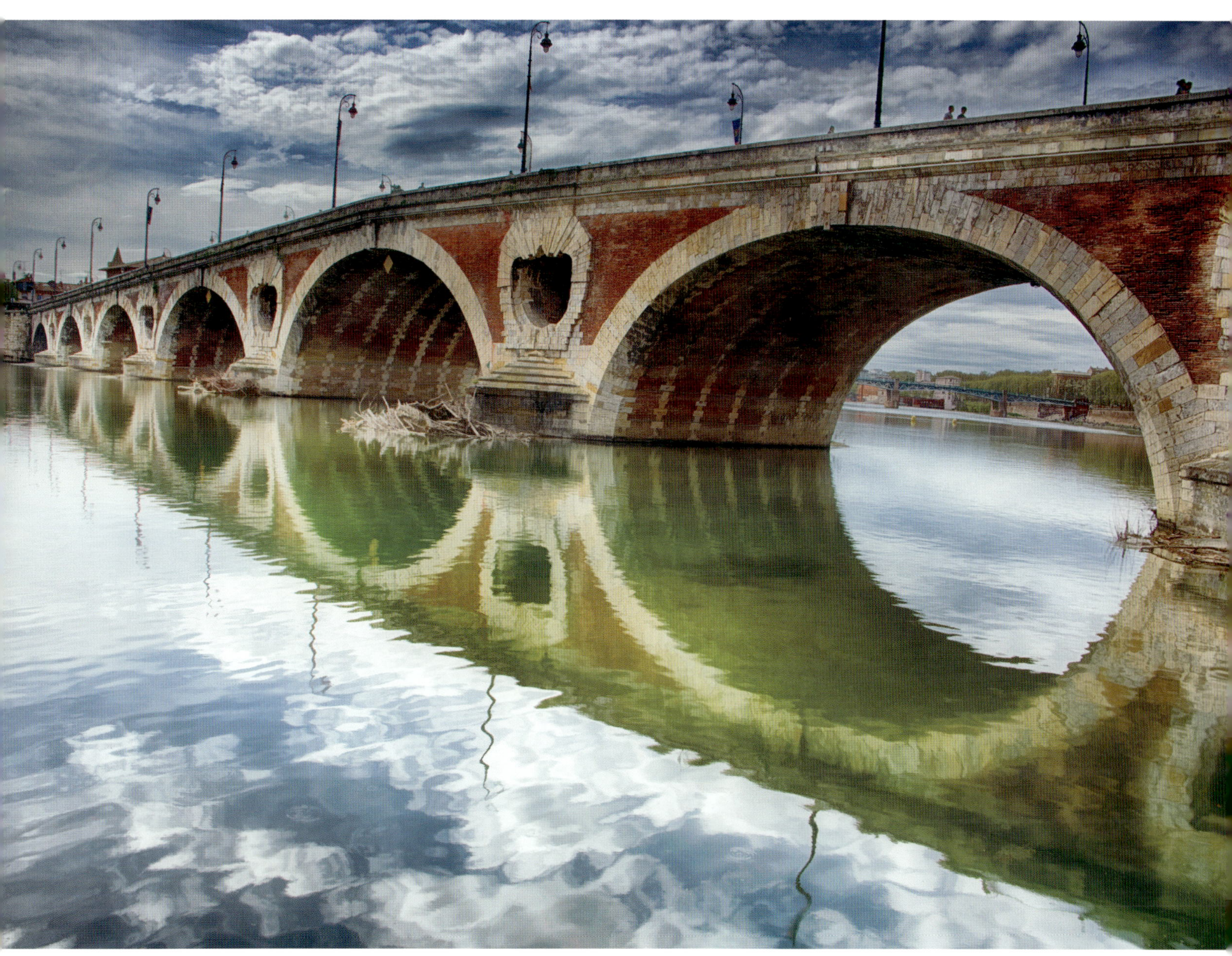

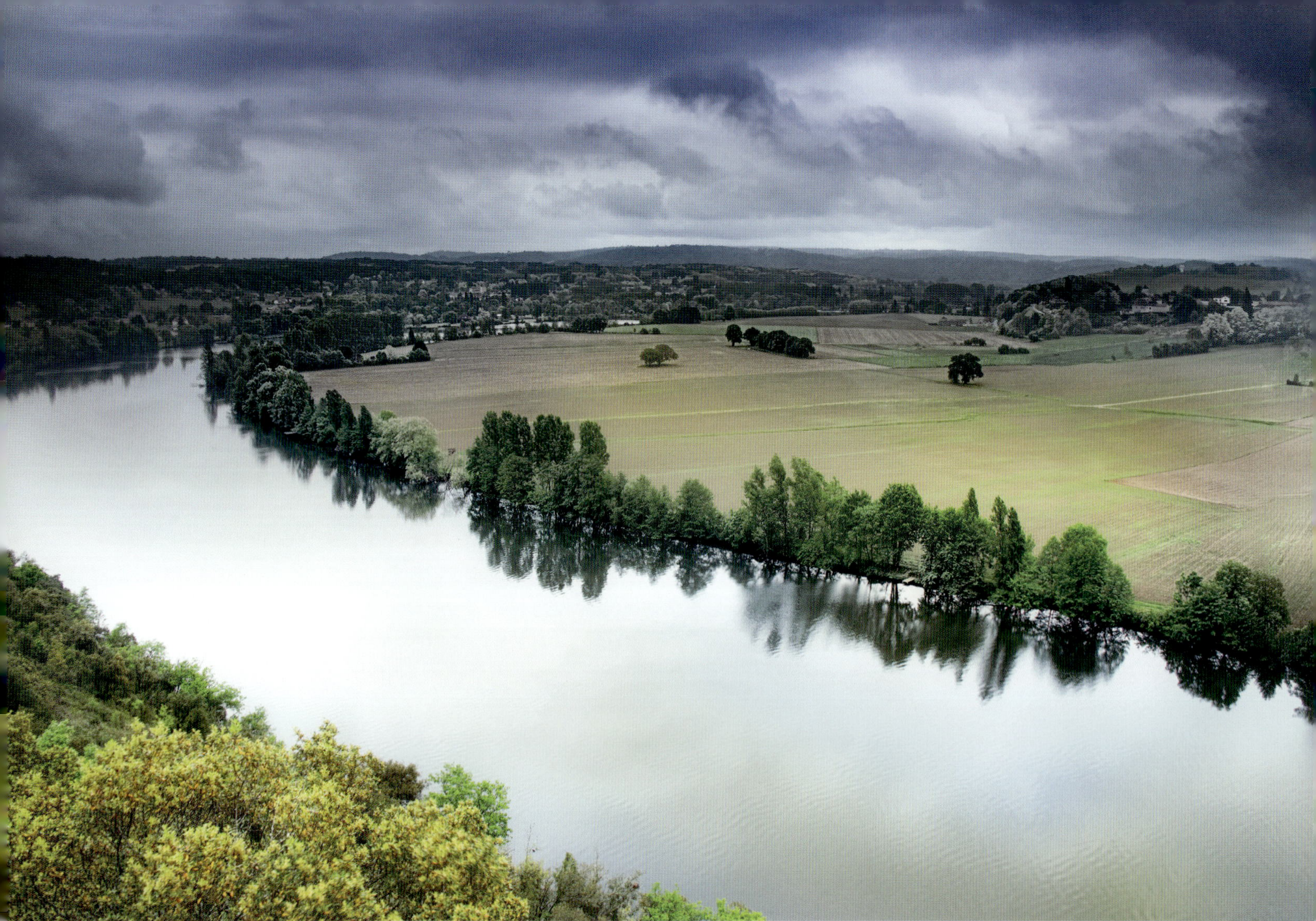

Bend in the River, Dordogne—Based in the ancient monastery town of Cadouin, France, I was exploring the surrounding countryside of the Dordogne. My hosts, who ran an organic strawberry farm, told me about an excellent hidden overlook above a bend in the Dordogne River. Apparently, this was not a very well-known spot, and would take a bit of effort to find.

On a bright but cloudy day with intermittent rain, I set out with my detailed Michelin map to try to find this location. Following my map and intuition through picturesque, cliffside villages, I came across the right spot, opposite an abandoned hotel. The tumble-down hotel building was gloomy and I couldn't see the river. I knew I was close, but didn't know which way to go until I noticed an unmarked trail leading away from the hotel's parking lot.

Setting out on the trail with my camera, backpack, and tripod, I found my way to the top of the bluff that my hosts had described to me. The storm was blowing in with large

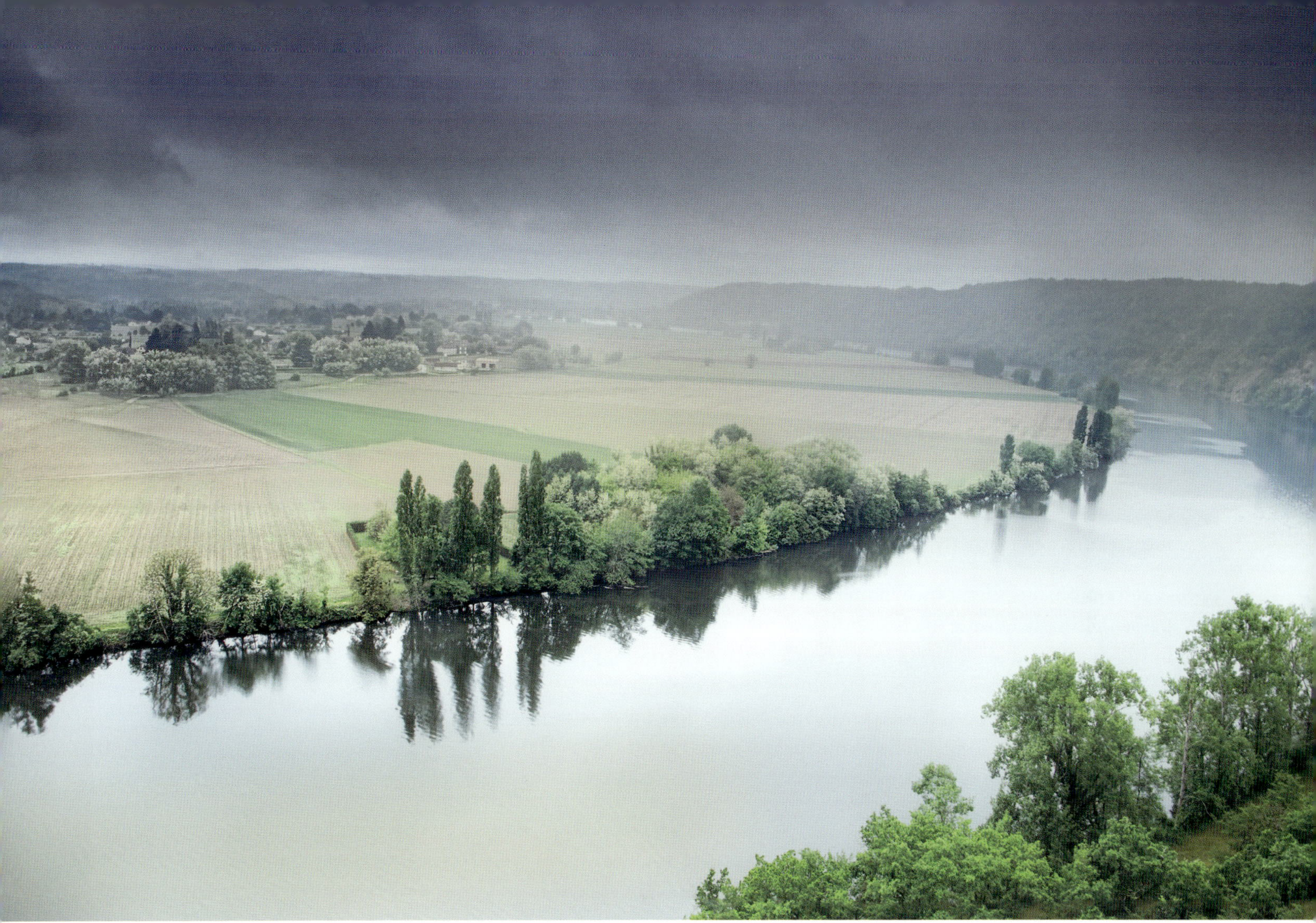

raindrops starting to fall on my camera and tripod.

To make this image, I ignored the rain and mounted my camera vertically on the tripod and photographed three sets of exposures. The idea was to stitch the bracketed sets together to make a panorama.

The panorama shows a wide-angle view, but without the distortion that an extreme wide-angle lens would give. There are three vanishing points, the most important one in the center of the image, roughly located where the camera was pointed. The other two vanishing points follow the curvature of the river with the view to left into the brighter sky, and the view to the right into the oncoming squall.

Nikon D800, 28-300mm Nikkor zoom at 28mm, three sets each of five bracketed exposure sets, each set with shutter speeds ranging from 1/125 of 1/8 a second, all exposures at f/11 and ISO 100, tripod mounted; bracketed sets merged into a panorama using Photoshop.

Refraction, Curvature, and the Perspective Model

It's a fundamental principle of photography that you cannot actually photograph an object. All you can photograph is the light reflected or emitted from the object. This implies that any model of perspective is using reflected or emitted light rather than the actual scene itself.

With it understood that one is capturing light, then it is clear that you can alter the perspective of almost anything if you can curve or bend the light. The most common way to play with light is to use reflection and refraction. A reflection mirrors existing light, and thus will create multiple perspective points if the camera is correctly positioned.

A refraction alters light by bending it. For example, when light passes through a bottle filled with liquid, the light within the bottle bends and any objects in the bottle, such as a spoon, will appear distorted. A curtain blowing in the breeze with shadows projected onto it follows normal perspective for the curtain, but no longer follows normal perspective for the shadows because they will appear curved (for an example, see pages 86–87).

Another example is a reflection in a curved surface, such as a building with large, curved panes of mirrored glass. The reflections in this building no longer follow normal rules of perspective and may show other buildings and scenery that wiggles across the glass. This mirrored scene in no way follows what we think of as normal perspective. The response is not to understand that this is an alternative projection, but rather to see it as a weird reflection.

When working in my studio, I often try to see what weird effects I can come up with using mirroring, curvature, and reflection. The odder the visual effect, the more impact the image has. This is true out in the wider world as well as in the studio.

Window on the Ancient Abbey— Exploring the historic and picturesque village of Conques in the southwest of France, my photography workshop group and I walked across the central square. While we were looking at the Abbaye Sainte-Foy de Conques, a World Heritage Site, some of us noticed a small wine bar across the way with a second-story window looking out on the square.

Checking in with the proprietor, we got permission to photograph from the window. I ran up the ancient, cramped stairs to the second floor, opened the windows, and was intrigued to notice the reflections on the left and right.

Setting up for this shot was a little nerve-racking because space was limited, there was a two-story drop out the window, and it was hard to position the tripod so it was stable in the space, and so that I was able to get exactly the right camera position. Notice how the towers at the top of each reflection are complete with a little bit of sky above them. I worked hard for this! Small movements of the camera position in this kind of situation have a huge impact on the final composition.

This image has three apparent vanishing points: the Abbaye straight ahead, and the two reflected church facades, one on the left and one on the right.

Nikon D800, 16mm Nikkor fisheye, seven exposures with shutter speeds ranging from 1/8,000 to 1/40 of a second at f/6.3 and ISO 200, tripod mounted.

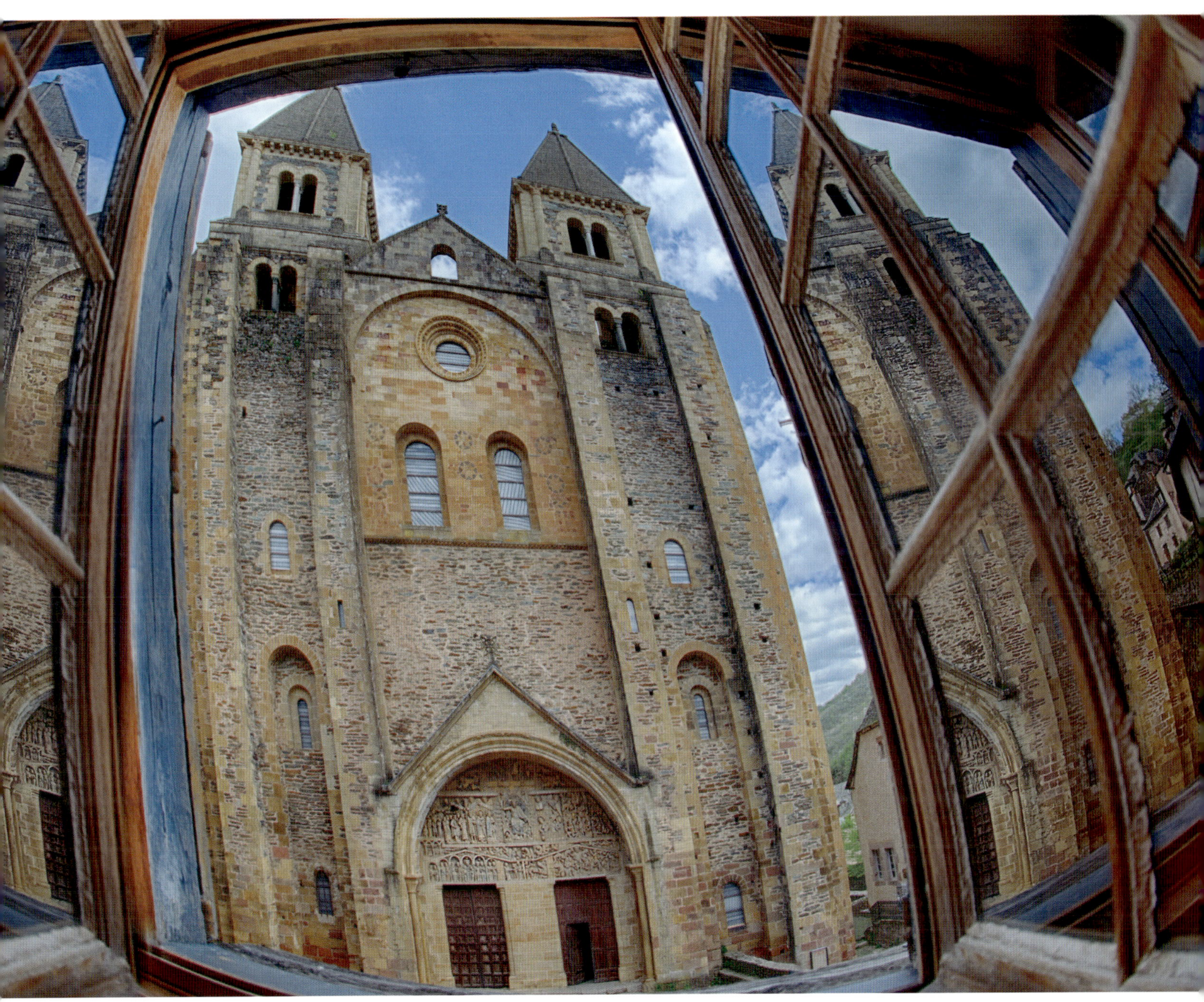

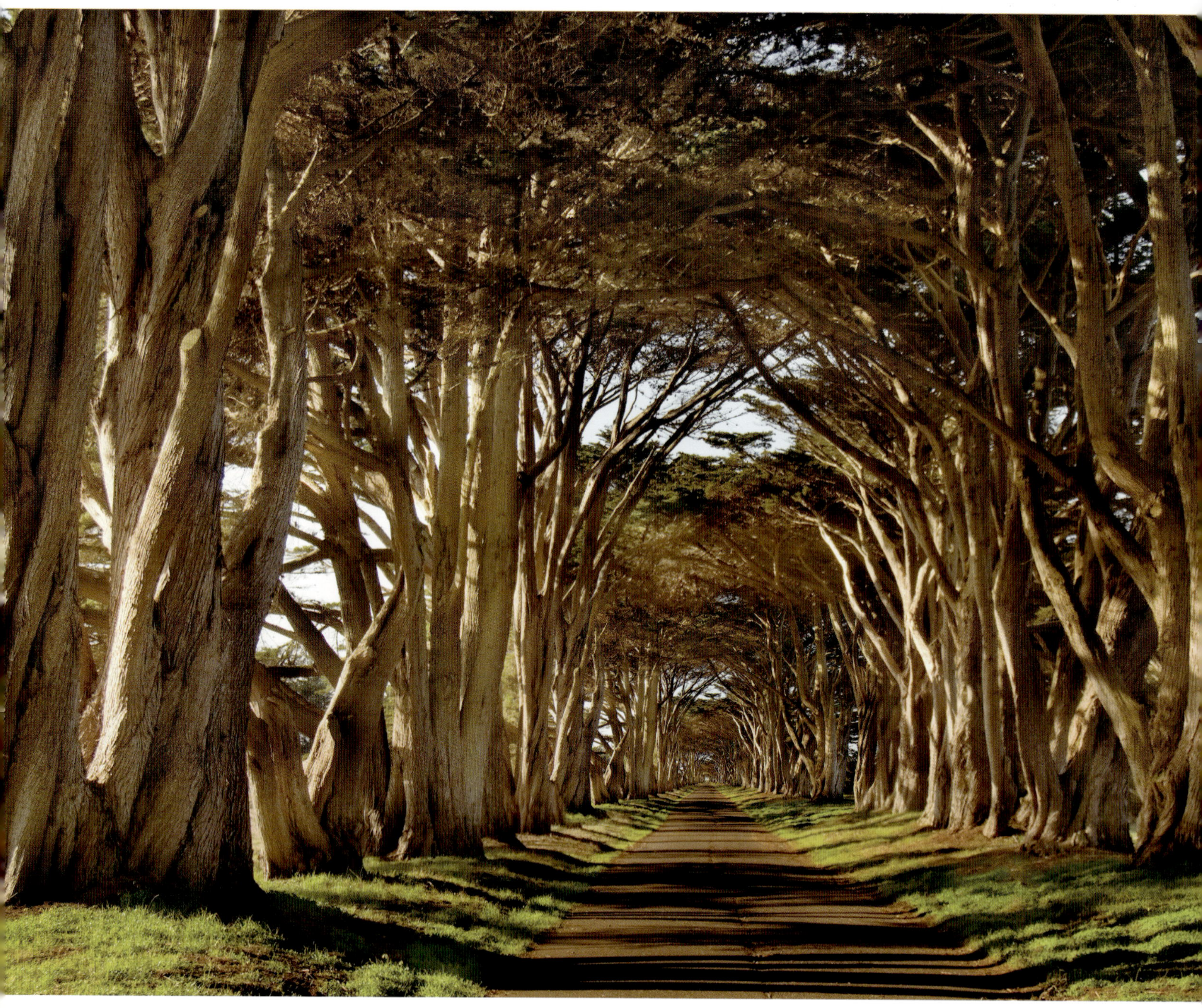

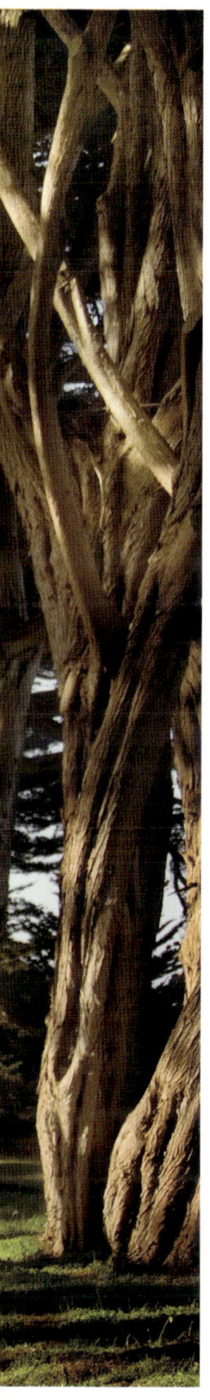

The Destination Recedes—This tunnel of Monterey cypress trees (*Cupressus macrocarpa*) leading away from the Marconi Station in Point Reyes National Seashore, California, presents an obvious single vanishing point. Don't be fooled! True, the vanishing point following a road down a row of trees is likely to be a great example of single-point perspective.

In this case, I took the single-point perspective and extended it to the max. Let me explain!

In the actual row of trees you can see the end of the aisle about 2/3 of the way down the road. There, the tunnel of trees opens to the sky. I composited the image with a resized version of itself several times, placing each successive reduced image in the center of the image further down. This creates an illusion of a tree-lined vanishing point that seems to go on an impossible distance.

In some sense, this is a double-fractal image. Not only did the trees grow in a fractal fashion, but also my extension of the vanishing point was created using fractals (to find out more about fractals, turn to page 128).

If you look at the magnification on the upper right, you'll see that it appears almost the same as the entire image. In fact, this portion of the image is actually a small area of the original image, as shown in the diagram at the lower right.

Nikon D300, 18-200 Nikkor zoom at 40mm, 1/250 of a second at f/6.3 and ISO 100, hand held; composited with itself in Photoshop.

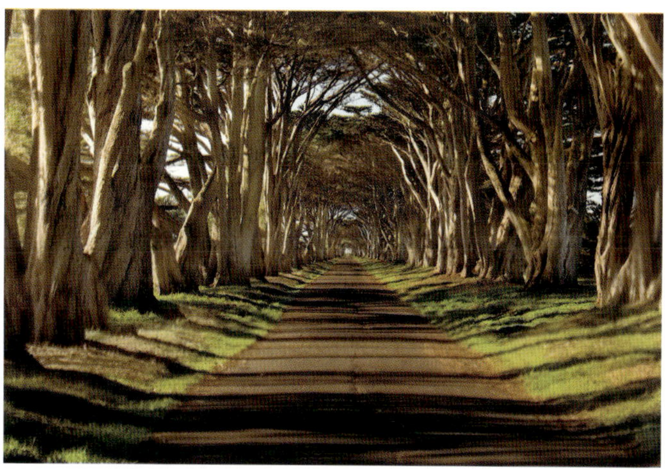

The image shown above is not the original image that you see to the left! It is a small, magnified portion of the image.

At first glance, this magnification looks like the original. Look hard to find the differences. The vanishing point is the same in both images. Does this also remind you of fractals? For more about fractals, turn to page 128.

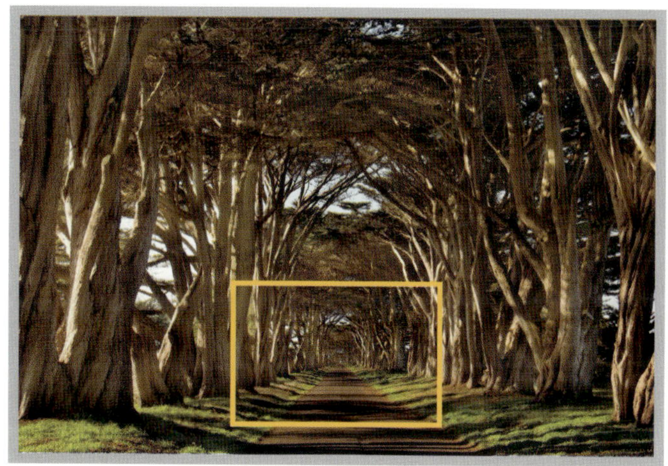

The yellow rectangle shows the area from where the magnified version (top) of the original image was taken. Proportionally, it is the same as the original image (left).

Changing Perspective in Post-Production

Last but not least, it is possible to change perspective using Photoshop or other post-production tools. The advantage of changing perspective in post-production is essentially that the sky is the limit. You can modify all aspects of the perspective in your image as much as you want.

The disadvantages of modifying perspective in post-production are that it is surprisingly difficult to pull off with *élan*, and the results are all too likely to look artificial, faked, and "Photoshopped." It's often best to look for situations where what you are doing is enhancing or modifying reality, rather than creating from scratch.

One of my favorite techniques for modifying perspective in post-production involves duplicating an image, horizontally or vertically mirroring the duplicate, and then using portions of the mirrored duplicate to composite with the original image.

In addition, many photo-manipulation software tools allow you to alter perspective. For example, Photoshop's Edit ▸ Transform menu provides a number of tools that can be used to alter the perspective in an image. These tools include Distort, Perspective, Skew, and Warp.

Photo-manipulation tools, such as the transformation tools in Photoshop, allow the image manipulator to alter perspective in a variety of ways either locally, for a portion of an image, or globally, for an entire image.

KEY IDEAS

- Positioning vanishing points in an image is extremely important. Experiment! Keep your eyes open and have fun!

- When it comes to perspective, slight shifts in camera position can make a huge difference.

- Generally, you want to move the camera position in the opposite direction from the direction you want the vanishing point in an image to shift. If you want the vanishing point higher up, move the camera down, if you want it more to the right, move the camera left, etc.

- Look beyond single-point perspective!

Quad—This is an evening photograph of covered pedestrian arcades at Stanford University in Palo Alto, California. The walkways presented two corridors meeting at a right angle, which lent themselves to a two-point perspective image when I used a fisheye lens.

My tripod was located behind a puddle from recent rains. As I looked at the scene, it occurred to me that if only the puddle were bigger and reflections more complete, I would have four vanishing points.

Voila! No sooner said than done. Well, not quite. I spent some time working in Photoshop. First, I duplicated the original image, flipped it horizontally, and then rotated it. Carefully combining portions of the duplicate with the original to be as seamless as possible, I created the full image with four vanishing points that you see here.

Nikon D300, 10.5mm Nikkor fisheye, 2 seconds at f/20 and ISO 100, tripod mounted; composited with itself in Photoshop.

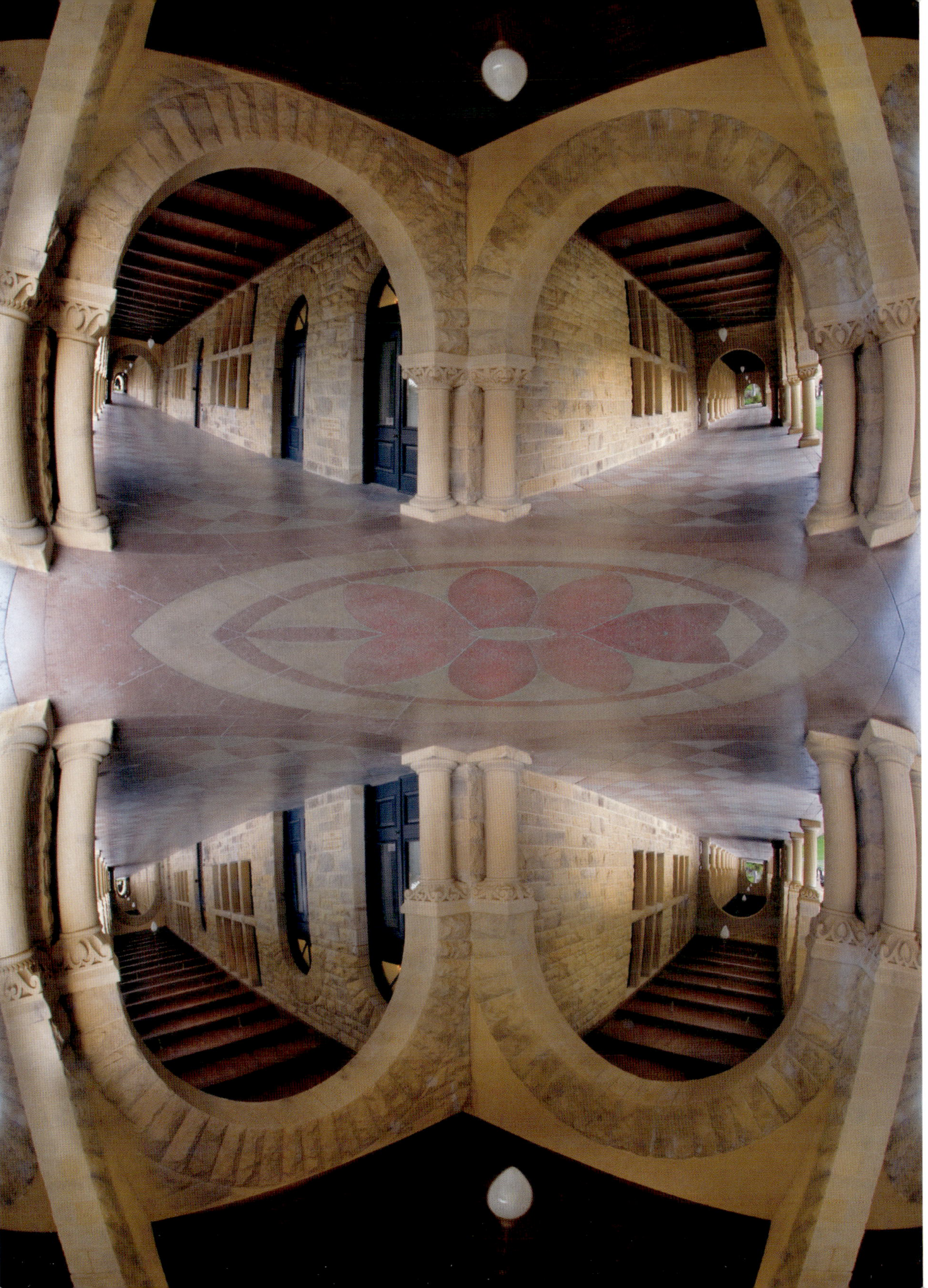

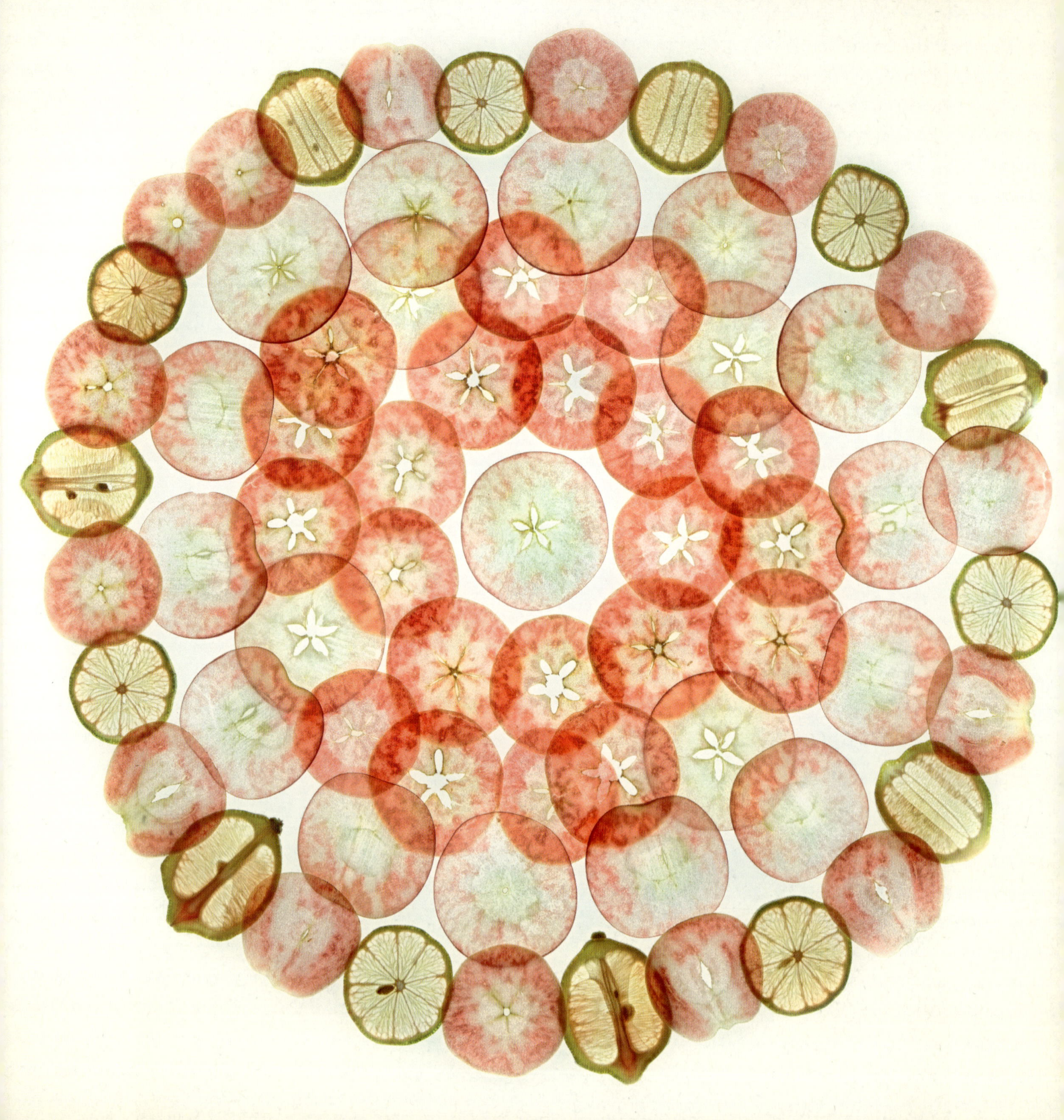

SYMMETRY & ASYMMETRY

"Tyger Tyger burning bright,
In the forests of the night:
What immortal hand or eye,
Dare frame thy fearful symmetry?"

—*William Blake*

Lady Pink Apple Slices with Lemons—When I made this image, I was spending much of my creative time photographing slices of fruits and vegetables on my light box. I was lucky enough to score some beautiful Pink Lady apples and a few variegated pink lemons.

One of the most difficult things about photographing backlit fruit slices is cutting them thin enough. To achieve this, I used a mandoline food slicer. If you try this at home, please be very, very careful!

I started with the apple slice in the center of the image. This slice itself shows partial symmetry around a vertical medial axis. From the central slice, I enlarged the composition using radial symmetry, trying to keep a pattern of colors so that the symmetry was in balance. Since each slice of fruit is necessarily different, symmetry of this kind of subject matter can only be approximate. The viewer takes in the partial symmetry, and perceives it as mostly symmetrical to see the pattern as a whole.

The final image delivers a symmetrical pattern that is reminiscent of a flower or a mandala.

Nikon D850, 50mm Zeiss Makro-Planar, eight exposures with shutter speeds ranging from 1/60 of a second to 4 seconds, each exposure at f/14 and ISO 64, tripod mounted.

One of the most important organizing principles of life, the universe, and everything is symmetry. As Michio Kaku puts it, "To a physicist, beauty means symmetry and simplicity."

What's true for a physicist also applies to the visual arts. Graphic designer Darrin Crescenzi speaks of the "unique visual tension between comforting symmetry and compelling asymmetry." Crescenzi believes that the "thoughtful application [of this tension] can bring beauty and harmony and intrigue to all manner of designed things."

This chapter explores what it means to be visually symmetrical, and the different kinds of visual symmetry. Symmetry can apply to an entire frame, or proportionally to part of an image.

Visual symmetry occurs frequently and often in some kinds specific kinds of shapes, such as mandalas and spirals.

When we think of symmetry, most often we think of *bilateral symmetry*—symmetry along two sides of a median axis, so that there are two halves, one on each side of the axis. In addition to bilateral symmetry along a horizontal or vertical axis, *radial symmetry* and *reflective symmetry* are also important to the photographer.

Symmetry—or lack thereof—also has some rather unexpected consequences for photographs, and plays a role with the source of light, color balance, and more, depending upon the image.

What are the differences between symmetry and asymmetry, and how can asymmetry be exploited by the photographer? There's an automatic assumption that being asymmetric means being visually out of balance. Put another way, breaking symmetry causes a certain amount of tension. If so, how can this out-of-balance tension be exploited? Creating an asymmetric image that seems balanced is a neat trick to pull off, but it can be done.

Ultimately, the image maker needs to realize that symmetry is important to viewers. Symmetry can be used as tool to draw the viewer in, and to add emotional emphasis.

In science, symmetry is seen as an important organizing basis for life that helps enforce simplicity. As visual artists, perhaps it makes sense to look at symmetry similarly, and regard symmetry and partial symmetry as helpful organizational constraints.

Plaça d'Espanya, Barcelona—Built on the occasion of the 1929 International Exposition, the Plaça d'Espanya is one of the most important public spaces in Barcelona. Located at the foot of Montjuïc, this is a grand public square with a central statue designed by a collaborator of Antoni Gaudi, a bull ring, and two mammoth Venetian towers that were the entrance to the exposition.

Photographing the Plaça d'Espanya presented me with a bit of a problem, as I didn't just want to make a documentary image. What I found striking were the modern buildings that surrounded all the pomp-and-circumstance architecture from the last century.

Before deciding to just photograph the central monument, I took a moment to take stock of the situation. Looking around me, I turned 180 degrees away from the Gaudi-esque monument. Rather than aiming my camera directly at the statue, I decided to capture the contrast between the reflections of the elaborate statue and a stark, modern building on one side of the square. It seemed to me that the contrast was the most interesting photographic subject in the area and I was particularly intrigued by the partial symmetry between the two reflected images.

I was very pleased to discover that I was able to frame an image that showed two different reflections of the tower in the center of the square. Best of all, these two reflections were interspersed with the modern masonry of an office tower.

Framing this image with its symmetry of both the reflections and the panels of the modern building required me to be in exactly the right place and pay close attention to the camera position.

Nikon D810, 28-300mm Nikkor zoom at 190mm, circular polarizer, 1/160 of a second at f/8 and ISO 400, hand held.

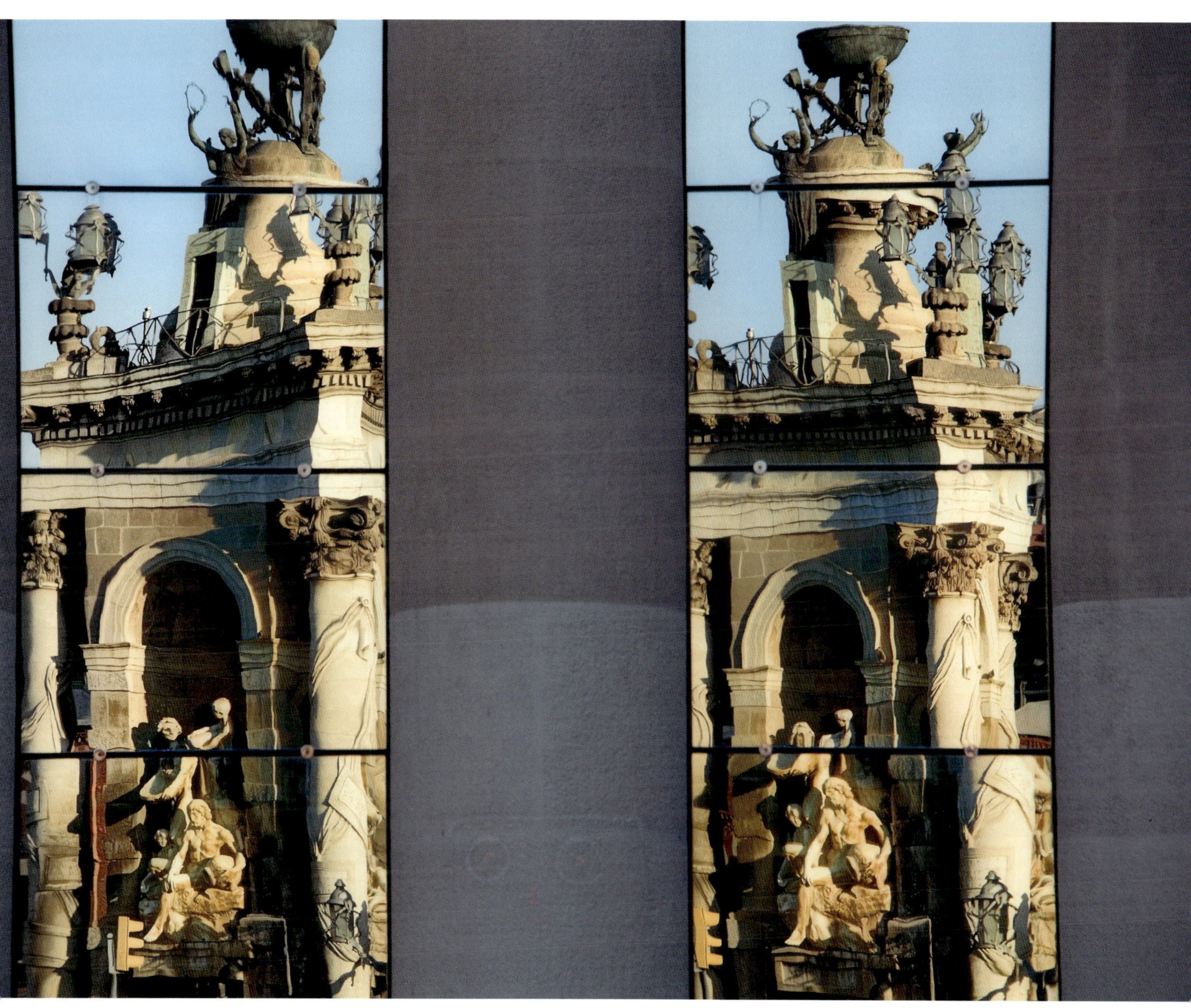

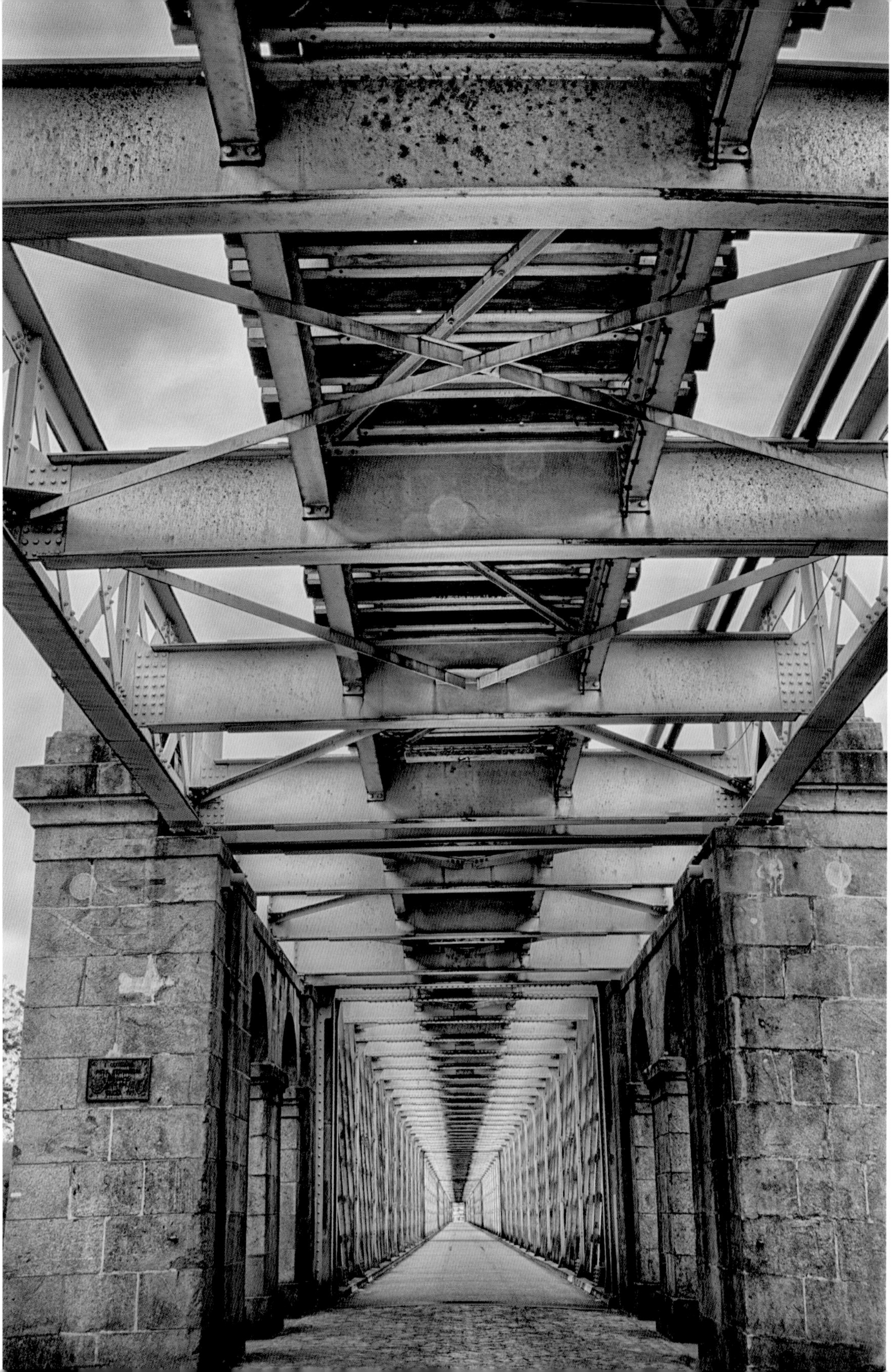

Kinds of Symmetry

The world contains a lot of symmetry. It's almost a given that any particular photographic frame will contain some symmetry or near-symmetrical elements. You really can't avoid symmetry even if you want to—and why would you want to?—because symmetry, longing for symmetry, absence of symmetry, and asymmetry help provide the spice that makes the visual world interesting.

Once we're clear that symmetry will almost always be involved, it makes sense to identify the most important kinds of symmetry. They are:

Lower Deck—The Ponte Rodo-Ferroviária de Valença crosses the River Minho from Tui in Galicia, Spain, to Valença, Portugal. It is a double-decker, cast-iron bridge with train tracks on top and room for cars and foot traffic on the lower deck—sometimes pedestrians have to scramble out of the way of the cars, and traffic is mostly one way at a time.

I positioned the camera on the tripod precisely in the center of the road. Every time a car came by, I had to grab the camera and tripod and scamper to safety. If you try something like this, please be very careful!

Bridges, particularly those constructed of cast iron, are often highly symmetrical constructions (for another example, turn to page 57). With this composition, I worked hard to emphasize the bilateral symmetry running on both the horizontal and vertical axes. It is asymmetrical only in a few areas; for example, the pattern of the train tracks above is not exactly symmetrical with the paved roadway below.

Nikon D850, 28-300 Nikkor zoom at 35mm, four exposures with shutter speeds ranging from 1/30 to 0.4 of a second, each exposure at f/25 and ISO 64, tripod mounted.

- *Vertical symmetry*: This is usually along a vertical axis, often the median axis.

- *Horizontal symmetry*: Usually along a horizontal axis, often the median axis.

- *Radial symmetry*: Most often seen in compositions that involve circles, spirals, or fractals.

- *Reflective symmetry*: Often involving mirrors, reflections in water, and shadows. This kind of symmetry flips the subject in a mirror-like fashion.

A key issue with vertical and horizontal symmetry is where the axis falls. When the axis is close to the center of the image, the symmetry is considered *bilateral*. Horizontal and vertical symmetry that is not bilateral is sometimes called *proportional* symmetry.

Composition and Symmetry

From a compositional viewpoint, the most important thing that the photographer can do is to consider the placement of the axis. When this axis is perpendicular to the image frame, then the symmetry is bilateral. Once the angle of the axis is no longer exactly at 90 degrees to the border frame, then the symmetry becomes proportional, and can quickly begin to verge on asymmetry.

As in some other aspects of photographic composition, the details of positioning the camera in relationship to the subject have a huge impact on the rendition of symmetry. So keep this in mind as you are composing your image.

If you intend the image to be symmetrical along an axis, like *Lower Deck*, shown on page 183, then you need to position yourself smack-dab in the middle of the road, even at the possible risk of being run over (as I did).

On the other hand, if you are trying to create a radically asymmetric image, then you should go for it! Don't even put up a pretense of symmetry, and position the camera off to one side of the image, perhaps along an image entry point. (For more about entry and exit points, turn to page 136.) Small camera movements can make a big difference when it comes to symmetry.

Radial Symmetry

With radial symmetry, the elements of the image circle around an important element. What is this element? Why is it important? What is the radial pattern surrounding the central element?

Keep in mind that—with the possible exception of floral work—radial symmetry is relatively rare, and therefore special.

In nature, flowers almost always exhibit radial symmetry. Spirals, such as those that make up the matter of the universe, are exercises in radial symmetry. Domes are an architectural application of radial symmetry. Some examples of radial symmetry include mandalas, such as *Lady Pink Apple Slices* on page 178 (for more about mandalas, turn to page 49), flowers, such as the *Coreopsis* on page 197, and the *Galleria Vittorio Emanuele II* shown opposite.

Approaching radial symmetry with a camera, it's important to behold and acknowledge the full extent of the symmetrical design. One strategy is to embrace a full circle; perhaps, the edges of the circle almost brush the inner border frame and are tangent to the border.

In some other cases, a circle may be too vast to capture in its entirety. The idea here would be to capture enough of the circle, perhaps a quarter of a turn, so that the entire circle is "completed" mentally by the viewer. The circle has been implied and strongly suggested but has not been shown in its entirety. For an example, take a look at *Bottle Light Study* on page 187.

Galleria Vittorio Emanuele II—Located across from the Duomo in Milan, Italy, the Galleria Vittorio Emanuele II is perhaps the world's oldest covered shopping mall. The central octagonal space, shown in the image here, is topped with a glass dome.

Walking through the Galleria, staring up at this cast-iron marvel, I was struck by the incredible amount of symmetry in the architecture. The dome itself exhibits radial symmetry, the buildings on each side are symmetrically designed, and the galleries attaching to the dome were designed in pairs. When I looked up I could see not only radial symmetry in the dome, but also bilateral symmetry along both horizontal and vertical axes of the gallery as a whole.

To capture this symmetrical view, I got down as close to the ground as I could among the rush of fashionable shoppers, and used a horizontal fisheye lens.

Nikon D810, 16mm Nikkor horizontal fisheye, 1/320 of a second at f/8 and ISO 640, hand held.

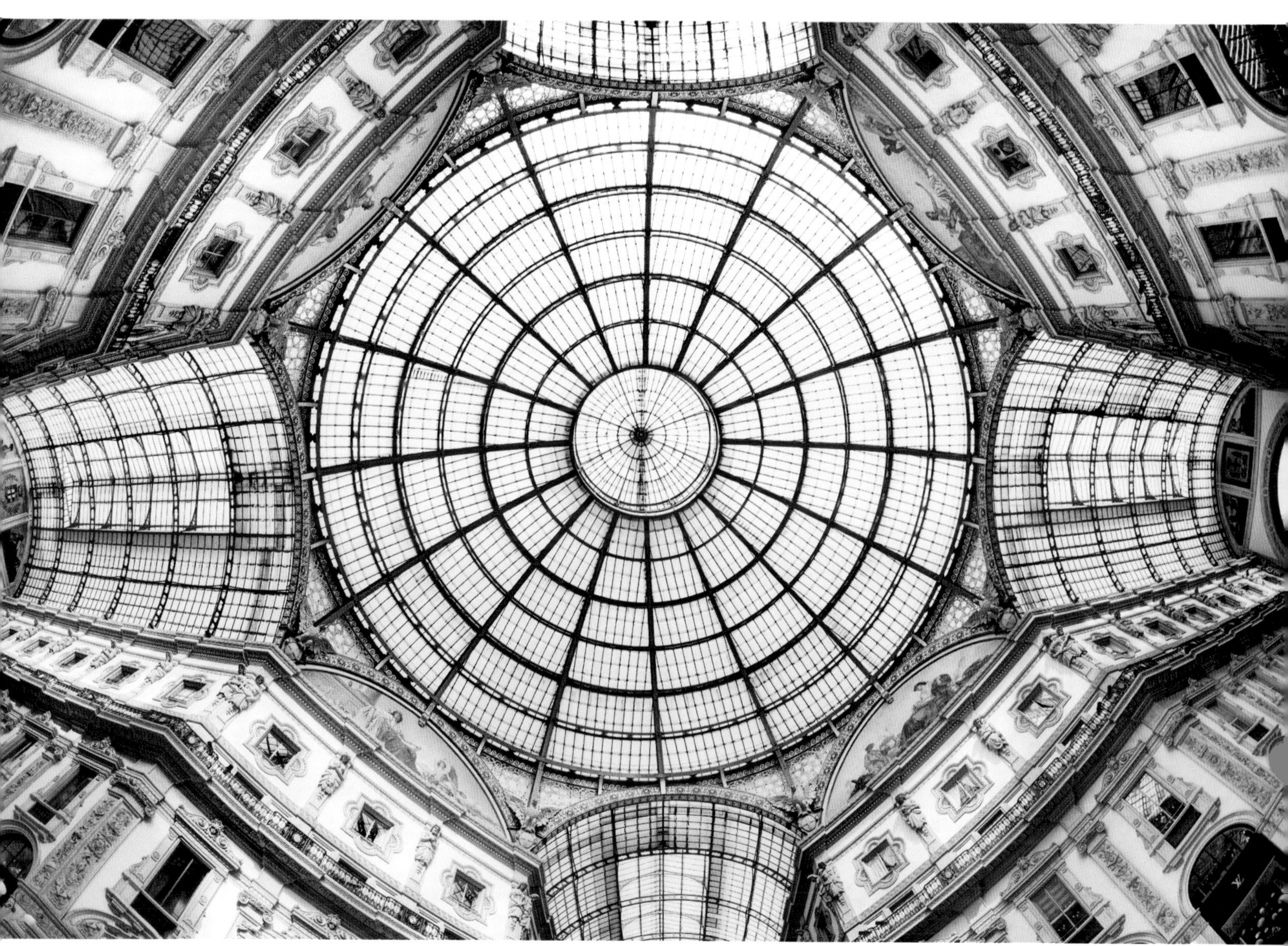

Symmetry and Reflection

A different and important kind of symmetry is reflective. Reflective symmetry is really common and can be spectacular when used correctly.

There are many surfaces that can create reflective symmetry—plate glass windows in a skyscraper, a puddle, polished marble, a mirror, and more. A common photographic subject that uses reflective symmetry involves a landscape reflected in a body of water. *Dawn on Lake Como* on pages 192–193 is one example of this.

Reflective symmetry is uniquely manipulable and in some cases can even be created by the photographer. I once knew a photographer, Julius Vitali, who carried a portable puddle around so he could create reflections wherever he wanted.

The best starting place for understanding reflections is the Fundamental Law of Reflection, which states that *the angle of reflection equals the angle of incidence* (see the diagram above). In other words, this means that incoming light bounces off a reflective surface and exits at the same angle in relationship to the surface at which it entered.

Understanding the Fundamental Law of Reflection helps you to time your reflective photographs by waiting for the sunlight to hit a reflective surface such as lake or river at the right time.

To increase the amount of reflection, you can move the camera position as necessary to be located at the angle that corresponds to the angle of incidence. Putting this another way, if you want

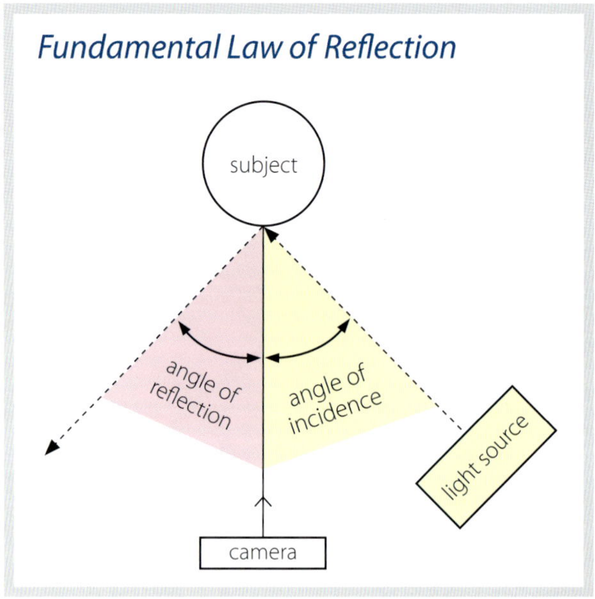

Bottle Light Study—This image shows sunlight coming through a small glass bowl with blue-colored water in it. I used a Lensbaby to make the capture. The Lensbaby is a specially designed optic that presents the center as sharp and everything else as pleasantly out of focus when used (as here) wide open (at f/1.6).

The point of this image was to create an abstraction where the viewer doesn't necessarily know how the image was made (for more about abstractions, turn to page 210).

This image shows several different kinds of symmetry, as many images do. From an overall viewpoint, the viewer can assume that the radial pattern of light rays continues around the circumference of the bowl to create a complete circle. In addition, there is a symmetric and diminishing relationship between the progression of the individual light rays.

Nikon D850, 85mm Lensbaby Velvet, 1/500 of a second at f/1.6 and ISO 200, hand held.

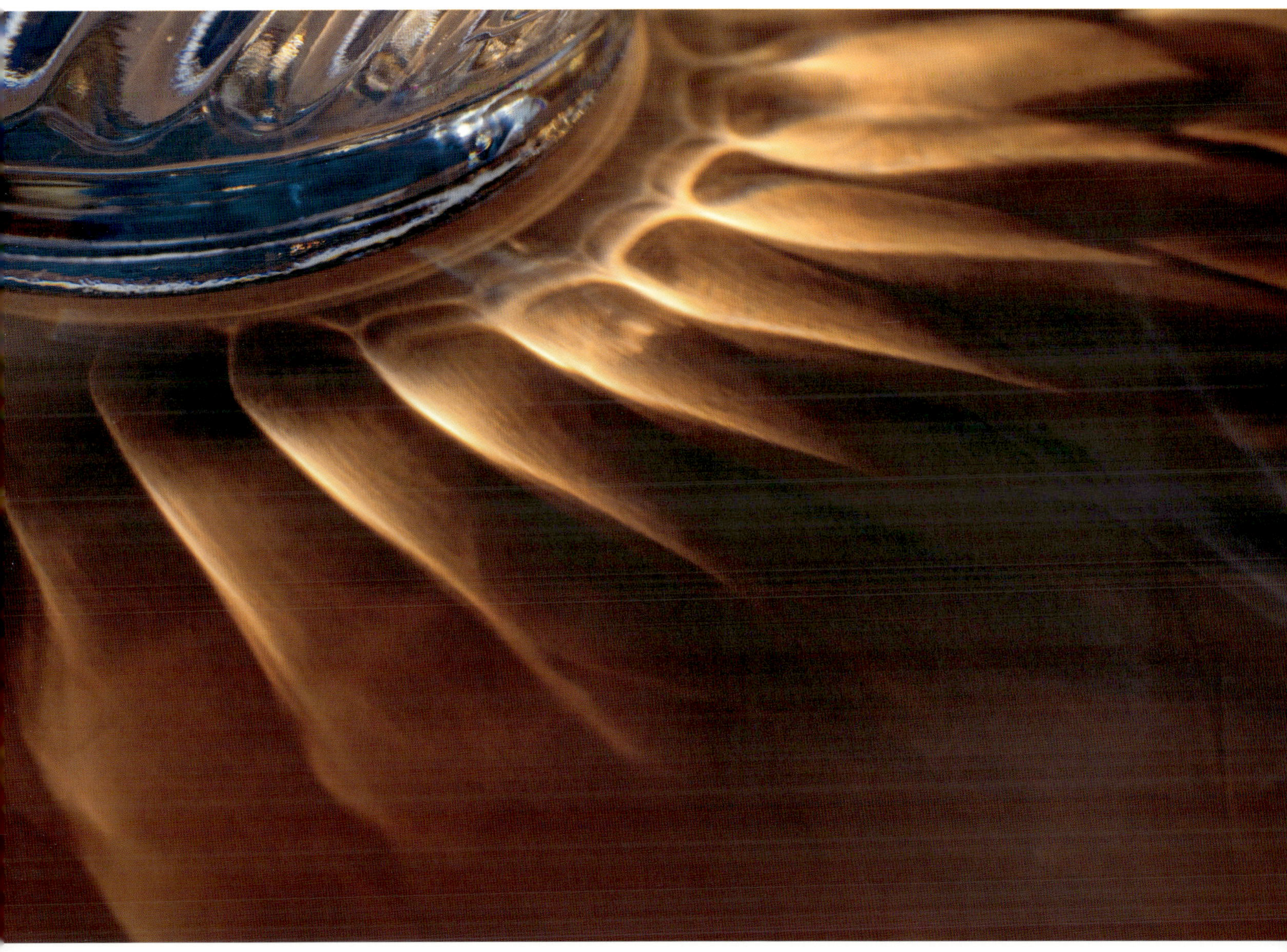

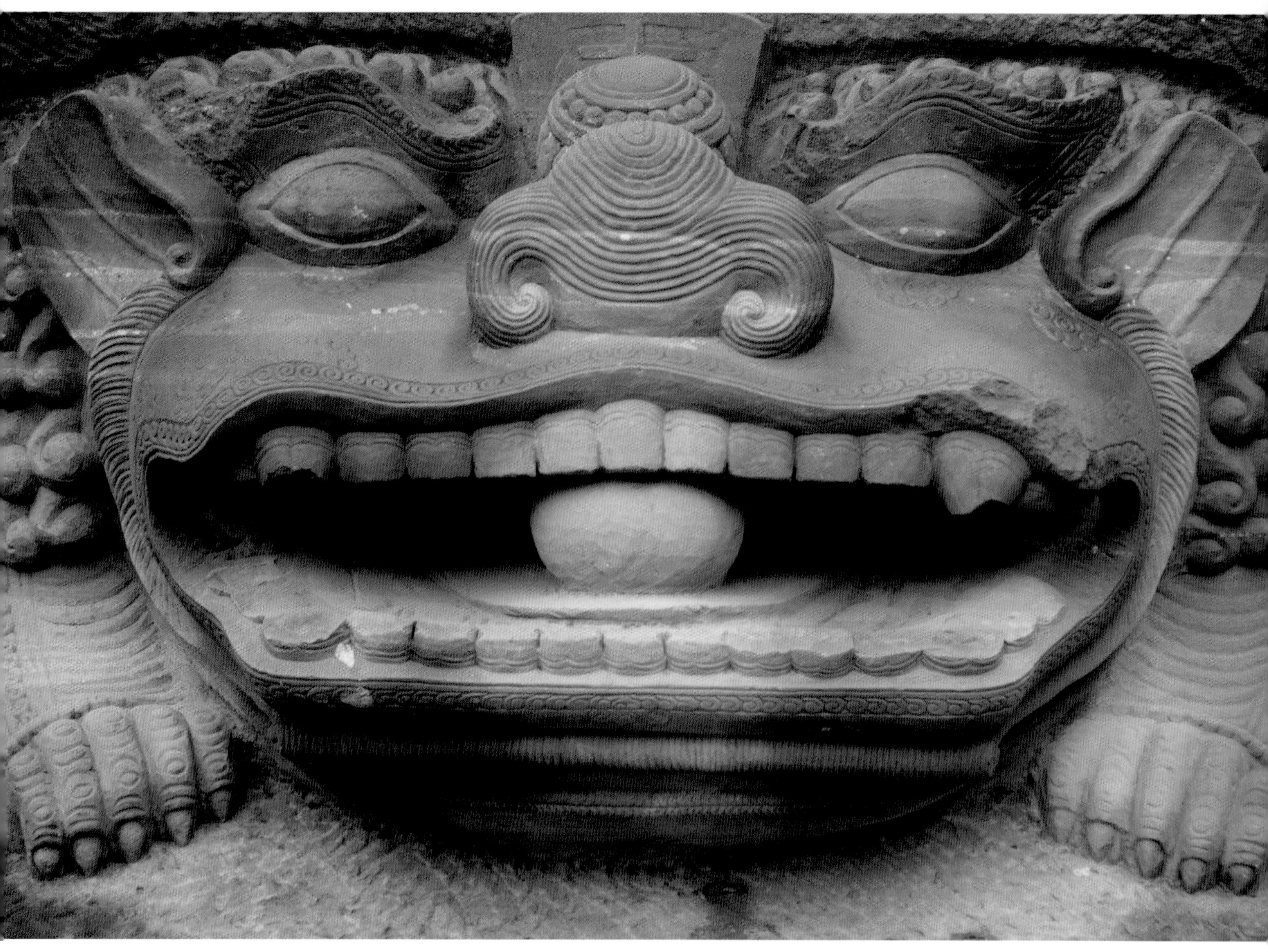

Thought Experiment

What would the world be like without symmetry? What would you see in this world without symmetry when you looked into a mirror? Would you have body parts in the wrong place like in a Picasso painting? Would everyone in this world have the vampire-like quality of being invisible when looking in a mirror?

Can you make a photograph that shows no symmetry, and completely ignores symmetry, and the possibility of symmetry?

Now, make a completely symmetrical image using a mirror or reflective surface. Can you change this image by taking one small element out to make an interesting asymmetrical image? Which element? How does making a small change impact the overall effect of reflectivity?

Making Faces—This photograph shows the sculpted face of a Vietnamese lion, taken from a Buddhist temple. I found this sacred lion on the grounds of the National Museum of Vietnamese History in Hanoi, Vietnam.

Like all faces, the face of this stone lion shows extensive symmetry. The primary symmetry in a face reflects around the vertical axis. As an example, we have two eyes that are fairly equidistant from the nose.

This stone lion additionally shows symmetry between the sharp-taloned paws, curly ears, and pretty much everything else. In addition, the prominent teeth are symmetrical across the horizontal axis that bisects the symbolic jewel in the lion's mouth.

Nikon D810, 28-300 Nikkor zoom at 125mm, 1/100 of a second at f/5.6 and ISO 400, hand held.

the most reflection in your photograph, then the angle of reflection should be as close as possible to the angle of incidence. Working backwards, you can get a good idea of the angle of incidence by looking at how the light strikes your subject. This should tell you how to position your camera at the angle of reflection.

Every subject has a surface. Another factor to consider is the surface's index of reflectivity. The greater the index of reflectivity, the more you will get perfect reflective symmetry. For example, a lake in the morning when the water is perfectly calm has close to 100% index of reflectivity, and the buildings on the shoreline will be symmetrically reflected in the water. On the other hand, if a squall blows in, and the surface of the water becomes disturbed and choppy with whitecaps and waves, then the index of reflectivity decreases to close to 0% and there will be no reflections.

Any partial reflections under stormy conditions may be attractive to photograph, but they will not be symmetrical because the distortion in the water surface will distort the reflections.

Also, a reflective surface can be curved—for example, convex and concave mirrors, and water drops. In this case, when conditions are right, you will see a reflection that has been distorted due to refraction. The refracted reflection will not be entirely symmetrical—in fact, it may be wildly asymmetrical—but it can be striking and interesting in a photographic composition. For instance, take a look at *Falling Flowers* on pages 92–93.

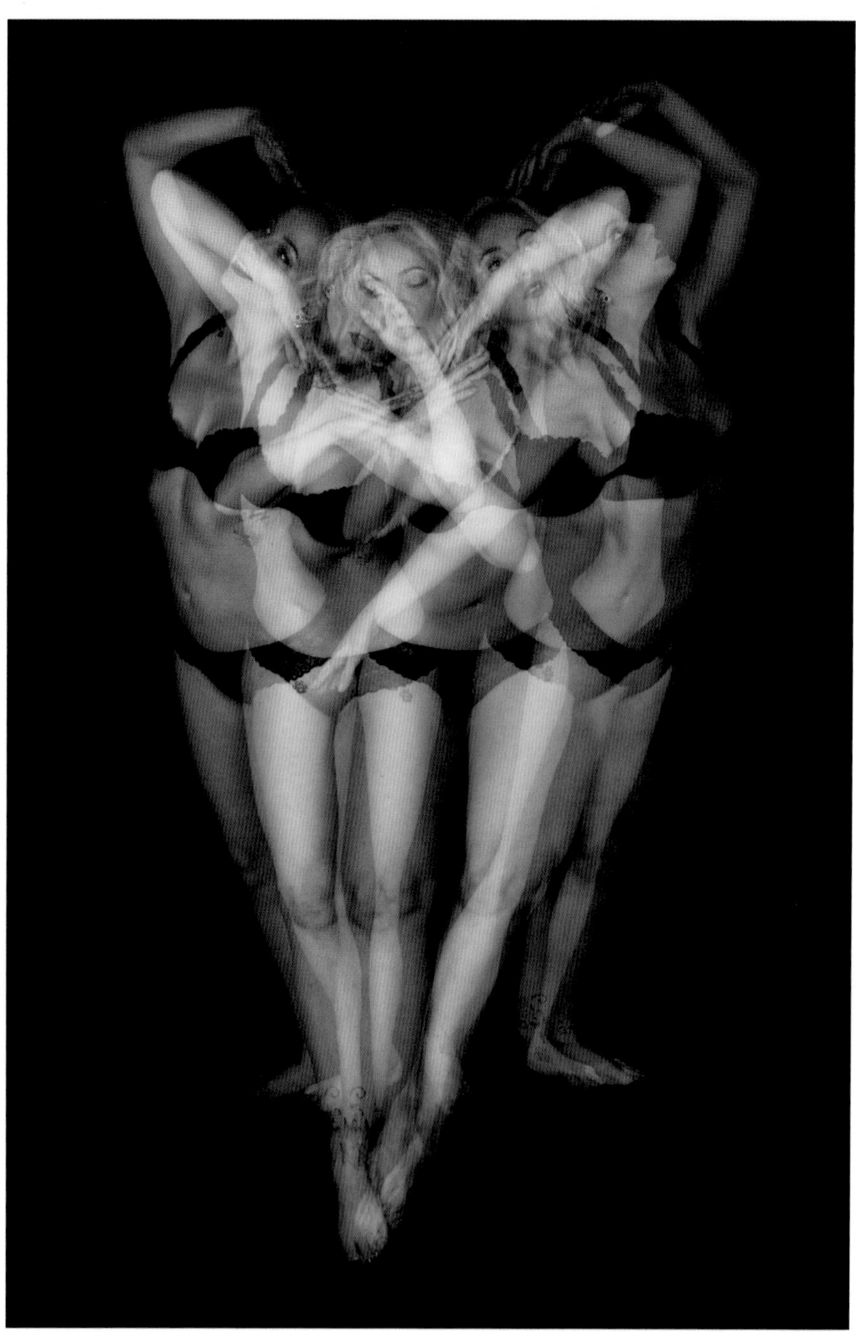

Left: *Vagaries of the Heart*
Right: *Near Symmetry*

With these in-camera multiple exposures, I clicked the shutter and fired the strobe each time the model moved into a new position. The model and I worked according to a plan to establish an outer shape. This shape would become the perimeter of the image.

With *Vagaries of the Heart*, on the left, we used five exposures to create the rough outlines of a heart. The partial symmetry here is along the vertical axis, and creates a mirroring effect.

With *Near Symmetry* to the right, the goal was to create a spiral shape, so this is an example of radial symmetry. In addition, there is also reflected symmetry from left to right over the vertical axis.

In both images, you can see examples of internal symmetry if you take a look at the models' gestures and apparel.

To some extent, these figure studies can be regarded as examples of abstraction (turn to page 210 for more about abstractions). An image of this sort works if the viewer visually connects with it. In this case, the symmetry embodied in each image is an important part of a successful composition.

Both: Nikon D810, 28-300mm Nikkor zoom, single in-camera multiple exposure at 1/160 of a second, tripod mounted.

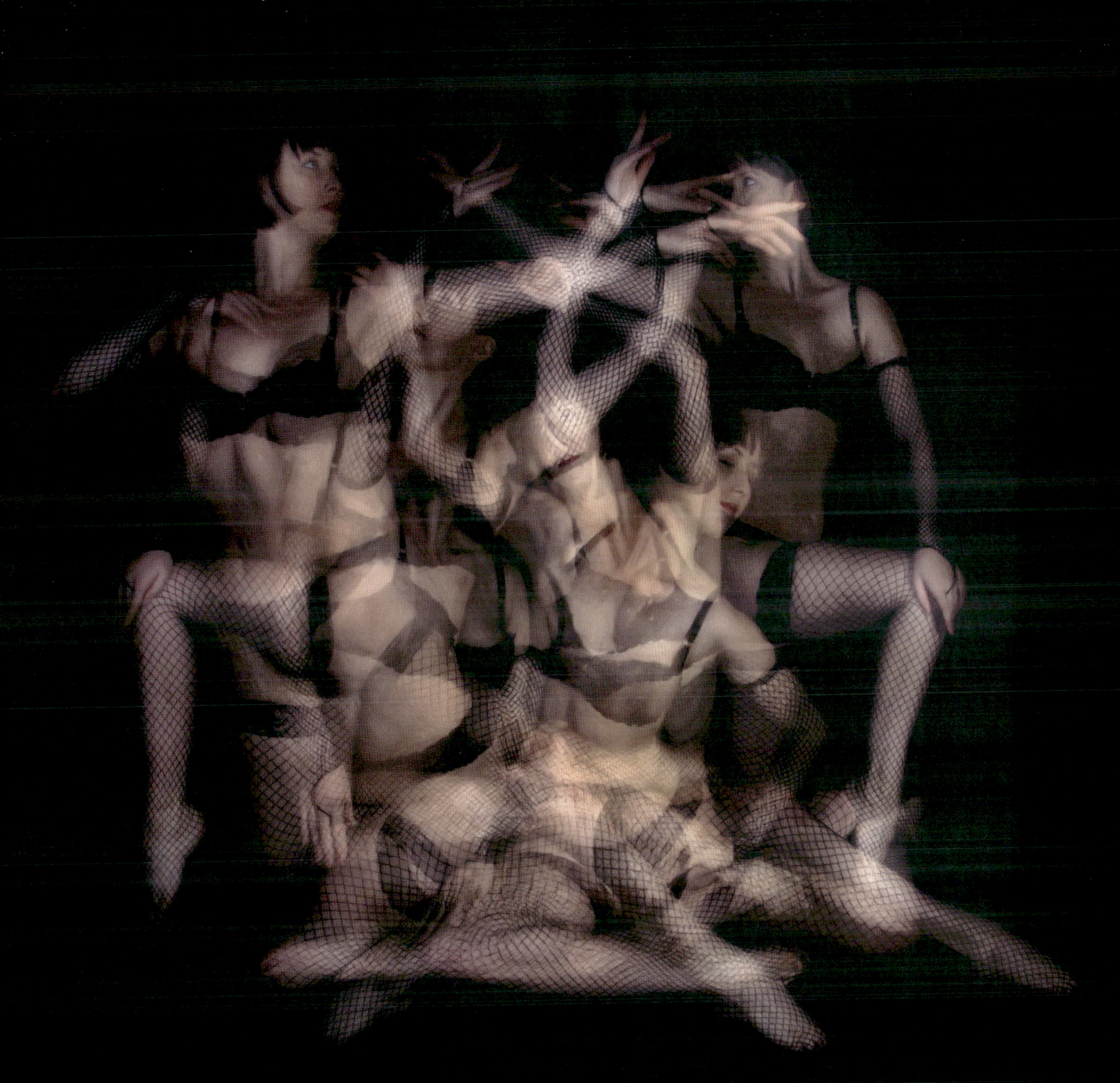

Using a Polarizer

When it comes to reflections, one important tool in the photographer's bag is the *polarizer*. A polarizer is a filter, also called a secondary lens, that fits at the end of the primary lens. The polarizer blocks some light from certain polarization angles, and allows other light to pass through it. There are two kinds of polarizers, *linear* and *circular*. A linear polarizer only allows horizontal or vertical light waves to enter the filter. Circular polarizers, which are usually better for photographic purposes, allow light waves that move in a circular direction to enter.

With a circular polarizer, there are two optical lenses sandwiched together. The outer optic rotates 360 degrees, compared to the inner optic, which is static once it has been affixed to the primary lens. As you rotate the outer optic, you change the effective angle of light that can enter and pass through the filter, an effect called *polarizing.* Perhaps you have seen this with polarized sunglasses: if you are oriented in the right direction, the sunglasses remove glare and reflection.

Having a circular polarizer mounted on a camera's lens means that you can rotate the polarizer to cut out the light frequencies you don't want and the emphasize the ones you do. This comes in handy when you are dealing with reflective water.

When you try it out on reflective water, depending on the angle of light striking the water, you can rotate the polarizer through almost complete transparency— meaning you can see down through the water—to almost complete opacity— which, depending on the conditions, emphasizes the reflections on the surface of the water. If the goal is to create an image with maximal reflective symmetry,

(continued on page 196)

Dawn on Lake Como—On a cold autumn morning in pre-dawn darkness, I found myself on the shores of Lake Como in Italy. I positioned myself across from the lights of the town of Lecco. As the sun rose, it became clear that the best position for the tripod was in shallow water. Shall we say that getting my feet soaking wet did not help to warm me up? But anything for a photo!

Like with many landscapes, reflective symmetry adds interest to this scene. It is particularly notable because of the soft luminescent blue of the predawn light.

In addition to the symmetry reflected along the shoreline of the lake opposite where I was positioned, the photograph shows some of the lake bed through the water. I used a polarizing filter to add clarity to the portion of the view through the water. The view of the lake bed adds compositional interest to the overall symmetry of the image.

Nikon D810, 28-300 Nikkor zoom at 28mm, circular polarizer, 3 seconds at f/8 and ISO 64, tripod mounted.

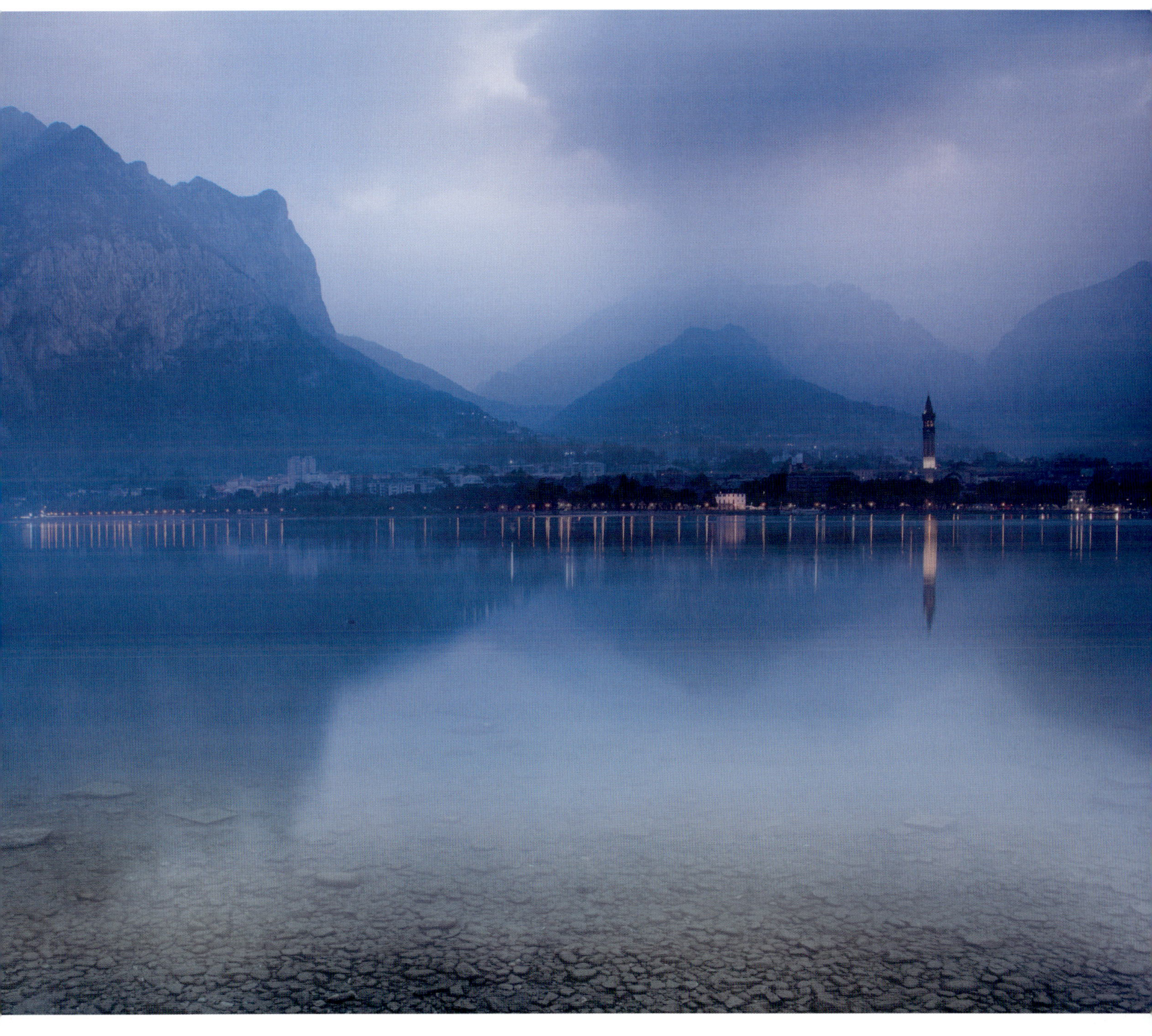

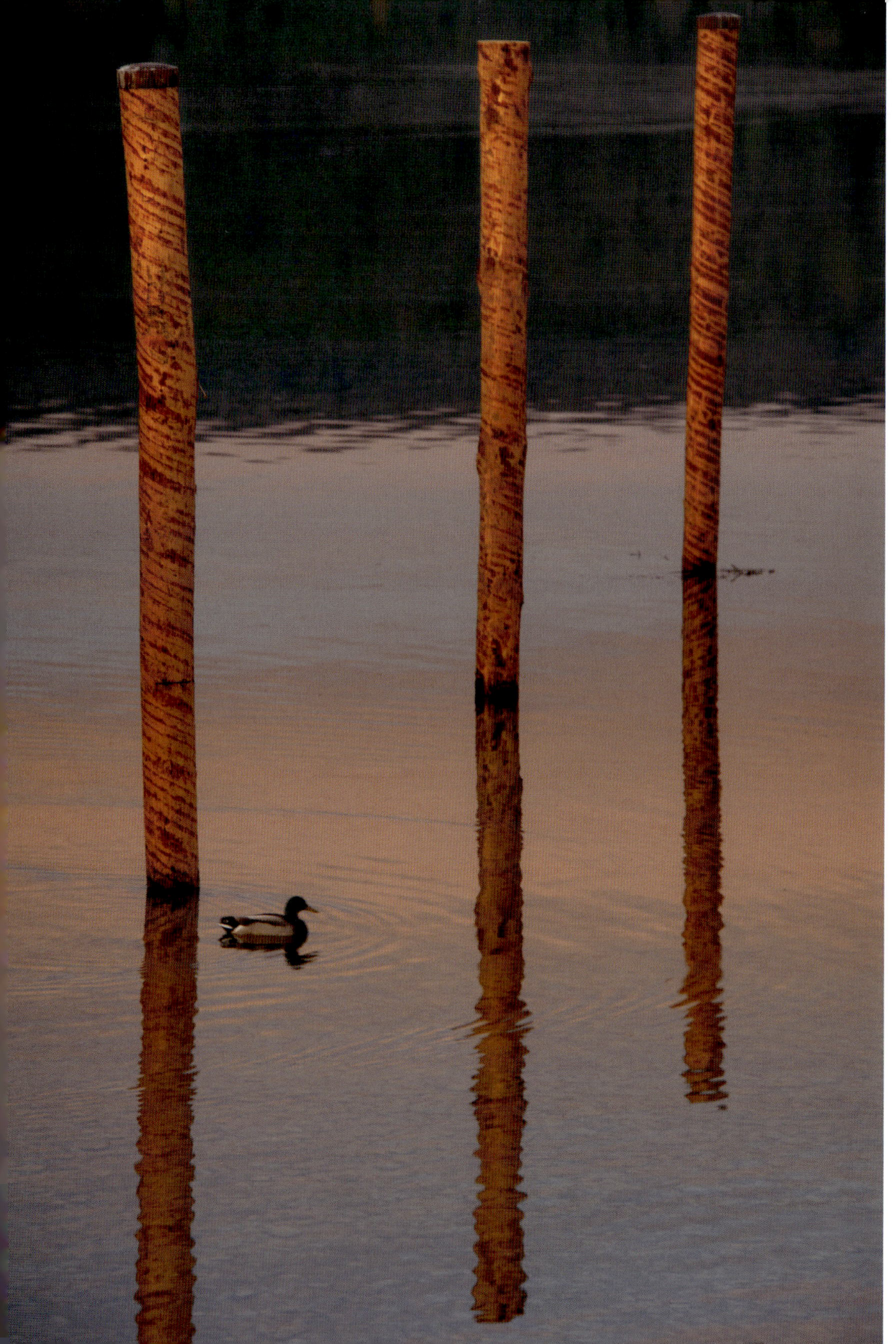

Reflections in the Untersee—
I photographed this composition with reflections on the shores of the Untersee, which is between Germany and Switzerland and is part of Lake Constance.

The image reads as a realistic scene either as shot, or when flipped upsidedown. In this way, I think of it as a visual palindrome.

A palindrome is a phrase that can be read backward and forward. Some examples are: *Madam I'm Adam*, *Able was I ere I saw Elba*, and *A man a plan a canal Panama*.

While my photographic palindrome works top to bottom and bottom to top, rather than left to right and right to left, I still think it is fun!

Can you determine which of the two images is the original? And, how can you tell for sure? For the answer, turn to page 237.

Nikon D850, 28-300 Nikkor zoom at 180mm, 1/13 of a second at f/8 and ISO 64, hand held.

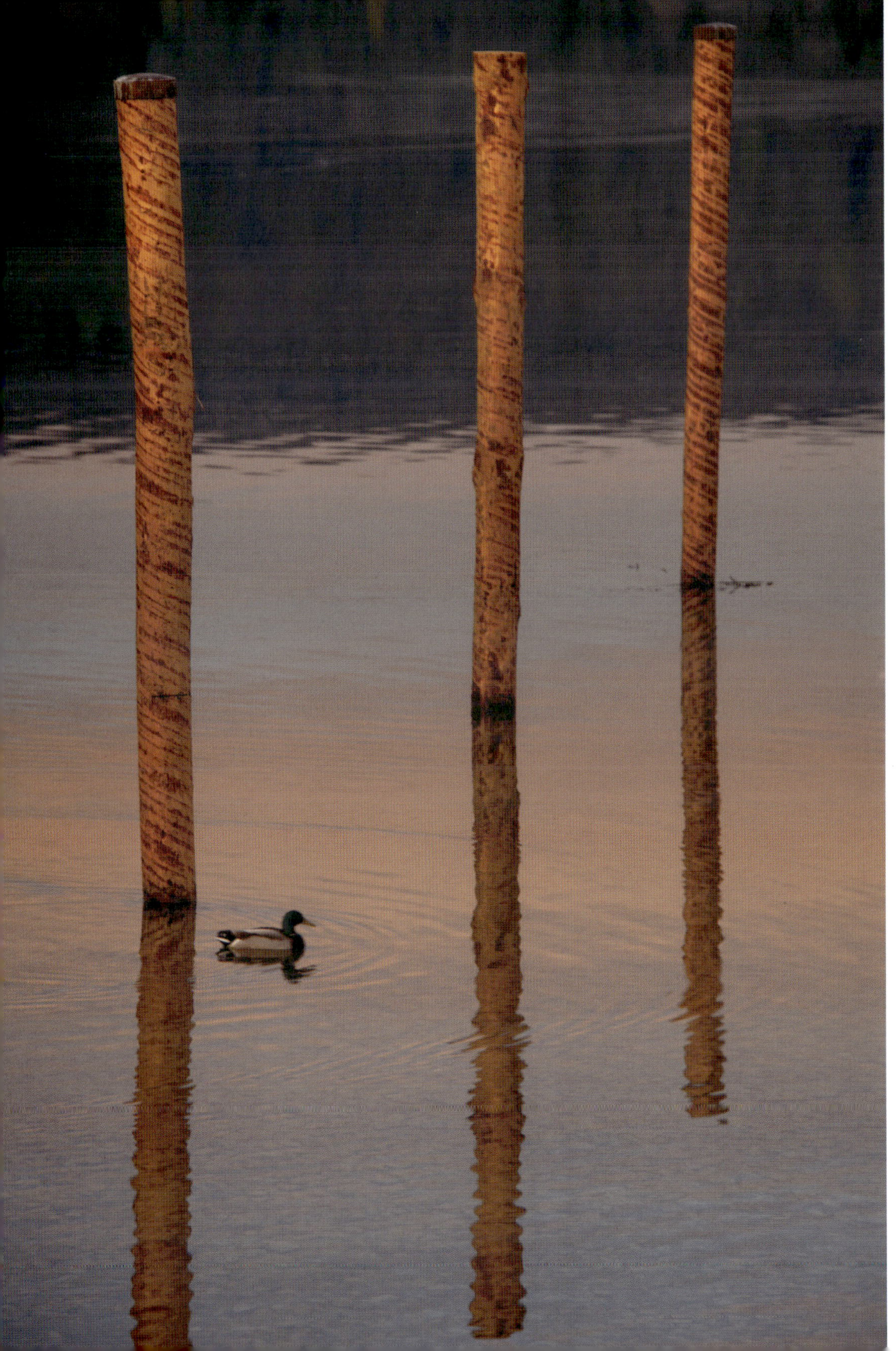

Reflections in the Untersee—
I photographed this composition with reflections on the shores of the Untersee, which is between Germany and Switzerland and is part of Lake Constance.

The image reads as a realistic scene either as shot, or when flipped upsidedown. In this way, I think of it as a visual palindrome.

A palindrome is a phrase that can be read backward and forward. Some examples are: *Madam I'm Adam, Able was I ere I saw Elba,* and *A man a plan a canal Panama.*

While my photographic palindrome works top to bottom and bottom to top, rather than left to right and right to left, I still think it is fun!

Can you determine which of the two images is the original? And, how can you tell for sure? For the answer, turn to page 237.

Nikon D850, 28-300 Nikkor zoom at 180mm, 1/13 of a second at f/8 and ISO 64, hand held.

(continued from page 192)

then you may want to use a circular polarizer to help with this effect. For a photographer interested in reflections, a polarizer is their best friend.

Keep in mind that a polarizing filter fits on the end of your lens and is therefore part of the optical setup that captures your photographs. If you are interested in photographing reflections, you should invest in an optically high-quality polarizer. Also, the thickness of the polarizer matters, because a polarizer that is too thick can lead to optical distortion and vignetting, particularly with wide-angle lenses.

Symmetry & Emphasis

Why is symmetry so important to us? To start with, for the most part we are symmetrical beings along a medial horizontal axis. We see the world in symmetrical patterns and seeing this symmetry helps us see the balance in things. We often recognize symmetry as an action that completes an image and will respond to symmetry in an image with an inner sigh of contentment.

Just as complete symmetry conveys satisfaction, breaking symmetry is a significant event that we notice. When an image is set up to be symmetrical but, in fact, is not entirely, it is a statement.

Symmetry can enhance a composition and lack of complete symmetry can call attention to portions of an image. Whatever your intentions are as an image creator, you should not ignore the potential of symmetry and asymmetry to create emphasis in your compositions.

KEY IDEAS

- The world around us is filled with symmetry. Kinds of symmetry include bilateral, radial, and reflective symmetry.

- Use the Fundamental Law of Reflection to guide you in positioning the camera relative to reflections.

- A polarizar can enhance reflective symmetry.

- Symmetry in an image can convey a sense of balance.

- Asymmetry is as important as symmetry and can convey unsettling emotions.

Coreopsis—The coreopsis is a small but mighty flower! Shown here, photographed on a light box, the symmetry of the irregularly shaped petals is radial and mirrored across the vertical and horizontal axes.

While many macro photographs of small flowers are intriguing, this image gets the viewer's attention because of the extensive symmetry involving irregularly shaped petals. All the petals are basically similar, but they are each uniquely patterned, colored, and variegated. Similarly, the spacing between the petals is close, but not exact.

It is noteworthy that at first glance this image seems highly symmetrical, but after studying it in detail, the viewer understands the natural and irregular aspects of the flower while still recognizing its symmetrical qualities.

Nikon D810, 85mm Zeiss Otus, 12mm extension tube, seven exposures with shutter speeds ranging from 1/4 of a second to 8 seconds, each exposure at f/16 and ISO 64, tripod mounted.

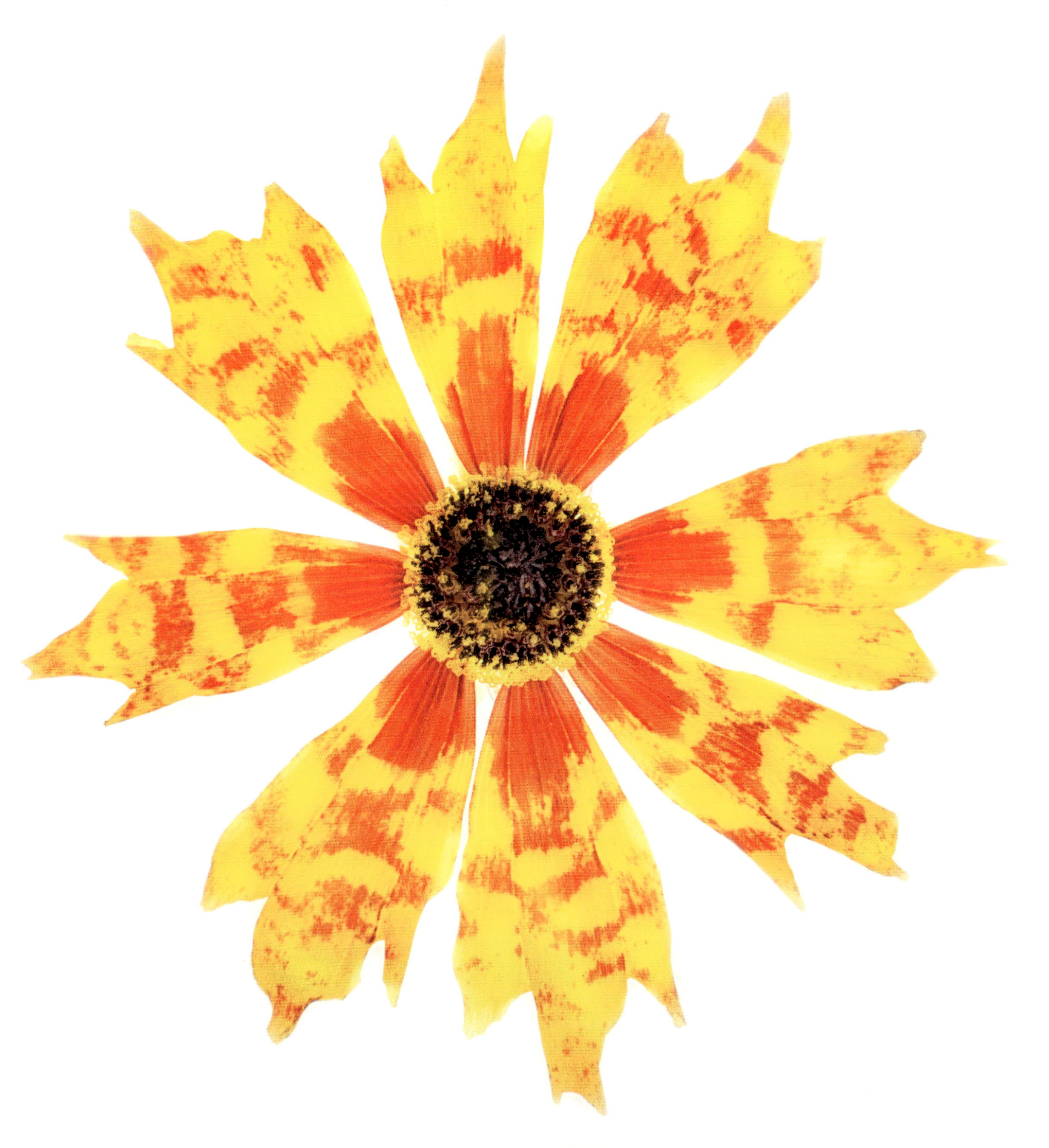

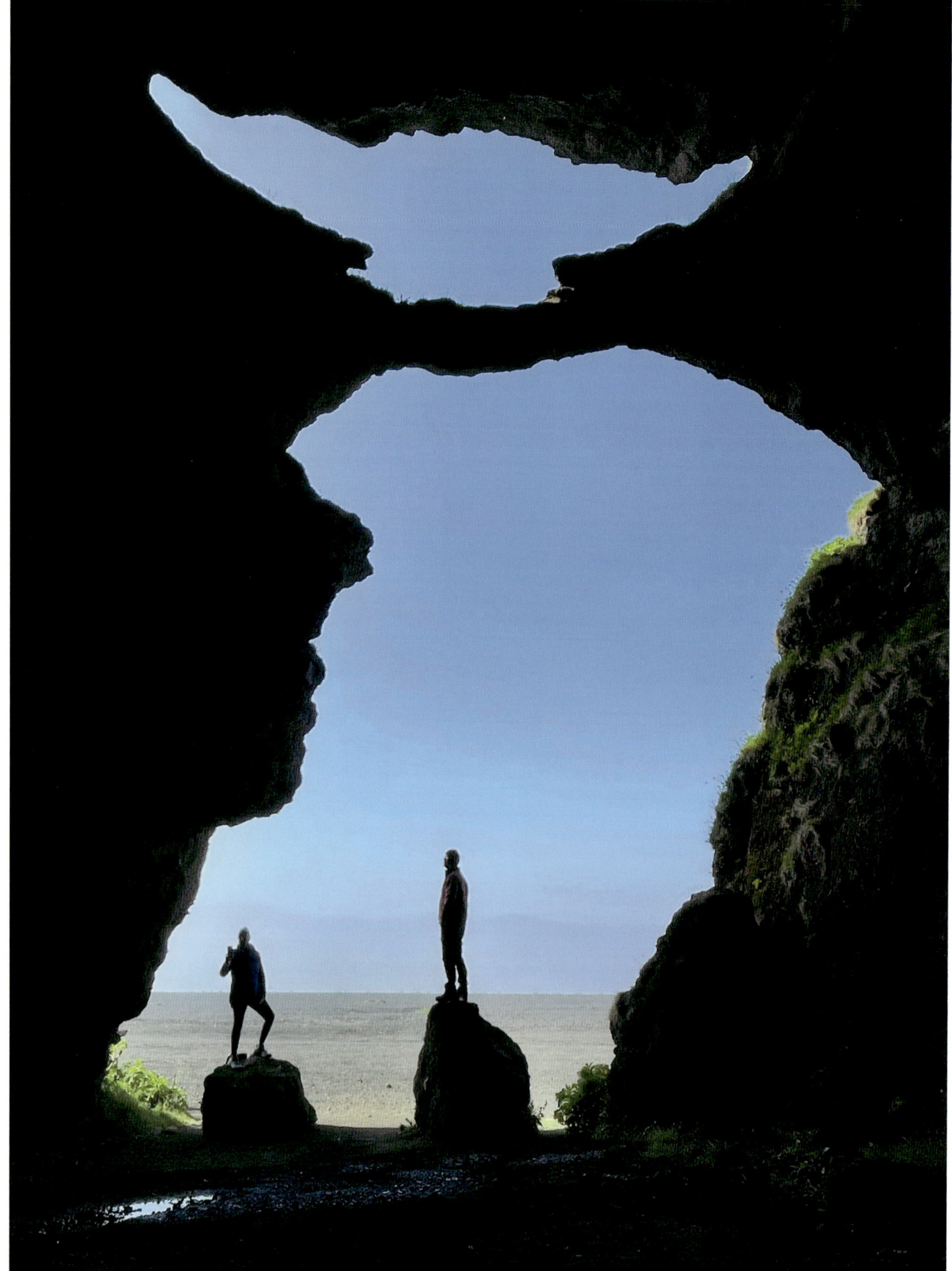

POSITIVE & NEGATIVE SPACE

"We put thirty spokes together and call it a wheel; But it is on the space where there is nothing that the utility of the wheel depends.…We pierce doors and windows to make a house; And it is on these spaces where there is nothing that the utility of the house depends. Therefore just as we take advantage of what is, we should recognize the utility of what is not." —Carl Jung

At first glance, the whole issue of positive and negative space seems really straightforward. The subject is the positive space and the background is the negative space.

While it is generally true that the subject is the positive space and the background is the negative space, like many simple statements this turns out to be far more complex in the real world. This complexity often starts with the question of what exactly the subject is.

Keep in mind that positive and negative space is one more formal mechanism for analyzing the design within an image. In this sense, positive and negative space can be used in parallel with other mechanisms such as shapes, entry and exit points, and so forth. Take your pick! A starting place is often to contemplate what modality is key to a given image.

It's important to note that the relationship of positive and negative space has a major impact on the *context* of the subject within an image. Generally, when the context is clear, so are the assignments of space as positive or negative, and vice versa. Depending on the intent of the creator, some images benefit from clarity of context, and others (such as abstractions, see page 210) do not.

Yoda Visits a Cave—On the south coast of Iceland my workshop group visited a cave. Iceland has been inhabited for over a millennium and in the early years, when survival was tenuous, caves like this one were crucial to the survival of the Viking civilization.

This image uses positive and negative space to present a visual pun. It's easy to see the figures standing silhouetted in the cave's entrance. Can you also see that Yoda walks among us? Perhaps you also see Aladin's lamp, or the profile of a face.

iPhone 12 Pro Max.

The Color of Space

I want to get something off my chest at this point: this section should really have been called "color does not define positive or negative space," but I thought "The Color of Space" was catchier. So, yeah, positive and negative space analysis is pretty much not about color. Sometimes color plays a role, but it's only a bit player and supporting actor, and not the lead.

Put another way: color does not define positive or negative space, and in a color image, the color is irrelevant to positive and negative space.

In a monochrome image, generally either black or white could be the positive space, and either white or black could be the negative space. There's no rule about this and I have seen many examples of each. It's probably more common for positive space to be black, and negative space to be white. A great example of this is *Trees in the Fog* on pages 208–209, where the black silhouettes of the trees are positive space and the white spaces between the trees are negative space.

Color is a good place to start looking for positive and negative spaces in an image. On the other hand, it is very clear that any color could be either kind of space depending on the image. For example, in *Havana Cross* on page 139, the cross in the sky is really the positive space even though it is seen through the buildings, and even though it is the sky. The uniform color of the surrounding buildings helps make them the background of the image rather than the foreground, and therefore the negative space. This is in marked contrast to a normal architectural photo where a building is the subject and the positive space, and the sky would usually be the background or negative space.

Another example is shown to the right in *Towers of San Gimignano*. This is an image with a fairly typical configuration for a landscape photo. Part of what makes it striking are the vibrant colors in the clouds. But, as the image is constructed, these beautiful clouds are part of the background. If it were framed somewhat differently so the clouds were the primary subject with one or two towers in the background, then the brightly colored clouds would be considered positive space.

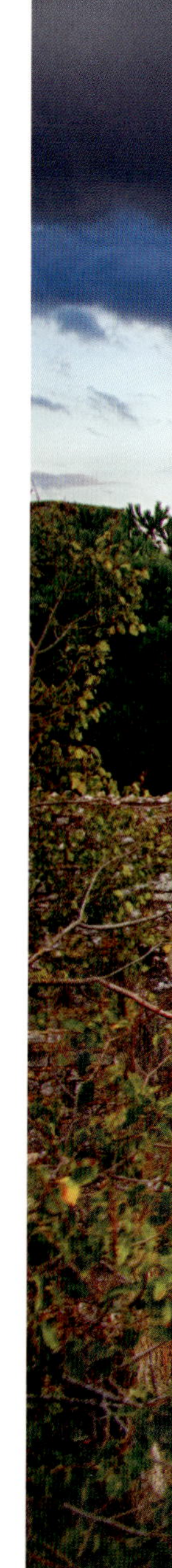

Towers of San Gimignano—With sunset coming on in a light rain, I hurried to find a high vantage point in the fabulous Tuscan city of San Gimignano, Italy. The towers of San Gimignano are notorious because they were built as status symbols—the higher the tower, the greater the status. As the rain passed, I photographed across the towers during the oncoming sunset.

With a landscape photo of approximately this composition, normally the landscape and buildings are the subject—meaning the positive space—and the sky is the negative space. That analysis works well for this image.

Towers of San Gimignano can hardly be called a minimalist image. But, in fact, analysis of positive and negative spaces is useful whether or not an image is minimal, and helps one understand compositional space even in a very full and colorful landscape like this one.

Nikon D810, 28-300mm Nikkor zoom at 28mm, seven exposures with shutter speeds ranging from 1/125 to 0.8 of a second, each exposure at f/8 and ISO 64, tripod mounted.

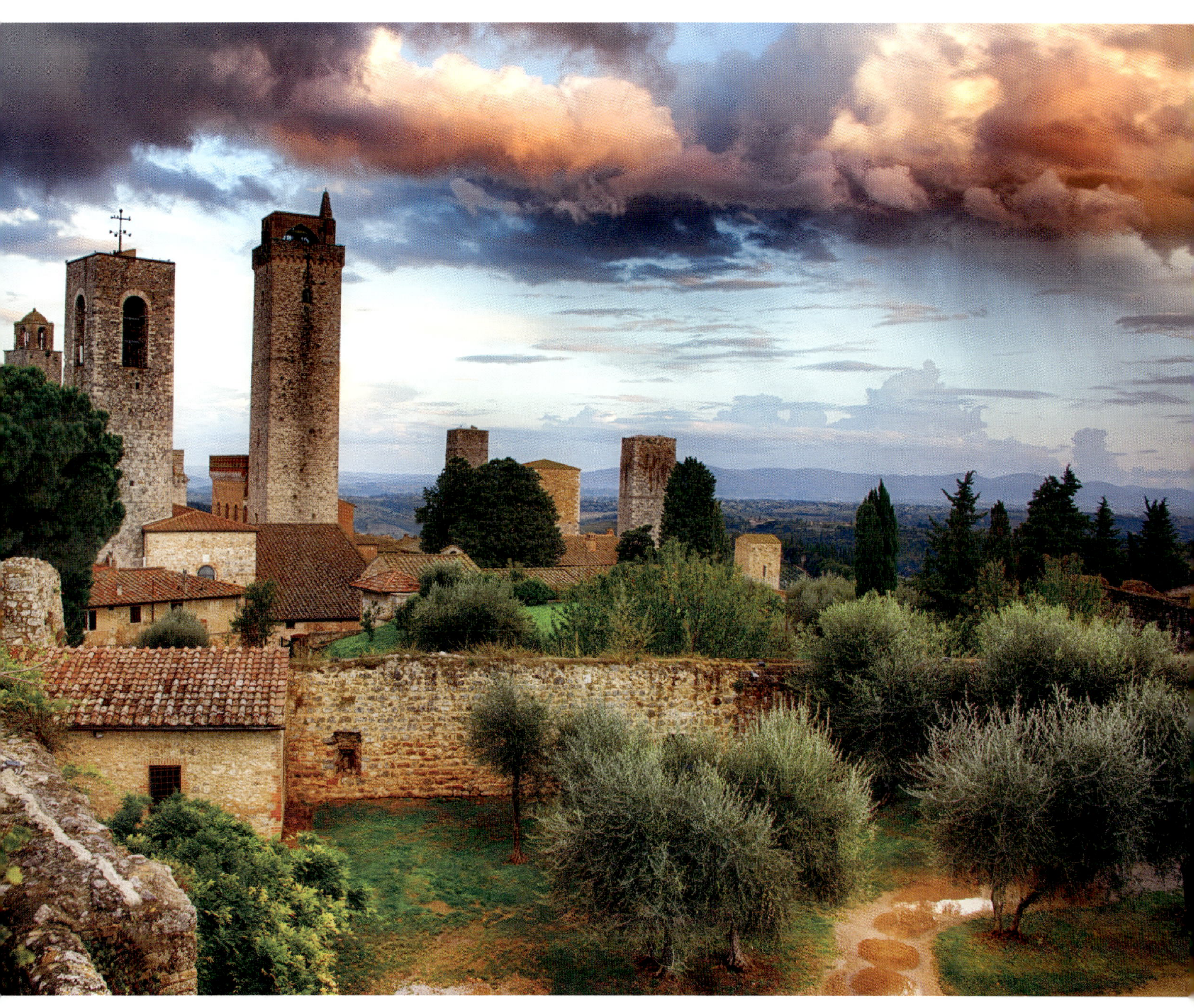

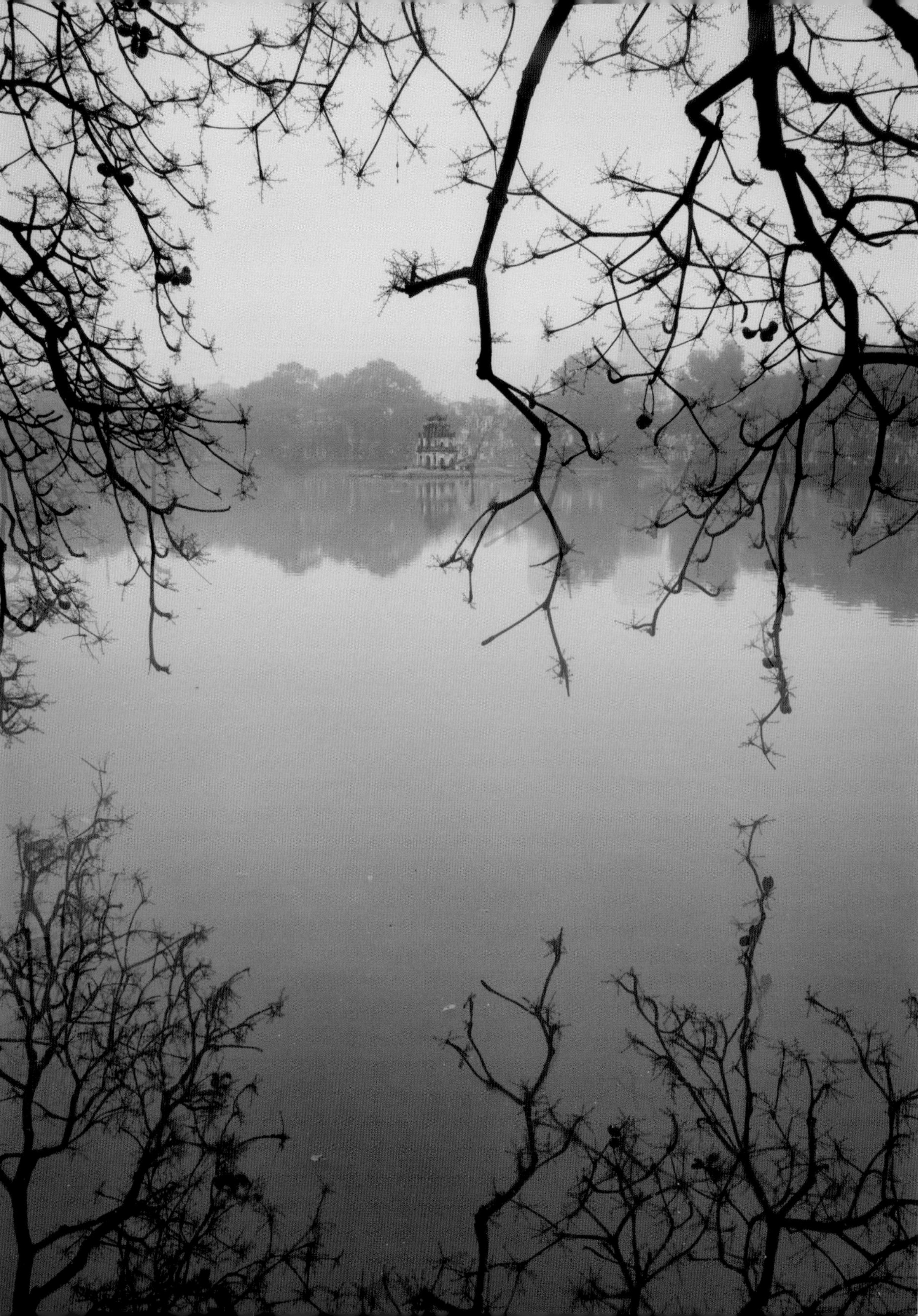

Hoan Kiem Lake—Hanoi, Vietnam, is a city with many charms and constant bustle. On a steamy, early evening, I took refuge from the city's blaring motorbikes and the press of people on the banks of Hoan Kiem Lake. Located in the center of old Hanoi, this lake has an ancient crumbling tower, a temple on an island, and peaceful vistas.

In making this image, my idea was to use the dark branches to create the feeling reminiscent of an antique Asian brush painting.

There's some complexity to this image regarding positive and negative space. Are the branches in the lower portion reflections or actual branches? In fact, they are reflections. The best way to read the image is that the branches are the positive space and the lake, tower and all, is the negative space. But stare at the image long enough, and it's possible to go the other way: the tower and waterscape can be read as the subject and positive space, and the dark branches merely a negative intrusion into this primary space.

Nikon D810, 28-300mm Nikkor zoom at 28mm, 1/13 of a second at f/22 and ISO 64, tripod mounted.

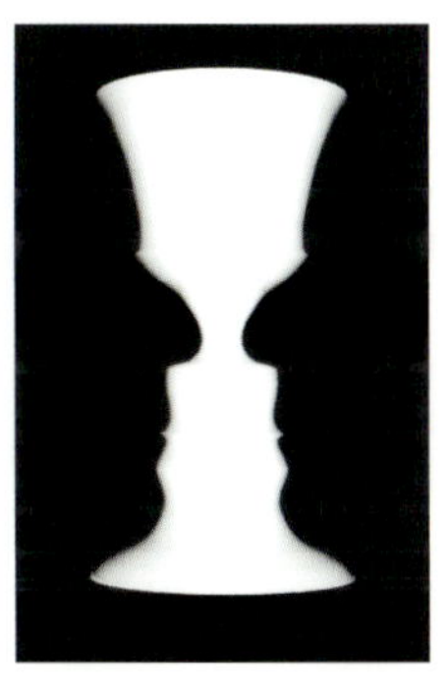

Rubin's vase, developed by Danish psychologist Edgar Rubin, is a famous example of ambiguous use of positive and negative space. Depending upon how you look at the image, it is either a white vase on a black background, or two black silhouettes with white space between them.

That Which Is Not Said

The relationship between positive and negative space is often undoubtedly complex. This is another way of putting the truism: that which is not said is as important as that which is said.

Good photographers have long known that to make a good image, you need both foreground and background. A portrait can be wonderfully emotive, but if the background is undistinguished, then the image as a whole doesn't work. Recognizing this, street photographers will sometimes find the right background and then wait patiently for the right foreground subject to come along.

Once one is clear that attention must be paid to the background (negative space) as much as the foreground (positive space), it is possible to work with positive-negative relationship in a more thoughtful way. Nothing can exist without its opposite. In that sense, think of the negative space as an actual subject just as much as the positive space.

So this means that negative space is not just a default area that happens to be there. It's as important in any image as the positive space. Think of it this way: If you are creating a portrait, you don't just "plop" the subject somewhere. You are thoughtful about positioning, lighting, and camera angles.

The same kind of thought needs to go into "that which is not said," negative space: create it, use it, appreciate it, and don't just fill it because it is there.

The Importance of the Background

As I've noted, the background is as important as the fore-ground. Positive and negative space are partners and must work together with balance and in harmony.

An image breathes in its background. If you have no nega-tive space or only very little negative space, then the image can seem to be claustrophobic. The eye wanders through an undifferentiated mass of subject with no place to pause and contemplate. On the other hand, if there's too much negative space, then the image loses clarity of context. The negative space swallows the clarity and becomes an entry point that has no exit (for more about entry and exit points, turn to page 136).

I like to think of the question of how much negative space an image needs as one that deserves a "Goldilocks" solu-tion: not too much space, but not too little space. It's really a question of visual balance.

Balance was in my mind when I composed *Hoan Kiem Lake*, shown on page 202. It was really a challenge to com-pose this image so that the lake provided respite from the curved and gnarled branch silhouettes. Too much space, and compositional cohesion would be lost. Too little space, and the background would not assume its position of importance in the composition.

What's the best way to approach acknowledging the impor-tance of negative space in an image? I often like to see my compositions in terms of their negative space before I even consider the positive space (take a look at the sidebar above about LAB color for one helpful technique for viewing positive and negative space). Looking at negative space first runs counter to our normal way of seeing, but it can be very helpful as a technique for creating interesting compositions.

turn to page 136

Using LAB Color to "See" Positive and Negative Space

LAB is a color space that you can use in software such as Photoshop. In LAB, each color channel contains all values and their opposites. As a practical matter, this means that it is easy to flip color values using Photoshop's Image ► Adjustment ► Invert. For example, in a monochrome image that is inverted in LAB, white becomes black and black becomes white.

There's no doubt that LAB color can be used to great creative effect when you are working on images. Another way that I like to use LAB color is to invert my images on a trial basis. This helps me immediately grasp the positive and negative space elements in my image.

Dandelion—I photographed this dandelion in the field, underexposing the image and using a tripod. Back in the studio, I allowed the background of the image to go very dark.

In this version of the image, clearly the white dandelion is the positive space, and the black background is the negative space. The relationship between positive and negative space remains the same in *Dandelion Inversion* on page 124, even though black has been exchanged for white, and white for black, using an LAB color L-channel inversion.

Nikon D850, 50mm Zeiss macro, 1/13 of a second at f/20 and ISO 200, tripod mounted.

   COMPOSITION & PHOTOGRAPHY

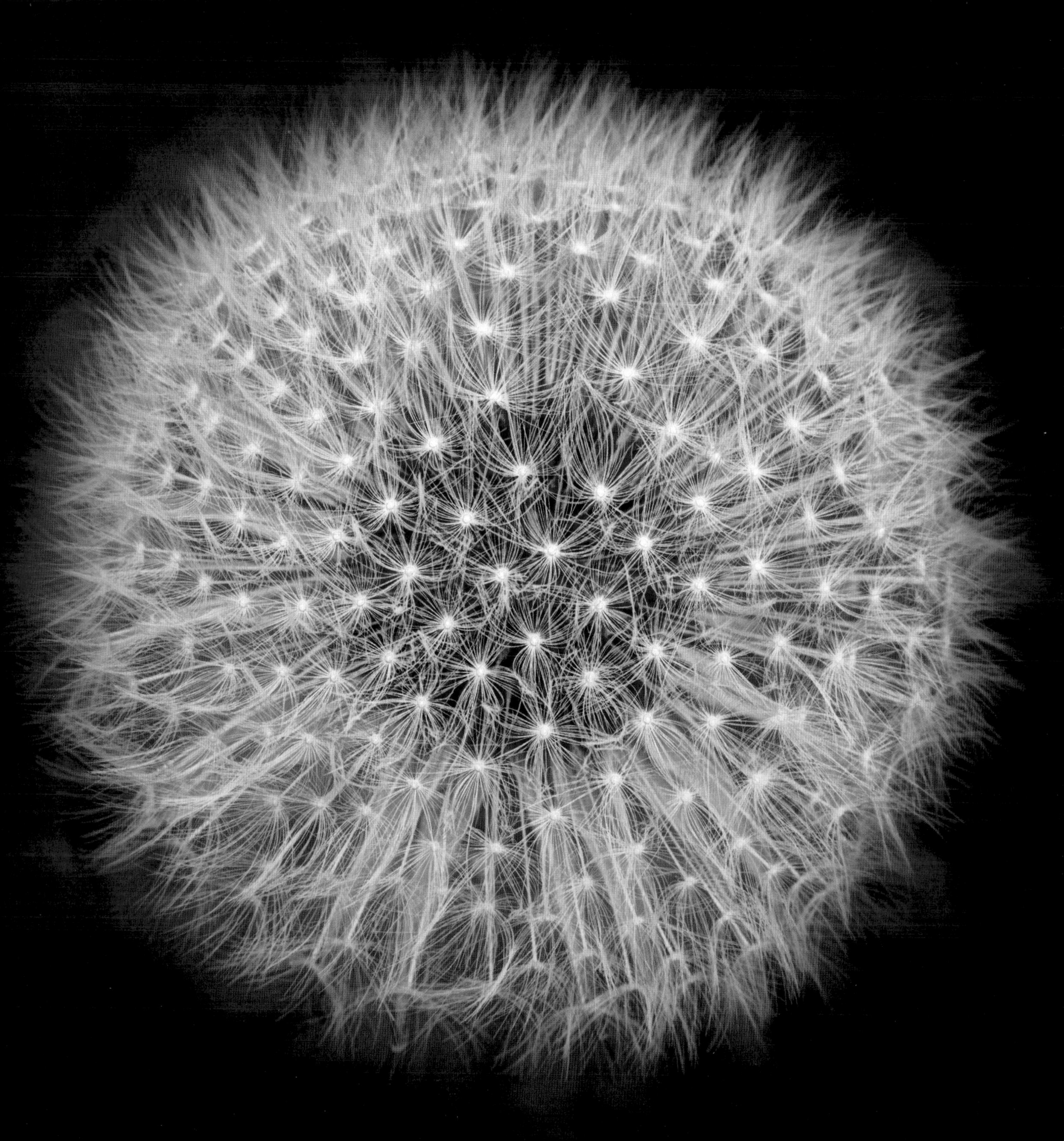

Nothing Could Exist without Its Opposite

The complex interrelationship between positive space and negative space is rarely simple.

At first glance, *Lady Boot Arch*, right, shows a massive arch formation in the foreground, representing the positive space, with a star-trail-studded sky as the background and negative space.

Look at the image a little longer and the hole in the arch, the "lady boot," becomes the real subject of the photograph, and therefore the positive space. The negative space has become a positive space, and this is a complete shift of perception.

This analysis is great as far as it goes, but looking at the image a little longer still, one might wonder about the role of the snowy mountains in the distant background. My point here is that images can be complex, and not to be too dogmatic.

An analysis of positive and negative space is an important compositional tool, and one that I often use when I contemplate a subject, but not the be-all and end-all of every photographic composition.

The way I like to think of it is that the relationship of positive to negative space strongly suggests the context of the image. By context, I mean the "story" that the image is telling, and the relationship of the subject to that story.

In a photograph, "story" refers to a narrative that the photograph may be showing or telling. From a compositional viewpoint, the story of an image also responds to a number of questions: What is important in the image? What does the photographer want the

Lady Boot Arch—Between the lowest point in the continental United States, Death Valley, and the highest point, Mount Whitney, lies a tremendous and gorgeous "badlands" of tumble-down desert, canyons, valleys, and boulder formations. One particularly spectacular area, above Lone Pine, California, is known as the Alabama Hills.

Lady Boot Arch is one of the most spectacular formations in the Alabama Hills. I made this photograph at night with the snow-crested Sierra Nevada mountains showing through the arch.

On the face of things, the subject—or positive space—of this photo is the arch, and the star-trail-filled sky is the negative space. Look again! This arch has a hole in it, supposedly in the shape of a lady's boot. If you take the boot as the subject of this photo—meaning the positive space—then the arch and sky all become background—or negative space.

Nikon D300, 12-24mm Nikkor zoom at 12mm; Background (star trails): forty-two 1 minute exposures at f/4 and ISO 200; Foreground (arch): three exposures, one at 90 seconds at f/14 and ISO 200, one at 211 seconds at f/14 and ISO 200, one at 390 seconds at f/8 and ISO 640, all tripod mounted.

Thought Experiment

Create a series of images in which the negative space is more important than the positive space. How hard was this to do?

What does this reversal tell you about the relationship between positive space and negative space?

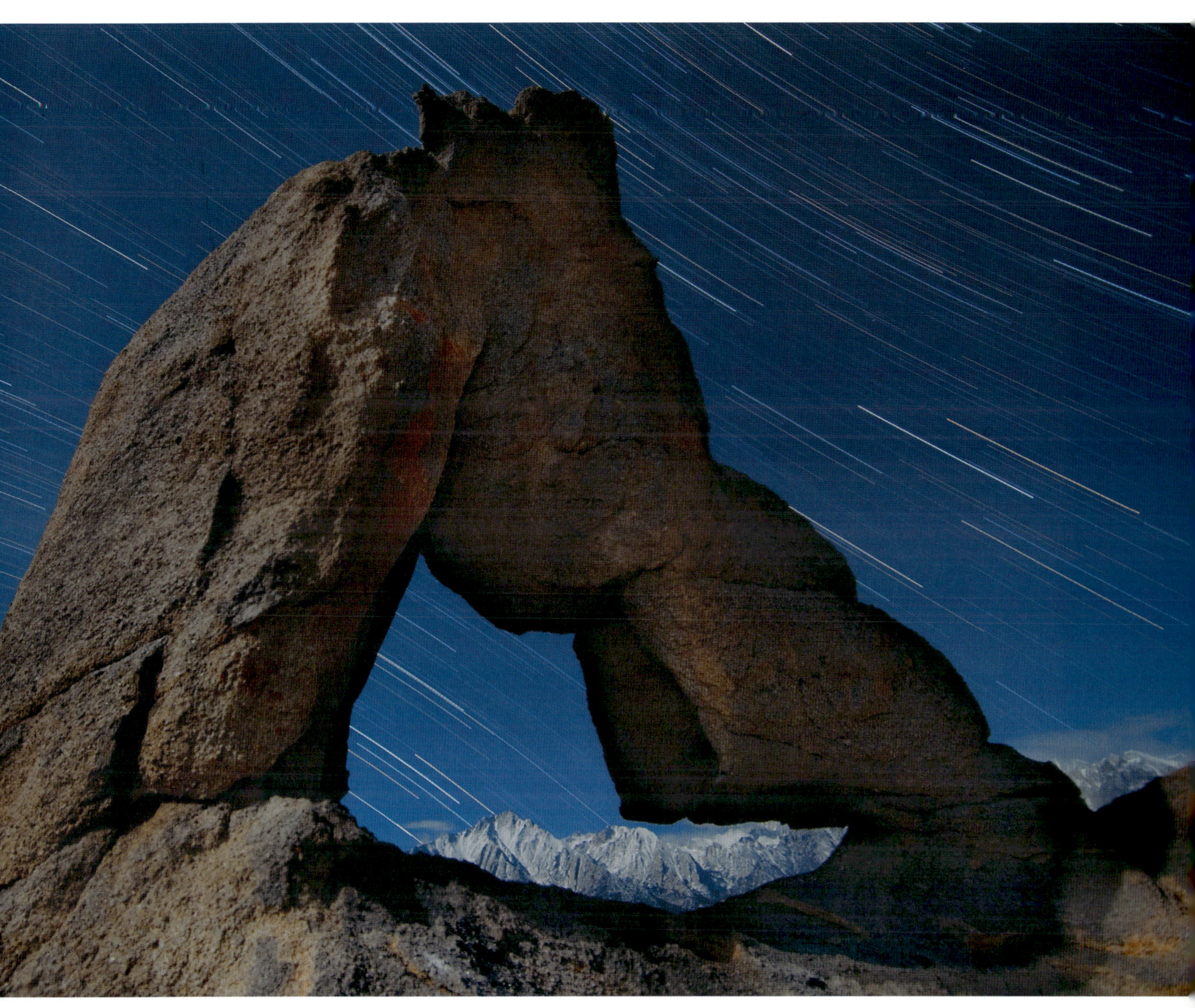

viewer to feel? And, what are the takeaways from the image?

The way the photographer has delineated the subject matter using positive space, and using negative space as the demarcation for the positive space, tells the viewer a great deal about the story of the image.

Some stories that are told—and every image has a story—are bold and direct. You don't have to wonder much about what is going on. Other photographs have an element of slyness. They can work by misdirection. These images often cause the viewer to stop and think twice about what they are seeing. The scale of the subject matter may be entirely unclear, important elements may be reversed or optically confused, and what is being shown may not even be clear. A sly image of this sort can be much more powerful than a literal image, but requires working with negative space.

To create an image that takes advantage of ambiguity, it's important to both look at the shapes that are being captured and also to look at the world with negative space in mind. Remember, the positive cannot exist without the negative.

By shaping the negative first, one is altering the sense of the positive in a way that brings out the space in otherwise less seen portions of the image—for example, in deep shadow areas.

Working with positive and negative space is only one tool in the photographic composition arsenal. It's not always useful. But when applied—particularly to images that are intended to contain ambiguity—it is extremely powerful.

KEY IDEAS

- Positive versus negative space seems simple until it meets the real world.

- There's no direct correspondence between color and positive or negative space.

- Negative space, that which is not said, is as important as positive space.

- Looking at the world from a negative-space perspective can yield fascinating compositional insights.

Trees in the Fog—On the Pacific coast of San Francisco, California, I came to photograph the crashing surf on the ocean, but it was totally obscured by fog. Turning around, in the opposite direction I saw intense, orange street lighting coming through the trees across the beach parking lot.

In this image, the silhouettes of the trees are the positive space, and the negative space is the fog itself with beams of light accentuating the fog.

The takeaway here is that the positive space of the trees needs the negative space of the lit fog between the trees. Without the fog—the negative space—there would be no image.

Nikon D300, 18-200mm Nikkor zoom at 56mm, 52 seconds at f/4.8 and ISO 100, tripod mounted.

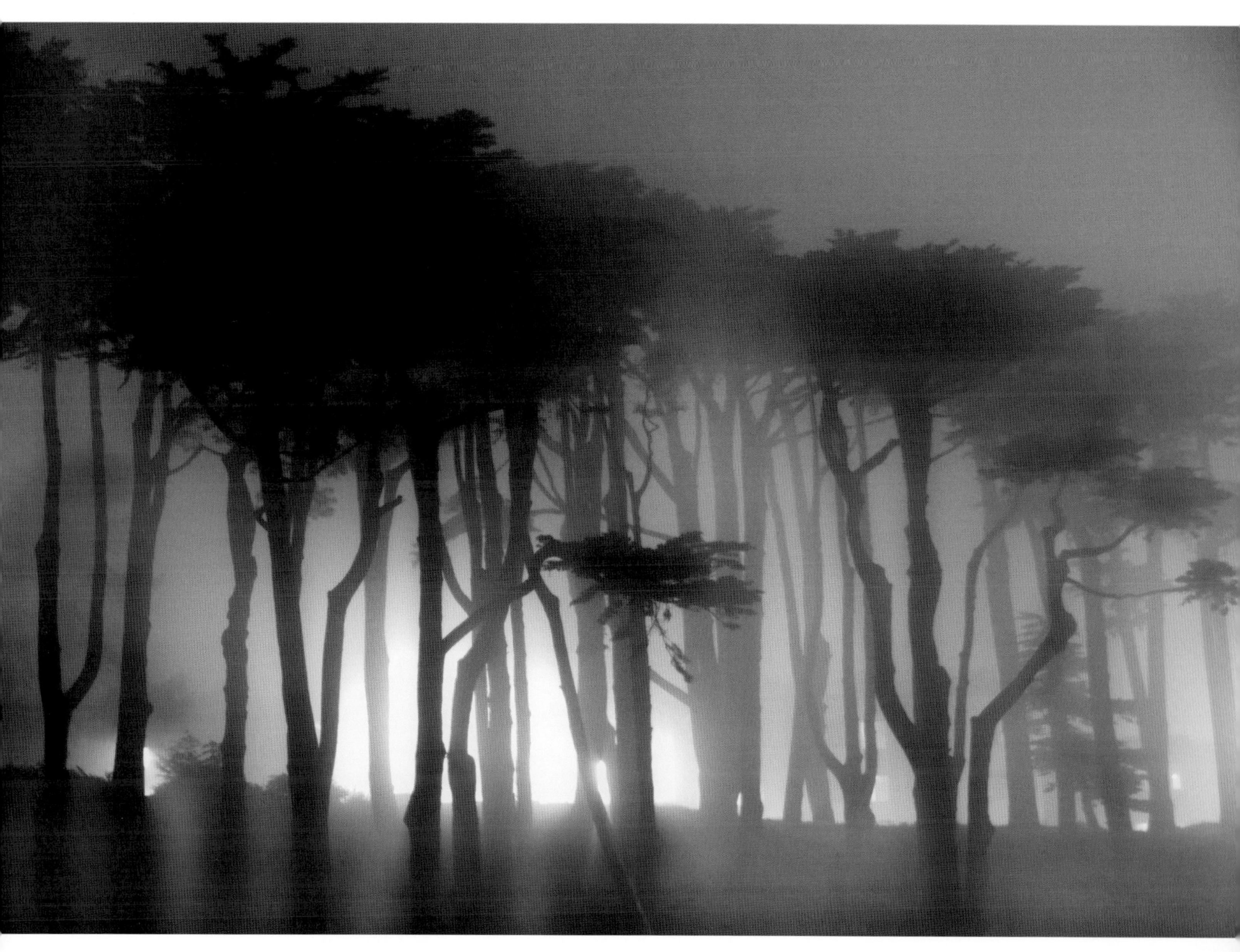

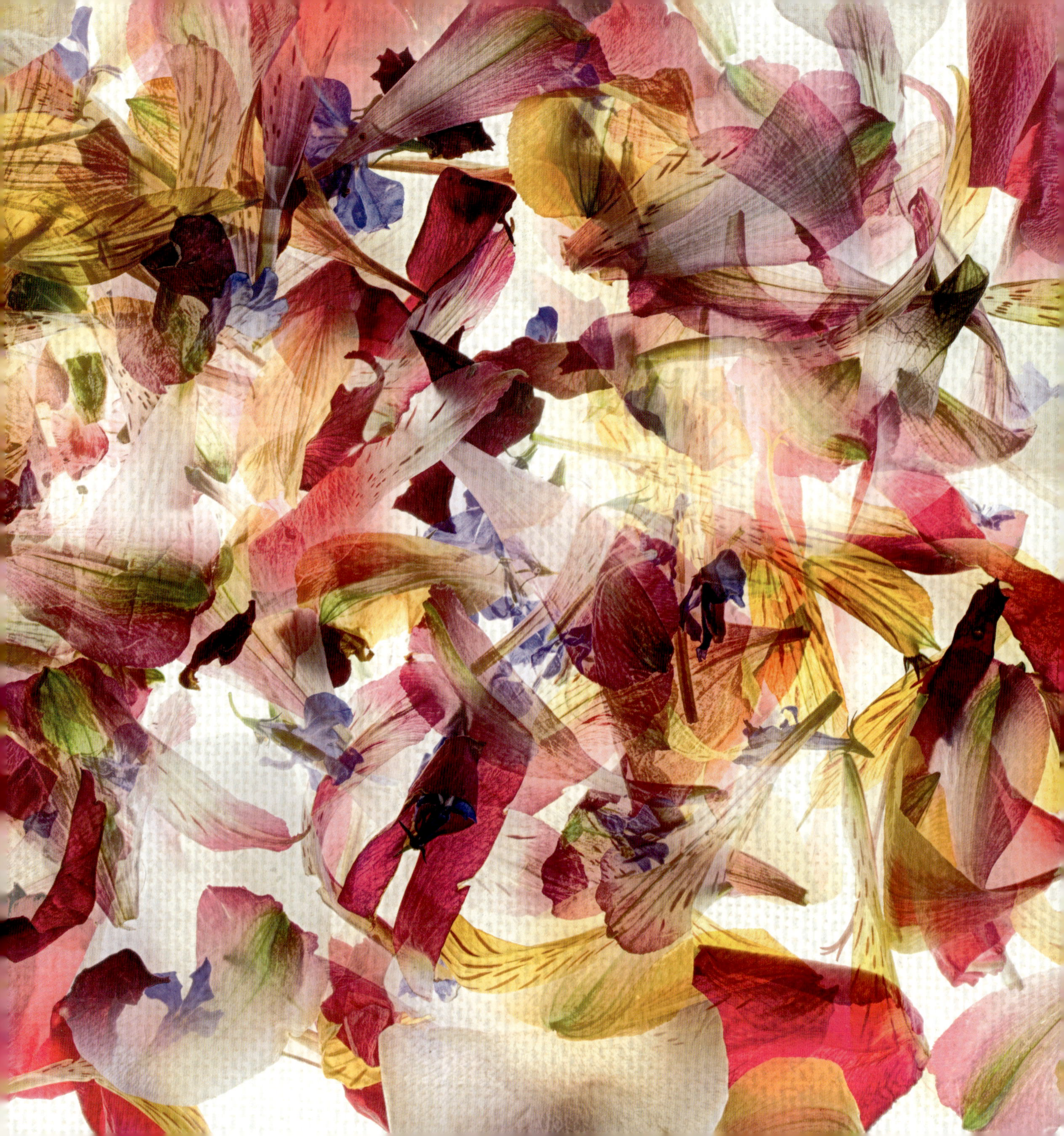

ABSTRACTION

In nineteenth-century France and elsewhere, the rigors of academic painting softened to the more-forgiving-of-reality Impressionism. This was partly due to the invention of photography: what was the point of all that rigor if a camera could render "reality" more simply?

As time went by, and the bonds that tied art to realism further loosened, Impressionism morphed into more free-form, two-dimensional art movements, including Fauvism, Cubism, and Surrealism. Eventually, by the 1950s in New York City, Abstract Expressionism was the dominant mode in the art world, and the already tenuous connection between art and "reality" had frayed well beyond the breaking point.

To *abstract* literally means to take something out of something else. In science, an "abstract" is a synopsis-in-brief of the results of an experiment or a scientific theory. In art, to abstract means to change a literal subject to something more symbolic. This kind of abstraction exists on a spectrum, with abstract art that has almost no visual connection to the literal real world.

Photography has always had a more fraught relationship with abstraction than other forms of art. This is because a photograph is often taken

If Jackson Pollock Dripped Using Flower Petals—Jackson Pollock was my inspiration when I made this image. I stood near my light box with piles of different flower petals. Saying a prayer to the gods of Zen serenity, serendipity, and simultaneously embracing chaos, I started tossing petals onto the light box. I tried to retain randomness while embracing an underlying cohesive pattern in how I tossed the petals.

Nikon D850, 55mm Zeiss Otus, seven exposures with shutter speeds ranging from 1/8 of a second to 4 seconds, each exposure at f/16 and ISO 64, tripod mounted.

to be a literally truthful rendition of reality. But as I explained earlier (see page 160), it is simply not logically possible to create a two-dimensional version of our three-dimensional reality.

Despite the ambiguous and ambivalent connection of the camera to reality, it has long been recognized—at least since the well-known 1951 Museum of Modern Art exhibition *Abstraction in Photography*—that photographs can be abstractions. Photographs work as abstractions both in the sense of abstracting and loosening reality, and also further along the spectrum as a tool and source material for the creation of fully abstract, non-literal art.

These possibilities provide powerful compositional fodder for the creative photographer.

Along the Abstraction Spectrum

From the very beginning, photography—despite its association with a literal rendition of the world—was clearly regarded as a medium for abstraction. This is clear, if nowhere else, in the very name *photography*, which translates to "drawing with light" or "writing with light." Drawing generally is, itself, a process of abstraction. Writing is by its very nature a symbolic process of abstraction. Adding light to the mix merely reinforces the sense that something involving magical transformation is involved, and that the process is not just literal.

When the photographic subject is abstracted, but to some extent literal, meaning that portions of the image can be realized but the image is presented in a poetic or metaphorical kind of way, the process is relying on two related phenomena: *pareidolia* and *anthropomorphism*.

Pareidolia refers to the human propensity for assigning meaning to an apparently random or ambiguous visual pattern—for example, when someone sees shapes in the clouds, or looks at patterns of sand on the beach and sees a mountain range, as in *Mountains on the Beach*, opposite.

Personally, I sometimes think of the pareidolia phenomenon in terms of the swaggering Captain Jack Aubrey character in Patrick O'Brian's classic Aubrey-Maturin sea stories set during the Napoleonic Wars. In these books, Aubrey often gets away with feats of cloaked derring-do, slipping by without being observed because people "only see what they expect to see."

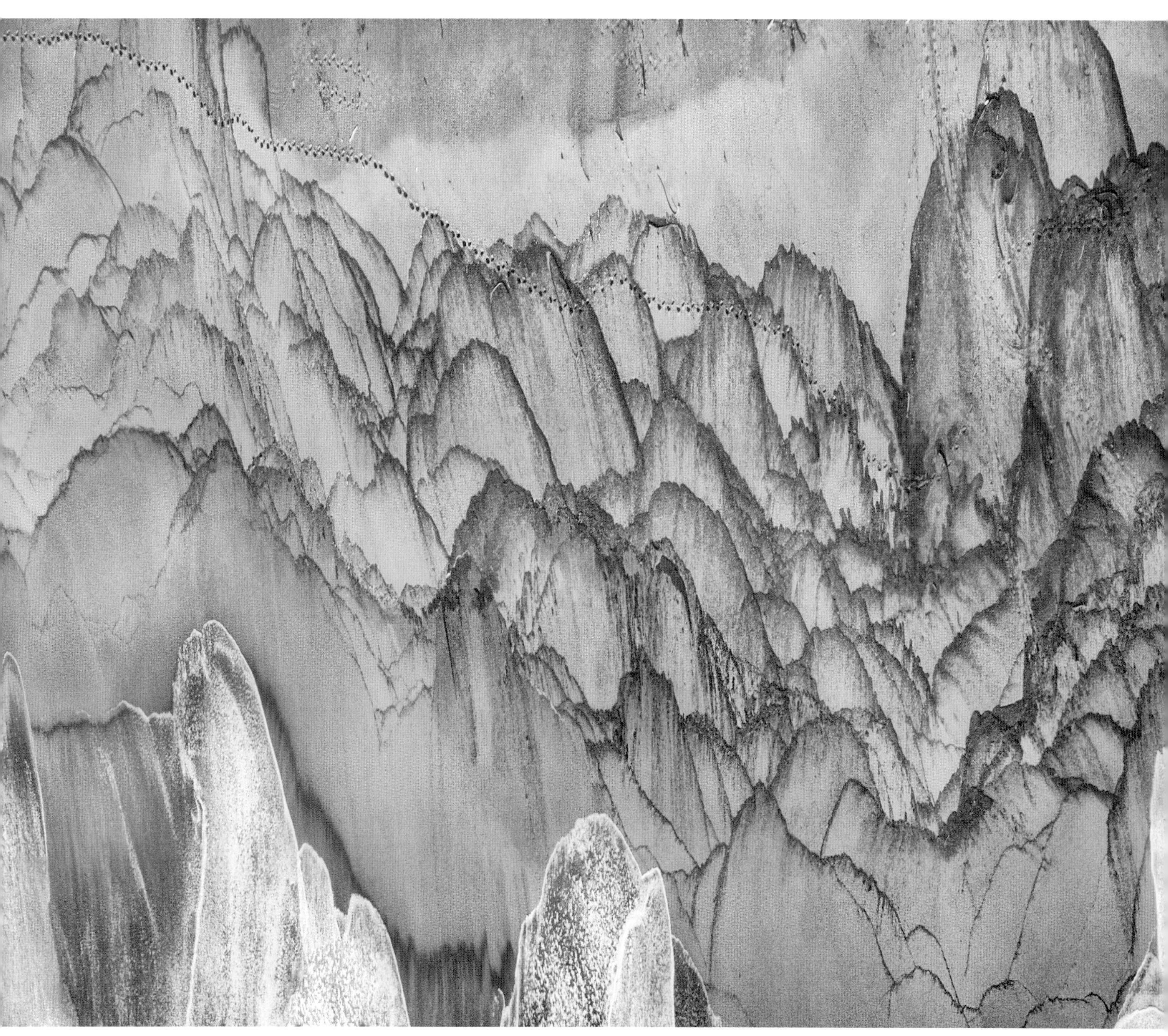

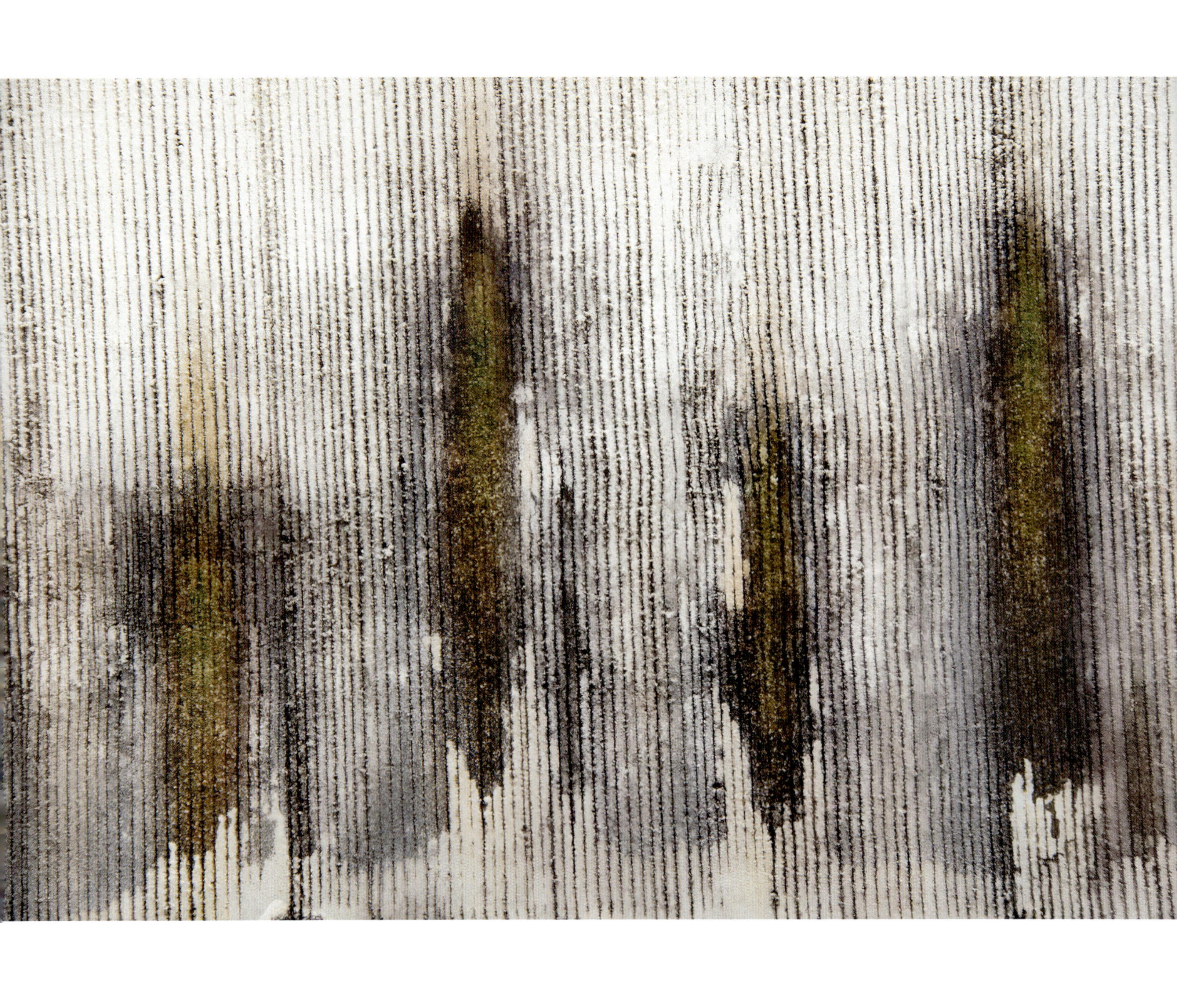

Garden Wall, Nara—Wandering in the gardens of the old imperial city of Nara, Japan, I looked away from the cultivated plantings, and noticed that one garden wall had seeps and stains from lichen. I carefully framed the image to create an abstraction.

One of my goals when I made this composition was to be careful to capture a recognizable pattern as part of the image. The green bars alternate short and long, and the whole creates a pleasing sense of balance without being so symmetrical that the viewer's eye skims over the image without being engaged.

Nikon D800, 28-300mm Nikkor zoom at 135mm, 1/125 of a second at f/9 and ISO 400, hand held.

Anthropomorphism is the human tendency to translate shapes into human, and by extension animal, form. For example, when someone looks up at a cloud in the sky and says, "I see a whale!" this is anthropomorphism (actually, "animal-morphism," but let's not quibble!).

Both pareidolia and anthropomorphism are related to the idea behind the Rorschach test. The Rorschach test uses apparently abstract art as a projective device where the subject picks out supposed meanings based on patterns and anthropomorphisms. Trained psychologists can then, supposedly, derive insights about the test subject.

So along the more reality-based end of the abstraction spectrum, the artist is rendering a real object. That object can be stylized, distorted, or exaggerated, using colors and textures to communicate emotions and feelings, rather than with the goal of producing a replica. As an example, consider the Russian artist Wassily Kandinsky, a founder of Abstraction, and the author of *On the Spiritual in Art*, written in 1911 and one of the most influential theoretical books on abstract art. Kandinsky was born with *synaesthesia*—a rare condition that for him translated sounds into colors. He believed that his paintings used different shades of color to provoke a range of sounds and emotions, and to touch the portions of the brain connected with music.

Heading further along the abstraction spectrum, abstract art gets even more abstract, meaning it goes well beyond any representation of "the facts." Abstract art attempts to build a new self-contained reality. In the case of a photograph, this reality is on a two-dimensional plane. One point of view is that abstract art on a two-dimensional plane should be created by pure patterns of form, color, and line. This is a line of aesthetics that goes back at least as far as Plato.

The Platonic ideal of beauty consists of an arrangement of integral parts into a coherent whole, according to order, proportion, and symmetry. In this world view, the main purpose of abstraction in art is not to tell a story, but to encourage involvement and imagination.

Abstraction goes back a long way, perhaps to the birth of humanity. The Paleolithic cave paintings in Lascaux—from more than 15,000 years ago—contain abstractions.

Even once you grant that the purpose of a photograph is to create a symbolic generalization, there remains the question of whether this should be done following neat, ordered, and structured patterns, or as a matter of emotional gesture. Abstract Expressionism has room for both the order of a Mark Rothko color-field painting and the drippings of a Jackson Pollack.

Certainly, a completely abstract work of art—at the far end of the abstraction spectrum—can convey emotion. For example, Mark Rothko's black paintings in the Rothko Chapel in Houston, Texas, are deeply moving. And as the 1986 Los Angeles County Museum of Art landmark exhibition *The Spiritual in Art: Abstract Painting 1890–1985* amply demonstrated, a common goal in abstract art is the conveyance of emotion and the ineffable in the universe.

The only question remaining is whether photography is an art that is capable of participating in the ability to abstract that is the birthright of all other two-dimensional art forms. In this, there can be no real doubt. Photography's ability to render literal scenes can make it easier for people to forget its power of abstraction. This is an issue of opening one's eyes and grasping the myriad tools and techniques that are available.

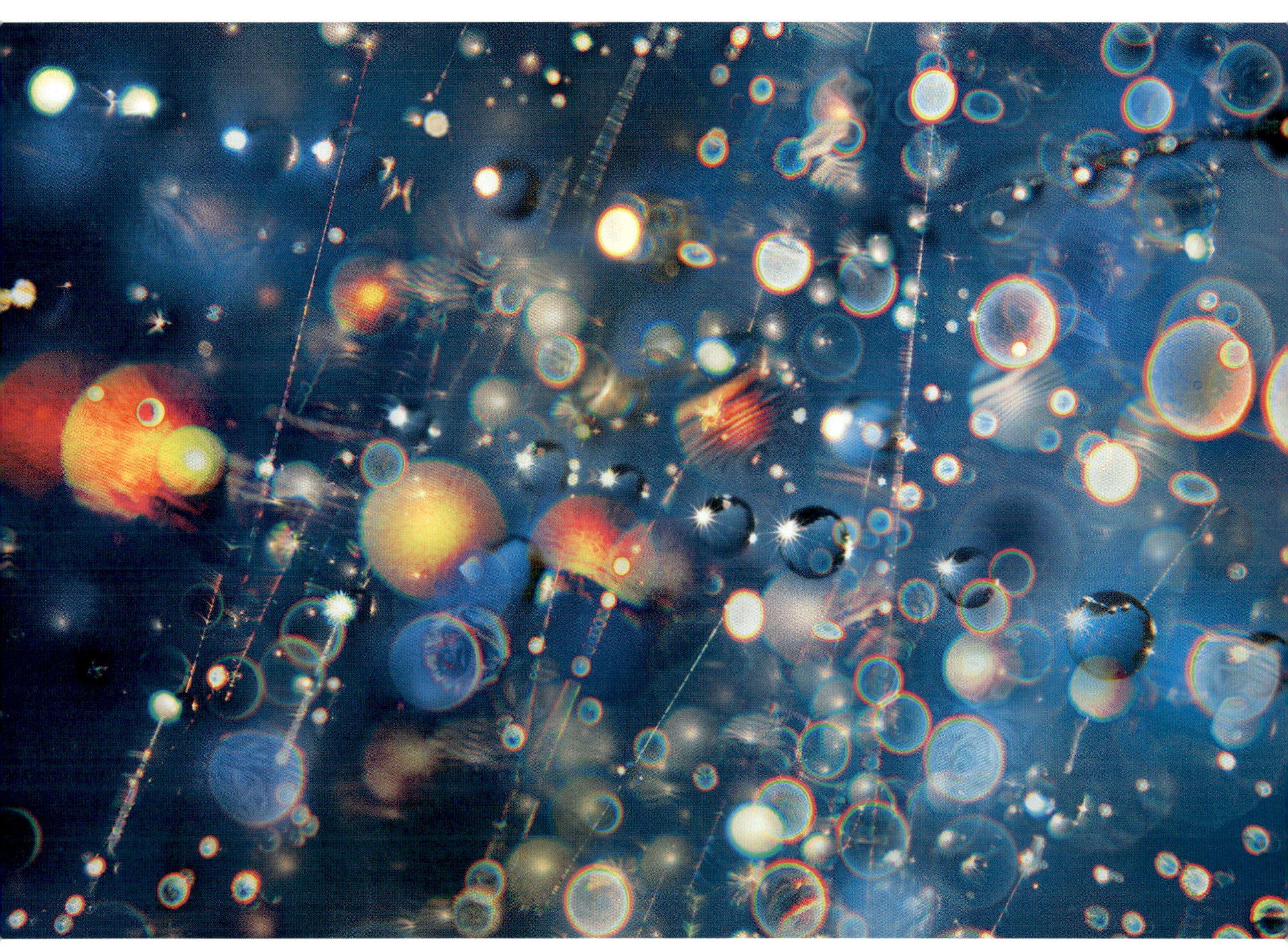

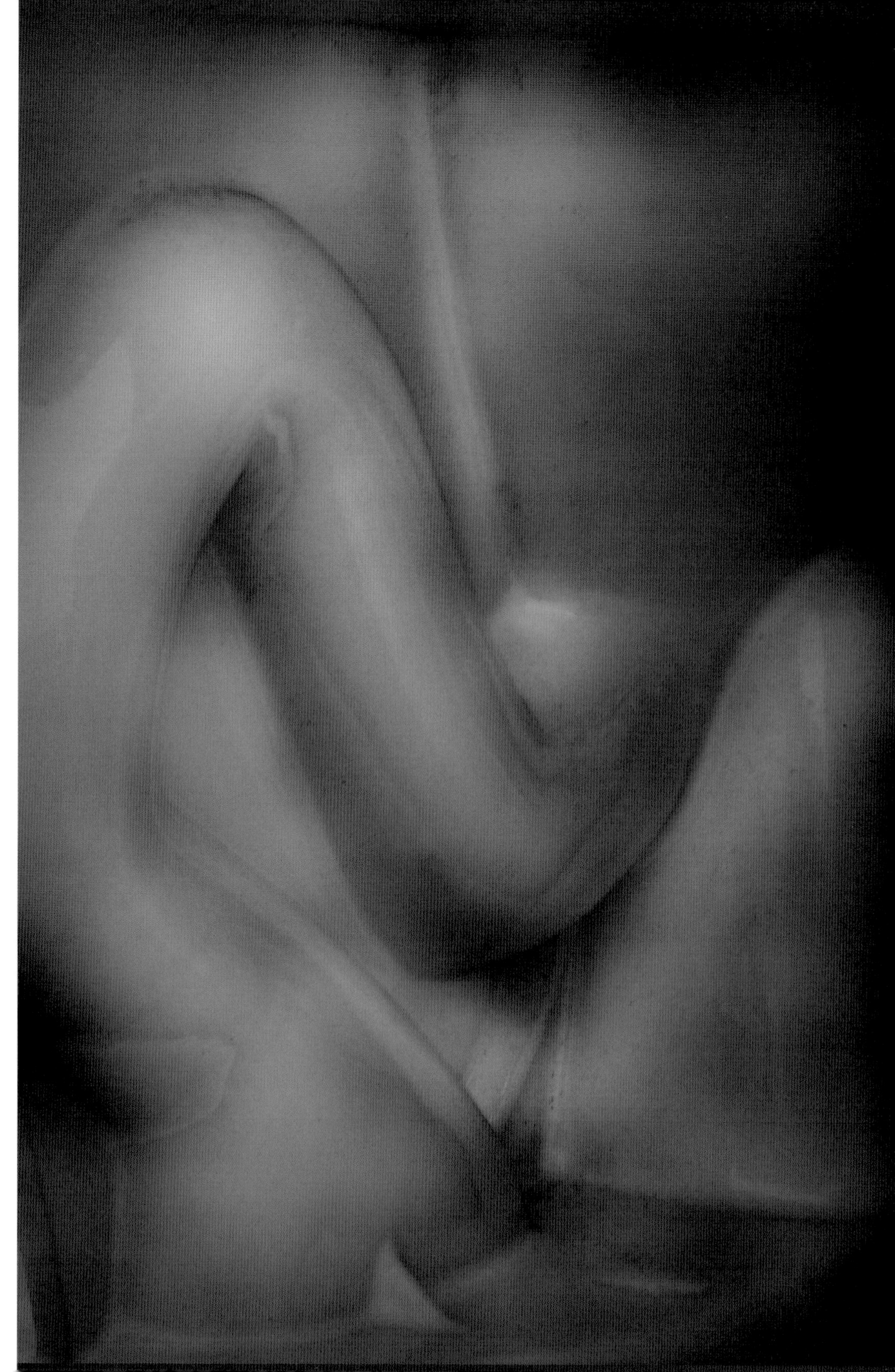

Key Ideas for Abstraction

Your eyes, and your ability to previsualize, are your best tools for creating photographic abstractions. The trick here is to train yourself to see photographic subjects as a potential basis for an abstraction. Does that rock look like a bear? Would there be a possibility for an interesting image if you collaged certain things together?

There's no end of possibilities. But it all has to start with your personal vision. This *can* be learned and can be trained.

Start by slowing down. Be sure to always look around you. If you are someplace special, don't settle for the obvious. What else is there to see? Turn your camera away from the Taj Mahal or the Eiffel Tower or the majesty of a waterfall in Yosemite and see what is behind you, or above you, or below you. Remember, the best camera to use is the one you have with you, and photographic vision is almost never about gear.

With that in mind, here are some of the most important tools and techniques for creating abstract, rather than literal, photographic images:

Porcelain Series No. 1—At a local salvage yard, I got low to the ground with my camera on a tripod to photograph beneath a plumbing fixture, and pointed the camera up at the underside of the porcelain. The result is this largely abstract image where the subject matter is not obvious at first glance.

Nikon D300, 85mm Nikkor macro, 1/15 of a second at an adjusted aperture of f/64 and ISO 100, tripod mounted.

Macros—Often closeups, the more extreme the better, present a view of the world that one has never seen before. Many of these new vistas are at least partly abstract, and it can be hard for the viewer to recognize the literal subject matter.

Camera angles—It's astounding how shifts in your camera's position and point of view can change things and create abstractions. Sometimes all it takes is getting down on the ground and photographing from far below—for an example, take a look at *Porcelain Series No. 1*, opposite.

Changing orientation—There's nothing set in stone about the orientation of your images. A horizontal can be shifted to the vertical, or vice versa, or even at some angle in between. You can change this orientation in your camera, or change it in post-production. For example, *Mountains on the Beach* on page 213 was rotated 90 degrees in post-production.

In-camera techniques—There are a variety of techniques you can use in your camera to create abstractions. Some of these are: in-camera motion (ICM), used to create *Bus Window 1* on page 96; in-camera multiple exposures used to make *Devotion* on page 141; and something as simple as a long exposure to abstract waves, clouds, and other moving subjects, as in *Cayucos Pier* on pages 142–143.

Alternative processing—In the wet darkroom, alternative tools included solarization, cross-processing, and other chemical interventions were used experimentally. Most of these film-era techniques can be simulated digitally. In addition, there are some alternative processing techniques that belong solely to the digital realm. A good example is the use of LAB color; as an example, take a look at *Colored Apple Slices* on pages 52–53.

▥ *Alternative spectrums*—Digital captures can be made using light waves in spectra that are not normally visible to the human eye, or for that matter, to the camera. For example, Infrared (IR) and Gamma rays can both be recorded using appropriate gear. IR and Gamma rays are not part of the visible light spectrum. Gamma rays are used in x-ray imaging. As an example of an image that used x-ray capture, check out *Sunflower X-Ray Fusion* on page 235.

▥ *Collaging*—Collages can be created literally by cutting and pasting pieces of paper or other substrate together. An example is David Hockney's use of small Polaroid photographs to create alternative perspectives and avoid the one-eyed "paralysed Cyclops" of photography (see page 159).

Collages can also be created virtually. Much of my work involves virtual collaging using post-production—for example, *Down the Rabbit Hole* on page 158. It has been said that in addition to being a photographer, I am an artist that uses my photographs as the source material for my virtual collages. Pro tip: If you think you may be interested in virtual collaging,

when you are in the field on location, take every angle, point of view, and closeup, even if you don't know for sure that you will end up using it. It's hard to go back and photograph this kind of thing again, and frustrating to find you're missing something important when you begin the virtual collaging process in post-production.

There are many other techniques for creating photographic abstractions. The ones I have listed here are a good starting place, and you will find many examples of their use throughout *Composition & Photography*.

It all comes down to seeing. Enjoy the process of looking around you and observing. Furthermore, try to practice seeing the world with "beginner's" eyes. This is a reference to the Zen term "beginner's mind": the idea that if you start without preconceptions, you will see and find more in your practice in the everyday world that surrounds you with so many possibilities and such interest and joy.

Homage to Rothko—Mark Rothko was an Abstract Expressionist painter, best known for his canvases with regions of vibrant color, abstracted into rectilinear shapes.

With Rothko in mind, I created this abstract image by adding food color to water, with the colored water placed in a glass vase. I photographed sunlight coming through the water, using a wide-open aperture (f/1.6). To complete the image, I rotated it 90 degrees in post-production, and added a slight canvas effect.

Nikon D850, 85mm Lensbaby Velvet, 1/500 of a second at f/1.6 and ISO 64, hand held.

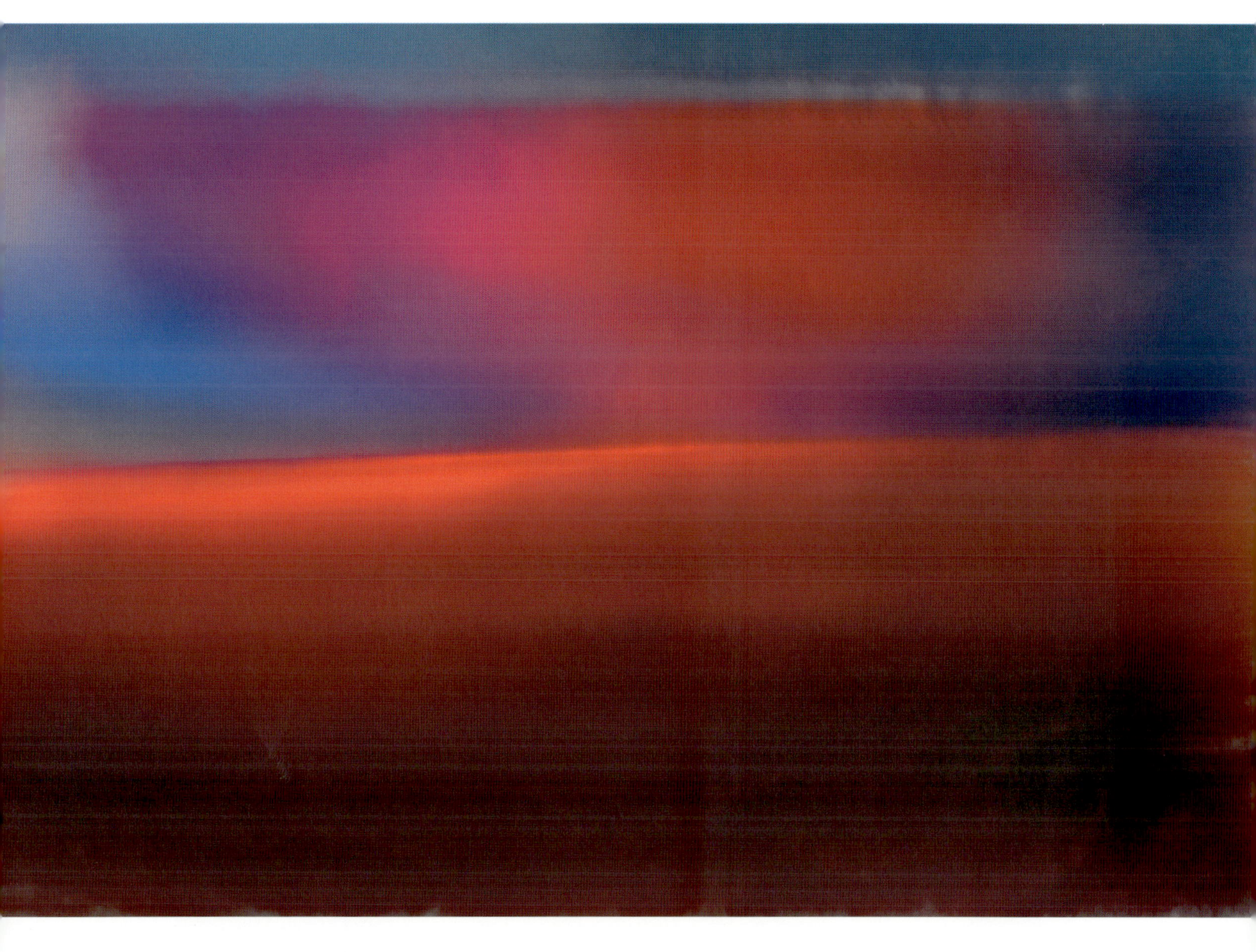

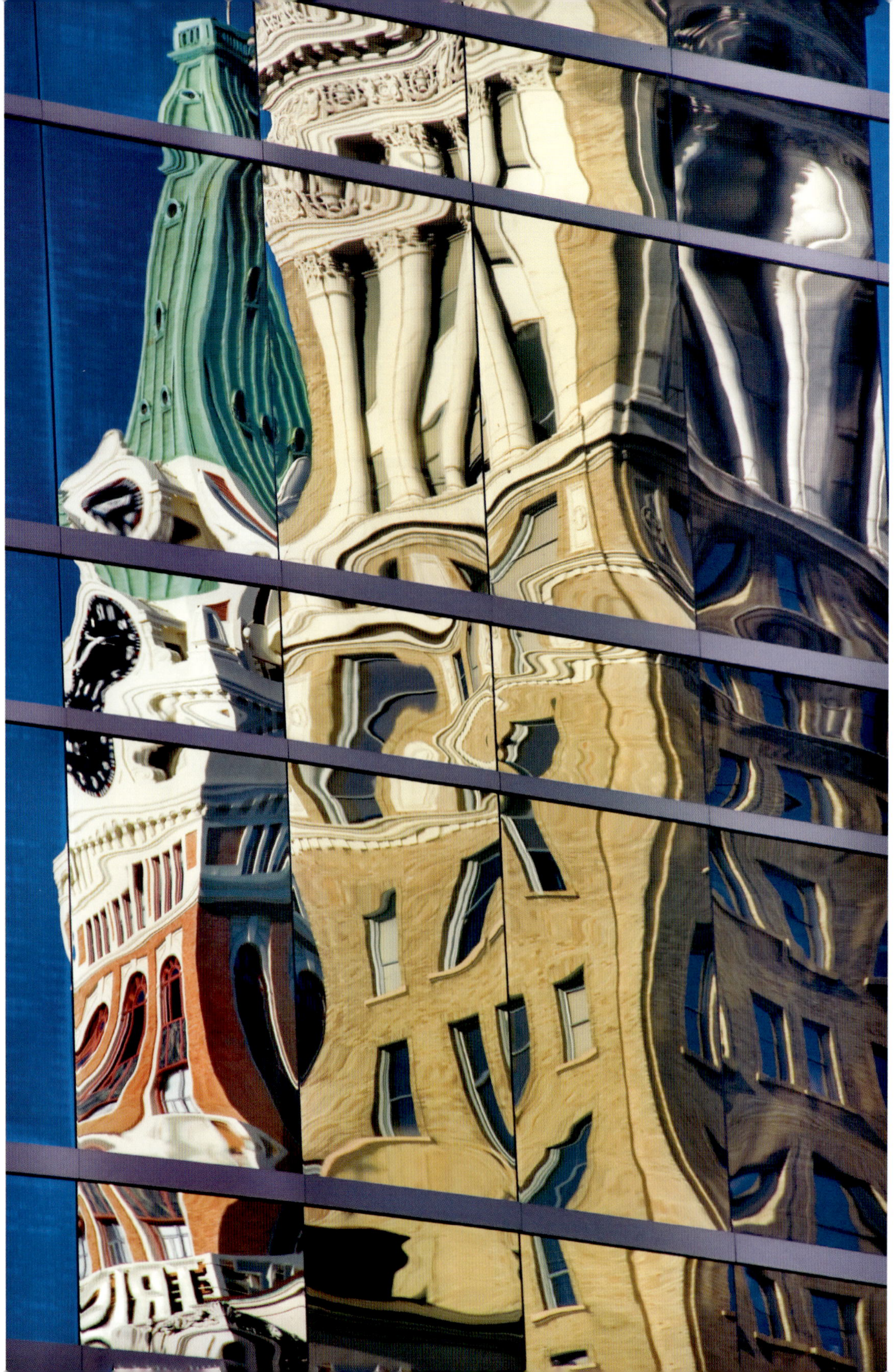

THE PRACTICE OF COMPOSITION

A *composition*, as in a photographic composition, is a noun. However, the act of creating a composition is denoted by a verb, *to compose*, or in participle form, *composing*. To compose is an active verb. It is not passive. Composing is something the photographer does, not something that is done to the photographer. It is very important to take an active part in becoming fluent with the language of composition, and with using the power of composition to enhance your creative work.

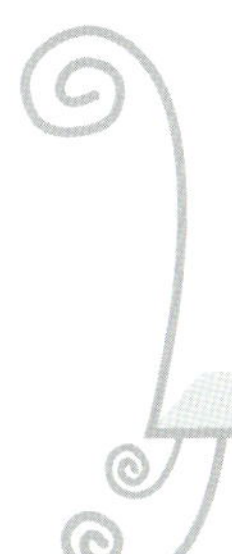

Persistence of Reflection—Wandering in downtown Oakland, California, with my camera, I came across a modern office tower with curved reflective glass windows. The older buildings refracted and reflected in this curvature created a fascinating partial abstraction in this composition. I used a polarizer to help accentuate the reflections.

Nikon D300, 28-300mm Nikkor zoom at 170mm, circular polarizer, 1/250 of a second at f/7.1 and ISO 500, hand held.

I began *Composition & Photography* with a quotation from Edward Weston that suggested that "to consult the rules of composition before making a picture is a little like consulting the law of gravitation before going for a walk." This seems true to me. You don't think when you breathe.

At the same time, to become proficient at photography, one must master composition. So how is the novice to obtain and internalize the skills to be able to reflexively create compelling compositions?

This is not a process, or practice, that happens automatically. You must work at it, and for one thing, literally practice! The more photographs you make and the more attention you pay to composition, the more likely your photographs are to improve.

A *practice*, as a noun, is a way of doing something, the actual application of an idea or method,

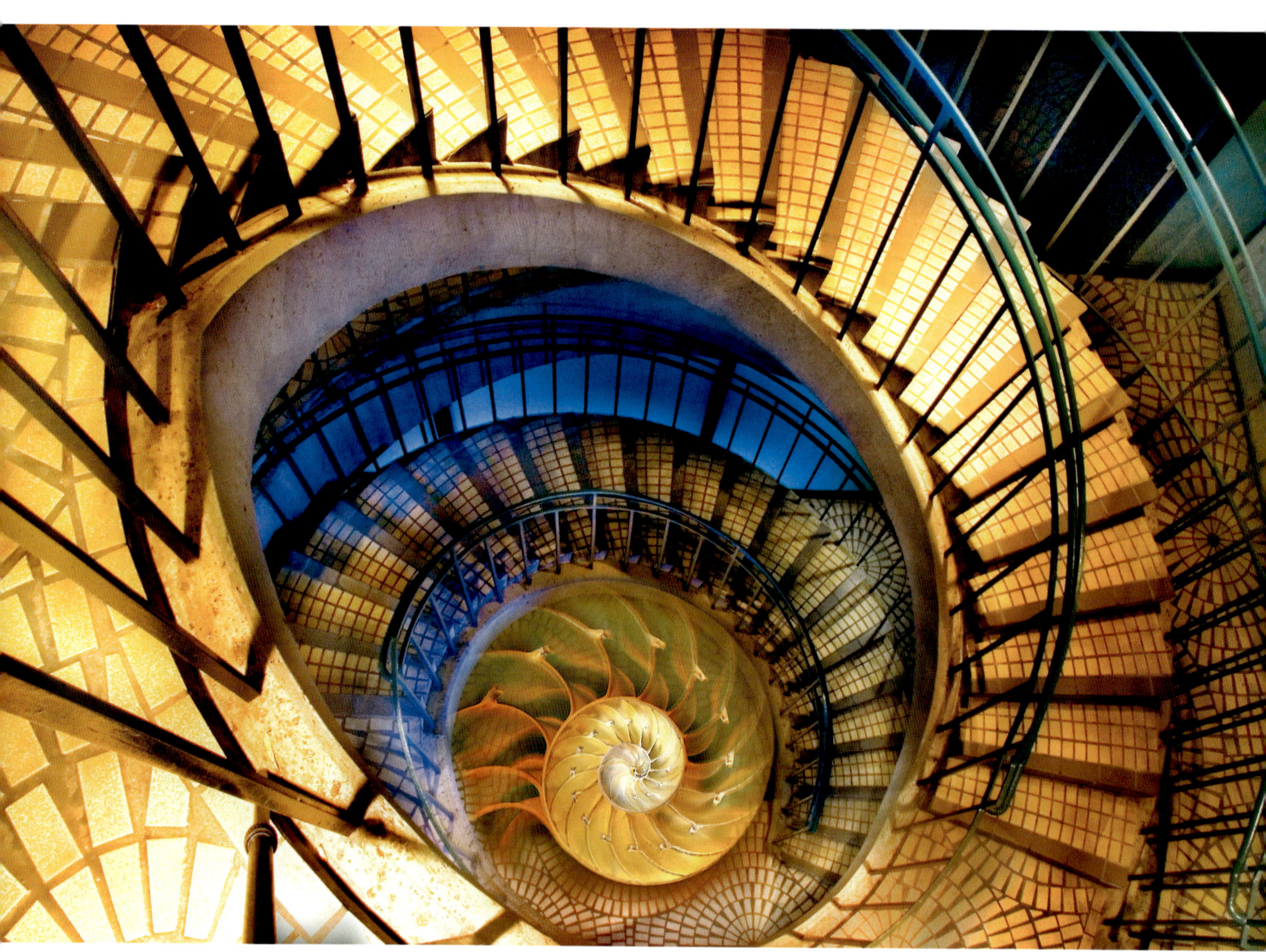

a process and procedure. As a verb, *to practice* means to perform or to exercise in order to improve one's proficiency at something.

I chose *practice* as part of the title of this chapter because I believe that practicing composition is a lifelong endeavour. Composition involves practicing skills that will improve over time; it also means learning to see the world with a particular mindset related to design.

The second epigraph at the beginning of *Composition & Photography* is from Ansel Adams, a fount of pithy but accurate quips about all aspects of photography. Adams stated that "there are no rules for good photographs, there are only good photographs."

In other words, we know good photography when we see it, but there are really no objective rules concerning its creation. This presents an additional difficulty for the photographer who wishes to internalize "good" composition—there are no rules to internalize.

I believe that the answers to these twinned dilemmas lie along two tracks.

Key Ideas in Composition

The first and broadest track in the practice of composition involves living a full life as a human being. As part of this, one should develop as complete a set of ideas and tools as a person, artist, and photographer (in this order) as possible. One also needs to understand oneself as well as one can (see the "Thought Experiment" on page 226).

More narrowly, the study of composition itself is important. I believe that composition is correctly categorized in the context of two-dimensional art generally. This implies that it is important not to limit compositional studies to photography, and to keep an eye on the broader range of visual art. It is my premise in *Composition & Photography* that the most fruitful study of composition involves placing imagery in the context of design.

Since, as Adams put it, there are no rules, how should this study of composition proceed?

Two-dimensional art, such as photography, is usually formally bounded by a frame (page 54). The photographer can design within that frame starting with lines (page 18), circles (page 36), and rectangles (page 54).

It's absolutely amazing how expressive a simple line can be, and how complex images can be created using only lines. Circles are a universal shape that are related to wholeness, our relationship to the universe, and our position on Mother Earth. The circle is a valuable shape to become familiar with because it means so much.

The frame is a rectangle, but in the context of a photograph also contains and bounds the image. While the concept of framing—not a picture frame!—often confuses people, once you've become clear about framing, the power of your compositions will be significantly enhanced.

A composition can get more complex and interesting when you add patterns and repetition (page 82) and spirals and fractals (page 108). To take one of these important shapes, the fractal is astounding because a simple shape slightly varied and repeated can lead to almost infinite variations. An appreciation for patterns, spirals, and fractals is greatly enriching and can yield a harvest of subtle and complex imagery.

Thought Experiment

Who are you? What pictures have you seen? What books have you read? What music do you listen to? Who do you love? What do you like? What do you like to photograph?

Jot down your answers to these questions. Feel free to add anything else you like that is important to your inner being.

Rinse and repeat this experiment in self-discovery periodically.

Sagrada Família—Sagrada Família, formally the Basilica de la Sagrada Família, is an unfinished Roman Catholic church that is about 135 years old, located in Barcelona, Catalonia. It is a UNESCO World Heritage Site, and the masterpiece of Catalan architect Antoni Gaudí.

Gaudí's work was largely influenced by nature, although he was also known for his introduction of new techniques and materials in construction, particularly his use of ceramics. The Sagrada Família echoes important Gothic and Asian structures while incorporating natural motifs in every aspect of its design. For example, the columns holding up the cathedral roof are carved to be reminiscent of trees, and their shape is definitely fractal-like.

For me, the experience of visiting the Sagrada Família is more like being in a very special organic and natural shape than like visiting a conventional cathedral. Perhaps it is this conflation of nature with the ineffable that makes the Sagrada Família such a special and other-worldly space.

When I made this photo inside the Sagrada Família, I used an extreme wide-angle lens (15mm) to help capture the organic and forest-like nature of the cathedral ceiling. Since I could not use a tripod, I raised my ISO to 1000 so that I could get decently sharp results even while hand holding.

Nikon D810, 15mm Zeiss Distagon, 1/100 of a second at f/2.8 and ISO 1000, hand held.

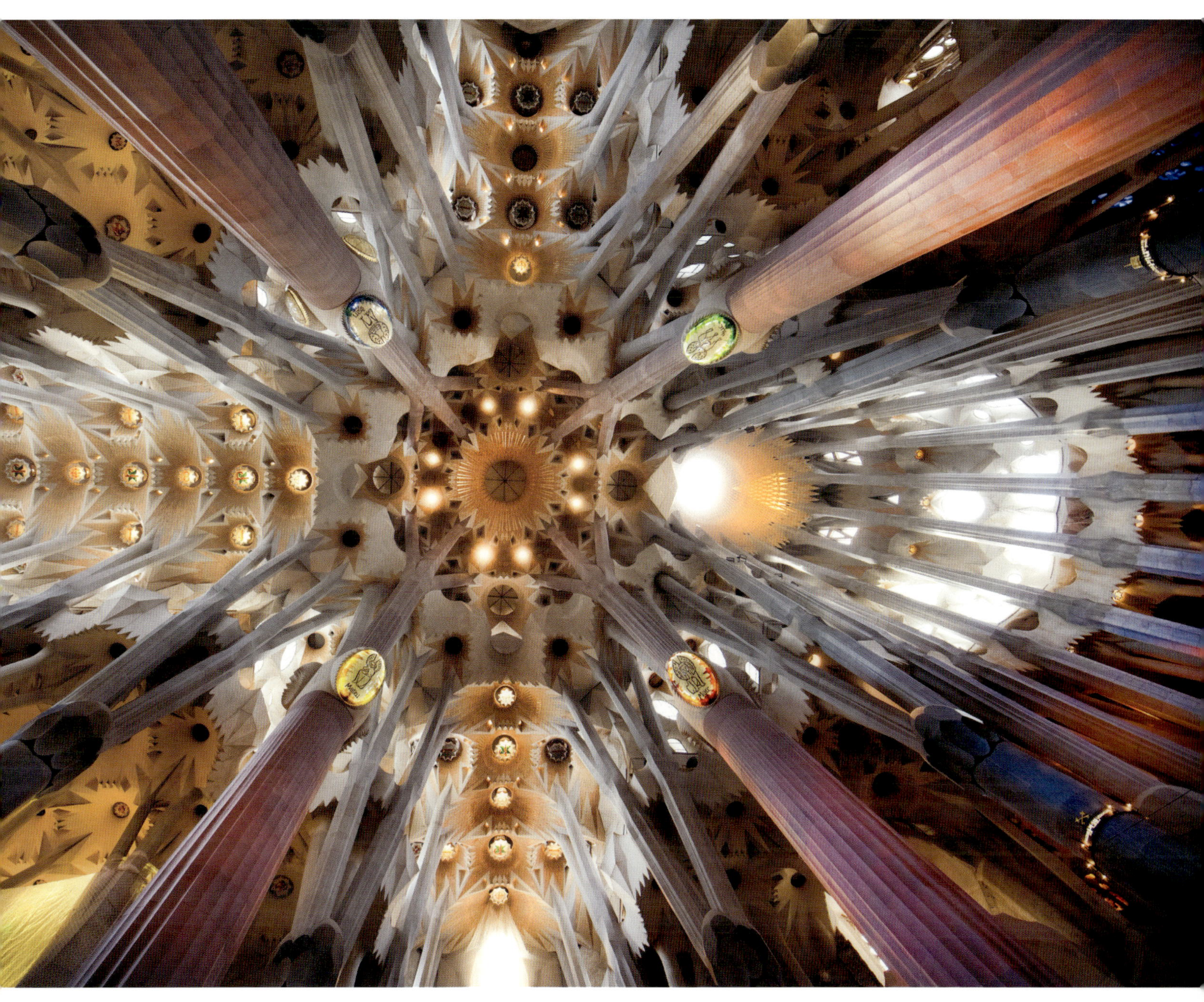

Once placed within a frame, a photographic composition has visual entry points and exit points (page 136). The way a viewer visually approaches a photograph is a completely different system of formal design, but it can be manipulated, and this is extremely powerful once you grasp how it works.

If there is a depiction of "reality" in a photograph, vanishing points and perspective must be considered. Since single-point perspective is expected in a photograph, why not take this expectation and turn it on its head? You'll find ideas about how to do this starting on page 158.

Symmetry and asymmetry (page 178) and positive and negative space (page 198) are visual motifs that spice compositional interest up a notch. And, contrary to many expectations, photographs, like any other art form, are often partially or completely abstract (page 210).

I hope you've enjoyed the journey and process of composition in my book. Hopefully these tools will help you analyze photographs and compositions. Most important, I hope you find the ideas in *Composition & Photography* useful in your own creative work.

Heceta Head Lighthouse—Along the rocky and storm-bound coast of Oregon, Cape Perpetua rises almost 1,000 feet above the Pacific Ocean. Isolated, with connection to the world only by water or dangerous trail until the 1930s, the Hecata Head Lighthouse was built to safeguard shipping in this perilous region.

As the golden light of late afternoon faded into evening, from across Cape Cove near Devil's Elbow, I photographed the Heceta Head Lighthouse with a telephoto lens (230mm). I bracketed my exposures from 1/500 of a second, which captured the waves, to 1/30 of a second, which allowed me to render some of the details in the comparatively dark forest.

In post-production, I worked on combining the different layers that made up this image to add a painterly effect so that my image would show the overall romantic nature of this scene.

Nikon D850, 28-300 Nikkor zoom at 230mm, five exposures with shutter speeds ranging from 1/500 to 1/30 of a second at f/8 and ISO 200, tripod mounted.

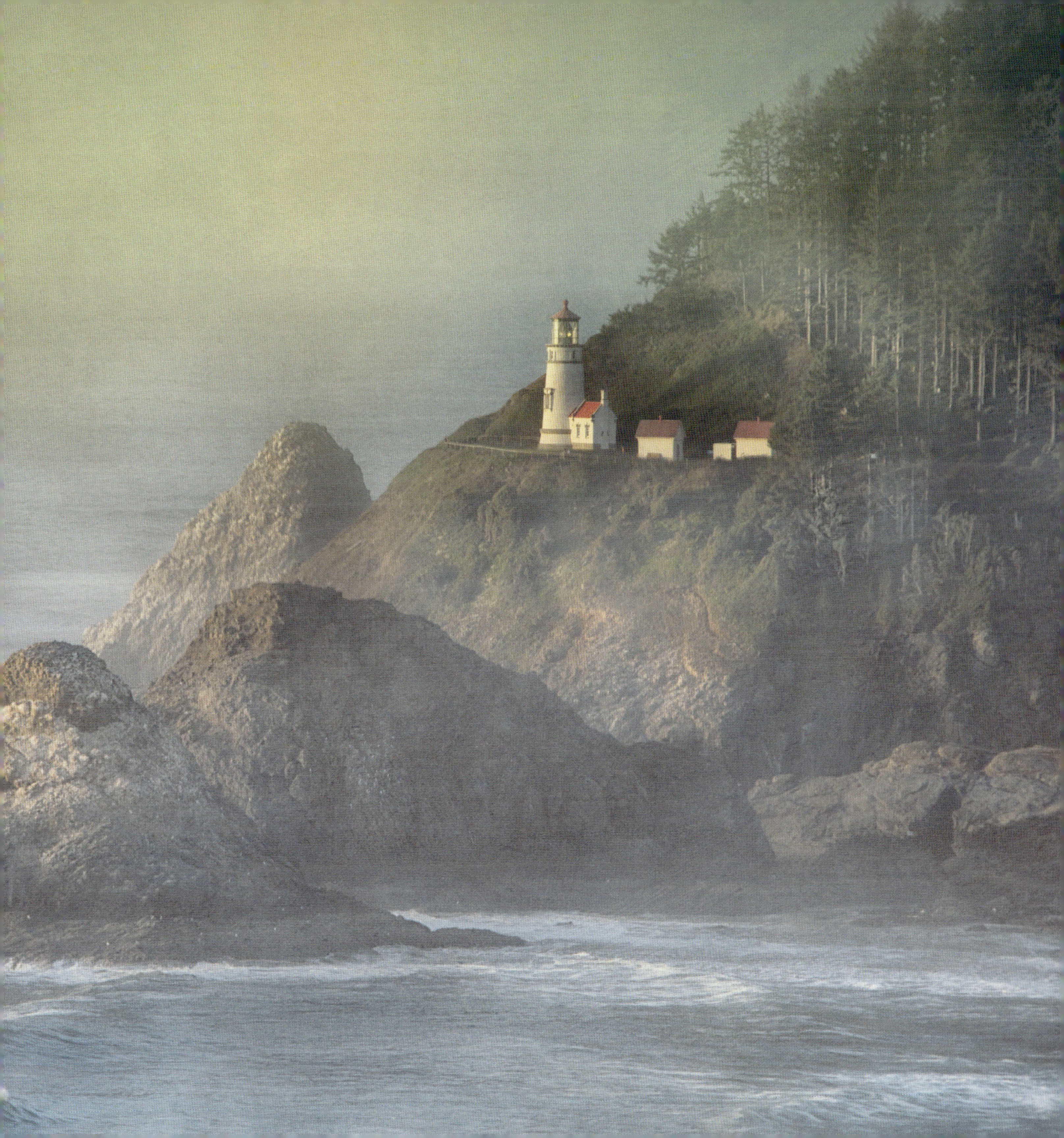

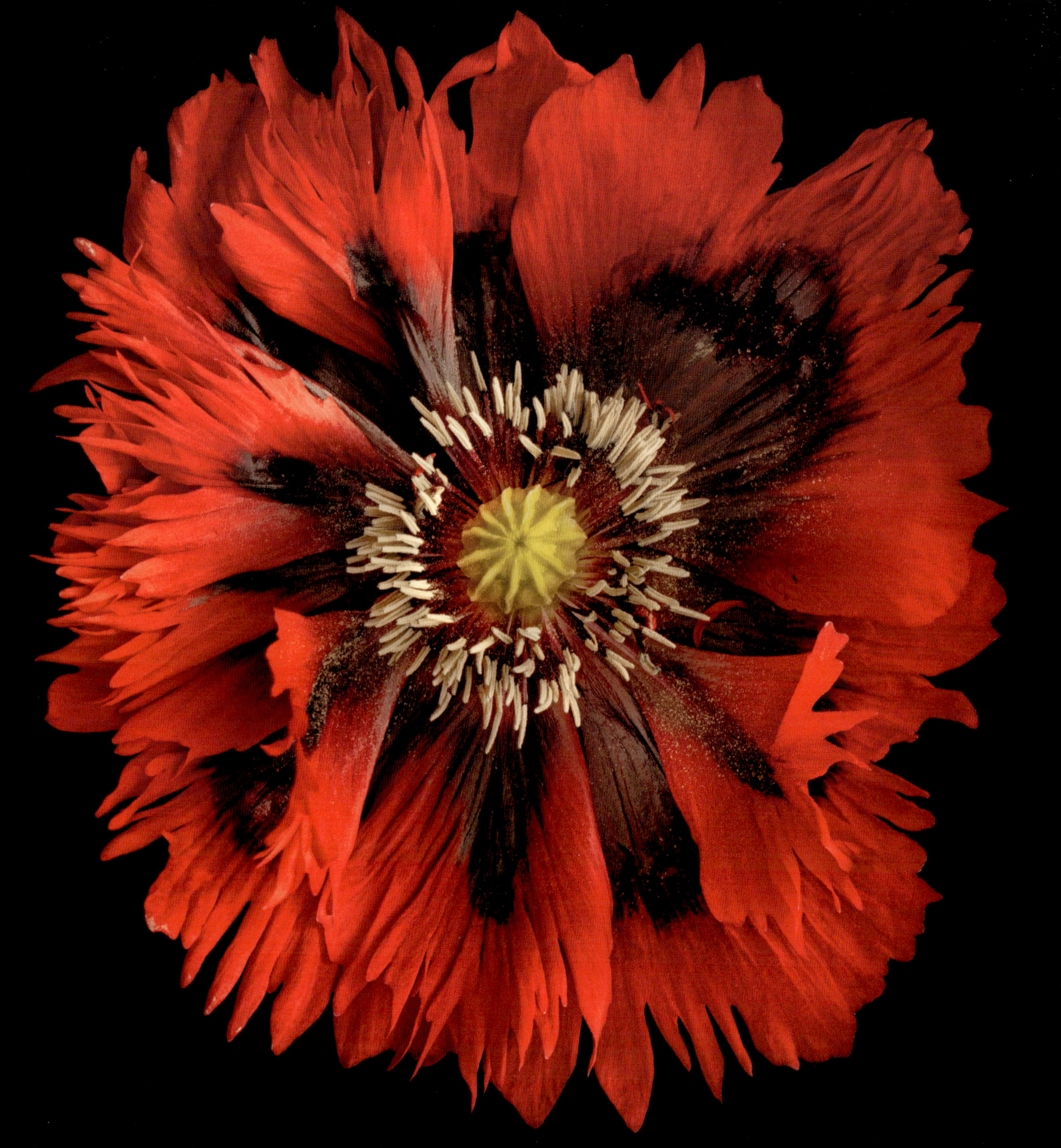

NOTES & RESOURCES

Please visit my website at digitalfieldguide.com. My website has FAQs, learning resources, and photos (of course!). You'll also find a photography blog with thousands of stories about many aspects of photography. You can find my blog at digitalfieldguide.com/blog.

You can find many of my webinar recordings at digitalfieldguide.com/learning, or search for *Harold Davis Photography* on YouTube.

Go to digitalfieldguide.com/about/subscribe to subscribe to my newsletter. If you are interested in following me on photographic social media, you can find me on Flickr, and on Instagram I am @haroldldavis. If you would like to contact me, please write me at harold@digitalfieldguide.com.

Composition & Photography touches many aspects of photography but, of course, cannot be a complete reference. There's additional information on a variety of topics in my two most recent books:

- *Creative Garden Photography* (Rocky Nook, 2020)
- *Creative Black & White, 2nd Edition* (Rocky Nook, 2019)

You can find many of my books on my Amazon author page, amazon.com/author/harold.

Learning Photoshop

Most of the photographs in this book would not have been made without Adobe Photoshop and other software. But what if Photoshop seems intimidating to you?

If you were in one of my workshops, I would tell you that *now* is the time to learn Photoshop, "fear is the mind killer," and go on and get started learning!

Learning to become fluent in Adobe software, specifically Lightroom Classic and Photoshop in the context of photography, is admittedly a major endeavor. I tell workshop students that the best approach to learning this software will depend on their learning style. For some folks, a course at a local community college might be a great way to learn Lightroom and Photoshop.

If you are the kind of person who learns from books, you might want to check out my books *The Photoshop Darkroom* (Focal Press, 2009) and *The Photoshop Darkroom 2* (Focal Press, 2011).

About EXIF Data

Sensor size information in the technical captions in this book primarily comes from the EXIF data automatically compiled by the camera and transferred to the computer when my RAW files are processed.

EXIF data as recorded in a RAW file is quite accurate for the aperture (f-stop) and ISO used on each exposure, with the caveat that the aperture recorded is sometimes the *effective* aperture. For example, the effective aperture for a macro lens focused close can be a smaller opening than the lens nominally will stop down to. This explains why a lens may have a minimum aperture of f/22, but be recorded at an effective aperture of, for example, f/45, when using an extension tube. Of course, the reduction in aperture also reduces the light hitting the sensor.

Shutter speeds are recorded accurately for single exposures. They are a little more problematic in the case of HDR blends (see "Why Bracket Exposures?" on page 233), where the EXIF

data is either left blank, or records the data of the first exposure in the blend. With the HDR photos shown in this book, I either noted the shutter speeds at the time I made the images, or went back to the RAW files and checked out the shutter speeds by inspecting the individual files.

In summary, leaving the issue of effective apertures aside, the technical information in the captions is primarily drawn from the EXIF data recorded by the camera, occasionally supplemented by my own observations and notes.

Focal Length

With the focal length of the lens used—when the focal length is recorded in the EXIF data—it is accurate, but what the focal length *means* depends upon the sensor size of the camera. Not all sensors are the same size. The smaller the sensor, the closer a given focal-length lens brings you to your subject. For example, if a sensor has half the area of another sensor, then a specific focal-length lens will bring you twice as close on a camera with the smaller sensor.

Since different cameras have different-sized sensors, it is not always possible to have a uniform vocabulary of lens focal lengths. Thus, people compare focal lengths to their 35mm film equivalent by adjusting for the sensor size.

To make the comparison with 35mm film focal lengths, you need to know the ratio of your sensor to a frame of 35mm film, which is called the *focal-length equivalency*. For reference, a 50mm lens on a full-frame camera is considered "normal." This is roughly comparable to the central angle of view of a human eye, which is between 40–60 degrees.

Lenses that are shorter than 50mm on a full-frame camera are considered wide angle, and lenses that are longer and bring things closer are telephotos.

To compute the comparable focal lengths on your own camera if your sensor has a different sensor size than mine, you need to know the focal-length equivalency factor of your sensor. You can check your camera manual for this information.

Cameras and Lenses

In *Composition & Photography*, the camera I used for each image is included as part of the technical capture data. The Nikon D850, D810, and D800 cameras, which were used for the bulk of the images in this book, are all full-frame cameras. The Nikon D300, D200, and D70 cameras, which were used for some of the photos, all have a 1.5 focal-length equivalency.

In other words, a 28mm focal length on a Nikon D300 would be equivalent to a 42mm focal length on a full-frame camera, such as the Nikon D850.

Some of the photographs in this book were made with an Apple iPhone, primarily the iPhone 6s and iPhone 12 Pro Max. These models have dual front and back mobile phone cameras; in all cases, I used the higher-resolution back camera. With the iPhone, I have omitted EXIF data from the technical caption data that accompanies

each photo, since it is not particularly helpful; however, where appropriate, I have noted apps that were used in making each photo.

Why Bracket Exposures?

I am often asked why so many of my exposures consist of bracketed sequences. This is not always an easy question to answer. Bracketing sequences the way I do it is a labor-intensive process, requires the use of a tripod, and usually works best when the subject is stationary.

The short answer is that I bracket sequences to gain dynamic range. Certainly, these days there's a great deal of inherent dynamic range in a single RAW exposure, and using this dynamic range via multi-RAW processing is your best bet in a situation where you can't use a tripod, or where the subject is moving rapidly.

But if one is nice, then five to ten are even nicer! It's a fact of life that you get more dynamic range from multiple captures than you do from a single capture. I don't always use all the captures from a bracketed sequence, but what's the harm?

I'm already on location with my camera on a tripod, so why not shoot more exposures? As I like to say, "film is so expensive!" There's no incremental cost for bracketing exposures, even if I end up using only one capture from a bracketed sequence.

The way I look at it, the big cost is getting somewhere and preparing to make a photo.

Taking the time to bracket a sequence has almost no downside.

If you would like to learn more about my technique for taking and processing bracketed sequences of RAW photographs, please check out my books *Monochromatic HDR Photography* (Focal Press, 2013) and *Creating HDR Photos* (Amphoto, 2012).

Optical Quality versus Depth of Field

If you take a look at the technical captions in *Composition & Photography*, you'll see that many of the photos were taken with the lens fully stopped down at apertures such as f/16, f/32, and even effective apertures of f/64. I have sometimes been asked about this by those who note that a lens is not likely to be optically sharpest when it is fully stopped down.

Optical performance depends on the specific lens you are using, and varies tremendously. You *must* get to know the performance of your lenses at their various apertures.

Some lenses—for example, the 55mm Zeiss Otus that I use for most of my light box work—have excellent optical performance across their entire range of apertures. In the case of the Zeiss Otus, the lens performs well across the entire range of apertures from f/1.4 to f/16. A different lens would need to be tested at each aperture to understand how well it performs.

With a mediocre lens, it is true that the optically best apertures will most likely be in the middle of the aperture range, usually f/8 or f/11. Great lenses may also perform well when wide open.

The craft of photography always involves trade-offs. You get greater depth of field as you stop your lens down. Conversely, in low-light, hand-held situations, you might decide to use a wide-open aperture, such as f/1.4, even with the trade-off of losing optical quality.

Despite a certain amount of agony and ecstasy regarding optical performance based on aperture, there is usually not that much incremental impact. I often elect to choose depth of field over a shallower aperture that, at best, provides slightly better optical performance.

Sunflower X-Ray Fusion—I have been very excited to work with x-ray equipment to produce unusual images of subjects like flowers and shells. The virtue of light in the x-ray spectrum, as opposed to the visual spectrum, is that it can show the insides of things, not just their external surfaces. On the other hand, the output of an x-ray machine is monochromatic. X-rays don't "see" in color.

With this image, I created an x-ray of the sunflower, then carefully moved the sunflower over to a light box. With the sunflower on the light box, I created a color photograph, which I then combined in post-production with the x-ray. In some sense, this is the best of both possible worlds, because the image shows both the inside and the outside of a sunflower.

Digital x-ray capture using Hologic mammography machine at a wavelength of roughly 0.04nm; Digital Imaging and Communications in Medicine (DICOM) file processed and inverted in Photoshop; DICOM image combined with light box photograph of the sunflower.

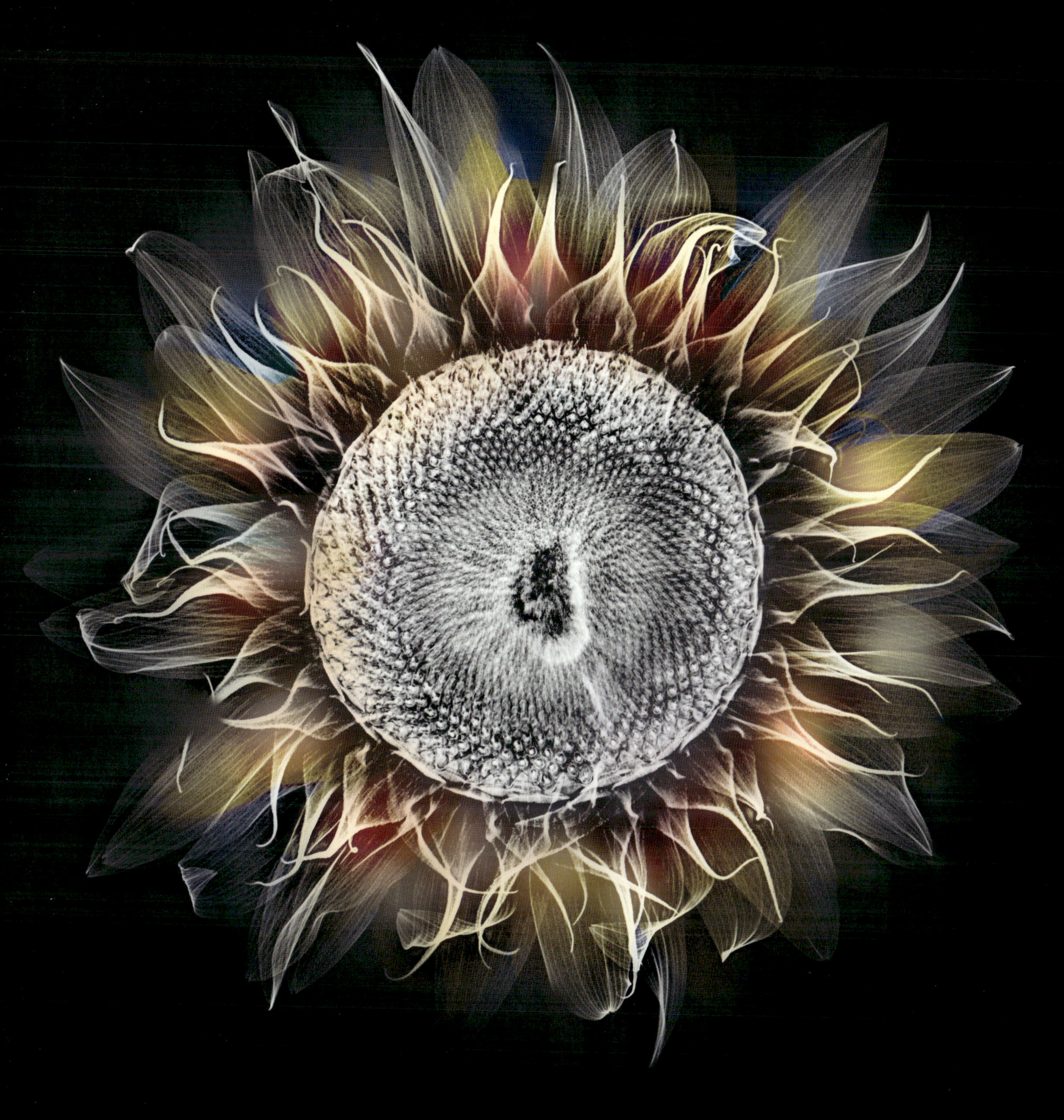

GLOSSARY

Design Terms

Archetype: A visual archetype is symbolic on a deep level.

Crop, cropping: The way an image or print is framed in post-production; the proportions used for presentation of an image or print.

Entry point: Refers to where the viewer's gaze begins going into an image.

Exit point: Where the viewer's gaze leaves the image.

Fractal, fractal-like: A fractal image is one in which small areas of the image as a whole are replicated in different sizes across the entire image; a simple transformation used on a portion of an image to eventually create a highly complex overall image; an image that resembles a fractal.

Frame: A border or boundary of something, particularly within or around a two-dimensional work of art; the context of a work of art, as in the way a concept is *framed*.

Framing: In a photographic composition, positioning the image in relationship to its edges.

Mandala: A circular shape that may represent paradise, sacred space, or the world.

Minimalism, minimalist: The philosophy that less is more; a work of art that is simple, unadorned, and stripped to its essentials.

Perspective: Representation of three-dimensional subjects on a two-dimensional surface to give the impression of height, width, depth, and position.

Recursive: In math, a procedure or function that invokes itself; in art, a work that is self-referential, and may seem to continue indefinitely.

Single-point perspective: Perspective rendering with a single vanishing point.

Spiral: A three-dimensional curve rotating around a fixed position.

Tondo: A circular work of art or image.

Vanishing point: The point at which parallel lines viewed in perspective appear to converge.

Photographic Terms

Adobe Camera Raw (ACR): Used to convert RAW files into files that Photoshop can open.

Ambient light: The available, or existing, light that naturally surrounds a scene.

Aperture: The size of the opening in the iris of a lens. Lens apertures are designated by f-numbers. The smaller the f-number, the bigger the opening, and the less depth of field.

Bracketing: Shooting many exposures at a range of settings. It often works better to bracket shutter speed rather than aperture.

Camera obscura: A dark room or box with a pinhole or lens on one side. The scene outside the camera obscura is projected onto the wall opposite the hole.

Chiaroscuro: Moody lighting that shows contrasts between shadows and brightness.

Close-up filter: A piece of optical glass that screws into the front of a lens and provides magnification.

CMYK: Cyan, Magenta, Yellow, and Black. The four-color color model used for most offset printing.

Color space: A color space, sometimes called a color model, is the mechanism used to display the colors we see in the world, in print, or on a monitor. CMYK, LAB, and RGB are examples of color spaces.

Composite: Multiple images that are combined to create a new composition.

Depth of field: The field in front of and behind a subject that is in focus.

DICOM file: Digital Imaging in Communication in Medicine file format.

Diffraction: Bending of light rays; unwanted diffraction can cause loss of optical sharpness, particularly at small apertures.

DSLR: Digital single-lens reflex camera.

Dynamic range: The difference between the lightest tonal values and the darkest tonal values in a photo.

Effective aperture: The aperture recorded by EXIF data as opposed to the aperture set on the camera. In close focus, the effective aperture is often a smaller opening than the set aperture.

EV (Exposure Value): Denotes any combination of aperture, shutter speed, and ISO that yields the same exposure. −1 EV means halving the exposure, and +1 EV means doubling the exposure.

Exposure: The amount of light hitting the camera sensor. Also, the camera settings used to capture this incoming light.

Exposure histogram: A bar graph displayed on a camera or computer that shows the distribution of lights and darks in a photo.

Extension tube: A hollow ring that fits between a lens and the DSLR, used to achieve closer focusing.

f-number, f-stop: The size of the aperture, written f/n, where n is the f-number. The smaller the f-number, the larger the opening in the lens; the larger the f-number, the smaller the opening in the lens.

Focal length: Roughly, the distance from the end of the lens to the focal plane.

Focal plane: The sensor's position on a plane parallel to the lens. For more information, turn to page 61.

Focus stacking: Extending the field of focus beyond

that possible in a photo by combining multiple photos, each photographed at a different point of focus.

Grayscale: Used to render images in a single color from white to black; in Photoshop a grayscale image has only one channel.

Hand-HDR: The process of creating an HDR image from multiple photos at different exposures without using automatic software to combine the photos.

HDR: Extending the dynamic range in an image using techniques including multi-RAW processing, hand-HDR, and automated HDR software.

High key: Brightly lit photos that are predominantly white, often with an intentionally "overexposed" effect.

Histogram: A graph that represents a distribution of values; an *exposure histogram* is used to display the distribution of lights and darks in an image.

Image stabilization: Also called *vibration reduction*, this is a high-tech system in a lens or camera that attempts to compensate for, and reduce, camera motion.

In-camera multiple exposure: Exposures made on a single captured frame in the camera, and blended in the camera.

Infinity (∞): The distance from the camera that is far enough away so that any object at that distance or beyond will be in focus when the lens is set to infinity, regardless of aperture.

Inversion: A Photoshop adjustment that inverts the color in a channel or channels.

ISO: Scale used to set a camera's sensitivity to light.

JPEG: A compressed file format for photos that have been processed from an original RAW image.

LAB color: A color model consisting of three channels.

Lensbaby: A special-purpose lens that may have a flexible barrel that allows you to adjust the "sweet spot" (area in focus).

Low key: Dimly lit photos that are predominantly black, often with an intentionally "underexposed" effect.

Macro lens: A lens that is specially designed for close focusing; often a macro lens focuses close enough to enable a 1:1 magnification ratio, so that the image on the sensor is as large as the image in real life.

Magnification ratio: The correspondence of an object and its actual size on the sensor.

Monochrome, monochromatic: A monochrome image is presented as nominally consisting of tones from white to black; however, "black and white" images can be tinted or toned, and usually vary from straight grayscale.

Multi-RAW processing: Combining two or more different versions processed from the same RAW file to extend the dynamic range and create a more pleasing final image.

Open up, open wide: To open up a lens, or to set the lens wide open, means to set the aperture to a large opening, denoted with a small f-number.

Overexpose: An overexposed photo appears too bright; the exposure histogram is bunched toward the right side.

Pinhole camera: A camera that uses a literal, very small hole as the lens to capture an image.

Polarizer: A filter that lets in some kinds of polarized light and blocks other kinds; useful to enhance reflections.

Previsualization: Understanding, or seeing in one's "mind's eye," before making an exposure how an image will come out after capture and processing.

RAW: A digital RAW file is a complete record of the data captured by the sensor. The details of RAW file formats vary among camera manufacturers.

Refraction: Alteration of light waves by bending when light reflects or passes through substances such as glass and water.

RGB: Red, Green, and Blue; a three-color color model, used for displaying photos on the web and on computer monitors.

Sensitivity: Set using an ISO number; determines the sensitivity of the sensor to light.

Shutter speed: Shutter speed is not a speed. Rather, it is the duration of time that the shutter is open. This interval of time controls how objects in motion are rendered.

Solarization: Reverses or partially reverses blacks and whites. In film photography, uses re-exposure to make partially developed material lighter; simulated in digital photography.

Stop down: To stop down a lens means to set the aperture to a small opening; denoted with a larger f-number.

Tonal range: The range of color and light and dark values in an image.

Underexpose: An underexposed photo appears too dark; the exposure histogram is bunched toward the left side.

X-Ray: Radiation shorter in wavelength than visible light.

Harold's Vase: for more about this optical illusion, see page 203.

Answer to the question on pages 194–195: The image on page 194 is the original orientation. You can tell because there are faint water ripples on the duck in the flipped version on page 195.

INDEX

A

Abstract Expressionism, 211
abstraction, 211–221
Abstraction in Photography (MOMA exhibition), 212
Adams, Ansel, 9, 223, 225
Adobe Photoshop
    composite, 41, 67–69, 132–134, 159, 175
    LAB color, 33, 220
        inversions, 50, 53, 70, 133
            positive and negative space, viewing in, 204
        perspective, changing in, 176
        transformations, in, 132–134, 176
anthropomorphism, 212–215
aperture, effective, 232
apotropaic, 138
archetype, visual, 41–46

B

Berkeley, Busby, 128
Blake, William, 179
Bosch, Hieronymus, 148
boundary, 62–63, 80
    rectangular, 91
    vanishing point, and, 165
bracketing, exposure, 233–234
Brunelleschi, Filippo, 159

C

camera obscura, 159–163
camera position, moving, 61
Carroll, Lewis, 131
Cartier-Bresson, Henri, 10
circle(s), 37–53, 67, 83, 137, 226
    archetype, in, 41–46
    balance, and, 50–52
    concentric, 91
    definition of, 37
    infinity, and, 38
    mandala, as, 41
    patterns, and, 91–92
    radial symmetry, 184
    squaring, the, 46
    virtuous and vicious, 37–38

Cohen, Leonard, 49
collaging, virtual, 220
color
    lines, and, 21
    negative space, and, 200
    positive space, and, 200
    using LAB to invert, 50, 53
    versus contrast, 151
composite, 41, 67–69, 132–134, 159, 175
composition
    abstraction in, 211–221
    as process, 10, 223–229
    asymmetry in, 179–197
    background, importance of, 204
    circles, using, 37–53
    design principles, and, 14
    emotion using direction, 156
    entering and exiting, 137–157
    entry point, 27, 137–157
        in portraiture, eyes as, 148
    exit point, 27, 131, 137–157
    fractal(s), 109–135, 175
    framing, and, 55–81
    good, 9
    grid, as, 91–92, 99
    lines, using in, 34
    moving camera for, 61
    multi-point perspective, 166–171
    narrative in, 151, 206–208
    open vs. closed, 146
    patterns, and, 83–107
    perspective, and, 172
    positive and negative space, 199–209
    practice of, 223–229
    repetition, and, 83–107
    rules, and, 9–10, 14
    spirals, and, 109–135
    squaring the circle, 92
    symmetry, in, 179–197
    vanishing point, working with, 162–166
cropping square, 46
Cubism, 211

D

decisive moment, 10
design and photography, 28
design patterns, 104–106, 110
    architecture, in, 104
    in imagery, 104–106
    A Pattern Language: Towns, Buildings, Construction (book by Christopher Alexander et al.), 104
    software development, using, 104
direction
    emotion, and, 156
    language of, 142–145
    misdirection, and, 146–148
    patterns, and, 152–155
dot, 19, 25

E

effective aperture, 232
entry point, 27, 137–157
    eyes in portraiture, 148
Escher, M.C., 75, 128, 131
EXIF data, 232
exit point, 27, 131, 137–157
exposure bracketing, 233–234

F

Fauvism, 211
fisheye lens, 70, 91
focal-length equivalency, 232–233
focal plane, 56, 61
fractal(s), 109–135, 137, 175, 226
    branching patterns, and, 120
    composites, 132–134
    composition, kinds of, 128
    creative use of, 135
    definition of, 128
    fractal art, 109, 126
    framing, 131
    lens, 128
    mathematical, 126, 128
    natural, 120–125, 128
    nature, in, 109
frame(s), framing 55–81, 91, 100, 137

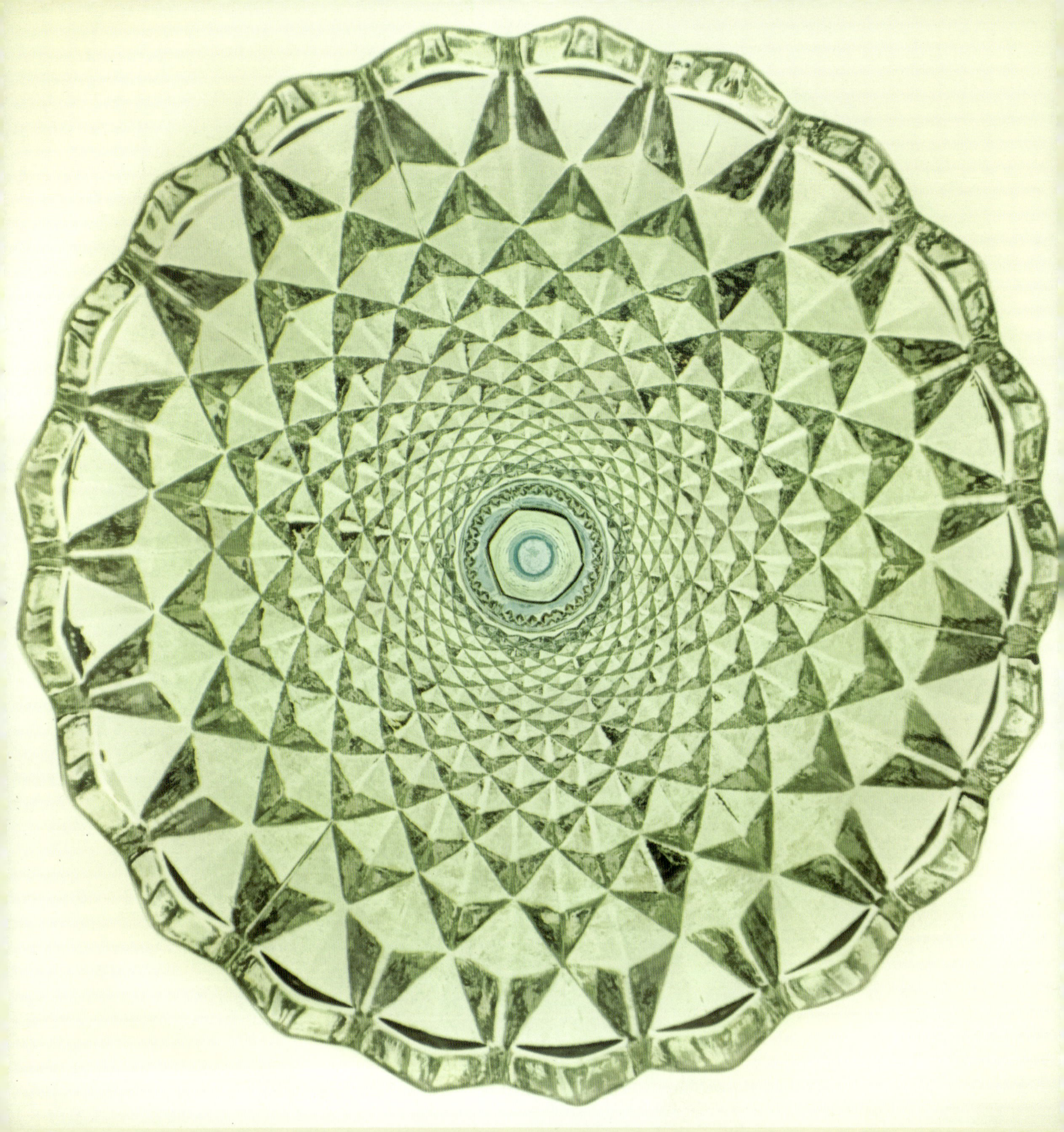